Interpretations of Marx

Interpretations of Marx

Edited with an Introduction by

TOM BOTTOMORE

Basil Blackwell

Selection and editorial material copyright © Tom Bottomore 1988

First published 1988

Basil Blackwell Ltd
108 Cowley Road, Oxford, OX4 1JF, UK

Basil Blackwell Inc.
432 Park Avenue South, Suite 1503
New York, NY 10016, USA

British Library Cataloguing in Publication Data

Interpretations of Marx.
1. Society. Theories of Marx, Karl,
1818–1883
I. Bottomore, Tom, *1920–*
301'.092'4

ISBN 0-631-15256-3 Pbk

Library of Congress Cataloging in Publication Data

Interpretations of Marx.
Bibliography: p.
Includes index.
1. Marx, Karl, 1818–1883. I. Bottomore, T.B.
HX39.5.I565   1988   335.4   88-14444
ISBN 0-631-15256-3 (pbk.)

Typeset in 10 on 11½ point Ehrhardt
by Alan Sutton Publishing, Gloucester
Printed in Great Britain by Billing and Sons Ltd, Worcester

Contents

Introduction

Tom Bottomore

Marx's social theory was one of the great intellectual achievements of the nineteenth century, comparable – and often compared – with Darwin's theory of evolution. Its remarkable synthesis of ideas from philosophy, history and the nascent social sciences, the originality of the conceptions which it expressed, were unrivalled in the work of any other contemporary thinker. The theory was unique, moreover, in its close relationship with the political movements of the time. Marx set out to change the world, as well as to interpret it; and his theoretical analysis of the course of social development, especially in the modern capitalist societies, was also intended to have a practical effect by helping to form the consciousness of the industrial working class – the class, in Marx's words, 'to which the future belongs'.

Yet the very breadth of Marx's synthesis, which he was far from elaborating in all its aspects, and the problems posed by the connections between Marxist theory and Marxist practice through a century of profound social changes have given rise to diverse formulations of the Marxist theory itself. These different, often conflicting, interpretations have been affected both by changing political circumstances and by the piecemeal discovery and publication of some of Marx's manuscripts, which have raised new questions about the development of his thought.[1]

---

1 A critical, scholarly edition of the complete works of Marx and Engels – *Karl Marx/Friedrich Engels. Historisch-Kritische Gesamtausgabe (MEGA)* – was planned and begun in the 1920s by David Riazanov, the founder and director of the Marx – Engels Institute in Moscow; but his dismissal and subsequent disappearance, as one of the early victims of Stalinism, brought the enterprise to an end when only twelve of the projected forty-two volumes had been published. Only in 1975 was publication undertaken of a new edition of the collected writings of Marx and Engels in the original languages, with an elaborate critical apparatus: *Karl Marx/Friedrich Engels Gesamtausgabe* (Berlin: Dietz Verlag, 1975 onwards); and in the same year publication of a complete English edition also began: *Karl Marx/Frederick Engels, Collected Works* (London: Lawrence and Wishart, 1975 onwards).

Thus, the *Economic and Philosophical Manuscripts* of 1844, first published in 1932,[2] but not extensively discussed until two decades later,[3] have often been treated as marking a point of transition between the 'young Marx' and the 'mature Marx' – the former a humanist philosopher, the latter the author of a deterministic social theory known as 'historical materialism'. In the discussion of these manuscripts since the mid-1950s, two main issues have been raised: first, whether the transition does represent a total break in Marx's thought – the replacement of one theoretical scheme by another – or whether there is an underlying continuity of ideas; and secondly, the nature of the relation in Marx's theory between philosophy and social science, or in a narrower sense, between his socialist aspirations and his analysis of the historical development of the working-class movement in capitalist society.[4]

The widespread discussion of Marx's early writings reflects political as well as intellectual interests. Those who have emphasized most strongly Marx's 'humanism' have been engaged in a struggle (which has evolved in many different forms since the crisis marked by the Polish and Hungarian revolts of 1956) against the Stalinist version of Marxism and its expression in political movements and institutions. They have sought deliberately to revise the interpretation of Marx's thought that prevailed from the 1930s to the 1950s by calling attention to other themes in his work, above all his conception of human nature and its needs, and the implicit moral doctrine of human liberation for which it provides a basis; and in so doing they have drawn upon ideas derived from currents of thought outside Marxism – from phenomenology and existentialism or from sociology.

The revision, which is also in part a revival, of Marxist thought has been given a new impetus by the still more recent publication and discussion of Marx's preliminary drafts of *Capital*, published in Moscow from 1939 to 1941 under the title *Grundrisse der Kritik der politischen Oekonomie (Rohentwurf)*.[5] This

---

2 In an incomplete version in S. Landshut and J. P. Mayer, *Karl Marx. Der historische Materialismus. Die Frühschriften*, and fully in *MEGA*, I/3.

3 Some scholars recognized their importance at the time, but no general discussion took place. For example, Henry de Man published (in the journal of the Austro-Marxists, *Der Kampf* [1932]) an essay entitled 'The newly discovered Marx', in which he argued that these manuscripts showed 'more clearly than any other work the ethical-humanist themes which lie behind Marx's socialist convictions and behind . . . his whole scientific work.' In England, H. P. Adams, in *Karl Marx in his Earlier Writings*, published an interesting analysis of the manuscripts and other early writings, making use of the *MEGA* edition, but his work was ignored at the time. Only in the 1960s did many of Marx's early writings become available in English translation: see especially T. B. Bottomore (ed.), *Karl Marx: Early Writings*; L. Easton and K. Guddat (eds), *Writings of the Young Marx on Philosophy and Society*; D. McLellan, (ed.), *Karl Marx: The Early Texts*.

4 For a useful collection of essays and bibliographical references on Marx's early writings, see *Annali*, VII (1964–65).

5 The *Grundrisse* did not attract much attention until a new edition was published after the war by Dietz Verlag (Berlin, 1953). Excerpts were published in English in T. B. Bottomore and Maximilien Rubel (eds), *Karl Marx: Selected Writings in Sociology and Social Philosophy*, where the

text was first discussed comprehensively, in English, in an essay by Martin Nicolaus, 'The unknown Marx'.[6] Nicolaus argued, first, that the *Grundrisse* shows a direct line of continuity with the *Economic and Philosophical Manuscripts* insofar as it develops the notion of alienation, and the analysis of money as a social bond (so that a rigorous separation of the 'young' from the 'mature' Marx becomes implausible),[7] and second, that it formulates, more explicitly than is done in *Capital*, Marx's newly gained insight into the fundamental contradiction of capitalist society and the conditions of its breakdown. On this view, the *Grundrisse* is of crucial importance in providing the starting point for a comprehensive analysis of the development of capitalism – such as Marx himself was unable to complete – that would take account of the social and political factors, as well as the economic processes, affecting the capacity of capitalism to survive and of socialism to come into existence as a new form of society.

The controversies over the interpretation of Marx's thought will not arise in the future, as they have done in the recent past, from the revelation of new texts; but they are unlikely to subside quickly, for they are continually reanimated by cultural changes and by the rise and decline of political movements. Nevertheless, the present circumstances seem particularly favourable for attempting to assess the structure and development of Marx's social theory in a more comprehensive, more dispassionate way. The diverse interpretations have taken shape in more or less distinct 'schools', and they can now be viewed in the light of our knowledge of the whole corpus of Marx's major writings. At the same time, many of Marx's conceptions have been absorbed into the general intellectual stock of the social sciences, while Marxism (in any of its versions) as an all-embracing theory of man and society is increasingly questioned, and in varying degrees abandoned, even by those thinkers whose work has been mainly inspired by this tradition, but who now find the Marxist system inadequate especially for understanding the main trends of social development in the late twentieth century.

In the passionate debates of recent years about the proper scope and methods of the social sciences, Marxism has been one of the chief sources of critical and politically radical ideas. But as a theoretical system, it is itself an object of criticism. After a century of turbulent economic and political changes, and in

---

importance of the manuscripts as outlining a comprehensive study of modern capitalism, going far beyond an economic analysis, is stressed. Since then, an English translation has been published: *Karl Marx, Grundrisse*, translated with a foreword by Martin Nicolaus (Harmondsworth: Penguin Books, 1973), and the text has been widely discussed.

6 *New Left Review*, XLVIII (March-April, 1968).

7 David McLellan, in the introduction to his selections (1971) advances this as the principal reason for considering the *Grundrisse* 'the centerpiece of Marx's thought'.

8 See the discussion in Norman Birnbaum's essay, 'The crisis in Marxist sociology', included in his book *Toward a Critical Sociology*, pp. 94–129; and also the earlier criticisms of Marxism in C. Wright Mills, *The Marxists*.

4   *Tom Bottomore*

the face of entirely new problems, we have to ask what is still living and what is
dead in Marx's theory. I propose to explore this question by looking first at
those ideas and preoccupations of Marx's own time that helped to shape his
thought; then tracing the stages in the formation of his theory, and examining
some of its distinctive elements; and finally considering those aspects of it
which remained undeveloped, or which seem questionable in the light of
historical experience and of later social thought about that experience.

The formation of Marx's thought

The earliest intellectual influences upon Marx came from the French
Enlightenment and the Revolution.[9] The Rhineland where Marx was born, at
Trier in 1818, had been strongly affected by French ideas and became a centre
of liberal, and even socialist, doctrines in the 1820s and 1830s. Marx's father –
described by his granddaughter Eleanor as a 'true eighteenth-century
Frenchman' who 'knew his Voltaire and Rousseau by heart' – was a moderate
liberal; and so too was the principal of the high school which Marx attended.
His future father-in-law, Ludwig von Westphalen, was more radical and had
embraced the Saint-Simonian doctrines that were circulating widely in the
Rhineland; it was he who introduced Marx to Saint-Simon's writings.

Later at the University of Berlin, another Saint-Simonian, Eduard Gans, the
professor of law, had a strong influence upon Marx. In 1836 Gans published a
book[10] in which he expounded the ideas of the Saint-Simonians, using phrases
which foreshadow those of the *Communist Manifesto*:

> amidst all this intellectual confusion the Saint-Simonians have said something of
> importance, and have put their finger on a public scandal of the day. They have
> correctly observed that slavery has not really disappeared; though it has been
> formally prohibited, in practice it still exists in the fullest form. Once there was the
> opposition between master and slave, then between patrician and plebeian, and
> later still between feudal lord and vassal; now we have the idle rich and the
> worker. . . . It will be more necessary now for future history to speak of the
> struggle of the proletariat against the middle classes.[11]

Marx himself did not become a Saint-Simonian, and he remained sceptical
about all the new socialist and communist doctrines until 1843; but the social
ethic of the Saint-Simonians – above all their concern with the future of the
'poorest and most numerous class' – entered deeply into his outlook, animated

9 A good short account of Marx's life which gives particular attention to his early environment is
that by Werner Blumenberg, *Karl Marx*. The most comprehensive biography of Marx and Engels is
Auguste Cornu, *Karl Marx et Friedrich Engels* of which four volumes have so far been published.
10 E. Gans, *Rückblicke auf Personen und Zustände*.
11 Quoted in Blumenberg. *Karl Marx*, pp. 45–6.

his critical attitude toward Hegel's philosophy, and eventually led him into the socialist movement. The extent to which Marx's moral views derived from the humanism and rationalism of the Enlightenment and from the development of Enlightenment ideas in the thought of the early socialists is suggested by a passage in *The Holy Family* (1845) where he observes: 'When one studies the materialist theories of the original goodness of man, the equality of intellectual endowment among men, the omnipotence of education, experience, and habit, the influence of external circumstances upon man, the great importance of industry, the value of pleasure, etc., there is no need for extraordinary penetration to discover what necessarily connects them with communism and socialism.'[12]

Marx's reservations about the socialist and communist doctrines as he encountered them at the beginning of the 1840s arose mainly from his judgement that while they expressed a new world view they did not connect their moral aspirations with a philosophical or theoretical conception of reality.[13] In his philosophical studies in Berlin Marx had been preoccupied with the problem of the conflict between what is and what ought to be; and in describing the development of his views in a letter to his father[14] he notes that, setting out from the idealism of Kant, Fichte, and Schelling, he had 'hit upon seeking the Idea in the real itself' and had arrived at Hegel's system. At this time Marx joined a Hegelian discussion group, the Doctors' Club, in which some of Hegel's disciples, inspired by the ideas of the French Revolution, were attempting to develop his philosophy in a more radical fashion. From these discussions, and from the writings of Feuerbach and other Young Hegelians,[15] several themes emerged which assumed importance in the development of Marx's own thought. One of these was the notion of 'praxis' expounded by August von Cieszkowski; in a short book published in 1838[16] he argued that philosophy should 'become a practical philosophy or rather a philosophy of practical activity, of "praxis", exercising a direct influence on social life and developing the future in the realm of concrete activity'. Far more significant in Marx's development, however, was the work of Ludwig Feuerbach, not only for its exposition of a radical naturalism and humanism, which reinforced Marx's

12 See, for the whole passage, Bottomore and Rubel (eds), *Marx: Selected Writings*, p. 243.
13 As editor of the liberal *Rheinische Zeitung*, Marx replied to an accusation by the *Augsburger Allgemeine Zeitung* that the paper had communist sympathies by declaring: 'The *Rheinische Zeitung* does not even concede *theoretical validity* to communist ideas in their present form, let alone desires their practical realization, which it anyway finds impossible, and will subject these ideas to a fundamental criticism.'
14 10 November 1837. The letter is translated in L. Easton and K. Guddat (eds), *Writings of the Young Marx on Philosophy and Society*, pp. 40–50.
15 For a general account of the milieu and ideas of the Young Hegelians, see David McLellan, *The Young Hegelians and Karl Marx*.
16 August von Cieszkowski, *Prolegomena zur Historiosophie*. See McLellan, *The Young Hegelians*, pp. 9–11.

own orientation,[17] but still more for its approach to the criticism of Hegel's philosophy. It was Feuerbach who first 'inverted' Hegel's system, transforming the subject of idealist philosophy (thought) into a predicate, and the predicate (man) into a subject,[18] a real individual from whose practical existence philosophical inquiry should begin. Marx went on to apply this method in his criticism of Hegel's political philosophy.

The crucial period in the formation of Marx's own social theory is that between March, 1843 (when he resigned as editor of the *Rheinische Zeitung*), and the autumn of 1844. During this time Marx wrote a long critique of Hegel's philosophy of the state,[19] published his two essays – 'On the Jewish question' and 'Contribution to the critique of Hegel's Philosophy of Right: Introduction' – in the *Deutsch-Französische Jahrbücher*, and composed the *Economic and Philosophical Manuscripts*. The most significant aspects of this intellectual development are, first, the formulation of Marx's conception of the proletariat, and second, the beginning of his critique of political economy.

A number of writers in France and Germany had already discussed the situation of the proletariat in modern society,[20] but the most systematic account of this new class was given by Lorenz von Stein in his book *Der Sozialismus und Kommunismus des heutigen Frankreich*.[21] There has been much controversy about the extent of Marx's indebtedness to Stein;[22] it seems likely that he read Stein's book soon after it was published in 1842, and although this was by no means his first acquaintance with the ideas of the French socialist thinkers, Stein's sociological interpretation of the role of the proletariat in industrial society was probably an important influence in clarifying his own views. At all events the conception of the proletariat as a new political force engaged in a struggle for emancipation had an immense significance, for here Marx at last discovered the 'idea in the real itself'. The working-class movement, a new and striking phenomenon in the political life of modern society, was also the source of the

17 Though Marx had some reservations; in a letter to Arnold Ruge, after Feuerbach's essay, 'Vorläufige Thesen zur Reformation der Philosophie' was published early in 1843 in the *Anekdota* (edited by Ruge), he commented: 'I approve of Feuerbach's aphorisms, except for one point: he directs himself too much to nature and too little to politics. But it is politics which happens to be the only link through which contemporary philosophy can become true.'
18 See the discussion in Shlomo Avineri, *The Social and Political Thought of Karl Marx*, pp. 10–12.
19 The manuscript was first published in *MEGA*, I, 1/1 (1927), under the title *Kritik des hegelschen Staatsrechts*. An English translation has now been published, edited by Joseph O'Malley, *Karl Marx: Critique of Hegel's 'Philosophy of Right'*.
20 Gans, as I noted earlier, had written of the class struggle of the proletariat; and there were many other references to this phenomenon, as Avineri shows in the selection included in this volume (see pp. 236–8 below).
21 First published in 1842, a second revised and enlarged edition appeared in 1848, and the final version, under the title *Geschichte der sozialen Bewegung in Frankreich von 1789 bis auf unsere Tage*, in 1850. There is an English translation of major sections of Stein's book, edited with an introduction by Kaethe Mengelberg, *The History of the Social Movement in France, 1789–1850*.
22 See the discussion by Kaethe Mengelberg, ibid., pp. 25–31.

new social doctrines of socialism and communism. So Marx could conclude his essay on Hegel's Philosophy of Right by proclaiming that the mission of the proletariat as a 'universal class' was to dissolve existing society and bring about a general human emancipation; he could also express in a more precise way the philosophy of 'praxis': 'as philosophy finds its *material* weapons in the proletariat, so the proletariat finds its *intellectual* weapons in philosophy.'

But the proletariat, as Marx noted, was a product of the industrial movement; and in order to understand fully its social situation and role it would be necessary to study the economic structure of modern societies and the process of its development. Marx embarked on these new studies all the more willingly since as editor of the *Rheinische Zeitung* he had been 'embarrassed at first . . . in discussions concerning so-called material interests'; and he was encouraged, and initially guided, by the work which Engels had already done in political economy, and had published in an essay 'Umrisse zu einer Kritik der Nationalökonomie', in the *Deutsch-Französische Jahrbücher* (1844). Thus from October 1843, when he moved to Paris, until the end of 1844, Marx read voraciously in the works of the economists – among others J. B. Say, James Mill, List, Ricardo and Adam Smith – and filled a series of notebooks with excerpts from, and critical comments on, their writings.[23]

The first fruits of these studies were the *Economic and Philosophical Manuscripts*, in which Marx embarked on a critique of political economy that was to occupy him for the rest of his life. The manuscripts mark the transition in Marx's thought from philosophical criticism to a critical social theory – the transformation of philosophical ideas into social concepts. Marx's argument develops two main themes. First, the Hegelian conception of the spiritual self-creation of man is reinterpreted in the language of political economy, according to which labour is the source of all wealth. But at the same time the significance of human labour is more broadly conceived; through his labour man not only creates wealth, but develops his human qualities and a whole form of social life:

> It is just in his work upon the objective world that man really proves himself as a *species-being*. This production is his active species-life. By means of it nature appears as *his* work and his reality. The object of labour is, therefore, the *objectification of man's species-life*; for he no longer reproduces himself merely intellectually, as in consciousness, but actively and in a real sense, and he sees his own reflection in a world which he has constructed.[24]

Secondly, Marx uses the notion of alienation, which Feuerbach had employed to criticize religion, in order to describe a condition of society in which, although the process of labour *should* involve the development of man's

---

23 Published in *MEGA*, I/3, 411–583.
24 *Economic and Philosophical Manuscripts*, in Bottomore (ed.), *Karl Marx: Early Writings*, p. 128.

human potentialities and the creation of a world of human enjoyment, it actually produced, through private property, acquisitiveness, exchange and competition, a devaluation and dehumanization of the worker:

> We shall begin from a *contemporary* economic fact. The worker becomes poorer the more wealth he produces and the more his production increases in power and extent. The worker becomes an ever cheaper commodity the more goods he creates. The *devaluation* of the human world increases in direct relation with the *increase in value* of the world of things. Labour does not only create goods; it also produces itself and the worker as a *commodity*, and indeed in the same proportion as it produces goods. This fact simply implies that the object produced by labour, its product, now stands opposed to it as an *alien being*, as a *power independent* of the producer. . . . The performance of work appears in the sphere of political economy as a *vitiation* of the worker, objectification as a *loss* and as *servitude to the object*, and appropriation as *alienation*.[25]

All the elements of Marx's theory of society were now present – the moral commitment to a humanist doctrine of progress and human self-realization, which assumed the precise form of a commitment to the socialist movement, the idea of the proletariat as the embodiment of an ideal in the real world, the conception of labour and the system of economic production as generating the forms of society, the notion of private property and alienation as the sources of social antagonisms – and after an interlude in which he wrote, with Engels, a long and rather tedious critique of his former associates among the Young Hegelians,[26] who had remained immured in the sphere of 'critical philosophy', Marx began to formulate a positive outline of the general view at which he had arrived. This view was expressed first in *The German Ideology* (1845–6):

> This conception of history, therefore, rests on the exposition of the real process of production, starting out from the simple material production of life, and on the comprehension of the form of intercourse connected with and created by this mode of production, i.e. of civil society in its various stages as the basis of all history, and also in its action as the State. From this starting point, it explains all the different theoretical productions and forms of consciousness, religion, philosophy, ethics, etc., and traces their origins and growth, by which means the matter can of course be displayed as a whole (and consequently, also the reciprocal action of these various sides on one another).[27]

Similarly, in a letter written in December 1846, to P. V. Annenkov, commenting on Proudhon's book *Philosophie de la misère*, Marx set forth succinctly his own outlook:

---

25 Ibid., pp. 121–2.
26 *The Holy Family* (1845).
27 Bottomore and Rubel (eds), *Marx: Selected Writings*, p. 54.

What is society, regardless of its particular form? The product of men's interaction. Are men free to choose this or that social form? Not at all. Assume a certain stage of development of men's productive powers and you will have a particular form of commerce and consumption. Assume certain levels of development of production, commerce, and consumption, and you will have a particular type of social constitution, a particular organization of the family, of ranks or classes; in short a particular form of civil society. Assume a determinate form of civil society and you will have a particular type of political regime, which is only the official expression of civil society.[28]

The next stage for Marx was to analyse in detail the system of production and to depict its interrelations with the other aspects of social life, especially in the modern capitalist societies; in fact, to carry out the programme announced in the preface of the *Economic and Philosophical Manuscripts* where, after completing his study of political economy, Marx proposed to publish his 'critique of law, morals, politics, etc. . . . and finally, to present the interconnected whole, to show the relationships between the parts, and to provide a critique of the speculative treatment of this material'.[29]

The structure and development of capitalist society

However, Marx was unable to carry out his youthful plans. The critiques of 'law, morals, politics, etc.' were never written, except in the form of occasional pieces on current political events,[30] or as fragmentary discussions in manuscripts, notably the *Grundrisse*. Even Marx's analysis of the economic structure of society remained unfinished. After sketching the outlines of his theory of history in *The German Ideology*, and beginning the major work which he referred to as his *Economics*, Marx was then diverted from his studies for the next decade by an active involvement in politics in the revolutions of 1848, and by the journalism in which he had to engage in order to support himself.

Only in 1857 did Marx resume his economic studies seriously; and he then drafted a new plan for his work on political economy, and wrote large sections of it in the thousand-page manuscript of the *Grundrisse*. His plan envisaged a work in six parts, preceded by a methodological introduction in which he established a distinction between 'production in general' and the historical forms of production; and in the light of this, examined the categories of political economy – production, consumption, distribution, exchange:

28 Marx and Engels, *Ausgewählte Briefe* (Berlin, 1953).
29 Bottomore and Rubel (eds), *Marx: Selected Writings*, p. 63.
30 Especially his articles in the *Neue Rheinische Zeitung* (1848–9), and in the *New York Daily Tribune* (from 1851 to 1862); his Address, on behalf of the General Council of the International Working Men's Association, on the Paris Commune (1871); and his notes on the Gotha Programme of the German workers' party (1875).

Whenever we speak of production, therefore, we always refer to production at a certain stage of social development, to production by social individuals. Hence, it might appear that in order to speak of production at all we must either trace the historical process of development through its various phases, or else make clear at the outset that we are dealing with a specific historical period, for example, with modern bourgeois production, which is in fact the real theme of this work. But all stages of production have certain features and determining factors in common. *Production in general* is an abstraction, but a rational abstraction in so far as it highlights and establishes the common features, thus saving us repetition. These *general* aspects or common features discovered by comparison are themselves very complex, and their constituent elements develop along different lines. Some of these elements belong to all epochs, others are common to a few. Some are common to the most modern and to the most ancient epochs. . . . The conditions which regulate production in general must be distinguished in order not to lose sight of the essential differences within the uniformity which arises from the fact that the subject – mankind – and the object – nature – remain the same.[31]

Indeed, Marx devoted a long section of the *Grundrisse* to an analysis – the most systematic that he ever wrote – of the different stages of production and the process of economic evolution.[32] But the main theme, as Marx noted, was modern bourgeois production; and he proposed to deal with this in six books concerned with capital, landed property, wage labour, the state, foreign trade and the international relations of production, the world market and crises.[33] Only the first of these books was written (even then, not in its complete and final version) and published as *Capital*, although it contained references to many problems that would have been discussed fully in the other books.[34] The *Grundrisse* deals in a preliminary fashion with some of these problems, and reveals more clearly than does *Capital* the scope of Marx's work, as a study of the *social system* of capitalist production rather than a narrowly economic analysis. But this does not exhaust the significance of the text. It constitutes, as many commentators have pointed out, an essential link between Marx's early and late writings, revealing the way in which philosophical ideas were transformed into economic and sociological concepts; and it provides a much more detailed account of the trend of capitalist development, the contradictions that will lead to a breakdown of capitalism, and the conditions for a transition to socialism, than is to be found in the volumes of *Capital*.

31 *Grundrisse*, pp. 6–7. Unless noted otherwise, all translations from the *Grundrisse* are mine.
32 *Grundrisse*, pp. 375–413.
33 See Bottomore and Rubel (eds), *Marx: Selected Writings*, pp. 16–18.
34 It is evident, for example, that the fragment on social classes which Engels published as the final chapter of *Capital*, vol. III, is the draft of an analysis of classes which was meant to come at the end of the three books dealing with the 'main constituent elements' of bourgeois society – capital, landed property and wage labour.

Use-value and exchange value

The *Grundrisse* develops in a new way, and through a much more profound critique of political economy, the central concern of the *Economic and Philosophical Manuscripts* with the problem of alienated labour by elaborating the distinction between use-value and exchange value, and by introducing the concepts of 'labour power' and 'surplus value'. Marx characterizes capitalism, in the first place, as a society based upon exchange and the market, in which exchange value predominates over use-value, or to express the same idea in another way (which relates the phenomenon to the system of production): 'the product becomes a commodity'. Capitalism is a form of society in which money is the social bond:

> The universal reciprocal dependence of individuals who remain indifferent to one another constitutes their social bond. This social bond is expressed in *exchange value.* . . . [The individual] has to produce a general product – *exchange value* – or, in its isolated, individualized form – *money*. On the other side, the power that each individual exercises over the activity of others, or over social wealth, is based upon his possession of exchange values, money. He carries his social power and his bond with society in his pocket.[35]

The predominance of exchange value, and the power of money, constitutes an alienated form of social life:

> The social character of activity, and the social form of the product, as well as the participation of the individual in production, appear here as alien, material things in opposition to the individual; not in their behaviour to each other, but in their subordination to relations which exist independently of them and arise out of the collisions between indifferent individuals. The universal exchange of activities and products, which has become a condition of life for each individual, and the bond between individuals, appears to them as something alien and independent, like a thing.[36]

Marx's analysis of capitalist society as one in which the social bond assumed the impersonal character of a relationship between *things* provided one of the major themes of sociological thought in Germany in the late nineteenth

---

35 *Grundrisse*, pp. 74–5.
36 Ibid., p. 75. The affinity of these passages with the discussion of money in the *Economic and Philosophical Manuscripts* is unmistakable; see Bottomore (ed.), *Marx: Early Writings*, pp. 189–94. See also Marx's critique of utilitarianism in *The German Ideology*, where he wrote that: 'The apparent absurdity which transforms all the various interrelationships of men into the single relationship of utility, an apparently metaphysical abstraction, follows from the fact that in modern civil society all relationships are in practice subordinated to the single abstract relationship of money and speculation' (Bottomore and Rubel (eds), *Marx: Selected Writings*, p. 161).

century, although at that time his influence could arise only from the brief references in the essays in the *Deutsch-Französische Jahrbücher*, the *Communist Manifesto*, the criticism of Proudhon in *Misère de la philosophie* and *Capital* – not from the more extensive discussion in the manuscripts which have subsequently been published. Tönnies' distinction between two types of society, *Gemeinschaft* (community), characterized by direct personal relationships, and *Gesellschaft* (society), characterized by impersonal, especially economic, relationships, was inspired directly by Marx's thought.[37] Similarly, the major study of social relationships in a money economy, Simmel's *Philosophie des Geldes*,[38] was greatly influenced by reflection upon Marx's work. In his study Simmel deals not only with the impersonal character of social life in a developed money economy and the effects of the division of labour in restricting the individual's sphere of life, but also with the positive aspects of modern society – the growth of rationality exemplified by the development of an increasingly abstract measure of value, and the increase of social differentiation with all its possibilities for greater individual freedom. These ideas, however, were not entirely discordant with Marx's view, for he too regarded capitalism as a stage – the most significant stage – in the progress of human reason, and he recognized that it created more favourable conditions for the emergence of individuality:

> Relations of personal dependence (at first completely natural and spontaneous [*naturwüchsig*]) are the first forms of society, in which human productivity develops only to a limited extent and at isolated points. Personal independence, based upon dependence on *things*, is the second great form, in which for the first time a system of general social exchange, universal relationships, universal needs, and universal capacities, is established. Free individuality, based upon the universal development of individuals, and the subordination of their communal, social productivity as their own social powers, is the third stage. The second stage creates the conditions for the third.[39]

---

37 Ferdinand Tönnies, *Community and Association*. Tönnies' relation to Marx can be seen clearly from the study of Marx which he published later, *Karl Marx: His Life and Teachings*.
38 Georg Simmel, *Philosophy of Money*.
39 *Grundrisse*, pp. 75–6. See also the discussion in *The German Ideology*: 'But in the course of historical development, and precisely as a result of the assumption of independence by social relationships, which is the inevitable outcome of the division of labour, there emerges a distinction between the personal life of the individual and his life as it is determined by some branch of labour and the conditions pertaining to it. . . . In a system of estates (and still more in the tribe) this is still concealed: for instance, a nobleman always remains a nobleman, a commoner always a commoner, irrespective of his other relationships, a quality inseparable from his individuality. The distinction between the personal and the class individual, the accidental nature of conditions of life for the individual, appears only with the emergence of class, which itself is a product of the bourgeoisie' (Bottomore and Rubel, (eds), *Marx: Selected Writings*, pp. 249–50).

Labour power and surplus-value

The second aspect of alienated labour is analysed by Marx with the aid of the newly developed concepts of 'labour power' and 'surplus-value'. In capitalist society, in which all products and activities are converted into exchange values, labour power itself becomes an exchange value – i.e., a commodity. But it is a commodity very different from others in two ways. First, labour (the realization of labour power) is, as Marx describes it in the *Grundrisse*, 'living, purposeful activity', or as he says in the *Economic and Philosophical Manuscripts*, it is 'life activity, productive life . . . free, conscious activity', which is the characteristic of man as a species-being. The transformation of labour power into a commodity is an alienation of man's nature that deforms and cripples him.

Second, labour power as the capacity for productive activity has the unique characteristic of being able to create more value than is given in exchange for it. It creates 'surplus-value', and since this labour power has been acquired by the capitalist through an act of exchange, the surplus-value which it produces becomes the property of the capitalist. Thus, Marx concludes, 'all the progress of civilization, or in other words every increase in the *social powers of production*, if you want, in the *productive powers of labour itself* – as it results from science, inventions, the division and organization of labour, improved means of communication, the creation of a world market, machinery, etc. – does not enrich the worker, but capital; consequently it enhances still more the power which dominates labour, and only increases the productive capacity of capital.'[40]

Marx's analysis of labour power as a commodity is intended to show that in capitalist society, in spite of the appearance of equal exchange, surplus value is created and is appropriated by a particular class. In a slave society, or a feudal society, the production and appropriation of surplus value is obvious; the slave works for the slave-owner, the serf works for a part of the year on his lord's demesne. In capitalist society this process takes place in a concealed form, but it still constitutes the basis of the whole social system. As Marx later formulated his general proposition:

> The specific economic form in which unpaid surplus labour is pumped out of the direct producers determines the relation of domination and servitude, as it emerges directly out of production itself and in its turn reacts upon production. Upon this basis, however, is founded the entire structure of the economic community, which grows up out of the conditions of production itself, and consequently its specific political form. It is always the direct relation between the masters of the conditions of production and the direct producers which reveals the innermost secret, the hidden foundation of the entire social edifice and therefore also of the political form of the relation between sovereignty and dependence, in short, of the particular form of the State.[41]

40 *Grundrisse*, p. 215.
41 *Capital*, vol. III; in Bottomore and Rubel (eds), *Marx: Selected Writings*, p. 99.

It is plain from this analysis that the fundamental opposition in capitalist society, as in previous forms of society, is that between the 'masters of production' and the 'direct producers'. But what is the course of development through which this opposition will reach a point of crisis; what are the conditions in which a social transformation can occur; and what factors will determine the form of a new society? Marx gives diverse answers to these questions. In *Capital* he emphasizes the periodic economic crises which will become increasingly destructive; and it was along these lines that Marxists in the 1930s analysed what they termed the 'general crisis of capitalism'. From this standpoint Marx conceived an eventual struggle between the bourgeoisie and a proletariat reduced to a condition of extreme misery. As he expressed it in a well-known passage of *Capital*: 'Along with the constantly diminishing number of the magnates of capital . . . grows the mass of misery, oppression, slavery, degradation, and exploitation; but with this too grows the revolt of the working class . . .'[42]

But in the *Grundrisse* Marx lays stress rather on the development of the *social character* of production within the capitalist system, through the advance of science and technology; and he refers in much vaguer terms to the supersession of capitalism as the process of material production is 'divested of its impoverished and antagonistic form', and the conditions of social life are 'subjected to the control of the general intellect':

> To the extent that large-scale industry develops, the creation of real wealth comes to depend less upon labour time and the quantity of labour expended, than upon the power of the instruments which are set in motion during labour time, whose powerful effectiveness is likewise unrelated to the labour time directly involved in their production, but depends rather upon the general state of science and the progress of technology, or the application of this science to production. . . . Labour no longer appears as an integral part of the process of production; instead, man acts as the supervisor and regulator of this process. . . . With this transformation, what appears as the mainstay of production and wealth is neither the labour which man directly expends, nor the time he spends at work, but his appropriation of his own general productive powers, his understanding and mastery of nature; in short, the development of the social individual. The *theft of other men's labour time, upon which present-day wealth depends*, appears a miserable basis compared with this new one which large-scale industry has created. As soon as labour in its direct form has ceased to be the great wellspring of wealth, labour time ceases, and must cease, to be its measure, and consequently exchange value must cease to be the measure of use-value. The *surplus labour of the masses* has ceased to be a condition for the development of wealth in general; just as the *non-labour of the few* has ceased to be a condition for the development of the general powers of the human mind. Production based upon exchange value then collapses, and the process of direct

42 *Capital*, vol. I; in Bottomore and Rubel (eds), ibid., p. 141.

material production is divested of its impoverished and antagonistic form. Individuals can then develop freely ... and the reduction of necessary social labour to a minimum is accompanied by the development of education in the arts, sciences, etc. for all individuals, through the free time and means which have become available. Capital is itself a contradiction in action, for it strives to reduce labour time to a minimum, while at the same time it posits labour time as the only measure and source of wealth. Thus it reduces labour time in its necessary form in order to augment it in its superfluous form. ... On one side it brings to life all the powers of science and nature, of social organization and intercourse, in order to make the creation of wealth (relatively) independent of the labour time expended on it; but on the other side it wants to use labour time as a measure for the gigantic social powers thus created, and to confine them within the limits which are required in order to maintain already created values as values. Productive forces and social relations – which are different aspects of the development of the social individual – appear to capital only as a means, and are only a means, to produce on its own restricted basis. But in fact they are the material conditions to blow up this basis.... The development of fixed capital indicates the extent to which general social knowledge has become a *direct productive force*, and thus the extent to which the conditions of the social life process have themselves been brought under the control of the general intellect and reconstructed in accordance with it.[43]

It can be argued from this exposition in the *Grundrisse*, as Nicolaus has done in his essay 'The Unknown Marx', that Marx, far from envisaging the breakdown of capitalism in terms of a revolt by starving, degraded, and oppressed proletarians in the midst of a profound economic crisis, conceived it as a much longer-term process in which, ultimately, the immense productive forces based upon advanced science and technology and directed by educated, technically competent workers, would prove incompatible with the capitalist system, and would, in some manner, 'divest' themselves of this social framework.[44] But this conception poses some difficult problems. It is no longer clear how the transition from capitalism to socialism will be made, for the working class, as Marx conceived it in his earlier writings, seems to be progressively eliminated from any important role in the system of production; and thus the principal agent of social transformation vanishes from the scene.

There are two interpretations of social and political evolution that might be derived from Marx's discussion here. One is that the development of technology and the consequent changes in the economic system bring into existence a new class – distinct from the bourgeoisie and the proletariat – composed of the highly qualified technicians and administrators who pass from the

---

43 *Grundrisse*, pp. 592–4.
44 This view has also been formulated positively in the argument that production based upon advanced science and technology is *more* compatible with a socialist form of society, especially in the work by Radovan Richta and his associates, *Civilization at the Crossroads*, which draws extensively upon the discussion in the *Grundrisse*. See also my recent discussion in *Theories of Modern Capitalism*, ch. 1.

domination of the system of production to a struggle for general social power. This would resemble the process in which the bourgeoisie emerged as a class, between the feudal landlords and the serfs, in feudal society.

The second interpretation is that the increasingly predominant role of science and technology in production will create the conditions in which the organization and control of production by society as a whole is the essential next stage of development. For on one side, the application of science to production creates immense wealth, making possible high levels of living and greatly increased leisure time; and on the other side, it brings into existence a more educated population whose members can now formulate more clearly the goals of individual self-expression and self-realization. From this viewpoint the creation of a new society can be seen as a long-term process in which, through the progress of the 'general intellect', human beings gradually extend their control over the social conditions that affect their lives. Or, to use an expression which Marx employed in discussing the growth of joint-stock companies, there may be (there may in fact have occurred in the twentieth century) a progressive 'abolition of the capitalist mode of production within capitalist production itself'.

Neither in the *Grundrisse* nor elsewhere does Marx examine the political implications of these ideas about the future development of capitalist production. His political theory was never expounded in a systematic form. But by looking at its partial formulations in Marx's account of the class structure and in his commentaries on the development of the working-class movement, we may be able to grasp how it would have been worked out in the context of his later economic analysis.

The theory of classes

The theory of social classes is at the centre of Marx's thought. For as he wrote in his early criticism of the Young Hegelians: '*History* does *nothing*; it "does *not* possess immense riches", it "does not fight battles". It is *men*, real, living men, who do all this, who possess things and fight battles. . . . History is *nothing* but the activity of men in pursuit of their ends.'[45] Whatever the contradictions within a given form of society, and whatever abstract forces (such as the progress of science and technology) may be at work, they can only become effective through the conscious, purposive actions of human beings. And these actions arise out of, are shaped by, the real life experiences of individuals within the division of labour and the class structure.

The great importance of the concept of class was referred to earlier, when I noted that Marx's discovery of the proletariat as the bearer of a social ideal in the world of reality was a crucial element in the evolution of his thought. In fact,

45 *The Holy Family*; in Bottomore and Rubel (eds), *Marx: Selected Writings*, p. 63.

those parts of Marx's theory of class which are elaborated at all fully concern particularly the formation and development of the proletariat in capitalist society. His general view is well set out in *The Poverty of Philosophy*:

> Economic conditions had in the first place transformed the mass of the people into workers. The domination of capital created the common situation and common interests of this class. Thus this mass is already a class in relation to capital, but not yet a class for itself. In the struggle, of which we have only indicated a few phases, this mass unites and forms itself into a class for itself. The interests which it defends become class interests. But the struggle between the classes is a political struggle.[46]

A similar conception is formulated in Marx's discussion of the role of the peasantry in France, in *The 18th Brumaire of Louis Bonaparte*:

> The small-holding peasants form a vast mass, the members of which live in similar conditions but without entering into manifold relations with one another. Their mode of production isolates them from one another instead of bringing them into mutual intercourse. In so far as millions of families live under economic conditions of existence that separate their mode of life, their interests and their culture from those of the other classes, and put them in hostile opposition to the latter, they form a class. In so far as there is merely a local interconnection among these small-holding peasants, and the identity of their interests begets no community, no national bond and no political organization among them, they do not form a class.[47]

The proletariat, unlike the peasantry, is a modern – not a traditional – class, created by the growth of large-scale industry, and able, because of its concentration in factories and towns, to develop a class consciousness and independent political organizations. Marx emphasizes strongly the distinctive character of modern classes – the bourgeoisie and proletariat – in relation to earlier social groups such as feudal estates;[48] and the elaboration of his general theory would have required a systematic analysis of the different forms that social classes (in the broad meaning of 'class', which refers to all the historical social groups constituted by the 'masters of the system of production' and the 'direct producers') had assumed in the various stages of social development. As it is, Marx only indicates very briefly some of the specific features of modern classes by suggesting that the conditions of capitalist society permit the rapid development of classes on a national, rather than a local, scale; and at the same time capitalist society brings out more clearly the economic character and interests of the classes. The bourgeoisie and the proletariat are, in this sense, 'pure' classes.

46 Bottomore and Rubel (eds), *Marx: Selected Writings*, p. 187.
47 Ibid., pp. 188–9.
48 See above, p. 12, n. 39.

However, the most distinctive feature of modern classes is that they are also the 'final' classes; and capitalism is, in Marx's words, 'the last antagonistic form of society'. Just as the third estate abolished estates when it rose to power, so the working class will abolish classes and inaugurate the classless society. This idea of the social mission of the working class runs through Marx's work from his very early writings (the essay on Hegel's Philosophy of Right in the *Deutsch-Französische Jahrbücher*, 1844)[49] to one of his last publications (the preface to the *Enquête Ouvrière*, 1880).[50] It may well have had, as Avineri argues,[51] a speculative origin, as a reformulation of Hegel's concept of a 'universal class'; and Marx certainly attributed this historical importance to the proletariat before he had undertaken any serious analysis of the economic structure of modern society. But it should not be forgotten that Marx was already very familiar with the more empirical writings of the French socialists, especially the Saint-Simonians, and with Lorenz von Stein's study of the situation of the working class in the modern industrial system. His life's work can be regarded as an attempt to show, by an empirical investigation, how the development of modern capitalism necessarily leads to a social transformation in which the working-class movement will abolish all classes.

At all events, this conception has generally been seen as the predominant and distinctive theme of Marx's social theory, so that, as Ossowski observes,[52] it became in a sense 'the symbol of his whole doctrine', expressed by such terms as 'class point of view'. But as I indicated earlier, the theory of modern classes was not expounded systematically by Marx, and the conception that he outlined in a fragmentary way presents both theoretical and empirical problems that appear even within the context of Marx's own analysis of capitalism. In his earlier writings Marx emphasized very strongly the polarization of classes; for example, in *The Communist Manifesto* he asserts that 'the epoch of the bourgeoisie possesses ... this distinctive feature: it has simplified the class antagonisms. Society as a whole is more and more splitting up into two great hostile camps, into two great classes directly facing each other – bourgeoisie and proletariat.' But in the unfinished chapter of *Capital*, vol. III, written much later when Marx was trying to advance from his fundamental economic analysis to an investigation of the social relations that developed from the economic basis, he observed that even in the most highly developed modern society, England, 'the class structure does not appear in a pure form. . . . Intermediate and transitional strata obscure the class boundaries even in this case'.

It may be argued, as Ossowski suggests,[53] that Marx was formulating a model of the class structure, an ideal type to which the real social world would

49 See Bottomore, (ed.), *Marx: Early Writings*, pp. 58–9.
50 See below, p. 263.
51 See the selection in this volume, pp. 235–44.
52 See the selection in this volume, pp. 215–25.
53 See below, p. 217.

gradually conform more closely in the final stage of development of the capitalist system. Even if this view were accepted, it would involve a much more protracted evolution towards the final breakdown of capitalism than Marx envisaged in his writings on class in the period between the 1840s and the 1860s. There is indeed evidence that as he pursued his economic analysis Marx began to conceive a more prolonged development of capitalism; but at the same time there emerged a discrepancy between his political writings (in which he continued to greet every new economic crisis as the harbinger of revolution) and his theoretical investigations. More important, however, is the fact that in his theoretical studies Marx began to sketch a course of social development that directly contradicts the notion of an increasing polarization of classes. The possibility that the intermediate strata in capitalist society would grow, rather than diminish, as a proportion of the population is suggested in a number of ways, and expressed most clearly in a comment on Ricardo in the manuscript of *Theories of Surplus Value*: 'What he [Ricardo] forgets to mention is the continual increase in numbers of the middle classes, . . . situated midway between the workers on one side and the capitalists on the other, who rest with all their weight upon the working class and at the same time increase the social security and power of the upper ten thousand.'[54] Elsewhere in *Theories of Surplus Value*, commenting upon Malthus, Marx observes: 'His greatest hope – which he himself considers more or less utopian – is that the middle class will grow in size and that the working class will form a continually diminishing proportion of the total population (even if it grows in absolute numbers). That is, in fact, the trend of bourgeois society.'[55]

These ideas are developed more fully in the *Grundrisse*. There, especially in the passage which I quoted earlier,[56] Marx seems to envisage a virtual disappearance of the proletariat as he and other nineteenth-century social theorists had generally understood it – the class of manual workers in modern factory industry – at a more advanced stage of capitalist development. The problem which this presents is not that the contradiction between the social character of the production of use-values and the private appropriation of surplus value through exchange is resolved, but that there no longer seems to be a human agency that will bring about the necessary social transformation; and both the process of social change and the form of a new society become unclear. In fact, there is a strong element of technological determinism in the discussion in the *Grundrisse*, as though Marx was insisting that the application of advanced science to production must of necessity bring into existence a society of free and equal individuals. One is tempted to expand another of Marx's more deterministic statements – 'The hand mill gives you a society with the feudal lord, the

54 See Bottomore and Rubel (eds), *Marx: Selected Writings*, pp. 190–1. I have revised my original translation of this passage, which was rather too free.
55 Translated from the German text in *Werke*, XXVI/iii, 57.
56 See above, pp. 14–15.

steam mill a society with the industrial capitalist' – by summarizing the doctrine of the *Grundrisse* in the phrase: 'The automated mill gives you a classless society.'

If Marx had been able to complete his social theory by expounding his theory of classes and his political theory, he would undoubtedly have done so in the same manner as he presented his economic analysis; that is to say, he would have combined a theoretical discussion with a comprehensive empirical study of the actual development of social classes.[57] Such an investigation would have to deal with three principal sets of problems:

1 The consequences for the class structure, and especially for the polarization of classes, of the rapid increase in productivity and in the size of the surplus, and the concomitant growth of the middle classes.
2 The various cultural and political influences which either favour or impede the development of working-class consciousness, and in particular a revolutionary class consciousness.
3 The conditions which are necessary, beyond the abolition of private property in the means of production, and the disappearance of classes in this sense, to establish the new society of liberated individuals that Marx called 'socialism' or 'communism'.

As to the first of these problems, we can only speculate, on the basis of Marx's brief reference to the 'growth of the middle classes', and his discussion in the *Grundrisse*, about what kind of solution he might have proffered. It is obvious that he would not have taken the naïve view, which has sometimes been put forward under the guise of Marxism, that the working class in advanced capitalist societies is to be defined as all those who work for a living and who are not self-employed. Marx clearly meant by the working class the industrial workers who *produce* surplus-value; and he distinguished them from the middle classes who *live from* surplus-value, but who assist in the realization and distribution of the surplus (and also from various other categories of workers, e.g., domestic servants, whom he described, following Adam Smith and Ricardo, as 'unproductive'). The consequences of the growth of the middle classes and the relative (or even absolute) decline in numbers of the working class would seem to strengthen bourgeois rule, as Marx himself notes; and the transition to a socialist society then becomes more problematic. It could be argued, in terms of Marx's own analysis, either that the transition will never be made at all (and that there will emerge from capitalism a type of society which none of the socialist thinkers had foreseen), or that it will be made in a different way from that which Marx originally expected, through social conflicts in which

57 Not only did Marx not accomplish this, but no later Marxist has even attempted a thorough historical and sociological study of modern social classes. What we have, for the most part, is either abstract philosophical discourse or the tedious repetition of political slogans.

the working-class movement will be only one – though an important – element. At the extreme, however, as Marx sketched the course of capitalist development in the *Grundrisse*, the role of the working class seems to become quite insignificant. It is difficult to interpret Marx's ideas here because of the tentative and fragmentary character of the text; but it seems reasonable to suppose that he had in mind a technologically advanced economy, something we should refer to as 'computerized' or 'automated', in which a large proportion of the population would be engaged in scientific, technical and administrative occupations. The nature of the social conflict that would then bring about the breakdown of capitalism and the creation of a socialist society remains unclear, and is not discussed by Marx; but it seems to me that it might take the form suggested by some recent sociological analyses,[58] in which a direct political struggle would develop between those who control the instruments of economic and political decision-making and those who have been reduced to a condition of 'dependence'. Whether such groups, engaged in a conflict about the future form of society, should be called 'classes', is partly a question of terminology, but mainly one to be settled by theoretical and empirical inquiry. They can fit perfectly well within Marx's general scheme of the opposition between the 'masters of the system of production' and the 'direct producers'; but just as the social classes of nineteenth-century capitalism had to be distinguished from feudal estates, so these new classes would have to be distinguished from the bourgeoisie and proletariat of nineteenth-century theory, even though there may be elements of continuity.

The second problem – concerning the development of class consciousness – has to be examined in the context of the preceding discussion. For the most part, Marx emphasized, especially in his earlier writings, those influences which were favourable to the development of working-class consciousness, though he also recognized, implicitly or explicitly, that there were strong countervailing forces: the dominant position of ruling-class ideas, the effects of social mobility,[59] the growth of the middle classes. But Marx neglected other powerful influences which have proved to be of great importance. One is the strength of national or ethnic consciousness, not only in the creation of new nation-states in nineteenth-century Europe and of a new rivalry between them, but also in the nationalism of the twentieth century, whether in the form of national liberation movements, conflicts between nations, or social movements

58 See especially Alain Touraine, *The Post-Industrial Society*.
59 In *Capital* vol. III, Marx noted that the situation in which 'a man without wealth, but with energy, strength of character, ability and business sense, is able to become a capitalist . . . brings an unwelcome number of new soldiers of fortune into the field, and into competition with the existing individual capitalists . . . [but it] also consolidates the rule of capital itself, enlarges its basis, and enables it to recruit ever new forces for itself out of the lower layers of society'. See Bottomore and Rubel (eds), *Marx: Selected Writings*, p. 190.

based upon national or ethnic groups within existing nation-states.[60] A second influence, which works in quite a different direction, comes from the increasing social differentiation in modern societies (analysed most fully by Simmel) that is associated with the more complex division of labour and with a growing cultural diversity and individualism. This social differentiation tends to break down the uniformity of working-class consciousness, to create a greater diversity of status positions (which, as Max Weber argued, constitute another form of stratification inhibiting the development of 'pure' class antagonism), and to strengthen the influence of the 'intermediate strata', or middle classes. The effect of the forces that impede the growth of working-class consciousness, especially a revolutionary consciousness, is naturally greater if there is a long-term trend for the middle classes to increase and the working class to decline in relative or absolute numbers.

An assessment of the strength of these positive and negative influences would require a profound sociological and historical investigation and would be, in fact, a proper continuation of Marx's own work. It is plain enough, however, that the growth of working-class consciousness in the most advanced capitalist countries during the twentieth century has not followed the course that Marx anticipated, at least in his earlier writings. In most of these countries (but not in the United States, which must be regarded as a highly significant exception) there has been a steady development of working-class consciousness, in the sense that independent workers' parties have been formed and have gained the allegiance of a major part of the working class. But in no country has the working class become predominantly revolutionary in outlook – that is to say, deeply committed to bringing about a rapid and radical transformation of society. The high point of revolutionary consciousness among workers (at that time even among American workers) was probably in the period just before the First World War, during the war, and immediately afterwards. Since then, the general evolution of the working-class movement has been towards more reformist policies, and there are few indications in the present course of economic and social development that this trend is likely to change abruptly. At all events it is now scarcely possible to conceive the political system of the advanced capitalist countries as fostering the kind of dramatic confrontation between bourgeoisie and proletariat which Marx, especially in his romantic youth, foresaw.

The last set of problems in Marx's theory of class concerns the transition to a socialist society. Occasionally, as I have already indicated, Marx wrote in the language of technological determinism, as if the advance of science and its

---

60 Among later Marxist schools only the Austro-Marxists, as might be expected from their situation in the multinational Habsburg Empire, paid serious attention to the problem of nationalism; the classic study is Otto Bauer, *Die Nationalitätenfrage und die Sozialdemokratie*. For the most part, however, Marxists have continued to neglect or underestimate such phenomena. See T. B. Bottomore and P. Goode (eds), *Austro-Marxism*.

application to production must necessarily bring into existence a classless, liberated society. But I do not think such passages represent his most profound thought on the processes of social change. Marx's fundamental conception is rather that the advance of science will create both the material conditions (the abolition of scarcity in the satisfaction of basic human needs) and the intellectual or cultural prerequisites (understanding of the means to control and shape social life in order to achieve the maximum of human enjoyment) for a new society.[61] The complex interplay between the development of production, the emergence of new human needs and aspirations, the development of political consciousness, and the formation of organizations to engage in a political struggle would have been the subject of Marx's political theory. Unfortunately this, like the theory of class, can only be examined in the fragmentary, incomplete form in which Marx left it.

Social movements and ideologies

When nineteenth-century writers referred to 'the social movement', they meant the labour movement in its various manifestations[62] – political clubs, trade unions, cooperatives, utopian communities, or mass movements such as Chartism – just as, in referring to 'the social question', they meant the labour question, the condition of the industrial working class. Marx too wrote of the labour movement, or workers' movement, but he also used the term 'party' for some of its forms; however, it is clear that he was not referring, in the main, to the modern type of political party,[63] and in fact used the term to describe very different kinds of organization.[64] For example, Marx referred to the Communist League (of which he was a member from 1847 to 1852) as 'our party', although this was a party only in the sense of a political club, or *société de pensée*. In a different context, he and Engels regarded the Chartist movement as 'the first working-men's party of modern times', and saw the Chartist traditions as a possible basis for the creation of a new working-class party in England.

Marx also spoke of 'our party' in a more transcendental sense, as Monty Johnstone has noted: 'For Marx the party in this sense was the embodiment of

61 This is unmistakably a version of the Enlightenment doctrine of the beneficent progress of human reason. See further on this subject T. B. Bottomore, *Theories of Modern Capitalism*, ch. 6.
62 See Lorenz von Stein, *The Social Movement in France*.
63 Only towards the end of Marx's life did the German workers' party begin to develop some of the characteristics of the modern mass party, and it was mainly Engels who observed and commented on this development. See J. P. Nettl, 'The German Social-Democratic Party 1890–1914 as a political model', *Past and Present*, (1965), pp. 65–95.
64 There has been surprisingly little discussion of Marx's ideas about the nature of a working-class party, partly no doubt because of the preeminence which the Bolshevik Party acquired as a universal model. One useful review of the subject is Monty Johnstone, 'Marx and Engels and the concept of the party', *The Socialist Register* (1967), pp. 121–58.

his conception of the "mission" of the working class, concentrating in itself the "revolutionary interests of society"'.[65] From this standpoint 'party' and 'class' are identical; the party is simply the class organized for a political struggle, the final stage in the development of the 'class for itself'. This conception, however, is quite compatible with the view that Marx seems generally to have expressed: namely, that the political development of the working class (its organization, in a broad sense) would give rise to a variety of particular organizations that would be linked together by the class itself, not by a centralized, disciplined party. Thus the Paris Commune, which was not at all the achievement of a party in the modern sense, was described by Marx as 'the political form at last discovered under which to work out the emancipation of labour'.[66] The predominant theme of all Marx's writing on the development of working-class politics is that it should result in the creation of autonomous organizations, independent of the bourgeois parties and movements; it would not necessarily culminate in the establishment of a single supreme organization that would direct the whole working-class struggle.

Marx did not live to see the full development of mass political parties, and so he did not have to confront, in its most acute form, the problem of a divergence between the party as an organization, with its central offices, funds, newspapers and journals, and large numbers of officials, and the class as a potential community or social movement. When, later, Michels analysed the socialist parties, particularly the German Social Democratic party, he concluded that there is an inescapable concentration of power at the top, or 'oligarchy', in all large-scale organizations, and a consequent division of interest between the leaders and officials and the masses who have combined to form the party.[67] The interests of the officials, Michels says, 'are always conservative, and in a given political situation these interests may dictate a defensive and even a reactionary policy when the interests of the working class demand a bold and aggressive policy'.[68] Michels buttressed his argument by analysing what he called the 'incompetence of the masses', who in his view 'are incapable of taking part in the decision-making process and desire strong leadership'. This is quite similar to the conception that Lenin formulated, though from a different perspective and in a different context, which also established a strong distinction between party and class by asserting that the working class by itself can never attain more than a 'trade union consciousness' (i.e., a preoccupation with immediate economic questions) and that a revolutionary consciousness has to be brought to the working class from outside, by the Marxist theorists of the

65 Ibid., p. 129.
66 *The Civil War in France* (London, 1871). It was first published anonymously.
67 Robert Michels, *Political Parties*. But see the criticism of Michels by Brym, *Intellectuals and Politics*, pp. 35–6, 41–2.
68 In the second edition of his work (1915) Michels claimed that the actions of the German Social Democratic leaders in abruptly reversing their policy and supporting the war provided an effective confirmation of what he had said about the future of socialist parties.

party. This notion, which Lenin expressed in practical political terms, was elaborated in a philosophical argument by Georg Lukács as one of the central themes in his distinctive interpretation of Marxism; in the form of a distinction between a 'psychological consciousness' (the empirically given consciousness of workers) and an 'imputed rational consciousness', which Lukács also described as 'the correct class consciousness of the proletariat and its organizational form, the communist party'.[69]

The arguments of Lenin and Lukács (influenced in one case by the backwardness of Russian society, and in the other by the failure of the European revolutions after 1917) seem to me historically false, since the working-class movement had already arrived at socialist ideas before Marx himself became a socialist or worked out his social theory. They are also inconsistent with the fundamental orientation of Marx's own thought, which places the main emphasis upon a spontaneous development of working-class consciousness. Nevertheless, these arguments, like those of Michels, raise serious problems that remain largely unexplored in Marx's work, and which have received less attention than they merit from later Marxist writers. There are two principal issues to consider. One concerns the relation of the party as an organization to the class – the problems of leadership, of the role of a revolutionary elite, of oligarchy and bureaucracy. Michels' view of the dominant position of party leaders and officials and the 'incompetence of the masses' was based partly upon a consideration of the profound differences of education and culture that separated the leaders from the rank-and-file members and from the working class as a whole. Another socialist thinker, Waclaw Machajski, expounded this line of thought still more forcefully, again with particular reference to German social democracy, by arguing that the socialist movement actually expressed the ideology of dissatisfied intellectuals, and that its outcome would be the creation of a new ruling class of intellectuals – though he continued to believe that a classless society might still be attained eventually as a result of a general improvement in the level of education and culture.[70] It is worth noting that the few Marxists who have responded to Michels' argument have likewise attached great importance to the development of popular education and culture; Bukharin,[71] for example, argued that the 'incompetence of the masses' was a product of economic and technical conditions 'expressing themselves in the general culture and in educational conditions', and would disappear in a socialist society. It might be claimed – going beyond Bukharin's

---

69 See below, p. 230. I have outlined a criticism of Lukács' argument in my essay 'Class consciousness and social structure', in Istvan Mészáros (ed.), *Aspects of History and Class Consciousness*.

70 W. Machajski, *The Intellectual Worker* (in Russian, 1905). The argument of the book is summarized in Max Nomad, *Rebles and Renegades*. See also the restatement of this view with reference to present-day socialist societies by G. Konrád and I. Szelényi, *The Intellectuals on the Road to Class Power*.

71 Nicolai Bukharin, *Historical Materialism: A System of Sociology*

argument, which deals only with the situation *after* the revolution – that a high
level of general education is a *precondition* for the social transformation which
will create a socialist society; and this accords quite well with Marx's own ideas
about the course of social and intellectual development in an advanced capitalist
society as they are sketched in the *Grundrisse*.[72] But such ideas are still not
adequate to dispose of the problem raised by Michels; for his main argument
was that the very structure of large organizations engenders a bureaucratic style,
a dominant elite group, and a sharp division between the leaders, the
rank-and-file members, and even more the class as a whole. This is a problem
which Marx himself, as I have said, did not have to confront, but it has become
ever more acute for later Marxist thinkers, for a variety of reasons. One is that
the scale and complexity of organizations in modern societies has greatly
increased since Marx's time, so that the question of mass participation and
control has itself become more complex and difficult. Another is that the
oligarchic tendencies in working-class political parties have appeared in new,
and still more blatant forms; these phenomena have now to be studied not only
in the social democratic type of party, but also in the Bolshevik type in a
single-party political system. And because Marxism itself was dominated for
decades by the Bolshevik ideology, there is still very little serious Marxist
political sociology capable of analysing systematically, by theoretical and
empirical investigations, these aspects of present-day society.

The second important issue raised by the ideas of Lenin and Lukács on the
development of working-class consciousness concerns the relation between
class, political doctrine, and social theory – and in a general way, the role of
intellectuals in the working-class movement. There seems to me little warrant
in Marx's own writing for the view that a working-class party has to become a
'Marxist' party. Indeed, late in life Marx explicitly dissociated himself from
some of the attempts to create such parties, especially in France, by declaring
that he himself was not a 'Marxist'. Marx's theory of society would, of course,
influence working-class consciousness and enter in various ways into the
political doctrines of the working class; as a theory, however, its principal
objective was to reveal the nature of class relations in capitalist society, to
analyse the economic and social tendencies in the development of capitalism,
and to depict the working class as an independent political force engaged in
conflict with existing society. The manner in which the working class in each
particular society would become organized as a political movement, and the
form in which it would express its opposition to capitalism and its aspirations for
a new society, would depend upon cultural traditions and historical circumstances; and its doctrine would necessarily go beyond any science, since it
would embrace an imaginative vision of the society of the future.

---

72 See above, p. 15. Among later Marxist writers Antonio Gramsci and the Austro-Marxists, with
their particular interest in the development of workers' education, gave most attention to these
cultural questions.

Marx clearly distinguished between scientific theory and social doctrine (or ideology) in his critique of political economy; the bourgeois economic doctrines were certainly ideological, in the sense of presenting a distorted, misleading picture of capitalist society, but at the same time the political economy of Adam Smith and Ricardo was a genuine theoretical science. The distinction is set in a historical context. Marx's view seems to be that a rising class (for example, the bourgeoisie in feudal society) is able to develop, through its representative intellectuals, a realistic science of society, whereas the social thought of a class that is established in power becomes more ideological as the need emerges to conceal the special interests and privileges of the rulers and to prevent social changes which would diminish their power.[73] From this point of view it can be said that Marx's theory stands in the same relation to the proletariat as classical political economy stood to the bourgeoisie. But further: the Bolshevik ideology can then be seen as the doctrine of a new dominant class, resembling the vulgar apologias for capitalism which in Marx's judgement had succeeded the classical works of political economy. Of course, this historical development is not what Marx himself expected. He seems to have conceived the future socialist society as having a thoroughly rational and scientific character so that human social relationships, and the human relation to nature, would be more or less completely transparent and accessible to reason, while the scope of ideological thought, with its distorting influence, would be severely restricted if not eliminated altogether.

It needs to be emphasized that although Marx discussed theory and ideology in their historical context, the distinction that he made between them had an absolute and universal character. Marx undoubtedly believed that genuine theoretical progress was possible in the science of society, and that he himself had contributed to this progress through his discoveries in political economy – a science which, as he observed to Engels, had not advanced since the time of Adam Smith and Ricardo until his own work was undertaken. There is a profound difference, therefore, between Marx's outlook and the later interpretations of Marxism by Lukács or Karl Mannheim. For in Luckács' essays in *History and Class Consciousness* the distinction between theory and ideology becomes blurred, and Marxist theory is presented mainly in its ideological form by being identified with the class consciousness of the proletariat. And in Mannheim's principal contribution to this problem, *Ideology and Utopia*, the distinction is explicitly dissolved in a conception that makes all social thought, including Marxism, inescapably ideological – that is, endowed with a particular, biased orientation because of the thinker's social position.[74]

73 This is not a matter of *conscious* deception. Marx always emphasized that the production of ideology is a social and cultural process that occurs without individual thinkers being aware of it.
74 In a confused way, however, Mannheim retained a vestigial hope (which became stronger in his later writings) that ideology could be transcended in a more comprehensive, more objective synthesis that might be achieved by a particular social group in which all the diverse streams of thought came together, the 'socially unattached intelligentsia.'

Marx's thought, which separates yet connects theory and ideology, and relates both to the development of classes, presents a number of difficulties that require critical examination.[75] One such difficulty concerns the role of social classes as the sole or principal source of ideologies. If we characterize an ideology, following Kolakowski's usage[76] (which I think represents quite faithfully the intention of Marx's thought), as the sum of conceptions by means of which a social group systematizes its values, then it is evident that there are many potential sources of ideology – ethnic and linguistic groups, occupational, religious and gender groups, generations, groups resulting from cultural or regional affinities and traditions, as well as social classes – and the question of where ideologies do mainly originate has to be settled by empirical study, not by conceptual discussion or philosophical reflection. I have already drawn attention to the importance of nationalist movements and ideologies; and in recent decades many other social movements and ideologies have developed from very diverse social groups that are quite distinct from, or only loosely connected with, social classes (e.g., the student movement, women's liberation, the peace movement and various forms of religious fundamentalism). Moreover, it can well be argued that the production of ideology is unlikely to come to an end even in a classless society as long as any differentiated social groups continue to exist.[77]

Other difficulties arise concerning the role of intellectuals – the 'thinking' representatives of classes or other groups who actually construct theories and ideologies. Marx's political theory makes use of an analogy between the rise of the bourgeoisie in feudal society, and the rise of the proletariat in capitalist society, but in several respects the analogy is not exact. So far as the intellectuals are concerned, the main difference is that while the intellectual representatives of the bourgeoisie were themselves, for the most part, bourgeois, and participated directly in the social life that they expressed in thought, those of the proletariat – the socialist intellectuals – are not proletarians; and there emerges a potential divergence between the practical life and aspirations of the working class and the interpretation of that life in socialist doctrines. This situation makes plausible Lenin's idea that a socialist consciousness is brought to the working class from outside, and on the other hand, the view of Machajski and others that socialism is after all only the ideology of the intellectuals in their struggle for political dominance.[78]

75 Some of the problems are treated in the selections from Leszek Kolakowski and Jürgen Habermas below, see pp. 295–8 and pp. 299–309.

76 See p. 295.

77 There is an interesting discussion of this question in the book by Radovan Richta, *Civilization at the Crossroads*, which I mentioned earlier (p. 15 above, note 44). See also Althusser's argument (p. 64 below) that no society, including communist society, could ever do without ideology.

78 Or as might now be said, of the experts and managers as 'a new class' or elite. See especially, on this subject, Milovan Djilas, *The New Class*; and also Konrád and Szelényi, *The Intellectuals*.

General view of Marx's social theory

The preceding discussion will have suggested the complexity of the problems confronting any attempt to analyse the relations, of dependence or mutual influence, between the development of a system of production, the formation of classes, and the crystallization of interests and values (of classes and other social groups) in political movements and doctrines. The immense historical significance of Marx's thought is that it formulated these problems in such a manner as to create a 'wholly new attitude to social and historical questions',[79] and to open up entire new fields of social inquiry. To a large extent these new fields constituted the domain of the emerging discipline of sociology, and it is not surprising, therefore, that Marxism came to be widely regarded, at the end of the nineteenth century, as a system of sociology[80] and in this form had an important influence upon many of the early sociological theorists, among them Tönnies, Max Weber, Simmel, Michels, Pareto and Mosca.[81]

This is not to say, however, that a distinctive Marxist sociology was systematically developed. On the contrary, as the problems that Marx had posed were absorbed into the mainstream of sociology and began to be studied from quite different perspectives, many Marxist thinkers made a sharp distinction between Marxism and any kind of sociology, and they were encouraged in this direction by the increasingly political character of Marxist thought as it became the official doctrine of organized parties. Among those Marxists who did attempt to present and develop Marx's thought as a sociological theory the Austro-Marxists[82] – and in particular, so far as purely theoretical questions are concerned, Max Adler – occupied a preeminent place. According to Adler, Marx's great discoveries were: first, the concept of man as a social being, or 'socialized humanity', which laid the basis for a general social science on the same level as the natural sciences;[83] secondly, the notion of social evolution as a sociological category, derived by a transformation of the

79 Isaiah Berlin; see below, p. 102.
80 It was treated from this point of view by Tönnies and others at the first international congress of sociology (*Annales de l'Institut International de Sociologie*, ed. René Worms, vol. I [Paris, 1895]); and Georges Sorel examined at length the differences between the social theories of Durkheim and Marx in an essay, 'Les théories de M. Durkheim', published in *Le Devenir social* (Paris, nos 1 and 2 [April and May, 1895]). For a more general account see T. Bottomore, *Marxist Sociology*.
81 Durkheim is the outstanding exception. His sociological theory was developed in quite a different context of ideas, deriving from Comte and positivism, and from the conservative reaction to the French Revolution; and within his own cultural tradition he had little occasion to confront the Marxist theory.
82 For an account of the Austro-Marxists and selections from their writings see Bottomore and Goode (eds), *Austro-Marxism*.
83 In the tenth thesis on Feuerbach, Marx asserts that 'the standpoint of the new materialism is human society or socialized humanity'.

philosophical idea of development; thirdly, the conception of human society as an antagonistic unity, divided by the class struggle, which also constitutes the driving force in social change. Adler's exposition is distinctive because of his emphasis upon Marxism as a social science which conceives human behaviour as law-governed and strives to formulate social laws, and at the same time his effort to find a place for purposive behaviour. His chief preoccupation is the logic of Marxism, and within this framework he poses and attempts to resolve the problems of causation and teleology, of the differences between the natural and social sciences, with which Max Weber, similarly, was wrestling at this time. The strong emphasis upon Marxism as a social science, which needs to be consolidated and extended, led the Austro-Marxists to undertake investigations that still deserve attention for their combination of theoretical analysis and empirical reference. Among these studies are Otto Bauer's work on nationality,[84] and Karl Renner's examination of law in capitalist society, which remains one of the very few serious contributions to an analysis of the relationship between the economic structure and the sphere of ideology.[85]

The other main attempt to expound Marxism as a sociological theory is Bukharin's popular textbook, *Historical Materialism*,[86] which also discusses, though in a less profound way (and drawing upon Max Adler's work), the problems of causation and teleology. One of the most interesting aspects of Bukharin's book, which was undeservedly neglected, mainly for political reasons, after his condemnation and execution by Stalin, is that it deals seriously with other sociological theories and with the criticisms of Marxism that arise from them, and attempts to meet these criticisms in a scientific way.[87]

Bukharin's work, though neglected in substance, is known through two critical essays by Lukács and Gramsci.[88] These essays provide a convenient starting point for considering the opposite view, in which Marxism is treated as a philosophy ('historical materialism') characterized by a distinctive method (the 'dialectic'), and is contrasted with sociology as a 'positive science' employing a natural science method. Thus Lukács writes of Bukharin that as a

necessary consequence of his natural-scientific approach, sociology ... develops into an independent science with its own substantive goals. The dialectic can do without such independent substantive achievements; its realm is that of the historical process as a whole, whose individual, concrete, unrepeatable moments

84 See above, p. 22, note 60.
85 See below, pp. 290–4.
86 See above, p. 25.
87 For example, Michels' analysis of oligarchy (see above, p. 24), and Max Weber's account of the Protestant ethic and the origins of capitalism.
88 Lukács' review, published in 1925, appears in an English translation under the title 'Technology and social relations' in *New Left Review*, 39 (1966). Gramsci's discussion of the book, written in prison, has been published in English in Quintin Hoare and Geoffrey Nowell Smith (eds), *Selections from the Prison Notebooks of Antonio Gramsci*, pp. 419–72.

reveal its dialectical essence precisely in the qualitative differences between them and in the continuous transformation of their objective structure. The *totality* is the territory of the dialectic. A 'scientific' general sociology, on the other hand, . . . must have its own independent substantive achievements allowing only one kind of law.

Gramsci's argument follows a similar course and is summed up in his claim that

. . . the philosophy of praxis is 'sufficient unto itself', that it contains in itself all the fundamental elements needed to construct a total and integral conception of the world, a total philosophy and theory of natural science, and not only that but everything that is needed to give life to an integrated practical organisation of society, that is, to become a total integral civilization.

Another major contribution to the development of Marx's thought as a critical philosophy was Karl Korsch's *Marxism and Philosophy* (1923). Korsch argued that Marxism, as a materialist dialectic, is the revolutionary philosophy of the working class, standing in the same relation to the working-class revolutionary movement as did German idealist philosophy to the bourgeois revolutionary movement; and like Lukács he regarded the concept of 'totality' as the decisive element in Marx's theory.[89] Later, however, he changed his views and rejected what he regarded as the 'distortion of the strongly empirical and critical sense of the materialistic principle', and the elaboration of Marxism as 'a general philosophical interpretation of the universe'. 'The main tendency of historical materialism', he concluded, 'is no longer "philosophical", but is that of an empirical scientific method'.[90]

Korsch and Lukács both played a part in the creation of the Institute for Social Research (the institutional basis of the Frankfurt School). They participated in the 'First Marxist Work Week' held in the summer of 1922, where the idea of the Institute was first conceived, and much of the time at this conference was spent in discussing the manuscript of Korsch's *Marxism and Philosophy*.[91] It is evident that the ideas of some of the leading members of the Frankfurt School, at the outset and subsequently, were very close to those of Korsch and Lukács, notably in their emphasis upon the philosophical sources of Marx's thought and especially its direct and crucial relationship with Hegel's

89 Lukács, *History and Class Consciousness*, p. 27. 'It is not the primacy of economic motives in historical explanation that constitutes the decisive difference between Marxism and bourgeois thought, but the point of view of totality. The category of totality, the all-pervasive supremacy of the whole over the parts is the essence of the method which Marx took over from Hegel and brilliantly transformed into the foundations of a wholly new science.' Similarly, Korsch refers to the 'totality of the historico-social process', and says of Marxism that it is 'a theory of *social development* seen and comprehended as a living totality; or, more precisely, it is a theory of *social revolution* comprehended and practised as a living totality', *Marxism and Philosophy*, p. 52.

90 *Karl Marx* (revised German edn, 1967), p. 203.

91 For details see Martin Jay, *The Dialectical Imagination*, ch. 1.

dialectic. This is apparent, for example in Horkheimer's essays on critical theory[92] published in 1937, and in Marcuse's *Reason and Revolution* (1941). Nevertheless, there were important differences between Korsch and Lukács on one side, and the Frankfurt School thinkers on the other. The former were active in political life (in 1923 both were leading members of communist parties, and Lukács remained a party member throughout his life except for the period 1957–69), and they saw the critical function of Marxist theory as one which is carried on by a revolutionary party. In *History and Class Consciousness* Lukács conceives Marxism as 'the expression in thought of the revolutionary process itself', and goes on to refer to 'the correct class consciousness of the proletariat and its organizational form, the communist party'. The Frankfurt School thinkers, on the other hand, were largely detached from political activity,[93] and they came to regard the critical reason embodied in Marx's social theory as being borne along, not by a party or a political movement, but by an intellectual group – a view not unlike that of the Young Hegelian 'critical critics', as George Lichtheim noted.[94]

This difference is particularly significant in respect of the connection between theory and practice, which all these thinkers emphasized as a vital element in the dialectical thought of authentic Marxism. Whereas Korsch and Lukács took the inherently plausible view that the unity of theory and practice is achieved in a revolutionary party or movement, and can themselves be said to have lived this unity, the Frankfurt School thinkers expressed a purely theoretical conception of theory and practice, engaged in no political practice, and proposed no way in which theory and practice could be brought into a valid and fruitful relation with each other. It is partly for this reason, I think, that much of the later writing of these thinkers is characterized by a preoccupation with the development of knowledge and culture, and a lack of attention to economic, and especially political, phenomena.[95]

This is not to say, however, that the difference can be summed up by concluding that Korsch and Lukács were consistent and correct in the position they adopted, while the Frankfurt School thinkers were inconsistent and

92 The term 'critical theory' has come to be used as a general description of the ideas of the Frankfurt School, though it perhaps refers more particularly to the later views of members of the School, and also to the views of thinkers who were not, in a strict sense, members at all.

93 See Jay, *Dialectical Imagination*, pp. 13–15.

94 Lichtheim, *From Marx to Hegel*. This outlook is most fully expressed, at a much later date, in the pessimistic concluding pages of Marcuse's *One-Dimensional Man*, where the critical thinker is represented as an isolated individual swimming hopelessly against the torrent of technological rationality; the critical theory of society no longer finds in society 'real forces' which are moving towards more rational and freer institutions, and it becomes 'incapable of translating its rationality into terms of historical practice'.

95 For some critical comments on Adorno from this point of view, see Gillian Rose, *The Melancholy Science: An Introduction to the Thought of Theodor W. Adorno*, ch. 7. See also T. Bottomore, *The Frankfurt School*.

mistaken. The matter is more complex than that. In the first place, it may be noted that both Korsch and Lukács, in the particular historical context of the postwar revolutionary movements in Europe, gave their allegiance to a party which eventually proved to be, not a liberating force, but, on the contrary, the instrument of a new despotism. Secondly, the ground of this allegiance, their conception of the proletariat as the subject of a historical process which can be cognized infallibly by dialectical reason (that is to say by Marxism, which is represented as being only the expression in thought of the process itself, or in other words the adequate, 'correct' self-consciousness of the subject) helped to transform Marxism into a dogmatic ideology and to exclude, as Korsch himself later recognized, those elements in Marx's own thought which gave it the character of an empirical, hence corrigible, social science.

The Frankfurt School thinkers, on the other hand, though they also grounded their thought on the idea of Marxism as dialectical reason, confronted more directly the disjunction between the pronouncements of reason (as they understood them) and the actual conditions and tendencies of social life, among which the non-revolutionary outlook and practice of the Western working class had a prominent place. In this sense it may be said that their thought was more 'critical', and that their detachment from the existing political parties and movements had a certain justification. But still there is something contradictory in accepting such a disjunction between the actual state of affairs (which can be known, presumably, only through some kind of scientific inquiry) and the judgements of critical reason (which seem to assume more and more the character of disguised or undisguised value judgements, where they are not concerned with purely epistemological questions) on the basis of an interpretation of Marxism which sees its uniqueness precisely in its overcoming of the dualism of fact and value, theory and practice.[96]

With the great renaissance of Marxist thought since the 1950s many new interpretations of Marx have appeared, but all of them (notwithstanding their individual variations) can be broadly assigned to one or the other of two principal, and more or less opposed, currents of thought which, as I have shown, also characterized the earlier interpretations. The first emphasizes the humanist, democratic or emancipatory content of Marxist theory, while the second focuses attention upon its scientific character and aims to elicit the distinctive conceptual scheme and epistemology which underlies it. As a matter of convenience I shall refer to these two general orientations as the 'humanist' and the 'scientific'.

The humanist versions of Marxism are characterized in general by a preeminent concern with the conscious actions of individuals and social groups, with cultural studies and historical interpretations, rather than with the analysis

---

96 See especially the discussion of this unique character by Lucien Goldmann below pp. 156–66. I have examined the relation between theory and practice more fully in my *Marxist Sociology*, ch. 4, and see also the discussion later in this Introduction.

of economic structure and processes. In recent writings, however, by contrast with the earlier formulations of Korsch, Lukács and Gramsci which emphasized the notions of 'historical totality' and a privileged 'historical subject' (the working class), the central concepts are those of 'human nature' and 'human needs'. This is apparent, for example, in a major collection of essays published in 1965 under the title *Socialist Humanism*,[97] and in the general orientation of one of the best-known Marxist journals of recent times, *Praxis*, which was published in Yugoslavia from 1964 to 1974 in Serbo-Croat and international editions.[98] Two of the contributors to the present volume, Petrović and Stojanović, were closely associated with the *Praxis* group, and it will be clear from the excerpts from their writings reprinted below[99] that their concern is not to construct an empirical science of human nature from which values could then be immediately derived, but to develop a normative theory, and in particular a Marxist ethics, which would formulate individual and social ideals as objectives of policy decisions. In the same way, one of the contributors to *Socialist Humanism*, Marek Fritzhand, expounds Marx's normative 'ideal of man', within which he distinguishes three related conceptions: that of the 'complete', rather than fragmented or limited, human being; that of the 'harmonious individual'; and that of the 'freely acting', creative individual.[100]

A similar dualism is apparent – although it shows itself in a less obvious way – in the thought of some recent 'critical theorists'. Thus Jürgen Habermas, in the course of his epistemological critique of positivism, distinguishes three human 'cognitive interests' (which are presumably, in some sense, components of 'human nature'): an interest in technical control which manifests itself in scientific knowledge; an interest in social interaction and self-understanding which manifests itself in hermeneutic knowledge; and an 'emancipatory' interest which is conceived as bringing together, in some way, theoretical and practical reason. Certainly, as Habermas' discussion of the emancipatory interest shows, his analysis is intended to lead to a monistic, rather than a

97 Erich Fromm (ed.), *Socialist Humanism*.

98 For a brief account of the history of *Praxis*, and of the philosophical and sociological debates which it encouraged, see Mihailo Marković, 'Marxist Philosophy in Yugoslavia: The Praxis Group', part 1 of M. Marković and R. S. Cohen, *Yugoslavia: The Rise and Fall of Socialist Humanism*. See also Mihailo Marković and Gajo Petrović (eds), *Praxis: Yugoslav Essays in the Philosophy and Methodology of the Social Sciences*. One particularly important feature of the contributions made by Yugoslav thinkers to these discussions is that they embodied serious and critical reflection upon the experiences, problems, needs and opportunities of a functioning socialist society which still presents today, as it has done for a quarter of a century, the most attractive model available for the future development of a democratic socialist system. This is not to say that it is by any means a perfect model; the fate of *Praxis* itself, which was obliged to cease publication in 1974, because its critical stance offended important political leaders and bureaucrats, shows that democracy and self-management are still far from being securely established in Yugoslavia. The journal reappeared in 1981, now published in Britain under the title *Praxis International*.

99 Chs 9 and 13, pp. 141–5 and 176–89 below.

100 Fromm, *Socialist Humanism*, pp. 157–65.

dualistic, conception; but it remains doubtful whether this unity of reason is convincingly established. Kolakowski, in a critical assessment,[101] has argued that:

> Habermas does not clearly define his key concept of 'emancipation'. It is evident that, in the spirit of the whole tradition of German idealism, he is seeking for a focal point at which practical and theoretical reason, cognition and will, knowledge of the world and the movement to change it, all become identical. But it does not appear that he has actually found such a point or shown us how to arrive at it. . . . It may be that, in some cases, acts of self-understanding by individuals or societies are themselves part of the practical behaviour leading to 'emancipation', whatever this term means. But the question will always remain: by what criteria are we to judge the accuracy of that self-understanding, and on what principle do we decide that 'emancipation' consists in one state of affairs rather than another? On the second point we cannot avoid making a decision that goes beyond our knowledge of the world.

In Habermas' thought, then, the identity of theoretical and practical reason appears to be less successfully established than their separateness as distinct forms of reason. This distinctiveness is also recognized implicitly by another critical theorist, greatly influenced by Habermas, when he writes that:

> In order to reformulate Marx's supposition about the prerequisites for a successful revolution in the case of the capitalist countries, it would be necessary to include socialist democracy, socialist justice, socialist ethics and a 'socialist consciousness' among the components of a socialist society to be 'incubated' within the womb of a capitalist order.[102]

The dualism expressed by the writers I have mentioned is certainly not intended to erect an impassable barrier between a realm of facts and a realm of values; nor to assert that the activity of reason is confined to the former, whereas will, or 'decisionism' (to use the term which Habermas applies to Max Weber's position), prevails in the latter. None of them would accept the view that in the sphere of practical activity reason is, and can be, only 'the slave of the passions'. Their aim is, rather, to demarcate the proper sphere and methods of scientific and philosophical inquiry, and to determine the role of philosophy within Marxist thought as a whole, especially in relation to the social sciences. Habermas, as we have seen, formulates a conception of the essential unity of reason, but this is best interpreted, I think, in a weak sense as a claim concerning the *relatedness* of the different forms of reason which he distinguishes. Such an interpretation seems to be warranted by some of Habermas'

101 Leszek Kolakowski, *Main Currents of Marxism*, vol. III, pp. 387–95.
102 Albrecht Wellmer, *Critical Theory of Society*, pp. 121–2. See also the excerpt below, ch. 12, pp. 167–75.

own presentations of his argument, as for example in *Legitimation Crisis* (p. 10) where he says that: 'To the truth claims that we raise in empirical statements there correspond claims of correctness or appropriateness that we advance with norms of action and evaluation.'

The Yugoslav thinkers, on the other hand, accept more fully the idea that reason has distinct, irreducible (but not unrelated) forms – that its procedures differ in diverse spheres, and that its scope and effectiveness are perhaps more restricted in some spheres than in others – and hence they are more inclined to formulate the specific problems of the social sciences, of the philosophy of value, or of the philosophy of science, as separate and distinct issues. The following passage from Marković's exposition of the research programme of the *Praxis* group illustrates this tendency:

> How to explain the fact that socialist revolutions did not occur in developed industrial countries of the West but in backward rural societies of the East? What really is a revolution if, after an apparent revolution, a bureaucratic society can emerge? How build up socialism in a relatively under-developed country? What does it mean for the state to wither away? How is a non-market modern economy possible? What is *Marxist* logic, ethics, aesthetics? Is there a Marxist anthropology? What is the essence of man with respect to which one speaks about alienation? If that essence is universal, how is history possible? If it is particular, how can we escape relativism? If man is a being of *praxis*, and *praxis* is (among other things) labour and production, how can the standpoint of *praxis* be a standard of critical evaluation? How reconcile the principle of determinism, according to which historical processes are governed by laws independent of human consciousness and will, with the principle of freedom according to which it is men who make their own history?[103]

The outlook of the humanist Marxists, however, confronts a major difficulty; for whereas a Marxist sociology or political economy can be, and has been, developed on the basis of Marx's own analysis and investigation of modes of production and social formations, there is no real starting-point in Marx himself – in the sense that he provided any systematic and comprehensive treatment of philosophical issues – for the elaboration of a Marxist conception in any of the principal fields of philosophical inquiry. In short, Marx was *not* a German philosopher.[104] Hence the fact that every attempt to construct a Marxist philosophy tends to depart from Marx's own work, and to draw heavily upon some non-Marxist scheme of philosophical thought: that of Hegel in the

103 Marković and Petrović, *Praxis*, Introduction, pp. xxii– xviii.
104 See the contrary assertion on page 1 of Kolakowski, *Main Currents*, vol. I. It may indeed be argued, as it was by Korsch in his later work, that the elaboration of Marx's thought into 'a comprehensive materialist philosophy embracing both nature and society, or a general philosophical interpretation of the universe' was a 'distortion of [its] strongly empirical and critical sense'. See above, p. 31.

case of Lukács, Gramsci (partly through the influence of Croce), and the Frankfurt School; of neo-Kantian and positivist philosophy of science in the case of the Austro-Marxists; of French rationalism, especially in the form given to it by Bachelard, and structuralist epistemology, in the case of Althusser.

What is present in Marx's own work, philosophically considered, is only a sketch of a normative social theory, expounded most fully in the *Economic and Philosophical Manuscripts*,[105] from which, as Stojanović observes, a Marxist ethics '. . . has yet to be constructed'.[106] Even here it might be more appropriate to speak of a 'socialist ethics', as does Wellmer, since the construction of such an ethical theory – requiring a systematic analysis and elaboration of such concepts as 'emancipation', 'human needs', 'justice', a 'good society' – must evidently draw upon the work of many thinkers besides Marx, go far beyond Marx's own fragmentary observations, and probably, in some important respects, fundamentally revise his conceptions.[107] Outside the sphere of ethical theory it is clear that Marx's contribution to philosophical inquiry was even more slight, or non-existent: there is in his work no attempt to develop in a systematic way an ontology, an epistemology, a logic, a philosophy of science, or an aesthetic theory (as distinct from his sporadic reflections upon a possible sociology of art and literature).[108] Thus, any elaboration of a 'Marxist' view in these spheres is, in a strict sense, non-Marxist, involving subsequent interpretation and elaboration of fragmentary observations and notes (which, in the case of Marx's occasional comments upon his own scientific method, can easily give rise to contradictory accounts), or of what are taken to be implicit philosophical orientations discoverable in Marx's texts; and relying to a very great extent, as I have indicated, upon ideas derived from quite varied philosophical traditions.

This poverty of Marxist philosophy is in sharp contrast with the substantial and largely autonomous development of Marxist social science on the foundation of Marx's own major investigations. In these circumstances it is scarcely surprising that one main current of Marxist thought should always have held that Marxism is primarily, or exclusively – and certainly most fruitfully – a science of society.[109] But this conception raises two distinct kinds of questions.

105 So that Hendrik de Man quite rightly claimed that they showed 'more clearly than any other work the ethical-humanist themes which lie behind Marx's socialist convictions and behind . . . his whole scientific work'. See above, p. 2.
106 See p. 176 below.
107 The view expressed here would be accepted by many humanist Marxists; see, for example, some of the contributions in, and Erich Fromm's introduction to, *Socialist Humanism*.
108 On the latter see the illuminating study by S. S. Prawer, *Karl Marx and World Literature*.
109 This view has also been taken by many non-Marxist commentators. Croce, for example, argued in his essay on 'The scientific form of historical materialism' that Marx's conception of history was not philosophical – 'within its limited field the elements of things are not presented in such a way as to admit of a philosophical discussion' – and in another essay, that historical materialism is 'simply a *canon* of historical interpretation', that is, 'an aid in seeking for [results] . . . entirely of empirical origin'. See Benedetto Croce, *Historical Materialism and the Economics of Karl*

First, we may inquire into the nature of this science: is it political economy, sociology, or historiography, or is it some quite distinctive kind of thought which incorporates and transcends these specialized disciplines? In other words, what are its fundamental concepts, and how are they connected in a theoretical model or paradigm? And further, what are its distinctive methods of research and of proof? Secondly, we may ask how the science should actually be developed substantively in diverse fields of inquiry.

The first of these questions poses general issues in the philosophy of science, and 'scientific Marxists' have taken very different positions in their attempts to establish the scientific character of Marx's theory, and to distinguish it from non-science, pseudo-science, or ideology. Such positions have been influenced primarily, as I have already indicated, by developments in the post-Marxian philosophy of science itself, and they take the form of meta-theoretical reflections upon Marx's thought. Max Adler, who provided the epistemological and methodological foundations of the Austro-Marxist conception of Marxism as a scientific sociology, with the aid of a neo-Kantian and positivist philosophy of science,[110] recognized this clearly when he argued that just as Kant's question about nature as an object of thought followed the emergence of Newtonian physics, so the neo-Kantian question about society as an object of thought followed the construction of Marx's social theory.

More recently, Louis Althusser also attempted, from an entirely different perspective, to establish the character of Marxism as a science.[111] In this case, the external influences upon Marxist thought are those of French rationalism,[112] and more particularly of structuralism, also largely French in inspiration, through the work of Lévi-Strauss. Hence the two fundamental ideas propounded by Althusser are his conception of science as a theoretical activity which consists above all in the construction of a 'problematic' (a conceptual scheme or theoretical system), and his assertion that the key concept of Marxist science, which is implicit, but not explicitly formulated, in Marx's work, is that of 'the effectivity of a structure on its elements'.

Marx, pp. 1–21, 77–8. Similarly, Schumpeter, while recognizing what he calls the 'prophetic' element in Marxism, says of Marx that 'Nowhere did he betray positive science to metaphysics', and further that 'his theory of history is not more materialistic than is any other attempt to account for the historic process by the means at the command of empirical science. It should be clear that this is logically compatible with any metaphysical or religious belief – exactly as any physical picture of the world is.' See J. A. Schumpeter, *Capitalism, Socialism and Democracy*, pp. 9–11.

110 See the selections from Adler's writings in Bottomore and Goode (eds), *Austro-Marxism*, section II. See also the critical discussion of Adler in Kolakowski, *Main Currents*, vol. II, pp. 258–76.

111 See the text below, ch. 2, pp. 60–71.

112 Especially that of Bachelard, who is the source of one of Althusser's most important ideas: that of the 'epistemological break' which divides pre-science (or ideology) from science, and in the case of Marx is held to separate the young Marx as a humanist philosopher sharply from the mature Marx (after 1845) who was a social scientist.

In recent decades structuralism has had a considerable influence, not only in the philosophy of science,[113] but in the social sciences and humanities generally. Thus, while Althusser's work was mainly confined to the philosophy of science, other Marxist structuralists such as Poulantzas[114] and Godelier[115] undertook empirical studies from this standpoint. Further, it is arguable that the diffusion of structuralist ideas has been largely responsible for an important shift of emphasis within recent Marxist thought towards the analysis of modes of production, which is evident not only in the general revival of Marxist political economy, but more specifically in the field of development studies.[116]

This last example is also significant as indicating that the present debates within Marxism are far from being limited to general discussions of epistemology and methodology. Many Marxist scholars, in fact, have been principally concerned with the second question that I posed earlier: namely, how should this science of society be developed substantively in specific fields of research?[117] Besides the extensive work on development and underdevelopment to which I have just referred, there have been major studies of the historical development of the capitalist economy[118] and of social formations;[119] of kinship and the social relations of production;[120] of the family (greatly influenced by radical feminist criticisms of traditional Marxism);[121] of social classes;[122] of property;[123] of the state;[124] and of culture and ideology.[125] It is

113 For example, the new 'transcendental realism', as expounded by Roy Bhaskar in *A Realist Theory of Science* and *The Possibility of Naturalism*, conceives causal explanation as comprehension of the deep structures of the world – both physical and social – which lie behind, and produce, patterns of events; and Bhaskar regards scientific realism as the philosophical foundation of Marxist social science, as does Ted Benton, *Philosophical Foundations of the Three Sociologies*, ch. 9.
114 See ch. 19 below. pp. 245–57.
115 See ch. 3 below. pp. 72–80.
116 For a general review and criticism of sociological theories of development and underdevelopment, and an outline of a theory of modes of production, see John G. Taylor, *From Modernization to Modes of Production*. There is an excellent comprehensive account of the revival of Marxist political economy in Karl Kühne, *Economics and Marxism*.
117 For an account of recent work in many different fields see the relevant entries in Tom Bottomore (ed.), *A Dictionary of Marxist Thought*, and also the references which follow in the text.
118 See Immanuel Wallerstein, *The Modern World System*.
119 See, for example, the two works by Perry Anderson, *Passages From Antiquity to Feudalism* and *Lineages of the Absolutist State*.
120 See the discussion and references in M. Godelier, *Perspectives in Marxist Anthropology*.
121 For a general account of recent work and discussion of some of the theoretical issues, see the essays in A. Kuhn and A. M. Wolpe (eds), *Feminism and Materialism*, and M. Barrett, *Women's Oppression Today*.
122 See Nicos Poulantzas. *Classes in Contemporary Capitalism*, and pp. 245–57 below.
123 See below pp. 203–14.
124 See Ralph Miliband, *The State in Capitalist Society*; Claus Offe, *Strukturprobleme des kapitalistischen Staates* and 'The theory of the capitalist state and the problem of policy formation'; and J. O'Connor, *The Fiscal Crisis of the State*.
125 See Goldmann, *The Hidden God*, and various essays in his *Marxisme et sciences humaines*. Much of the work of the Frankfurt School was, of course, devoted to cultural analysis; among the later

not the case, of course, that all the recent substantive studies in economics, sociology or anthropology have been undertaken by 'structuralists', or by scholars who would consider themselves 'scientific Marxists' even in a very broad sense; nevertheless, it seems to me that the most important work of the past two decades has been produced in an intellectual context which emphasizes the idea of Marxism as a social science, in whatever way the relation of science to philosophy or other modes of thought may be conceived.

It is clear that the general view of the scientific Marxists is dualistic, drawing a sharp distinction between science and other forms of knowledge; but the ways in which science is conceived to be related to these other forms are quite diverse. Max Adler examined this question at length in his first major work,[126] where he seems to argue that there are different perspectives on the world, of which science is only one. The task of a science of society is to provide causal explanations, but it reveals only one aspect of life, and 'the complete reality of our being' is to be found in practical, conative activity. He returned to the problem in later writings, where he argued that the causal mechanism of history is transformed into a teleology by the scientific illumination of it, since this scientific knowledge itself becomes a cause; and in one of his last works he embarked upon a fresh analysis of motives as causes.[127] The Austro-Marxists – with the exception of Otto Neurath, if he can properly be counted as a member of the school – were not positivists in the manner of the Vienna Circle, for they did not explicitly argue that only the statements of empirical science and logic are meaningful; but in a wider sense they were undoubtedly positivists. They gave primacy to scientific knowledge, the philosophy in which they were interested was the philosophy of science, not ethics or social philosophy,[128] and

---

works which deal particularly with ideology see Habermas, *Legitimation Crisis*, and also pp. 299–309 below. The essay by Althusser, 'Ideology and ideological state apparatuses', in *Lenin and Philosophy and Other Essays* has provoked much critical debate, and some investigations of ideology from a Marxist structuralist standpoint (for instance, by Godelier, in *Perspectives*).

126 Max Adler, *Kausalität und Teleologie im Streite um die Wissenschaft*. The view he expounds here is similar to that of other neo-Kantians, including Max Weber, who was also concerned to delimit the sphere of science as a distinct 'realm of value'. It also appears to be close to the ideas of some recent philosophers of science; thus Roy Bhaskar, in *The Possibility of Naturalism*, while arguing that it is *sometimes* possible to pass directly from a scientific explanation to a value judgement, concludes that 'science, although it can and must illuminate, cannot finally "settle" questions of practical morality and action, just because there are always – and necessarily – social practices besides science, and values other than cognitive ones' (pp. 82–3). On the other side there are Marxist philosophers who argue strongly that Marx's own thought was not dualistic; for a clear statement of such a view see Roy Edgley, 'Sociology, social criticism and Marxism', in W. Outhwaite and M. Mulkay (eds), *Social Theory and Social Criticism*.

127 Max Adler, *Lehrbuch der materialistischen Geschichtsauffassung*.

128 The Austro-Marxists paid relatively little attention to these subjects, and both Adler and Bauer rejected the ideas of those thinkers – influenced by another form of neo-Kantianism – who claimed that Marxism needed to be supplemented by an explicit ethical doctrine. However, in his essay on 'Marxism and ethics' Bauer recognized the value of Kant's doctrine in combating 'ethical scepticism' and in examining 'the question of which of the contending maxims (of practical reason)

they regarded Marxism as being preeminently, if not exclusively, a science of society.[129]

Althusser and other structuralist Marxists similarly assign primacy to science, but they dismiss in a more radical way any form of non-scientific thought – subsumed under the concept of 'ideology' – including the pre-scientific thought of Marx himself, expressed in the 'humanism' and 'historicism' of his early works. Althusser's view presents a number of difficulties. One is that of defining and explaining ideology.[130] Another concerns the epistemological status of Althusser's own philosophy of science (or more precisely, his philosophical reading of Marxism as science).[131] These questions, however, only pose in a particularly acute form problems which are inherent in any project to ground securely a scientific Marxism, or indeed any scientific sociology: (i) how, if at all, can science be demarcated from non-science; (ii) if so demarcated, what kind of relation is held to exist between science and non-science; and (iii) are the problems that arise in the non-scientific domain – in ethics, let us say – capable in principle of solution by reason and/or by reference to experience.

The Austro-Marxists, as we have seen, took a less extreme view of the primacy of science than do the Marxist structuralists. They did not intend to establish an impassable gulf between the spheres of cognitive/theoretical reason and practical reason; and they held that science can illumine, and profoundly influence, even if it cannot ultimately decide, matters of practical (especially political) conduct. For them, moreover, practical reason is still reason; their view was not that values are simply the result of arbitrary choices or decisions, set in a framework of determination by 'interests' – as for instance Max Weber's value theory asserted – but rather, as Bauer's essay indicates, that there can be universally valid reasons, such as are formulated in Kant's maxims, for choosing one course of action rather than another.

It is true, none the less, that the Austro-Marxists, like other scientific Marxists, devoted little of their intellectual effort to the problems of ethics and social philosophy; and it has been a major contribution of the humanist Marxists, exemplified in several of the following texts, to revive the discussion of ethical questions, of the Marxist conception of human nature, and of the

---

is supposed to guide us'. Only, he argued, 'science must come first, before we can successfully pose the moral question'. It is also worthy of note that *Der Kampf* (the theoretical journal of the Austro-Marxists) published a long essay by Hendrik de Man emphasizing the ethical-humanist themes in Marx's *Economic and Philosophical Manuscripts* (see note 3 above).

129 This view is set out very forcefully by Hilferding in his preface to *Finance Capital*.

130 See pp. 63–5 below. On the variations, and contradictions, in Althusser's accounts of ideology, see Jorge Larrain, *The Concept of Ideology*, pp. 154–64. See also the discussion of ideology by Godelier, in *Perspectives*, pp. 169–85, where a Marxist analysis of ideology is closely related to Lévi-Strauss' structural analysis of myth.

131 This is similar to the well-known problem of the status of the verification principle in logical positivism.

theory of needs. In his eleventh thesis on Feuerbach Marx set 'changing the world' above 'interpreting' it; in his life work, I would say, he gave equal importance to 'explanation' and 'action', to theory and practice, or in other terms, to theoretical and practical reason. But Marx himself never expounded his methodological views in the manner of Durkheim or Weber, and we cannot be sure how he would have dealt with the problems of method (in particular the relation between theoretical and practical reason) that have become the subject of later discussion. Nevertheless, I think it can be claimed – partly on the basis of Marx's references to the empirical nature of his studies, and to the similarities between the natural sciences and his own social science – that he regarded his work primarily as the construction of an empirical science, not as a new form of 'critical philosophy'. And there is one fairly long passage on method which seems to confirm this claim directly. In his preface to the second German edition of *Capital* in 1873, Marx responded to some of the criticisms of his work, especially those which alleged that it had a metaphysical character, by quoting and commenting upon the observations made by a Russian reviewer[132] of the first edition:

> After quoting from . . . the preface to my *Zur Kritik der politischen Oekonomie*, Berlin, 1859, in which I set forth the materialist foundation of my method, the writer continues as follows: 'For Marx, only one thing is important: to discover the laws of the phenomena he is investigating. . . . Consequently, Marx is concerned with only one thing: to show by exact scientific investigation the necessity of a definite and orderly succession in social conditions, and to establish, as accurately as possible, the facts that serve him as the starting point and grounds for his views. For this purpose it is quite enough if he proves, at one and the same time, the necessity of the present order and the necessity of another order into which the first must inevitably pass, regardless of whether men believe it or do not believe it, are conscious or unconscious of it. Marx regards the social movement as a natural sequence of historical phenomena, governed by laws which are not only independent of the will, the consciousness, and the purposes of men, but on the contrary, determine their volition, consciousness, and purposes.' . . . When the writer describes so aptly . . . the method I have actually used, what else is he describing but the dialectical method?

If this *is* the dialectical method, then it is scarcely distinguishable from the method of all empirical science. Of course, it raises all the problems with which studies in the logic of the social sciences have been concerned for the past century (and which Max Adler analysed within Marxist thought), and it is open to anyone to argue that such a scientific method is inappropriate for the study of human behaviour; but he should not then pass off his views as being those of Marx himself.

132 The review, published in a St Petersburg journal, *Vestnik Evropy*, no. 4 (1872), was written by I. I. Kaufmann, a professor at the University of St Petersburg, whom Marx later described in a letter as 'my very intelligent critic'.

What distinguishes Marx's social theory is not a unique method, nor is it the preeminence of a concept such as 'totality', upon which Lukács laid so much stress, for this idea has had an important place in almost all sociological thought. The distinctive feature is a particular conception of the scope and main problems of a general social science. Unlike other sociological systems which treat society as an autonomous subject and take its existence in the natural world as something given, Marx's theory is based firmly upon the idea of a relationship between society and nature. Its fundamental concept is 'human labour', viewed in a historical perspective; it is the developing interchange between man and nature, which at the same time creates, and progressively transforms, human social relationships. From this notion of labour, worked out for the first time in the *Economic and Philosophical Manuscripts*,[133] all the principal categories of Marx's social thought can be derived: the system of production, the division of labour, the alienation of labour, the formation of classes, the development of political movements and ideologies. Equally, Marx's conception of the future socialist society is expressed in terms of the same fundamental idea, for in the passage on freedom and necessity in the third volume of *Capital* he writes that: 'Freedom in this field [of material production] cannot consist of anything else but the fact that socialized mankind, the associated producers, regulate their interchange with nature rationally, bring it under their common control, instead of being ruled by it as by some blind power';[134] and the discussion of science and technology in the *Grundrisse* is only an elaboration of this theme.

In Marx's conception there is not a one-sided determinism of society by nature, or of nature by society, but an interchange and a mutual influence. Moreover, as social relations develop and cultural forms are elaborated in more complex ways, the various elements of social life assume the appearance, and to some extent the reality, of independent existence; and the general notion of human labour and production can provide only a guide for an analysis in detail of the interrelationships.[135] Thus, in assessing Marx's social theory we have to distinguish between questions concerning the value of his general approach and fundamental concepts, and questions concerning the truth or falsity of his

133 See especially the section, 'Private property and communism', where Marx writes, 'for socialist man, the *whole of what is called world history* is nothing but the creation of man by human labour, and the emergence of nature for man' (Bottomore, (ed.), *Marx: Early Writings*, p. 166). There is an excellent discussion of the crucial importance of this notion of human labour in Alfred Schmidt, *The Concept of Nature in Marx*, especially ch. 2.

134 Bottomore and Rubel (eds), *Marx: Selected Writings*, pp. 254–5.

135 As Marx observed in the course of discussing the fundamental relationship between the 'masters of production' and the 'direct producers': 'This does not prevent an economic basis which in its principal characteristics is the same, from manifesting infinite variations and gradations, owing to the effect of innumerable external circumstances, climatic and geographical influences, historical influences from the outside, etc. These variations can only be discovered by analyzing these empirically given circumstances' (*Capital*, vol. III; see Bottomore and Rubel (eds), *Marx: Selected Writings*, pp. 99–100).

44   *Tom Bottomore*

empirical propositions (and those of later Marxists) about particular forms of society at definite stages in their development. As to the first, it is difficult to dissent from Max Weber's judgement on the 'materialist conception of history': 'The analysis of social and cultural phenomena from the particular aspect of their economic conditioning and significance was a creative and fecund scientific principle . . . and will remain so for a long time to come.'[136] This is not to say that the principle or approach itself is incapable of any further development and modification, or that it can be accepted dogmatically without any confrontation with alternative principles and approaches, especially as these have been formulated in sociology and other social sciences since Marx's time.

Recent Marxist thought has been developing, and needs to develop further, in both the spheres that I have distinguished, taking up the kind of problems – some scientific, some ethical – outlined by Marković in the passage cited above.[137] But let us not be deceived either about the extent of the revisions that may be needed in the Marxist theory of society, or about the difficulty of elaborating a Marxist theory of practice. I do not agree entirely with Kolakowski's argument that 'the concept of Marxism as a separate school of thought will in time become blurred and ultimately disappear altogether. . . . What is permanent in Marx's work will be assimilated in the natural course of scientific development';[138] for it may also happen that Marxism, in a revised but still distinctive form, will provide the main elements of this scientific development, and become the most widely accepted and acceptable paradigm among the competing paradigms in theoretical sociology. But even if there were such an outcome, as I think is certainly possible, the kind of Marxist theory which eventually attained such a preeminent position would have been considerably affected by other methodological and theoretical orientations in the social sciences, as it has already been influenced by positivism and neo-Hegelianism, and more recently by structuralism, phenomenology and the realist philosophy of science.

We have also to consider how well established are Marx's empirical propositions concerning the stages of social development, the role of class conflict in history, the basic classes of capitalist society and their political role, the relations of dependence or reciprocity between the economy and the political system. We must also ask whether there has been any significant extension of Marx's 'new science' to those aspects of social life which he himself was unable to study with any thoroughness, or to the massive historical changes, including the emergence of 'post-capitalist' or 'socialist' societies, which have occurred since the end of the nineteenth century. In the latter field, as I showed earlier, major criticisms can be formulated which, if they do not

136 'Objectivity in social science and social policy', in Max Weber, *The Methodology of the Social Sciences*.
137 See p. 36 above.
138 Kolakowski, *Marxism and Beyond*, p. 204.

refute, at least cast doubt upon some of Marx's statements and raise a host of new problems. But perhaps the most serious criticism of all is that, in the course of the twentieth century, the scientific development of Marx's theory seems to have faltered. Where is an analysis of modern capitalism to be found that can be set beside Marx's *Capital*? Where is the Marxist theory of classes developed on the basis of profound historical and sociological research? Where is any comprehensive Marxist theory at all of modern political parties? The questions could be multiplied.

On the other hand, the difficulties to be faced in advancing Marxist social science still appear to me far less formidable than those involved in working out an adequate Marxist theory of practical action, that is to say, an ethical and political doctrine. Marxism does not have anything like the same preeminence, or offer the same prospects, in the analysis of ethical and social philosophical questions as in the scientific study of social life. This is due above all, as I suggested earlier, to the fact that there is only a very limited basis in Marx's own work for the development of such an analysis; for not only did he devote little sustained attention to these questions, but he showed far less originality in this field than in his scientific investigations, remaining content for the most part to adopt – and then express in his own way – the radical humanism and naturalism of the Enlightenment philosophers, the Saint-Simonians and Feuerbach.

I have considerable doubts, therefore, about the possibility of developing a specifically Marxist, rather than broadly socialist ethics, or a Marxist, as distinct from a socialist, humanism, except in the rather limited sense that the ethical theory or humanist outlook would necessarily be influenced by the findings of Marxist social science. For contrary to a widely held view, I do not consider that science cannot tell us anything at all about how we should live. In so far as science discloses the reality of the physical world, of human nature, and of human societies, it does undoubtedly offer *some* guidance in the conduct of practical life, at the very least perhaps in telling us how we should *not* live. But it is also evident that science cannot finally decide questions of conduct and morality, and we are obliged therefore to ask what kind of thought or knowledge can provide answers to such questions, and can do so with anything like the precision or reliability of science. As Ulrich, the 'man without qualities', reflected: 'science has developed a conception of hard, sober intellectual strength that makes mankind's old metaphysical and moral notions simply unendurable.'[139] Whether such intellectual strength is likely to emerge in the field of ethics and social philosophy may be a matter of doubt. What is certain is that these questions constitute a major intellectual problem for Marxist thinkers and that we still await the appearance of a great Marxist moral philosopher.

139 Robert Musil, *The Man Without Qualities*, vol. I, p. 48.

Part I Society and History

1 Marx the Sociologist

J. A. Schumpeter

. . . German-trained and speculative-minded as [Marx] was, he had a thorough grounding and a passionate interest in philosophy. Pure philosophy of the German kind was his starting point and the love of his youth. For a time he thought of it as his true vocation. He was a Neo-Hegelian, which roughly means that while accepting the master's fundamental attitudes and methods he and his group eliminated, and replaced by pretty much their opposites, the conservative interpretations put upon Hegel's philosophy by many of its other adherents. This background shows in all his writings wherever the opportunity offers itself. It is no wonder that his German and Russian readers, by bent of mind and training similarly disposed, should seize primarily upon this element and make it the master key to the system.

I believe this to be a mistake and an injustice to Marx's scientific powers. He retained his early love during the whole of his lifetime. He enjoyed certain formal analogies which may be found between his and Hegel's argument. He liked to testify to his Hegelianism and to use Hegelian phraseology. But this is all. Nowhere did he betray positive science to metaphysics. He says himself as much in the preface to the second edition of the first volume of *Das Kapital*, and that what he says there is true and no self-delusion can be proved by analysing his argument, which everywhere rests upon social fact, and the true sources of his propositions none of which lies in the domain of philosophy. Of course, those commentators or critics who themselves started from the philosophic side were unable to do this because they did not know enough about the social sciences involved. The propensity of the philosophic system-builder, moreover, made them averse to any other interpretation but the one which proceeds from some philosophic principle. So they saw philosophy in the most matter-of-fact

From J. A. Schumpeter, *Capitalism, Socialism, and Democracy*, 3rd edn (Allen and Unwin) pp. 9–20.

statements about economic experience, thereby shunting discussion on to the wrong track, misleading friends and foes alike.

Marx the sociologist brought to bear on his task an equipment which consisted primarily of an extensive command over historical and contemporaneous fact. His knowledge of the latter was always somewhat antiquated, for he was the most bookish of men and therefore fundamental materials, as distinguished from the material of the newspapers, always reached him with a lag. But hardly any historical work of his time that was of any general importance or scope escaped him, although much of the monographic literature did. While we cannot extol the completeness of his information in this field as much as we shall his erudition in the field of economic theory, he was yet able to illustrate his social visions not only by large historical frescoes but also by many details most of which were as regards reliability rather above than below the standards of other sociologists of his time. These facts he embraced with a glance that pierced through the random irregularities of the surface down to the grandiose logic of things historical. In this there was not merely passion. There was not merely analytic impulse. There were both. And the outcome of his attempt to formulate that logic, the so-called Economic Interpretation of History,[1] is doubtless one of the greatest individual achievements of sociology to this day. Before it, the question sinks into insignificance whether or not this achievement was entirely original and how far credit has in part to be given to predecessors, German and French.

The economic interpretation of history does *not* mean that men are, consciously or unconsciously, wholly or primarily, actuated by economic motives. On the contrary, the explanation of the role and mechanism of non-economic motives and the analysis of the way in which social reality mirrors itself in the individual psyches is an essential element of the theory and one of its most significant contributions. Marx did not hold that religions, metaphysics, schools of art, ethical ideas and political volitions were either reducible to economic *motives* or of no importance. He only tried to unveil the economic *conditions* which shape them and which account for their rise and fall. The whole of Max Weber's[2] facts and arguments fits perfectly into Marx's system. Social groups and classes and the ways in which these groups or classes explain to themselves their own existence, location and behaviour were of course what interested him most. He poured the vials of his most bilious wrath on the historians who took those attitudes and their verbalizations (the ideologies or, as Pareto would have said, *derivations*) at their face value and who tried to interpret social reality by means of them. But if ideas or values were not

1 First published in that scathing attack on Proudhon's *Philosophie de la misère*, entitled *Das Elend der Philosophie*, 1847. Another version was included in the *Communist Manifesto*, 1848.

2 The above refers to Weber's investigations into the sociology of religions and particularly to his famous study, *Die protestantische Ethik und der Geist des Kapitalismus* republished in his collected works.

for him the prime movers of the social process, neither were they mere smoke. If I may use the analogy, they had in the social engine the role of transmission belts. We cannot touch upon that most interesting post-war development of these principles which would afford the best instance by which to explain this, the Sociology of Knowledge.[3] But it was necessary to say this much because Marx has been persistently misunderstood in this respect. Even his friend Engels, at the open grave of Marx, defined the theory in question as meaning precisely that individuals and groups are swayed primarily by economic motives, which in some important respects is wrong and for the rest piteously trivial.

While we are about it, we may as well defend Marx against another misunderstanding: the *economic* interpretation of history has often been called the *materialistic* interpretation. It has been called so by Marx himself. This phrase greatly increased its popularity with some, and its unpopularity with other people. But it is entirely meaningless. Marx's philosophy is no more materialistic than is Hegel's, and his theory of history is not more materialistic than is any other attempt to account for the historic process by the means at the command of empirical science. It should be clear that this is logically compatible with any metaphysical or religious belief – exactly as any physical picture of the world is. Medieval theology itself supplies methods by which it is possible to establish this compatibility.[4]

What the theory really says may be put into two propositions: (1) The forms or conditions of production are the fundamental determinant of social structures which in turn breed attitudes, actions and civilizations. Marx illustrates his meaning by the famous statement that the 'hand-mill' creates feudal, and the 'steam-mill' capitalist societies. This stresses the technological element to a dangerous extent, but may be accepted on the understanding that mere technology is not all of it. Popularizing a little and recognizing that by doing so we lose much of the meaning, we may say that it is our daily work which forms our minds, and that it is our location within the productive process which determines our outlook on things – or the sides of things we see – and the social elbowroom at the command of each of us. (2) The forms of production themselves have a logic of their own; that is to say, they change according to necessities inherent in them so as to produce their successors merely by their own working. To illustrate by the same Marxian example: the system characterized by the 'hand-mill' creates an economic and social situation in which the adoption of the mechanical method of milling becomes a practical necessity that individuals or groups are powerless to alter. The rise and working of the

---

3 The German word is *Wissenssoziologie*, and the best names to mention are those of Max Scheler and Karl Mannheim. The latter's article on the subject in the German Dictionary of Sociology (*Handwörterbuch der Soziologie*) can serve as an introduction.

4 I have met several Catholic radicals, a priest among them, all devout Catholics, who took this view and in fact declared themselves Marxists in everything except in matters relating to their faith.

'steam-mill' in turn creates new social functions and locations, new groups and views, which develop and interact in such a way as to outgrow their own frame. Here, then, we have the propeller which is responsible first of all for economic and, in consequence of this, for any other social change, a propeller the action of which does not itself require any impetus external to it.

Both propositions undoubtedly contain a large amount of truth and are, as we shall find at several turns of our way, invaluable working hypotheses. Most of the current objections completely fail, all those for instance which in refutation point to the influence of ethical or religious factors, or the one already raised by Eduard Bernstein, which with delightful simplicity asserts that 'men have heads' and can hence act as they choose. After what has been said above, it is hardly necessary to dwell on the weakness of such arguments: of course men 'choose' their course of action which is not directly enforced by the objective data of the environment; but they choose from standpoints, views and propensities that do not form another set of independent data but are themselves moulded by the objective set.

Nevertheless, the question arises whether the economic interpretation of history is more than a convenient approximation which must be expected to work less satisfactorily in some cases than it does in others. An obvious qualification occurs at the outset. Social structures, types and attitudes are coins that do not readily melt. Once they are formed they persist, possibly for centuries, and since different structures and types display different degrees of this ability to survive, we almost always find that actual group and national behaviour more or less departs from what we should expect it to be if we tried to infer it from the dominant forms of the productive process. Though this applies quite generally, it is most clearly seen when a highly durable structure transfers itself bodily from one country to another. The social situation created in Sicily by the Norman conquest will illustrate my meaning. Such facts Marx did not overlook but he hardly realized all their implications.

A related case is of more ominous significance. Consider the emergence of the feudal type of landlordism in the kingdom of the Franks during the sixth and seventh centuries. This was certainly a most important event that shaped the structure of society for many ages and *also influenced conditions of production, wants and technology included*. But its simplest explanation is to be found in the function of military leadership previously filled by the families and individuals who (retaining that function however) became feudal landlords after the definitive conquest of the new territory. This does not fit the Marxian schema at all well and could easily be so construed as to point in a different direction. Facts of this nature can no doubt also be brought into the fold by means of auxiliary hypotheses but the necessity of inserting such hypotheses is usually the beginning of the end of a theory.

Many other difficulties that arise in the course of attempts at historical interpretation by means of the Marxian schema could be met by admitting some measure of interaction between the sphere of production and other spheres of social life.[5] But the glamour of fundamental truth that surrounds it depends precisely on the strictness and simplicity of the one-way relation which it asserts. If this be called in question, the economic interpretation of history will have to take its place among other propositions of a similar kind – as one of many partial truths – or else to give way to another that does tell more fundamental truth. However, neither its rank as an achievement nor its handiness as a working hypothesis is impaired thereby.

To the faithful, of course, it is simply the master key to all the secrets of human history. And if we sometimes feel inclined to smile at rather naïve applications of it, we should remember what sort of arguments it replaced. Even the crippled sister of the economic interpretation of history, the Marxian Theory of Social Classes, moves into a more favourable light as soon as we bear this in mind.

Again, it is in the first place an important contribution that we have to record. Economists have been strangely slow in recognizing the phenomenon of social classes. Of course they always classified the agents whose interplay produced the process they dealt with. But these classes were simply sets of individuals that displayed some common character: thus, some people were classed as landlords or workmen because they owned land or sold the services of their labour. Social classes, however, are not the creatures of the classifying observer but live entities that exist as such. And their existence entails consequences that are entirely missed by a schema which looks upon society as if it were an amorphous assemblage of individuals or families. It is fairly open to question precisely how important the phenomenon of social classes is for research in the field of purely economic theory. That it is very important for many practical applications and for all the broader aspects of the social process in general is beyond doubt.

Roughly speaking, we may say that the social classes made their entrance in the famous statement contained in the *Communist Manifesto* that the history of society is the history of class struggles. Of course, this is to put the claim at its highest. But even if we tone it down to the proposition that historical events may often be interpreted in terms of class interests and class attitudes and that existing class structures are always an important factor in historical interpretation, enough remains to entitle us to speak of a conception nearly as valuable as was the economic interpretation of history itself.

Clearly, success on the line of advance opened up by the principle of class struggle depends upon the validity of the particular theory of classes we make our own. Our picture of history and all our interpretations of cultural patterns and the mechanisms of social change will differ according to whether we choose, for instance, the racial theory of classes and like Gobineau reduce human history to the history of the struggle of races or, say, the division of labour theory of classes in the fashion of Schmoller or of Durkheim and resolve

5 In his later life, Engels admitted that freely. Plekhanov went still further in this direction.

class antagonisms into antagonisms between the interests of vocational groups. Nor is the range of possible differences in analysis confined to the problem of the nature of classes. Whatever view we may hold about it, the different interpretations will result from different definitions of class interest[6] and from different opinions about how class action manifests itself. The subject is a hotbed of prejudice to this day, and as yet hardly in its scientific stage.

Curiously enough, Marx has never, as far as we know, worked out systematically what it is plain was one of the pivots of his thought. It is possible that he deferred the task until it was too late, precisely because his thinking ran so much in terms of class concepts that he did not feel it necessary to bother about definitive statement at all. It is equally possible that some points about it remained unsettled in his own mind, and that his way toward a full-fledged theory of classes was barred by certain difficulties he had created for himself by insisting on a purely economic and over-simplified conception of the phenomenon. He himself and his disciples both offered applications of this under-developed theory to particular patterns of which his own *History of the Class Struggles in France* is the outstanding example.[7] Beyond that no real progress has been achieved. The theory of his chief associate, Engels, was of the division of labour type and essentially un-Marxian in its implications. Barring this we have only the sidelights and *aperçus* – some of them of striking force and brilliance – that are strewn all over the writings of the master, particularly in *Das Kapital* and the *Communist Manifesto*.

The task of piecing together such fragments is delicate and cannot be attempted here. The basic idea is clear enough, however. The stratifying principle consists in the ownership, or the exclusion from ownership, of means of production such as factory buildings, machinery, raw materials and the consumers' goods that enter into the workman's budget. We have thus, fundamentally, two and only two classes, those owners, the capitalists, and those have-nots who are compelled to sell their labour, the labouring class or proletariat. The existence of intermediate groups, such as are formed by farmers or artisans who employ labour but also do manual work, by clerks and by the professions is of course not denied; but they are treated as anomalies which tend to disappear in the course of the capitalist process. The two fundamental classes are, by virtue of the logic of their position and quite

6 The reader will perceive that one's views about what classes are and about what calls them into existence do not uniquely determine what the *interests* of those classes are and how each class will act on what 'it' – its leaders for instance or the rank and file – considers or feels, in the long run or in the short, erroneously or correctly, to be its interest or interests. The problem of group interest is full of thorns and pitfalls of its own, quite irrespective of the nature of the groups under study.

7 Another example is the socialist theory of imperialism. . . . O. Bauer's interesting attempt to interpret the antagonisms between the various races that inhabited the Austro-Hungarian Empire in terms of the class struggle between capitalists and workers (*Die Nationalitätenfrage*, 1905) also deserves to be mentioned, although the skill of the analyst only serves to show up the inadequacy of the tool.

independently of any individual volition, essentially antagonistic to each other. Rifts within each class and collisions between subgroups occur and may even have historically decisive importance. But in the last analysis, such rifts or collisions are incidental. The one antagonism that is not incidental but inherent in the basic design of capitalist society is founded upon the private control over the means to produce: the very nature of the relation between the capitalist class and the proletariat is strife – class war.

. . . Marx tries to show how in that class war capitalists destroy each other and eventually will destroy the capitalist system too. He also tries to show how the ownership of capital leads to further accumulation. But this way of arguing as well as the very definition that makes the ownership of something the constituent characteristic of a social class only serves to increase the importance of the question of 'primitive accumulation', that is to say, of the question how capitalists came to be capitalists in the first instance or how they acquired that stock of goods which according to the Marxian doctrine was necessary in order to enable them to start exploiting. On this question Marx is much less explicit.[8] He contemptuously rejects the bourgeois nursery tale (*Kinderfibel*) that some people rather than others became, and are still becoming every day, capitalists, by superior intelligence and energy in working and saving. Now he was well advised to sneer at that story about the good boys. For to call for a guffaw is no doubt an excellent method of disposing of an uncomfortable truth, as every politician knows to his profit. Nobody who looks at historical and contemporaneous fact with anything like an unbiased mind can fail to observe that this children's tale, while far from telling the whole truth, yet tells a good deal of it. Supernormal intelligence and energy account for industrial success and in particular for the *founding* of industrial positions in nine cases out of ten. And precisely in the initial stages of capitalism and of every individual industrial career, saving was and is an important element in the process though not quite as explained in classic economics. It is true that one does not ordinarily attain the status of capitalist (industrial employer) by saving from a wage or salary in order to equip one's factory by means of the fund thus assembled. The bulk of accumulation comes from profits and hence presupposes profits – this is in fact the *sound* reason for distinguishing saving from accumulating. The means required in order to start enterprise are typically provided by borrowing other people's savings, the presence of which in many small puddles is easy to explain or the deposits which banks create for the use of the would-be entrepreneur. Nevertheless, the latter does save as a rule: the function of his saving is to raise him above the necessity of submitting to daily drudgery for the sake of his daily bread and to give him breathing space in order to look around, to develop his plans and to secure cooperation. As a matter of economic theory, therefore, Marx had a real case – though he overstated it – when he denied to saving the role that the classical authors attributed to it. Only his inference does not

8 See *Das Kapital*, vol I, ch. 26: 'The secret of primitive accumulation'.

follow. And the guffaw is hardly more justified than it would be if the classical theory were correct.[9]

The guffaw did its work, however, and helped to clear the road for Marx's alternative theory of primitive accumulation. But this alternative theory is not as definite as we might wish. Force – robbery – subjugation of the masses facilitating their spoliation and the results of the pillage in turn facilitating subjugation – this was all right of course and admirably tallied with ideas common among intellectuals of all types, in our day still more than in the day of Marx. But evidently it does not solve the problem, which is to explain how some people acquired the power to subjugate and to rob. Popular literature does not worry about it. I should not think of addressing the question to the writings of John Reed. But we are dealing with Marx.

Now at least the semblance of a solution is afforded by the historical quality of all the major theories of Marx. For him, it is essential for the *logic* of capitalism, and not only a matter of *fact*, that it grew out of a feudal state of society. Of course the same question about the causes and the mechanism of social stratification arises also in this case, but Marx substantially accepted the bourgeois view that feudalism was a reign of force[10] in which subjugation and exploitation of the masses were already accomplished facts. The class theory devised primarily for the conditions of capitalist society was extended to its feudal predecessor – as was much of the conceptual apparatus of the economic theory of capitalism[11] – and some of the most thorny problems were stowed away in the feudal compound to reappear in a settled state, in the form of data, in the analysis of the capitalist pattern. The feudal exploiter was simply replaced by the capitalist exploiter. In those cases in which feudal lords actually turned into industrialists, this alone would solve what is thus left of the problem. Historical evidence lends a certain amount of support to this view: many feudal lords, particularly in Germany, in fact did erect and run factories, often providing the financial means from their feudal rents and the labour from the

9 I will not stay to stress, though I must mention, that even the classical theory is not as wrong as Marx pretended it was. 'Saving up' in the most literal sense had been, especially in earlier stages of capitalism, a not unimportant method of 'original accumulation'. Moreover, there was another method that was akin to it though not identical with it. Many a factory in the seventeenth and eighteenth centuries was just a shed that a man was able to put up by the work of his hands, and required only the simplest equipment to work it. In such cases the manual work of the prospective capitalist plus a quite small fund of savings was all that was needed – and brains, of course.

10 Many socialist writers besides Marx have displayed that uncritical confidence in the explanatory value of the element of force and of the control over the physical means with which to exert force. Ferdinand Lassalle, for instance, has little beyond cannons and bayonets to offer by way of explanation of governmental authority. It is a source of wonder to me that so many people should be blind to the weakness of such a sociology and to the fact that it would obviously be much truer to say that power leads to control over cannons (and men willing to use them) than that control over cannons generates power.

11 This constitutes one of the affinities of the teaching of Marx to that of K. Rodbertus.

agricultural population (not necessarily but sometimes their serfs).[12] In all other cases the material available to stop the gap is distinctly inferior. The only frank way of expressing the situation is that from a Marxian standpoint there is no satisfactory explanation, that is to say, no explanation without resorting to non-Marxian elements suggestive of non-Marxian conclusions.[13]

   This, however, vitiates the theory at both its historical and its logical source. Since most of the methods of primitive accumulation also account for later accumulation – primitive accumulation, as it were, continues throughout the capitalist era – it is not possible to say that Marx's theory of social classes is all right *except* for the difficulties about processes in a distant past. But it is perhaps superfluous to insist on the shortcomings of a theory which not even in the most favourable instances goes anywhere near the heart of the phenomenon it undertakes to explain, and which never should have been taken seriously. These instances are to be found mainly in that epoch of capitalist evolution which derived its character from the prevalence of the medium-sized owner-managed firm. Beyond the range of that type, class positions, though in most cases reflected in more or less corresponding economic positions, are more often the cause than the consequence of the latter: business achievement is obviously not everywhere the only avenue to social eminence and only where it is can ownership of means of production causally determine a group's position in the social structure. Even then, however, it is as reasonable to make that ownership the defining element as it would be to define a soldier as a man who happens to have a gun. The water-tight division between people who (together with their descendants) are supposed to be capitalists once for all and others who (together with their descendants) are supposed to be proletarians once for all is not only, as has often been pointed out, utterly unrealistic but it misses the salient point about social classes – the incessant rise and fall of individual families into and out of the upper strata. The facts I am alluding to are all obvious and indisputable. If they do not show on the Marxian canvas, the reason can only be in their un-Marxian implications.

   It is not superfluous, however, to consider the role which that theory plays within Marx's structure and to ask ourselves what analytic intention – as distinguished from its use as a piece of equipment for the agitator – he meant to serve.

---

12 W. Sombart, in the first edition of his *Theorie des modernen Kapitalismus*, tried to make the most of those cases. But the attempt to base primitive accumulation entirely on the accumulation of ground rent showed its hopelessness as Sombart himself eventually recognized.

13 This holds true even if we admit robbery to the utmost extent to which it is possible to do so without trespassing upon the sphere of the intellectual's folklore. Robbery actually entered into the building up of commercial capital at many times and places. Phoenician as well as English wealth offers familiar examples. But even then the Marxian explanation is inadequate because in the last resort successful robbery must rest on the personal superiority of the robbers. And as soon as this is admitted, a very different theory of social stratification suggests itself.

On the one hand, we must bear in mind that for Marx the theory of Social Classes and Economic Interpretation of History were not what they are for us, viz., two independent doctrines. With Marx, the former implements the latter in a particular way and thus restricts – makes more definite – the *modus operandi* of the conditions or forms of production. These determine the social structure and, through the social structure, all manifestations of civilization and the whole march of cultural and political history. But the social structure is, for all non-socialist epochs, defined in terms of classes – those two classes – which are the true dramatis personae and at the same time the only *immediate* creatures of the logic of the capitalist system of production which affects everything else through them. This explains why Marx was forced to make his classes purely economic phenomena, and even phenomena that were economic in a very narrow sense: he thereby cut himself off from a deeper view of them, but in the precise spot of his analytic schema in which he placed them he had no choice but to do so.

On the other hand, Marx wished to define capitalism by the same trait that also defines his class division. A little reflection will convince the reader that this is not a necessary or natural thing to do. In fact it was a bold stroke of analytic strategy which linked the fate of the class phenomenon with the fate of capitalism in such a way that socialism, which in reality has nothing to do with the presence or absence of social classes, became, by definition, the only possible kind of classless society, excepting primitive groups. This ingenious tautology could not equally well have been secured by any definitions of classes *and* of capitalism other than those chosen by Marx – the definition by private ownership of means of production. Hence there had to be just two classes, owners and non-owners, and hence all other principles of division, much more plausible ones among them, had to be severely neglected or discounted or else reduced to that one.

The exaggeration of the definiteness and importance of the dividing line between the capitalist class in that sense and the proletariat was surpassed only by the exaggeration of the antagonism between them. To any mind not warped by the habit of fingering the Marxian rosary it should be obvious that their relation is, in normal times, primarily one of cooperation and that any theory to the contrary must draw largely on pathological cases for verification. In social life, antagonism and synagogism are of course both ubiquitous and in fact inseparable except in the rarest of cases. But I am almost tempted to say that there was, if anything, less of absolute nonsense in the old harmonistic view – full of nonsense thought that was too – than in the Marxian construction of the impassable gulf between tool owners and tool users. Again, however, he had no choice, not because he wanted to arrive at revolutionary results – these he could have derived just as well from dozens of other possible schemata – but because of the requirements of his own analysis. *If* class struggle was the subject matter of history and also the means of bringing about the socialist dawn, and *if* there had to be just those two classes, then their relation had to be antagonistic on principle or else the force in his system of social dynamics would have been lost.

Now, though Marx *defines* capitalism sociologically, i.e., by the institution of private control over means of production, the *mechanics* of capitalist society are provided by his economic theory. This economic theory is to show how the sociological data embodied in such conceptions as class, class interest, class behaviour, exchange between classes, work out through the medium of economic values, profits, wages, investment, etc., and how they generate precisely the economic process that will eventually break its own institutional framework and at the same time create the conditions for the emergence of another social world. This particular theory of social classes is the analytic tool which, by linking the economic interpretation of history with the concepts of the profit economy, marshals all social facts, makes all phenomena confocal. It is therefore not simply a theory of an individual phenomenon which is to explain that phenomenon and nothing else. It has an organic function which is really much more important to the Marxian system than the measure of success with which it solves its immediate problem. This function must be seen if we are to understand how an analyst of the power of Marx could ever have borne with its shortcomings.

2 Marx's New Science

Louis Althusser

I

In 1845, Marx broke radically with every theory that based history and politics on an essence of man. This unique rupture contained three indissociable elements.

1 The formation of a theory of history and politics based on radically new concepts: the concepts of social formation, productive forces, relations of production, superstructure, ideologies, determination in the last instance by the economy, specific determination of the other levels etc.
2 A radical critique of the *theoretical* pretensions of every philosophical humanism.
3 The definition of humanism as an *ideology*.

This new conception is completely rigorous as well, but it is a new rigour: the essence criticized (2) is defined as an ideology (3), a category belonging to the new theory of society and history (1).

This rupture with every *philosophical* anthropology or humanism is no secondary detail; it is Marx's scientific discovery.

It means that Marx rejected the problematic of the earlier philosophy and adopted a new problematic in one and the same act. The earlier idealist ('bourgeois') philosophy depended in all its domains and arguments (its 'theory of knowledge', its conception of history, its political economy, its ethics, its aesthetics etc.) on a problematic of *human nature* (or the essence of man). For centuries, this problematic had been transparency itself, and no one had thought of questioning it even in its internal modifications.

The first excerpt is taken from Louis Althusser, *For Marx* (Librairie François Maspero; Allen Lane, 1969) pp. 227–36. The second excerpt is from Louis Althusser and Étienne Balibar, *Reading Capital* (Librairie François Maspero; New Left Books, 1970) pp. 177–81. Both excerpts are reprinted by permission of Verso.

This problematic was neither vague nor loose; on the contrary, it was constituted by a coherent system of precise concepts tightly articulated together. When Marx confronted it, it implied the two complementary postulates he defined in the Sixth Thesis on Feuerbach:

1 That there is a universal essence of man.
2 That this essence is the attribute of '*each single individual*' who is its real subject.

These two postulates are complementary and indissociable. But their existence and their unity presuppose a whole empiricist–idealist world outlook. If the essence of man is to be a universal attribute, it is essential that *concrete subjects* exist as absolute givens; this implies an *empiricism of the subject*. If these empirical individuals are to be men, it is essential that each carries in himself the whole human essence, if not in fact, at least in principle; this implies an *idealism of the essence*. So empiricism of the subject implies idealism of the essence and vice versa. This relation can be inverted into its 'opposite' – empiricism of the concept/idealism of the subject. But the inversion respects the basic structure of the problematic, which remains fixed.

In this type-structure it is possible to recognize not only the principle of theories of society (from Hobbes to Rousseau), of political economy (from Petty to Ricardo), of ethics (from Descartes to Kant), but also the very principle of the (pre-Marxist) idealist and materialist 'theory of knowledge' (from Locke to Feuerbach, via Kant). The content of the human essence or of the empirical subject may vary (as can be seen from Descartes to Feuerbach); the subject may change from empiricism to idealism (as can be seen from Locke to Kant): the terms presented and their relations only vary within the invariant type-structure which constitutes this very problematic: *an empiricism of the subject always corresponds to an idealism of the essence (or an empiricism of the essence to an idealism of the subject)*.

By rejecting the essence of man as his theoretical basis, Marx rejected the whole of this organic system of postulates. He drove the philosophical categories of the *subject*, of *empiricism*, of the *ideal essence* etc., from all the domains in which they had been supreme. Not only from political economy (rejection of the myth of *homo oeconomicus*, that is, of the individual with definite faculties and needs as the *subject* of the classical economy); not just from history (rejection of social atomism and ethico-political idealism); not just from ethics (rejection of the Kantian ethical idea); but also from philosophy itself: for Marx's materialism excludes the empiricism of the subject (and its inverse: the transcendental subject) and the idealism of the concept (and its inverse: the empiricism of the concept).

This total theoretical revolution was only empowered to reject the old concepts because it replaced them by new concepts. In fact Marx established a new problematic, a new systematic way of asking questions of the world, new principles and a new method. This discovery is immediately contained in the theory of historical materialism, in which Marx did not only propose a new theory of the history of societies, but at the same time implicitly, but necessarily, a new 'philosophy', infinite in its implications. Thus, when Marx replaced the old couple individuals/human essence in the theory of history by new concepts (forces of production, relations of production etc.), he was, in fact, simultaneously proposing a new conception of 'philosophy'. He replaced the old postulates (empiricism/idealism of the subject, empiricism/idealism of the essence) which were the basis not only for idealism but also for pre-Marxist materialism, by a historico-dialectical materialism of *praxis*: that is, by a theory of the different specific *levels* of *human practice* (economic practice, political practice, ideological practice, scientific practice) in their characteristic articulations, based on the specific articulations of the unity of human society. In a word, Marx substituted for the 'ideological' and universal concept of Feuerbachian 'practice' a concrete conception of the specific differences that enables us to situate each particular practice in the specific differences of the social structure.

So, to understand what was radically new in Marx's contribution, we must become aware not only of the novelty of the concepts of historical materialism, but also of the depth of the theoretical revolution they imply and inaugurate. On this condition it is possible to define humanism's status, and reject its *theoretical* pretensions while recognizing its practical function as an ideology.

Strictly in respect to theory, therefore, one can and must speak openly of *Marx's theoretical anti-humanism*, and see in this *theoretical anti-humanism* the absolute (negative) precondition of the (positive) knowledge of the human world itself, and of its practical transformation. It is impossible to *know* anything about men except on the absolute precondition that the philosophical (theoretical) myth of man is reduced to ashes. So any thought that appeals to Marx for any kind of restoration of a theoretical anthropology or humanism is no more than ashes, *theoretically*. But in practice it could pile up a monument of pre-Marxist ideology that would weigh down on real history and threaten to lead it into blind alleys.

For the corollary of theoretical Marxist anti-humanism is the recognition and knowledge of humanism itself: as an *ideology*. Marx never fell into the idealist illusion of believing that the knowledge of an object might ultimately replace the object or dissipate its existence. Cartesians, knowing that the sun was two thousand leagues away, were astonished that this distance only looked like two hundred paces: they could not even find enough of God to fill in this gap. Marx never believed that a knowledge of the nature of *money* (a social relation) could destroy its *appearance*, its form of existence – a thing, for this appearance was its very being, as necessary as the existing mode of production.[1] Marx never

1 The whole, fashionable, theory of 'reification' depends on a projection of the theory of alienation found in the early texts, particularly the *1844 Manuscripts*, on to the theory of 'fetishism' in *Capital*.

believed that an ideology might be dissipated by a knowledge of it: for the knowledge of this ideology, as the knowledge of its conditions of possibility, of its structure, of its specific logic and of its practical role, within a given society, is simultaneously knowledge of the conditions of its necessity. So Marx's theoretical *anti-humanism* does not suppress anything in the historical *existence* of humanism. In the real world philosophies of man are found after Marx as often as before, and today even some Marxists are tempted to develop the themes of a new theoretical humanism. Furthermore, Marx's theoretical anti-humanism, by relating it to its conditions of existence, recognizes a necessity for humanism as an *ideology*, a conditional necessity. The recognition of this necessity is not purely speculative. On it alone can Marxism base a policy in relation to the existing ideological forms, of every kind: religion, ethics, art, philosophy, law – and in the very front rank, humanism. When (eventually) a Marxist policy of humanist ideology, that is, a political attitude to humanism, is achieved – a policy which may be either a rejection or a critique, or a use, or a support, or a development, or a humanist renewal of contemporary forms of ideology in the *ethico-political* domain – this policy will only have been possible on the absolute condition that it is based on Marxist philosophy, and a precondition for this is theoretical *anti-humanism*.

So everything depends on the knowledge of the nature of humanism as an ideology.

There can be no question of attempting a profound definition of ideology here. It will suffice to know very schematically that an ideology is a system (with its own logic and rigour) of representation (images, myths, ideas or concepts, depending on the case) endowed with a historical existence and role within a given society. Without embarking on the problem of the relations between a science and its (ideological) past, we can say that ideology, as a system of

---

In the *1844 Manuscripts*, the objectification of the human essence is claimed as the indispensable preliminary to the reappropriation of the human essence by man. Throughout the process of objectification, man only exists in the form of an objectivity in which he meets his own essence in the appearance of a foreign, non-human, essence. This 'objectification' is not called 'reification' even though it is called *inhuman*. Inhumanity is not represented *par excellence* by the model of a 'thing': but sometimes by the model of animality (or even of pre-animality – the man who no longer even has simple animal relations with nature), sometimes by the model of the omnipotence and fascination of transcendence (God, the State) and of money, which is, of course, a 'thing'. In *Capital* the only social relation that is presented in the form of a *thing* (this piece of metal) is *money*. But the conception of money as a *thing* (that is, the confusion of value with use-value in money) does not correspond to the reality of this 'thing': it is not the brutality of a simple 'thing' that man is faced with when he is in direct relation with money; it is a *power* (or a *lack* of it) over things and men. An ideology of reification that sees 'things' everywhere in human relations confuses in this category 'thing' (a category more foreign to Marx cannot be imagined) every social relation, conceived according to the model of a money-thing ideology.

representations, is distinguished from science in that in it the practico-social function is more important than the theoretical function (function as knowledge).

What is the nature of this social function? To understand it we must refer to the Marxist theory of history. The 'subjects' of history are given human societies. They present themselves as totalities whose unity is constituted by a certain specific type of *complexity*, which introduces instances, that, following Engels, we can, very schematically, reduce to three: the economy, politics and ideology. So in every society we can posit, in forms which are sometimes very paradoxical, the existence of an economic activity as the base, a political organization and 'ideological' forms (religion, ethics, philosophy etc.). *So ideology is as such an organic part of every social totality.* It is as if human societies could not survive without these *specific formations*, these systems of representations (at various levels), their ideologies. Human societies secrete ideology as the very element and atmosphere indispensable to their historical respiration and life. Only an ideological world outlook could have imagined societies *without ideology* and accepted the utopian idea of a world in which ideology (not just one of its historical forms) would disappear without trace, to be replaced by *science*. For example, this utopia is the principle behind the idea that ethics, which is in its essence ideology, could be replaced by science or become scientific through and through; or that religion could be destroyed by science which would in some way take its place; that *art* could merge with knowledge or become 'everyday life' etc.

And I am not going to steer clear of the crucial question: *historical materialism cannot conceive that even a communist society could ever do without ideology*, be it ethics, art or 'world outlook'. Obviously it is possible to foresee important modifications in its ideological forms and their relations and even the disappearance of certain existing forms or a shift of their functions to neighbouring forms; it is also possible (on the premise of already acquired experience) to foresee the development of new ideological forms (e.g. the ideologies of 'the scientific world outlook' and 'communist humanism') but in the present state of Marxist theory strictly conceived, it is not conceivable that communism, a new mode of production implying determinate forces of production and relations of production, could do without a social organization of production, and corresponding ideological forms.

So ideology is not an aberration or a contingent excrescence of History: it is a structure essential to the historical life of societies. Further, only the existence and the recognition of its necessity enable us to act on ideology and transform ideology into an instrument of deliberate action on history.

It is customary to suggest that ideology belongs to the region of 'consciousness'. We must not be misled by this appellation, which is still contaminated by the idealist problematic that preceded Marx. In truth, ideology has very little to do with 'consciousness', even supposing this term to have an unambiguous meaning. It is profoundly *unconscious*, even when it presents itself in a reflected

form (as in pre-Marxist 'philosophy'). Ideology is indeed a system of representations, but in the majority of cases these representations have nothing to do
with 'consciousness': they are usually images and occasionally concepts, but it is
above all as *structures* that they impose on the vast majority of men, not via their
'consciousness'. They are perceived–accepted–suffered cultural objects and
they act functionally on men via a process that escapes them. Men 'live' their
ideologies as the Cartesian 'saw' or did not see – if he was not looking at it – the
moon two hundred paces away: *not at all as a form of consciousness, but as an object
of their 'world'* – as their *'world'* itself. But what do we mean, then, when we say
that ideology is a matter of men's 'consciousness'? First, that ideology is distinct
from other social instances, but also that men *live* their actions, usually referred
to freedom and 'consciousness' by the classical tradition, in ideology, *by and
through ideology*; in short, that the 'lived' relation between men and the world,
including History (in political action or inaction), passes through ideology, or
better, *is ideology itself*. This is the sense in which Marx said that it is in ideology
(as the locus of political struggle) that men *become conscious* of their place in the
world and in history, it is within this ideological unconsciousness that men
succeed in altering the 'lived' relation between them and the world and
acquiring that new form of specific unconsciousness called 'consciousness'.

So ideology is a matter of the *lived* relation between men and their world.
This relation, that only appears as *'conscious'* on condition that it is *unconscious*,
in the same way only seems to be simple on condition that it is complex, that it is
not a simple relation but a relation between relations, a second-degree relation.
In ideology men do indeed express, not the relation between them and their
conditions of existence, but *the way* they live the relation between them and
their conditions of existence: this presupposes both a real relation and an
'imaginary', *'lived'* relation. Ideology, then, is the expression of the relation
between men and their 'world', that is, the (overdetermined) unity of the real
relation and the imaginary relation between them and their real conditions of
existence. In ideology the real relation is inevitably invested in the imaginary
relation, a relation that *expresses* a *will* (conservative, conformist, reformist or
revolutionary), a hope or a nostalgia, rather than describing a reality.

It is in this overdetermination of the real by the imaginary and of the
imaginary by the real that ideology is *active* in principle, that it reinforces or
modifies the relation between men and their conditions of existence, in the
imaginary relation itself. It follows that this action can never be purely
instrumental; the men who would use an ideology purely as a means of action, as
a tool, find that they have been caught by it, implicated by it, just when they are
using it and believe themselves to be absolute masters of it.

This is perfectly clear in the case of a *class society*. The ruling ideology is then
the ideology of the ruling *class*. But the ruling class does not maintain with the
ruling ideology, which is its own ideology, an external and lucid relation of pure
utility and cunning. When, during the eighteenth century, the 'rising class', the
bourgeoisie, developed a humanist ideology of equality, freedom and reason, it

gave its own demands the form of universality, since it hoped thereby to enrol at its side, by their education to this end, the very men it would liberate only for their exploitation. This is the Rousseauan myth of the origins of inequality: the rich holding forth to the poor in 'the most deliberate discourse' ever conceived, so as to persuade them to live their slavery as their freedom. In reality, the bourgeoisie has to believe in its own myth before it can convince others, and not only so as to convince others, since what it lives in its ideology is *the very relation* between it and its real conditions of existence which allows it simultaneously to act on itself (provide itself with a legal and ethical consciousness, and the legal and ethical conditions of economic liberalism) and on others (those it exploits and is going to exploit in the future: the 'free labourers') so as to take up, occupy and maintain its historical role as a ruling class. Thus, in a very exact sense, the bourgeoisie *lives* in the ideology of *freedom* the relation between it and its conditions of existence: that is, *its* real relation (the law of a liberal capitalist economy) *but invested in an imaginary relation* (all men are free, including the free labourers). Its ideology consists of this play on the word *freedom*, which betrays the bourgeois wish to mystify those ('free men'!) it exploits, blackmailing them with freedom so as to keep them in harness, as much as the bourgeoisie's need to *live* its own class rule as the freedom of those it is exploiting. Just as a people that exploits another cannot be free, so a class that *uses* an ideology is its captive too. So when we speak of the class function of an ideology it must be understood that the ruling ideology is indeed the ideology of the ruling class and that the former serves the latter not only in its rule over the exploited class, *but in its own constitution of itself as the ruling class*, by making it accept the lived relation between itself and the world as real and justified.

But, we must go further and ask what becomes of *ideology* in a society in which classes have disappeared. What we have just said allows us to answer this question. If the whole social function of ideology could be summed up cynically as a myth (such as Plato's 'beautiful lies' or the techniques of modern advertising) fabricated and manipulated from the outside by the ruling class to fool those it is exploiting, then ideology would disappear with classes. But as we have seen that even in the case of a class society ideology is active on the ruling class itself and contributes to its moulding, to the modification of its attitudes to adapt it to its real conditions of existence (for example, legal freedom) – it is clear that *ideology (as a system of mass representations) is indispensable in any society if men are to be formed, transformed and equipped to respond to the demands of their conditions of existence*. If, as Marx said, history is a perpetual transformation of men's conditions of existence, and if this is equally true of a socialist society, then men must be ceaselessly transformed so as to adapt them to these conditions; if this 'adaptation' cannot be left to spontaneity but must be constantly assumed, dominated and controlled, it is in ideology that this demand is expressed, that this distance is measured, that this contradiction is lived and that its resolution is 'activated'. It is in ideology that the classless society *lives* the inadequacy/adequacy of the relation between it and the world, it is in it and by it that it transforms men's 'consciousness', that is, their attitudes and behaviour so as to raise them to the level of their tasks and the conditions of their existence.

In a class society ideology is the relay whereby, and the element in which, the relation between men and their conditions of existence is settled to the profit of the ruling class. In a classless society ideology is the relay whereby, and the element in which, the relation between men and their conditions of existence is lived to the profit of all men.

II

In the text I have just quoted [on the feudal mode of production, in *Capital*, vol. III, ch. 47, section ii] we have seen Marx prove that a certain form of combination of the elements present necessarily implied a certain form of domination and servitude indispensable to the survival of this combination, i.e. a certain *political* configuration (*Gestaltung*) of society. We can see precisely where the necessity and form of the political 'formation' is founded: at the level of the *Verbindungen* which constitute the modes of liaison between the agents of production and the means of production, at the level of the relations of property, possession, disposition etc.[2] These types of connection, according to the diversification or non-diversification of the agents of production into direct labourers and masters, make the existence of a political organization intended to impose and maintain the defined types of connections by means of material force (that of the State) and of moral power (that of ideologies) either *necessary* (class societies) or *superfluous* (classless societies). This shows that certain relations of production presuppose the existence of a legal-political and ideological *superstructure* as a condition of their peculiar existence, and why this superstructure is necessarily *specific* (since it is a function of the specific relations of production that call for it). It also shows that certain other relations of production do not call for a political superstructure, but only for an ideological superstructure (classless societies). Finally, it shows that the nature of the relations of production considered not only calls or does not call for a certain form of superstructure, but also establishes the *degree of effectivity* delegated to a certain level of the social totality. Irrespective of all these consequences, we can draw one conclusion at any rate where the relations of production are concerned: they relate to the superstructural forms they call for as so many conditions of their own existence. The relations of production cannot therefore be thought in their concept while abstracting from their specific superstructural conditions of existence. To take only one example, it is

2 One important specification. The term 'property' used by Marx can lead to the belief that the relations of production are *identical* with legal relations. But law is not the relations of production. The latter belong to the infrastructure, the former to the superstructure.

quite clear that the analysis of the buying and selling of labour power in which capitalist relations of production *exist* (the separation between the owners of the means of production on the one hand and the wage-workers on the other), directly presupposes, for an understanding of its object, a consideration of the *formal legal relations* which establish the buyer (the capitalist) as much as the seller (the wage-labourer) as legal subjects – as well as a whole political and ideological superstructure which maintains and contains the economic agents in the distribution of roles, which makes a minority of exploiters the owners of the means of production, and the majority of the population producers of surplus-value. The whole superstructure of the society considered is thus implicit and present in a specific way in the relations of production, i.e. in the fixed structure of the distribution of means of production and economic functions between determinate categories of production agents. Or in other words, if the structure of the relations of production defines the economic as such, a definition of the concept of the relations of production in a determinate mode of production is necessarily reached via the definition of the concept of the totality of the distinct levels of society and their peculiar type of articulation (i.e. effectivity).

In no sense is this a formal demand; it is the absolute theoretical condition governing the definition of the *economic* itself. It is enough to refer to the innumerable problems raised by this definition where modes of production other than the capitalist one are concerned to realize the decisive importance of this recourse: Marx often says that what is hidden in capitalist society is clearly visible in feudal society or in the primitive community, but precisely in the latter societies we can clearly see that *the economic is not directly and clearly visible*! – just as in these same societies we *can also clearly see* that the degree of effectivity of the different levels of the social structure *is not clearly visible*! Anthropologists and ethnologists 'know' what to confine themselves to when, seeking the economic, they come upon kinship relations, religious institutions etc.; specialists in medieval history 'know' what to confine themselves to when, seeking for the dominant determination of history in the 'economy', they find it in politics or religion.[3] In all these cases, there is no *immediate* grasp of the economic, there is no raw economic 'given', any more than there is any immediately 'given' effectivity in any of the levels. In all these cases, the identification of the economic is achieved by *the construction of its concept*, which presupposes a definition of the specific existence and articulation of the different levels of the structure of the whole, as they are necessarily implied by the structure of the mode of production considered. To construct the concept of the economic is to define it rigorously as a level, instance or region of the structure of a mode of production: it is therefore to define its peculiar *site*, its *extension*, and its *limits* within that structure; if we like to return to the old Platonic image, it is to 'divide

---

3 Cf. Maurice Godelier's article 'Objet et méthode de l'anthropologie économique' (*L'Homme*, October 1965, and in *Rationalité et irrationalité en économie*, Paris 1966).

up' the region of the economic correctly in the whole, according to its peculiar 'articulation', *without mistaking this articulation*. The 'division' of the 'given', or empiricist division, always mistakes the articulation, precisely because it projects on to the 'real' the arbitrary articulations and divisions of its underlying ideology. There is no correct division and therefore no correct articulation, except on condition of possessing and therefore constructing its concept. In other words, in primitive societies it is not possible to regard any *fact*, any *practice* apparently unrelated to the 'economy' (such as the practices which are produced by kinship rites or religious rites, or by the relations between groups in 'potlatch' competition), *as rigorously economic*, without first having constructed the concept of the differentiation of the structure of the social whole into these different practices or levels, without having *discovered* their peculiar meaning in the structure of the whole, without having identified in the disconcerting diversity of these practices the *region* of economic practice, its configuration and its modalities. It is probable that the majority of the difficulties of contemporary ethnology and anthropology arise from their approaching the 'facts', the 'givens' of (descriptive) ethnography, without taking the theoretical precaution of constructing the concept of their object: this omission commits them to projecting on to reality the categories which define the economic for them in practice, i.e. the categories of the economics of contemporary society, which, to make matters worse, are often themselves empiricist. This is enough to multiply aporia. If we follow Marx here, too, this detour via primitive societies etc., will only have been necessary in order to see clearly in them what our own society hides from us: i.e., in order to *see clearly* in them that the economic is *never clearly visible*, does not coincide with the 'given' in them any more than in any other reality (political, ideological etc.). This is all the more 'obvious' for the capitalist mode of production in that we know that the latter is the mode of production in which *fetishism* affects the economic region *par excellence*. Despite the massive 'obviousness' of the economic 'given' in the capitalist mode of production, and precisely because of the 'massive' character of this fetishised 'obviousness', the only way to the essence of the economic is to construct its concept, i.e. to reveal the *site* occupied in the structure of the whole by the region of the economic, therefore to reveal the articulation of this region with other regions (legal-political and ideological superstructure), and the degree of *presence* (or effectivity) of the other regions in the economic region itself. Here, too, this requirement can be faced directly as a positive theoretical requirement: it can also be omitted, and it then reveals itself in peculiar effects, either theoretical (contradictions and thresholds in the explanation) or practical (e.g. difficulties in planning techniques, whether socialist or capitalist). That, very schematically, is the first conclusion we can draw from Marx's determination of the economic by the *relations of production*.

The second conclusion is not less important. If the relations of production now appear to us as a regional *structure*, itself *inscribed* in the structure of the social totality, we are interested in this because of its *structural* nature. Here both the mirage of a theoretical anthropology and the mirage of a homogeneous space of *given* economic phenomena dissolve simultaneously. Not only is the economic a structured region occupying its peculiar place in the global structure of the social whole, but even in its own site, in its (relative) regional autonomy, it functions as a regional *structure* and as such determines its elements. Here once again we find the results of the other papers in this book: i.e. the fact that the structure of the relations of production determines the *places* and *functions* occupied and adopted by the agents of production, who are never anything more than the occupants of these places, in so far as they are the 'supports' (*Träger*) of these functions. The true 'subjects' (in the sense of constitutive subjects of the process) are therefore not these occupants or functionaries, are not, despite all appearances, the 'obviousnesses' of the 'given' of naïve anthropology, 'concrete individuals', 'real men' – but *the definition and distribution of these places and functions. The true 'subjects' are these definers and distributors: the relations of production* (and political and ideological social relations). But since these are 'relations', they cannot be thought within the category *subject*. And if by chance anyone proposes to reduce these relations of production to relations between men, i.e. *'human relations'*, he is violating Marx's thought, for so long as we apply a truly critical reading to some of his rare ambiguous formulations, Marx shows in the greatest depth that the *relations* of production (and political and ideological social relations) are irreducible to any anthropological inter-subjectivity – since they only combine agents and objects in a specific structure of the distribution of relations, places and functions, occupied and 'supported' by objects and agents of production.

It is clear once again, then, how the *concept* of his object distinguishes Marx radically from his predecessors and why criticisms of him have run wide of the mark. To think the concept of production is to think the concept of the unity of its conditions: the mode of production. To think the mode of production is to think not only the material conditions but also the social conditions of production. In each case, it is to produce the concept which governs the definition of the economically 'operational' concepts (I use the word 'operational' deliberately, since it is often used by economists) out of the concept of their object. We know which concept in the capitalist mode of production expressed the fact of capitalist relations of production in economic reality itself: *the concept of surplus-value*. The unity of the material and social conditions of capitalist production is expressed by the direct relationship between variable capital and the production of surplus-value. The fact that surplus-value is not a measurable reality arises from the fact that it is not a thing, but the concept of a relationship, the concept of an existing social structure of production, of an existence visible and measurable *only in its 'effects'*, in the sense we shall soon define. The fact that it only exists in its effects does not mean that it can be grasped completely in any one of its determinate effects: for that it would have to be *completely present* in that effect, whereas it is only present there, as a structure, in its *determinate* absence. It is only present in the totality, in the total movement of its effects, in what Marx calls the 'developed totality of its form of existence', for reasons bound up with its very nature. It is a relation of production between the agents of the production process and the means of production, i.e. the very structure that dominates the process in the totality of its development and of its existence. The *object* of production, the land, minerals, coal, cotton, the *instruments of production*, tools, machines etc., are *'things'* or visible, assignable, measurable realities: they are not *structures*. The relations of production are structures – and the ordinary economist may scrutinize economic 'facts' (prices, exchanges, wages, profits, rents etc. – all those 'measurable' facts) as much as he likes; he will no more 'see' any *structure* at that level than the pre-Newtonian 'physicist' could 'see' the law of attraction in falling bodies, or the pre-Lavoisierian chemist could 'see' oxygen in 'dephlogisticated' air. Naturally, just as bodies were 'seen' to fall before Newton, the 'exploitation' of the majority of men by a minority was 'seen' before Marx. But the concept of the economic 'forms' of that exploitation, the concept of the economic existence of the relations of production, of the domination and determination of the whole sphere of political economy by that *structure* did not then have any theoretical existence. Even if Smith and Ricardo did 'produce', in the 'fact' of rent and profit, the 'fact' of surplus value, they remained in the dark, not realizing what they had 'produced', since they could not think it in its concept, nor draw from it its theoretical consequences. They were a hundred miles away from being able to *think* it, since neither they nor the culture of their time had ever imagined that a 'fact' might be the existence of a *relation* of 'combination', a relation of complexity, consubstantial with the entire mode of production, dominating its present, its crisis, its future, determining as the law of its structure the entire economic reality, down to the visible detail of the empirical phenomena – while remaining *invisible* even in their blinding obviousness.

3 Structuralism and Marxism

Maurice Godelier

We can now see the epistemological conditions of a scientific analysis of the various means of production and the relations between economics and society gradually being defined and restored. An analysis of this kind is only possible when real structures are taken into account, remembering not to confuse, as empiricism does, the real with the visible; we also need a materialist approach without reducing the various structures and examples of social reality to the epiphenomena of man's material relations with his environment. If anthropology must be structural and materialist in order to be thoroughly scientific, should it not be inspired by the works of Claude Lévi-Strauss as much if not more than those of Marx? Though Lévi-Strauss devotes little space to the study of economics, it is vital to make a very close analysis of the main points of his methods of structural analysis and his study of both the relations between economics and society and society in relation to history, in order to evaluate the theoretical significance and limits of his materialist structuralism and to understand the difference between the thought of Lévi-Strauss and Marx.

There are two methodological principles, recognized by functionalism, structuralism and Marxism alike, which are basic to the scientific study of social facts. The first stipulates that analyses of social relations must not be analysed in isolation, but considered in their reciprocal relationships – as entities forming 'systems'. The second stipulates that these systems must be analysed in their internal logic prior to analysing their genesis and evolution. In a way these two principles mean that modern scientific thought has to confront nineteenth-century evolutionism, historicism and diffusionism, in so far as these doctrines – in spite of differing concepts as to the evolution of societies – were often

From Maurice Godelier, *Perspectives in Marxist Anthropology*, translated by Robert Brain (Cambridge: Cambridge University Press, 1977), pp. 44–51. Reprinted by permission of Cambridge University Press.

content with a superficial analysis of the real functioning of customs and institutions within the societies studied, and the bulk of their efforts were devoted to unearthing their origins and retracing their history through earlier stages of this purely conjectural evolution of mankind. But, apart from this agreement, which only concerns the abstract formulation of these two principles and not the concrete facts of putting them into practice, there is a total opposition between functionalism, as against structuralism, and Marxism when it comes to understanding the term 'social structure'. For Radcliffe-Brown and Nadel, a social structure is the 'order, the arrangement' of man's apparent relationships, an arrangement derived from the reciprocal complementarity of these relationships.[1] For functionalists, therefore, 'structure' is one 'aspect' of the real; they maintain that this reality exists outside the human mind. For Leach, on the other hand, structure is an ideal order which the mind brings to things converting the multiform flux of the real to simplified representations which allow reality to be grasped; it has pragmatic value and permits action and social practice.[2]

For Lévi-Strauss, structures are part of reality, are reality in fact, and here he is in agreement with Radcliffe-Brown and in opposition to the idealist empiricism of Leach. However, for Lévi-Strauss, as well as for Marx, structures are not directly visible or observable realities, but levels of reality which exist beyond man's visible relations and whose functioning constitutes the deeper logic of a social system – the underlying order by which the apparent order must be explained. This is the meaning of Lévi-Strauss's famous formula, which Leach and some structuralists have insisted on interpreting in an idealist and formalist sense. They prefer the first to the second phrase: 'The term "social structure" has nothing to do with empirical reality but with models which are built up after it. . . . social relations consist of the raw materials out of which the models making up the social structure are built.'

In replying to Maybury-Lewis, Lévi-Strauss had already insisted on the fact that:

Ultimate proof of the molecular structure is provided by the electron microscope which enables us to see the *actual* molecules. This feat does not mean that in the

1 Radcliffe-Brown, in D. Forde and A. R. Radcliffe-Brown (eds), *African Systems of Kinship and Marriage*, p. 82. 'The components of the social structure are human beings', the social structure itself being 'an arrangement of persons in relationships institutionally defined and regulated'. F. Nadel, *The Theory of Social Structure*, 'Preliminaries'.

2 E. Leach, *Political Systems of Highland Burma*, pp. 4–5, Introduction: 'I hold that social structure in practical situations (as contrasted with the sociologist's abstract model) consists of a set of ideas about the distribution of power between persons and groups of persons.' Then turning away from the model of informants to that of the anthropologist, Leach, somewhat like Radcliffe-Brown, states: 'We may discuss social structure simply in terms of the principles of organisation that unite the component parts of the system.' And in conclusion, as distinct from Radcliffe-Brown: 'The structures which the anthropologist describes are models which exist only as logical constructions in his own mind.'

future the molecule will become more visible to the naked eye. Similarly, it is pointless to expect that structural analysis will change the *perception* of concrete social relations. It will only explain them better.

And in his introduction to *From Honey to Ashes*, he again asserts in categorical terms:

> I have thus completed my demonstration of the fact that, whereas in the public mind there is frequently confusion between structuralism, idealism and formalism, structuralism has only to be confronted with true manifestations of idealism and formalism for its own deterministic and realistic inspiration to become clearly manifest.

In order to analyse structures whose reality, he claims, lies outside the human mind beyond the superficial aspect of social relations, Lévi-Strauss puts forward three methodological principles. He considers that:

(a)   all structure is a determined ensemble of relations all connected according to internal laws of change which have yet to be discovered;
(b)   all structure combines specific elements, which are its proper components and that for this reason it is useless to insist on 'reducing' one structure to another or 'deducing' one structure from another;
(c)   among different structures belonging to the same system, there is a relationship of compatibility whose laws must be discovered, but this compatibility should not be regarded as the effect of essential selection mechanisms for the success of a biological process of environmental adaptation.

It is obvious that Marx was working along the same lines when, after showing that economic categories of wages, profit and income are defined and dealt with in daily life by agents of the capitalist mode of production, he declares that these things express the visible relations between owners of labour, owners of capital and owners of land; they have a pragmatic value in this sense, as Leach would say, since they permit the organization and direction of these visible relations without having any scientific value; they conceal the fundamental fact that profit and income for one person is the unpaid labour of others:

> The *final pattern* of economic relations as seen *on the surface*, in their real existence and consequently in the conceptions by which the bearers and agents of these relations *seek to understand* them, is very much different from, and indeed quite the reverse of, their *inner but concealed essential pattern* and the *conception corresponding* to it.[3]

3 Karl Marx, *A Contribution to the Critique of Political Economy*, p. 20. '. . . these relations of production correspond to a given stage in the development of the material forces of production.

It must also be remembered that Marx's theoretical greatness was in demonstrating that industrial and commercial profits, financial interest and income from land – which seem to come from totally different sources and actions – are so many *distinct* yet *changed* forms of surplus value. They are forms of distribution among the different social groups which form the capitalist class, distinct forms of the global process of capitalist exploitation of wage-earning producers.

We know in fact that Marx was the first to formulate a hypothesis about the presence of essential relations of correspondence and structural compatibility between the forces of production and relations of production, as also between the mode of production and superstructures, without any intention of reducing the former to being merely epiphenomena of the latter. Does Lévi-Strauss's structuralism merge into Marx's historical materialism? It would seem so. But in order to answer this question, it is essential to get nearer to what Lévi-Strauss understands by history and to understand his ideas on causality in economics, as well as seeing how he has applied them in theoretical practice.

For Claude Lévi-Strauss, it is 'tedious as well as useless, in this connection, to amass arguments to prove that all societies are in history and change: that this is so is patent'.[4] History is not only 'histoire "froide"', where 'societies which create the minimum of disorder . . . tend to remain indefinitely in their initial state'.[5] It is also made from 'non-recurrent chains of events whose effects accumulate to produce economic and social upheavals'.[6] To explain these changes, Claude Lévi-Strauss accepts 'the incontestable primacy of infrastructures' as 'a law of order'.[7]

> I do not at all mean to suggest that ideological transformations give rise to social ones. Only the reverse is in fact true. Men's conception of the relations between nature and culture is a function of modifications of their own social relations . . . We are merely studying the shadows on the wall of the Cave.[8]

And Lévi-Strauss himself claims that, with his studies on myths and the 'savage mind', he wants 'to contribute' to a theory of superstructures hinted at by Marx.[9] We can only note that these theoretical principles are contradicted in

---

The totality of these relations of production constitutes the economic structure of society – the real foundation, on which legal and political superstructures arise and to which definite forms of social consciousness correspond.' And in *Capital*, vol. I, p. 82: 'Don Quixote long ago paid the penalty for wrongly imagining that knight-errantry was equally compatible with all the economic forms of society.'

4 C. Lévi-Strauss, *The Savage Mind*, p. 234.
5 C. Lévi-Strauss, *Conversations with G. Charbonnier*, p. 33.
6 Lévi-Strauss, *Savage Mind*, p. 235.
7 Ibid., p. 130.
8 Ibid., p. 117.
9 C. Lévi-Strauss, *La Pensée sauvage* (1962), p. 178.

From Honey to Ashes, where he discourses on the fundamental historical turmoil in ancient Greek society 'when mythology gave way to philosophy and the latter emerged as the necessary precondition of scientific thought'. Here we see 'one historical occurrence, which can have no meaning beyond its actual happening at that place and in that time'.[10] History, however, subject to a law of order by which the whole of society is organized, remains deprived of all necessity and the origins of western philosophy and science are explained away as simple accidents. 'I am not rejecting history. On the contrary, structural analysis accords history a paramount place, the place that rightfully belongs to that irreducible contingency without which necessity would be inconceivable.'[11] And Claude Lévi-Strauss quoted Tylor's phrase of 1871 for his epigraph to *Elementary Structures of Kinship*: 'The tendency of modern inquiry is more and more towards the conclusion that if law is anywhere, it is everywhere.' With this he finally finds himself in agreement with empiricism which sees in history a mere succession of accidental events.

> To return to ethnology, it was one of us – E. R. Leach – who remarked somewhere that 'the evolutionists never discussed in detail – still less observed – what actually happened when a society in Stage A changed into a society at Stage B; it was merely argued that all Stage B societies must somehow have evolved out of Stage A societies.'[12]

Now we have come back to the same standpoint as the functionalist empiricist.[13] 'The historian has changes, the anthropologist structures', and this is because the changes, 'the processes are not analytical objects, but the particular way in which temporality is experienced by a subject':[14] a thesis in radical opposition to the thesis of the law of order in social structure and their changes, which Lévi-Strauss took from Marx.

How does he arrive at this point? How can he obliterate, *annul* in his *practice*, those theoretical principles to which he refers, but which evidently remain largely inoperative? Here we are not going to make an internal analysis of Lévi-Strauss's work and we make no claims to estimate their scientific value. But let us admit straight away that his work has made an impact in two domains,

---

10 C. Lévi-Strauss, *From Honey to Ashes*, p. 473.

11 Ibid., p. 474.

12 C. Lévi-Strauss, 'Les limites de la notion de structure en ethnologie', in Roger Bastide (ed.), *Sens et usage au terme structure*, p. 45. The passage from Leach quoted by Lévi-Strauss comes from *Political Systems of Highland Burma*, p. 283.

13 The same as Leach, who states clearly: 'The generation of British anthropologists of which I am one has proudly proclaimed its belief in the irrelevance of history for the understanding of social organisation ... We functionalist anthropologists are not really "antihistorical" by principle; it is simply that we do not know how to fit historical materials into our framework of concepts', Leach, *Political Systems of Highland Burma*, p. 282.

14 Lévi-Strauss, 'Limites de la notion de structure en ethnologie', p. 44.

those of kinship theory and ideological theory, and that all progress now has to be made with the help of his successes as well as his failures. Fundamental questions such as the incest prohibition, exogamy and endogamy, cross-cousin marriage, dual organizations which were formerly treated separately and inadequately have all been linked together and explained as deriving from the basic fact of marriage as an exchange, the exchange of women; and that kinship relations are primarily relations between groups rather than relations between individuals. In distinguishing two possible mechanisms of exchange, restricted exchange and generalized exchange, Lévi-Strauss discovered an *order* in a vast ensemble of kinship systems which before seemed to have little in common and which were part of societies which had had no historical contact. And this order is an order of transformation. A huge Mendelian tableau of 'types' of kinship systems was gradually constructed. This tableau does not cover the 'complex' kinship structures, which only define a limited circle of kin, leaving other mechanisms, such as economics or psychology, the process of determining the interconnection.[15]

Nevertheless, structural analysis, while not denying history, cannot go hand in hand with it, since it has separated the analysis of 'types' of kinship relations from the analysis of their 'functions'. These functions are neither ignored nor denied, but they are never explored for what they are. And so the question of any *real articulation* between kinship relations and other social structures which characterize historically determined, concrete societies is never analysed: Lévi-Strauss confines himself to extracting from concrete facts a 'formal system' of kinship relations, a system which he then studies in its internal logic and compares with other types, either similar or different, but belonging, even in their differences, to the same group of transformations.

In this connection, it could be said that Lévi-Strauss, unlike the functionalists, never studies real societies and does not try to account for their diversity or internal complexity. Of course, it is not that he is unaware of these problems, but he has never treated them systematically. Thus, concerning Murdock's correlation of patrilineal institutions and 'highest levels of culture', Lévi-Strauss declares:

> It is true that in societies where political power takes precedence over other forms of organization, the duality which would result from the masculinity of political authority and the matrilineal character of descent could not subsist. Consequently, societies attaining this level of political organization tend to generalize the paternal right.[16]

---

15 C. Lévi-Strauss, *Les Structures élémentaires de la parenté* (PUF, 1949), p. ix.
16 *Elementary Structures of Kinship*, p. 116. Lévi-Strauss refers to G. P. Murdock's text, 'Correlation of matrilineal and patrilineal institutions', *Studies in the Science of Society*, presented to A. G. Keller (New Haven, Conn., 1937).

In spite of the woolly notion 'stage of political organization', Lévi-Strauss is here confronting the fact of the emergence, historically, of societies within which kinship relations are no longer playing a dominant role, and instead politico-ideological relations are beginning to take over. Why and under what circumstances did it become so? Why are patrilineal rights more compatible with this new type of social structure? Lévi-Strauss does not answer these questions, nor does he even explain under what circumstances such societies appear – societies in which kinship systems and marriage have little or nothing to say about the kind of person one may marry. Allusion is made to the fact that in these societies, wealth, money, bridewealth and social hierarchy play a determining role in the choice of marriage partners; but how is this so, and where does history come into it? Not that history, for a Marxist, is a category which explains; on the contrary, it is a category that has to be explained. Historical materialism is not another 'model' of history, nor another 'philosophy' of history. It is primarily a theory of society, a hypothesis about the articulation of its inner levels and about the specific hierarchical causality of each of these levels. And when it is able to discover the types and mechanisms of this causality and articulation, Marxism will show its ability to be a true instrument of historical science.[17]

To have more understanding on this point, we have to go beyond a structural analysis of kinship forms and the uncovering of formal codes and a grammar of Amerindian myths. These structural analyses may be indispensable, but they are not sufficient in themselves. Lévi-Strauss recognizes this himself when he criticizes with justification the principle of looking solely at the accidental events of history and at the diffusion of exogenous causes, for the *raisons d'être* of a kinship system:

> A *functional* system, e.g. a kinship system, can never be interpreted in an integral fashion by diffusionist hypotheses. The system is bound up with the *total structure* of the society employing it and consequently its nature depends more on the *intrinsic* characteristics of such a society than on cultural contacts and migrations.[18]

In order to go beyond a structural analysis of the types of social relations or modes of thought, we must practise this kind of morphological analysis in such a way as to discover the intrinsic connection between *form, function, mode of*

17 Karl Marx, Letter to the Editor of *Otechestvenniye Zapisky*, late 1877, addressed to Chukovsky in reply to Mikhailovsky, one of the Narodnik socialist party leaders: 'But that is too little for my critic. He feels obliged to transform my sketch of the origins of capitalism in Western Europe into a historical-philosophical theory of a universal movement necessarily imposed upon all peoples, no matter what the historical circumstances in which they are placed, and which will lead, in the last resort, to an economic system in which the greatly increased productivity of social labour will make possible the harmonious development of man. But I must protest. He does me too much honour, and at the same time discredits me.' *Marx–Engels Correspondence* (Lawrence and Wishart, 1956).
18 Lévi-Strauss, *Elementary Structures of Kinship*, p. 390. [Godelier's italics, Tr.]

articulation and conditions for the appearance and transformation of these social relations and the ways of thinking in specific societies studied by historians and anthropologists. In our opinion, it is only by a resolute involvement along these lines that we may hope to make any progress in a scientific analysis of a field usually neglected or maltreated by materialists, and where idealism, whether it derives from functionalism or structuralism, for this very reason has a privileged role. In the same way this is how we shall make progress in the field of ideology and, as a result, as far as symbolic forms of social relations and practice are concerned.

Elsewhere,[19] we have shown how Lévi-Strauss has made enormous advances in a theory of ideologies, which he has tried to develop along Marxist lines; using Amerindian myths, he revealed in precise detail that all those elements of ecological, economic and social reality are transposed into the myths, showing that they are the thoughts of men living in specific social and material relations. At the same time, he also reveals that, at the core of this mode of social thought, there is present and functioning a formal logic of analogy, i.e. the activity of human thought which reasons about the world and organizes the content of experience in nature and society into symbolic forms of metaphor and metonym. In fact, Lévi-Strauss, even should he take exception to the interpretation, has brought together under his unique phrase 'la pensée sauvage' a dual content; one refers to nature, that is to say to formal capacities of the mind whereby reasoning is done by analogy, and by equivalence, more generally, to 'pensée à l'état sauvage', 'a direct expression of the structure of the mind (and behind the mind, probably, of the brain)'.[20] The other element refers to 'la pensée des sauvages', to the way men think while they are actually hunting, fishing, or gathering honey, growing cassava or maize and living in bands or tribes. But what is neglected and missing from this gigantic theoretical exercise is an analysis of the articulation of form and content, of thought in its 'savage' state and the thought of 'savages', the social functioning of these representations and the symbolic practices which accompany them, the transformation of these functions and their content, the circumstances of their transformation. Finally, that which exists as a *void* in thought, which is like keeping an object of thought outside thought itself, is an analysis of forms and fundamentals in the 'fetishization' of social relations, an analysis which few Marxists have attempted; and on which depends not only a scientific explanation of political and religious elements in general, but also and foremost an explanation of the circumstances and stages of development of rank, caste or class societies, and even an explanation for the disappearance from history of former classless societies. It is precisely in order to achieve this complex task, a task which presupposes a combination of multiple theoretical practices, that Marx's

19 Maurice Godelier, 'Mythe et histoire, réflexions sur les fondements de la pensée sauvage', *Les Annales*, special issue, 'Histoire et structure', August 1971, pp. 541–68.
20 C. Lévi-Stauss, *Totemism*, p. 163.

hypothesis on the determination of types of society, and their evolution and modes of thought by the conditions of production and *reproduction* in material life, must be used as the central hypothesis: 'The history of religion itself, without its material basis, lacks criteria. Indeed, by analysis, it is easier to discover the content, the terrestrial nucleus of religion's mist-enveloped conceptions than, conversely, it is to reveal how the actual conditions of life gradually assume an ethereal form.'[21] We hope we have shown, despite appearances and contradictory statements, that it is to this central hypothesis that functionalism and structuralism must necessarily lead, as soon as they start penetrating more deeply into the logic of the societies under analysis.[22]

---

21 Karl Marx, *Le Capital*, vol. I, section 4, ch. 15, Ed. Sociales, vol. 2, p. 50 (trans. from French).
22 One cannot but admire the offhand way in which Edmund Leach, having shown that the analysis of property relations is 'of the utmost importance' for his general argument, writes in *Political Systems of Highland Burma*, p. 141: 'In the *last* analysis the power relations in *any* society must be *based* upon the control of real goods and the primary sources of production, but this Marxist generalization does not carry us very far.' (!) [Godelier's italics. Tr.]

4 Marx's Political Economy

Meghnad Desai

The previous chapters [of *Marxian Economics*] have concerned themselves with clarifying, explaining and sometimes developing Marx's economic theory. Not surprisingly, the dominant theme is of a competitive capitalism, accumulating and revolutionizing technology without interruption. In this stylized model of nineteenth-century competitive capitalism, the state hardly gets a mention either for its economic or its social and political role. By the same token, the workers enter into a wage contract where wage is fixed prior to and independent of the type of work they perform. Trade union organization, rise of social democratic parties (in the early sense of the word), impact of social reform legislation and the growth of political democracy are all post-Marxian historical phenomena as far as the stylized model is concerned.[1]

In this chapter we shall look at all various problems involved in using the Marxian economic theory to understand contemporary capitalism.[2] This not only raises all the familiar problems of proceeding from an abstract stylized model to a concrete historical situation, but much more, it raises the problem of the extent to which Marx's model should be updated or revised. Once it is updated or revised, the next task is how to make the transition from the

From Meghnad Desai, *Marxian Economics* (Oxford: Basil Blackwell, 1979), pp. 199–213. Reprinted by permission of Basil Blackwell.

1 This is not to say that trade unions did not exist in the nineteenth century but that their emergence as an important and recognized party in the wage bargain is a post-1914 phenomenon. Similarly, it is not usually appreciated that universal adult suffrage is an achievement of the twentieth century, since the abolition of property qualification, of sex discrimination and of racial discrimination in voting rights (for example in the USA) are very recent accomplishments.

2 This is not to say that we cannot understand pre-capitalist societies or post-capitalist societies such as the Soviet Union, China or Cuba from a Marxian perspective. Of the many attempts to do this, I shall cite but one. See M. Ellman (1975). He has used Marxian schemes imaginatively to analyse the source of surplus-value to finance the Soviet First Five Year Plan.

theoretical model to contemporary reality.[3] ... We now know that Marx addressed himself to questions that Hegel had taken up and offered an outline of an alternative solution as early as 1845–6. By 1846 Marx had arrived at the concept of the proletariat (contrasting with Hegel's notion of Bureaucracy) as the universal class. He had come to look upon private property as a fetter rather than a precondition of free development of human potential. He had also seen beyond Hegel's notion of the German State as the epitome of human development to communism as the ideal.[4]

In this context, we must remember that Marx, like Hegel, accepted the separation of Man (*homme*) and citizen (*citoyen*), the division between State and Civil Society as a fact. This was the Rousseau problem. Hegel thought the French Revolution had failed to bridge the gap, while Marx thought that it had only confirmed the gap. Civil society, the domain of contract and private property, of *economic relations*, was seen to be drifting away from political society and the state and to be developing autonomously. This separation of the economic and the political was caused by the breakdown of extra-economic coercion in economic life that was part of feudalism. The emergence of free labour ... was a central event in the development of capitalism.

This separation of the economic and the political, of the state from the civil society, was thus a starting-point of Marx's thought. The question of whether such separation was historically a fact in the early nineteenth century even in an advanced capitalist country such as England is an open question. Adam Smith had, however, shown convincingly that the civil society *could* develop without political interference and perhaps *ought* to do so. From this it was a small step to take as a starting-point for theoretical analysis that indeed the civil society *did* develop independently of the political.

Starting as a political philosopher and developing his arguments as a critique of Hegel's political philosophy, Marx concentrated his efforts increasingly on the understanding of the economic mechanism of the civil society. One can date this shift in his efforts after the failure of the 1848 revolution in France and the restoration of a Bonaparte. The twenty years between 1851 and 1871 were taken up with economic researches. (After 1871 and the collapse of the Paris Commune Marx took up study of the societies on the 'periphery' of the capitalist mode. He studied anthropology and developed an interest in Russia.)

---

3 While the theory-data transition has to be done in all subjects, Marxists discussing these problems have usually made a muddle of it. Marx himself did not keep different levels of abstraction separate. One person to emphasize these separate levels and to attempt to keep them separate is the Japanese scholar Prof. Uno, whose work is relatively little known. See, however, T. Sekine 'Uno-Riron' (1975). [An English translation of Prof. Uno's major work has been published by Harvester Press under the title *Principles of Political Economy* (1980) Ed.]

4 Some of what follows on Marx, Hegel and the state is a potted version of Joseph O'Malley's excellent introduction to Marx's *Critique of Hegel's Philosophy of Right* (1970). The interpretation of Adam Smith's work is, however, my own.

Throughout this period, the separation of state and civil society was maintained in his analysis.

This separation is the starting-point of many of the problems we have in updating Marx's analysis. An attitude of absolute reverence to every word he wrote (even when in contradiction with other words he wrote) does not help. But aside from that, the analytical problems are enormous. There is, to begin with, the problem that value categories are not directly perceived. A threefold account in terms of value, price and quantities, or equivalently of the commodity, money and physical circuits of capital, has to be given. Any crude matching of price, wage and profit data to value measures only makes analysis difficult. This is so even for the competitive capitalist model that is developed independently of political institutions. But if one had to take historical data from the nineteenth century and interpret them in terms of Marxian categories, there is the further problem that, as a historical description, the separation of civil and political society is not accurate. The major role the state played in the economic development of Germany, Japan, Italy and Russia in the late nineteenth century has been well documented. In France, the state has always played a major role. Only in England, and even there only after 1845 (after the passage of Free Trade legislation and Banking Acts), could one pretend that the state was absent from the civil society. Even in England the state played an active role in maintaining the overseas Empire.

One would need a major theoretical effort at synthesizing the state with Marx's model of competitive capitalism. The role of the state in sponsoring social welfare legislation, due either to the push given by the anti-bourgeois aristocracy, as in Britain, or as a result of calculation, as in the case of Bismarck, is already evident in the nineteenth century. Do we consider this as an attempt to socialize the cost of reproduction of labour power or as a palliative for the reserve army of unemployed? Such a question cannot be answered until one can redefine concepts such as the value of labour power in an abstract model which allows for the role of the state in reproduction of social relations. If the value of labour power is defined in the context of a two-class model with wage bargain as between the individual labourer and the capitalist, then all outside influences will seem arbitrary.

This is also reflected in the crude theory that the state is only an agent of ruling-class interests – a committee for the bourgeoisie. Recent works by Marxian political theorists have emphasized the autonomy of the state, its relative independence of the ruling classes.[5] In a two-class model of the civil society where at the beginning the state has been ruled out, one can introduce the state only by arbitrarily relating it to one class or another. Both at the level of abstract analysis and for understanding historical events this is a wrong approach.

5 Miliband, *Marxism and Politics*, among others.

Modern approaches to developing Marxian theory are also compounded by another difficulty. This is that following Hilferding and Lenin, it is said that capitalism entered a monopoly phase in the twentieth century. This monopoly phase is to be understood as being in addition to the class monopoly of ownership of means of production. This monopoly phase was described in terms of increase in size and concentration of industries, of the linkage between them provided by finance capital by Hilferding. Lenin used this concept (in conjunction with Bukharin's theory) to understand rivalry among imperialist powers in the First World War as motivated by struggle between national capitals for markets. Thus, in the monopoly phase increasing concentration of capital made it possible for Marxists to speak of national capital and to see the state as an agent of national capital in external relations.

Thus a somewhat simple dichotomy emerged. In the competitive phase, the state played a passive role in Marxian models. In the monopoly phase, the state is interlinked with capitalist society. This simple dichotomy has been a serious obstacle to development of Marxian economic theory. First because, as we said above, the separation of the state and the economy in the competitive phase is a simplification which is analytically unsatisfactory and historically inaccurate. On the other hand, it leads to an implicit belief that the competitive phase is the original or natural phase of capitalism. This is reflected in teleological labels such as the highest phase of capitalism, the last phase or the old age (*le troisième age* in Mandel's words) of capitalism reserved for recent periods. But historically capitalism emerged with mercantilism, where the state played an active role in mobilization of economic surplus from trade and empire. The monopoly phase with active role of the state precedes the competitive phase of capitalism historically.

But we have to deal with the analytical problem most of all. The separation of the state and the civil society in one age and the emergence of monopoly capitalism with state involvement are not subsequent stages in the hierarchy of models. We have an analytical model of competitive capitalism, in isolation from the state, in Marx's work, although it has many missing elements. The next step would be an analytical model of monopoly capital or a fusing of competitive model with the state. But we lack any analytical model of monopoly capitalism. We do not know, in other words, how for example the value-price transformation differs in monopoly capitalism from competitive capitalism. We do not know whether the wage relationship is reproduced differently or how accumulation and realization problems interact.

When discussing monopoly capitalism, one often takes the full competitive model and only adds monopoly as a complicating model (indeed as much neoclassical economic theory does). This is done frequently in measuring rates of exploitation from wage data. Or we get a combination of Marxian labels with mainstream economic analysis. Thus the theory of monopolistic competition of Chamberlin is often taken up along with Kalecki's theory as the Marxian theory of monopoly capital. The connection between value and price is severed and profits are linked not to surplus value but to high mark-up above costs maintained by market power. Such is the theory of Baran and Sweezy in their *Monopoly Capital*, which we have already discussed on an earlier occasion.[6]

Mandel in his *Late Capitalism* has put forward a sketch of how monopoly capitalism works. His work covers a broad panorama of developments during the last hundred years but here we shall concentrate on monopoly capitalism. Mandel begins with the idea that the equalization of profit rates across industries is only a long-run tendency. Actual economic movement takes place through uneven development and difference in level of profit rates. This is the dynamic disequilibrium path even in the competitive phase. There may be movements of capital in search of high profits tending to even out differences but this is not actually accomplished. But in monopoly capital, there is not even a theoretical tendency for profit rates to equalize. Although monopolies are never absolute and are subject to forces of competition, there is a constant reproduction of unequal profit rates.

Through accumulation and technical progress, monopoly seeks to make super-profits, higher-than-average profits. This may come about through differences in organic composition of capital between enterprises in the monopoly sector and out of it, by forcing down the price of labour and of constant capital purchased from outside and by constant improvements in productivity. Mandel argues, 'In all these cases we are dealing with surplus-profits which do *not* enter the process of equalization in the short term, and so do not lead simply to a growth in the average rate of profit.'

These surplus-profits do not, therefore, go into the pool of profits which are then distributed so as to equalize the rate of profit as in Marx's solution of the value-price transformation. To some extent, surplus-profits of the monopoly sector are due to a diversion of surplus value of the non-monopolized sector. Recall that price-value transformation breaks the link between surplus value produced by an individual firm/industry and its profits. Mandel is extending this idea to model the transfer of surplus value from a non-monopoly sector to a monopoly sector.

Thus one can think of an economy in two sectors – monopolized and competitive. They may produce different commodities but not necessarily so. Mandel's model can then be formulated as saying that there is one profit rate prevailing in the competitive sector and that the monopoly sector has either one or many rates which are all higher than the competitive rate. Monopolies sustain (reproduce) the differential profit rate by using barriers to entry, among other weapons. But they face limits to their ability to prevent the equalization of profit rates. Thus, while barriers may be placed against small capitals from within an industry or a country, large capitals from other industries or countries will enter into competition if the differential gets very large. Thus monopoly power is never absolute but always relative. Also it does not always reside in the

6 M. Desai, *Marxian Economic Theory*.

same firm. A monopolistic firm one day may find itself thrown on the scrap heap of competition by the superior technology of another firm.

Mandel's attempts to provide a numerical scheme to illustrate his thesis[7] are somewhat vitiated by the fact that he adopts both the erroneous price-value transformation method of *Capital* vol. III as well as an arbitrary accumulation behaviour reminiscent of the Scheme for Extended Reproduction of *Capital* vol. II. Thus accumulation rates are assumed without any market logic and input values are not, but output values are transformed into prices. This aside, Mandel tries to state a law of monopoly capital as follows: 'The higher the monopoly profit over the average profit, and the larger the monopolized sector, the faster must the monopoly profit drop to the level of the average social profit operative at the start, or decline together with it'.[8]

The only evidence Mandel offers in support of his law is a numerical example, which, as we said above, has many arbitrary features. Still, Mandel's assertion should form the subject of further investigation. Mandel's statements on monopoly capital form part of a wider historical and descriptive investigation. Thus he contrasts phases of long expansion with an undertone of optimism with phases that have an undertone of contraction. These phases are not so regular as to be called cycles and have more than purely economic causes underlying them. Thus the long expansionary phase from 1940–5 till the end of the 1960s could be traced to the weakened position of the working class at the end of the Depression, which led to a reduction in real wage growth, a boost of technological discoveries in the war that brought about the third technological revolution, and to an expansion of the market on an international scale. But in these developments, the state played a large role, guaranteeing the tempo of military investments, especially in research and development, easing the realization problem by fiscal policy and rescuing the loss-making enterprises by subsidy or nationalization.

The growth of state expenditure, viewed benevolently through the quarter-century following the Second World War, is now everywhere being viewed with alarm. Recent experiences of inflation and recession in all the developed capitalist countries have led to divisions among economists and disturbed the confident note of the 1960s. It seemed then that full employment and a more or less steady growth was a permanent feature, with inflation and balance-of-payments disequilibria only niggling worries. The seventies began with the collapse of the Bretton Woods system and witnessed increasing intervention in wage bargains and price setting by governments, the increasing sense of an ecological threat to the maintenance of existing life styles, the massive transfer of economic surplus to the OPEC countries and a period of high unemployment that has now lasted nearly five years.

7 *Late Capitalism*, pp. 532–4.
8 Ibid., p. 535.

Increased state expenditure has been linked to inflation by Marxist writers much as the monetarists have done, though their reasoning differs.

Marxist economists have emphasized the constraints put by the total mass of surplus-value on total realizable profits. They have often emphasized that fiscal expansion can ease the realization problem but not increase the mass of surplus-value. This remains a debatable point. As we said above, the concepts are taken from a purely capitalist model and transposed to the mixed economy. Thus the state's ability to raise surplus-value depends on whether one considers public sector employees productive or unproductive. The purest definition of productive labour . . . does not permit any government employee (except perhaps in nationalized manufacturing enterprises) to be labelled as productive. Much debate has been generated on this point but this is an instance in which citing chapter and verse from Marx is no help. One needs to understand what role the notion of productive labour plays in the model of pure capitalism and then seek to define similar concepts for the mixed model. Thus in the pure model exchange value of labour power coincides with the wage costs borne by the employer and the income received (and consumed) by the worker. But in an era of social security taxes, deductions for pensions, social and health care and insurance provided from public funds with free or subsidised educational and vocational facilities, there is a wedge between these two sides. What the employer pays, the worker does not receive, at least immediately. What the worker consumes, what reproduces him, is often not paid for by his income. The worker and the employer pay taxes to finance the 'social wage', but just as surplus-value and profits do not coincide for the firm, the payments and receipts do not coincide for the individual worker and often not even for the class. In such a context, it is hard to distinguish who is employed from revenue and who from capital. The complex of taxes and subsidies puts an additional layer of complication to the task of unravelling the price relationships in terms of value categories. What is more, we lack the appropriate value categories to handle the state–economy interaction even in an abstract model.

Much progress is, however, being made on the conceptual and the empirical fronts in this respect. Many economists are coming to grips with the task of unscrambling national income accounts in terms of value categories. On the theoretical side, we should mention James O'Connor's book *The Fiscal Crisis of the State*, which has many points of similarity with Mandel's *Late Capitalism*. O'Connor divides the economy into three sectors – the monopoly sector, the competitive sector and the state sector. The monopoly sector is technologically progressive, with high wages and high relative rate of surplus-value where trade unions play an active role in bargaining and where cost-plus pricing is the rule. The technologically progressive nature of the monopoly sector means that even in expansionary phases it expands its employment by small amounts. On average, it sheds labour instead of absorbing it. This labour, along with many less skilled and underprivileged workers (women, immigrants, blacks, youth) form the labour force in the competitive sector. Here the technology is not very progressive and absolute rate of surplus-value is the source of profit. Output expands by expanding employment. In this sector unions have to struggle for recognition. It includes the reserve army of unemployed – those who are 'hired last and fired first'. The cost of maintaining the reserve army – unemployment compensation, social security, poverty programmes and so on – is borne by the state sector. The state sector also bears the costs of research and development and the more risky undertakings – costs that are now socialized, though the benefits they generate accrue to the monopoly sector in the form of additional profits that are privately appropriated. The private appropriation of profits and the socialization of costs – costs of maintaining the labour force as well as of education and of research and development – represents for O'Connor the major contradiction that leads to increasing fiscal burden.

The monopoly sector needs the competitive sector as a supplier of reserve labour as well as of raw material and component inputs. The pricing system transfers surplus value from the competitive sector to the monopoly sector. The monopoly sector also needs the state, and its attitudes towards state activity are 'progressive' or benevolent. This is because of the willingness of the state to bear the social costs – social wage and research and development. But the unwillingness of either of the two private sectors to bear the costs in terms of taxation leads to continuous deficits. The state has to accommodate the political demands of surplus labour and of capital and herein lies the nub of the fiscal problem.

Mandel and O'Connor reject any crude theory of the state. They recognize that the state has relative autonomy and that its form does not correspond exactly to the production relationships. O'Connor sees the state as performing the twin tasks of accumulation and legitimation. In its accumulation task, the state's expenditure represents social capital. In this, *social constant capital* represents expenditure that will increase labour productivity and consequently the rate of profit. *Social variable capital* concerns the expenditures that lower the (private) reproduction costs of labour and hence raise the rate of profit. On the other hand, *social expenses* are projects required to maintain social harmony – to fulfil the legitimation function.

Obviously each item of expenditure may partake of one or more such features. But the crucial part of O'Connor's thesis has to do with limitations on the growth of employment in the monopoly sector and of productivity in the competitive sector which puts restrictions on the state's capacity to balance its budget. The state has to spend money on social expenses because of the slow growth of employment due to the failure of the monopoly sector to generate full employment. This is in turn due to limitations on the growth of market demand.

The monopoly sector generates surplus labour, that is, productivity grows faster than total demand and employment falls in the long run. The monopoly sector wages are determined by bilateral bargaining and follow productivity and price-level increases. But this is a high-wage island, entry to which is restricted. Prices in the monopoly sector are on a mark-up basis. But given stagnant or declining employment, and rising prices for its own products, the monopoly sector finds a limited market for its products among its wage-earners. The competitive sector is a sea of lower-wage, less than fully employed workers. Prices have fallen with productivity increases and profits are being constantly squeezed, while wages are determined by market forces of demand and supply in this sector. But, on the whole, the competitive sector does not represent a growing market for the monopoly sector. The terms of trade are going against the competitive sector; hence, its real purchasing power in terms of monopoly-sector products is shrinking. Thus the monopoly sector is producing surplus products to be disposed of either by state expenditure providing a market or by exports. Wages in the state sector are linked to the monopoly-sector wages but productivity does not grow here. This is one of the causes of the fiscal crisis.

O'Connor's book relates much more to US experience than to European experience, but it represents, along with Mandel's work, some common strands of thinking. Thus they both present a picture of differential profit rates in the monopoly as against the competitive sector. They both explore the dependence of the monopoly sector on the competitive sector as well as the dependence of the monopoly sector on the state sector. But both their theories are dependent on limitations of growth of market of the monopoly sector. This has not been satisfactorily demonstrated in their work.

As we said above, Marxists and monetarists have often sounded alike in their attack on Keynesian remedies and on the growth of state expenditure. The monetarists theorize about the natural rate of unemployment as an insuperable barrier that stands in the way of attempts by governments to reduce unemployment and they are sceptical of wage–price controls as counter-inflationary measures. The orthodox Keynesian answer has been to locate inflation in the wage–price spiral caused by trade union militancy and the tendency for wage increases to be passed on to price increases. Both these approaches appear in their Marxist guise in the form of limitations of market due to slow growth of employment and wages or of the mass of social labour. The wage explosion thesis is turned into an attack on capital by workers, as an example of the political determination of wages in the modern society.

The demand for higher state expenditure has traditionally come from working-class organizations. Full employment policies were adopted not merely as a cunning trick by big capital but after considerable struggle on the part of social democratic parties. It was the mobilization of population for the war effort which led in a number of countries, especially in the UK and USA, to the strengthening of this demand. Capitalist societies were now living in a democratic world, as they had not in the nineteenth century. The promises of the First World War – 'a land fit for heroes' – were not fulfilled, and massive deflation following the full employment and inflationary experience of 1916–21 led to unemployment and a long depression in the UK. The US Depression came later, but was none the less a massive blow to living standards. A repetition of such experience in the context of democratic politics, especially after 1945, was unthinkable. Even today, we think of high unemployment not as 10 per cent or 25 per cent but as 5 per cent. While Keynes provided the theory and the policy rules to guide in this task, it was not a demand granted from above but won from below.

This is not just a historical accident. The state has relative autonomy, and this autonomy is strengthened by widely spread franchise and the exercise of political democracy. In societies where either of these conditions are not fulfilled – in the nineteenth century or in contemporary 'socialist' countries – the state does become 'the committee of the ruling class'. Indeed, it is because the state is perceived as potentially autonomous – an institution which by political action can be made to realize its potential for autonomy – that over the past century trade unions and social democratic parties have concentrated on the demands that the state play a more active role. Thus in securing health care, unemployment benefits, a guaranteed wage, trade union rights, safety at work and so on through government action, the struggle over the past century has quite rightly succeeded. No doubt the capitalist can take advantage of these arrangements and manipulate them for profit, but that is no sign that capital, even big capital, *demanded* full employment and state intervention. The struggle to make these gains more beneficial to the lower-paid will continue, but this does not mean that the gains are illusory.

Even inflation must be seen in a class perspective. During the 1950s and 1960s inflation was viewed benevolently, as it aided personal and corporate wealth accumulation. But over the period, the share of wages in income was also rising. In the UK, at any rate, serious complaints about inflation began when it started to hurt middle- and higher-income groups. The wage-control policies began to narrow differentials (this again being a necessary price for a political incomes policy in a democratic society).

Thus in judging inflation one has to ask who it benefits and who it hurts. An inflation that eliminates the rentier is different from an inflation that hits the poor and unemployed. Similarly, in countering the growing budget deficit, one has to look for what expenditure cuts will mean in terms of their distributive impact on different classes. In the last three years or so, a 'Social Contract' has been accepted without widespread resistance in the UK because inflation has been seen as hurting workers. The idea that 'inflation hurts everybody' and especially the workers, has been conveyed by governments, and it is not entirely false consciousness that has led many to accept this idea.

This shift in attitudes towards state expenditure and inflation can be understood only through detailed analytical and statistical study of the various roles played by the state in the modern economy. Ian Gough has made one such attempt.[9] He begins with a critique of O'Connor while basically accepting the social capital/social expenses division. He rejects functional theories of the state that assign to it the task of ensuring profitability or legitimation. He rightly

9 'State expenditure in advanced capitalism'.

criticizes the appellation of unproductive labour for all state expenditure. Such a characterization can be made only if the state is viewed as an appendage to the civil society. Such a view gives no role for the class struggle. This is not to say that the state is completely autonomous or neutral, but that it is potentially so. Without the political background of adult franchise and democracy, as we said above, the state cannot be seen as autonomous.

Gough also points out that the growth in state expenditure was financed without a secular increase in borrowing in the 1950s and 1960s. It is only in the 1970s that the fiscal crisis has been serious, and one must not project recent events backward and forward through time. In the trend of expenditure, armaments have had a declining share and social services – the social wage – an increasing one. There has also been a growth in state aid to private industry and in legal and coercive apparatus. Gough also distinguishes between spending and transfers and counters the commonly held notion that the state takes resources away from the private ('productive') sector.

Gough quite rightly places the growth of state expenditure in a historical and international perspective. Though he does not point this out, some of the state aid to private industry in Europe came as a result of rivalry with American multinationals. It was to protect national capital, often publicly owned, against inroads by the larger, more efficient multinationals. On social expenses, Gough points out that 'the strength of working class pressure can roughly be gauged by the *comprehensiveness* and the *level* of the social benefits'.[10]

Any effort to understand contemporary capitalism in a Marxist framework is bound to be fraught with problems. We have concentrated on the need to develop analytical models that can encompass the state and the economy both in the classical competitive and the modern monopolistic competitive forms. But even the model of pure capitalism that Marx left behind was an unfinished one. The uncompleted nature of Marx's work has dictated a number of tasks of clarification and filling in the missing pieces. Thus an integration of money, commodity and physical circuits to provide a theory of crisis and cycles within the assumptions of *Capital* is still an open challenge.[11] We then need to re-examine the separation of state and civil society that Marx took as a starting-point, though his plan of work clearly indicates that he intended to return to the state in future volumes of *Capital*. Then we need to look at the models of 'monopoly capital' that have been put forward and subject them to the same scrutiny that the well-worn parts of Marx's work, such as the Transformation Problem, have undergone. At the same time the task of relating the models to historical data will always remain. There is no shortage of issues to consider.

10 Ibid., p. 75.
11 See the work of C. Palloix, 'The self-expansion of capital on a world scale', for use of the three circuits of capital framework.

5   Historical Materialism

Isaiah Berlin

No full or systematic exposition of historical materialism was ever published by Marx himself. It occurs in a fragmentary form in his early work written during the years 1843–8, it is briefly expounded in 1859, and is taken for granted in his later thought. He did not regard it as a new philosophical system so much as a practical method of social and historical analysis, and a basis for political strategy. Later in life he complained of the use made of it by some of his followers, who appeared to think that it would save them the labour of historical study by providing a kind of algebraic 'table' from which, given enough factual data, automatic answers to all historical questions could be mechanically read off. In a letter which, towards the end of his life, he wrote to a Russian correspondent, he gave as an example of dissimilar development, despite analogous social conditions, the history of the Roman plebs and of the European industrial proletariat. 'When one studies these forms of evolution separately,' he wrote, 'and then compares them, one can easily find the clue to this phenomenon; but one will never get there by using as one's master key a general historico-philosophical theory which explains everything because it explains nothing, the supreme virtue of which consists in being super-historical.'

The theory matured gradually in his mind. It is possible to trace its growth in the *Critique of Hegel's Philosophy of Right* and *On the Jewish Question*; in these the proletariat is for the first time identified as the agent destined to change society in the direction adumbrated by philosophy, which because it is as yet philosophy divorced from action, is itself a symptom and an expression of impotence. It is further developed in *The Holy Family*, an amalgam of polemical outbursts against the 'critical critics', that is, the young Hegelians – principally the

From Isaiah Berlin, *Karl Marx: His Life and Environment*, 4th edn. (Oxford: Oxford University Press, 1978), pp. 89–91, 98–105, 111–16. Copyright © 1978 by Oxford University Press. Reprinted by permission of the publisher.

brothers Bauer and Stirner – interspersed with fragments on the philosophy of history, social criticism of literature, and other oddities; it is most fully stated in a volume, over six hundred pages in length, which he composed with Engels in 1846, entitled *The German Ideology*, but never published. This verbose, ill-organised and ponderous work, which deals with authors and views long dead and justly forgotten, contains in its lengthy introduction the most sustained, imaginative and impressive exposition of Marx's theory of history. Like the terse and brilliant *Theses on Feuerbach*, which belong to the same period, and the *Economic and Philosophical Manuscripts* of 1844, with their new application of Hegel's concept of alienation, the greater part of *The German Ideology* did not see the light until some years after the author's death (the *Theses* in 1888, the rest only in the present century). It is philosophically far more interesting than any other work by Marx, and represents a submerged, but a most crucial and original stage of his thought, the total ignorance or neglect of which by his immediate followers (including the makers of the Russian Revolution) led to an exclusive emphasis on the historical and economic aspects, and defective understanding of the sociological and philosophical content, of his ideas. This fact is responsible for the clear, half-positivist, half-Darwinian interpretation of Marx's thought, which we owe mainly to Kautsky, Plekhanov, and above all to Engels – a tradition that has decisively influenced both the theory and the practice of the movement which goes by Marx's name.

The framework of the new theory is undeviatingly Hegelian. It recognizes that the history of humanity is a single, non-repetitive process, which obeys discoverable laws. Each moment of this process is new in the sense that it possesses new characteristics, or new combinations of known characteristics; but unique and unrepeatable though it is, it nevertheless follows from the immediately preceding state in obedience to the same laws, as this last state from its own predecessor. But whereas according to Hegel the single substance in the succession of whose states history consists, is the eternal, self-developing, universal Spirit, the internal conflict of whose elements is made concrete, in, for example, religious conflicts or the wars of national states, each being an embodiment of the self-realising Idea which it requires a super-sensible intuition to perceive, Marx, following Feuerbach, denounces this as a piece of mystification on which no knowledge could be founded. For if the world were a metaphysical substance of this type, its behaviour could not be tested by the only reliable method in our power, namely, empirical observation; and a theory of it could not, therefore, be confirmed by the methods of any science. The Hegelian can, of course, without fear of refutation, attribute anything he wishes to the unobservable activity of an impalpable world-substance, much as the believing Christian or theist attributes it to the activity of God, but only at the cost of explaining nothing, of declaring the answer to be a mystery impenetrable to normal human faculties. It is only such translation of ordinary questions into less intelligible language that makes the resultant obscurity look like a genuine answer. To explain the knowable in terms of the unknowable is to take away with one hand what one affects to give with the other. Whatever value such procedure may have, it cannot be regarded as equivalent to a scientific explanation, that is, to the ordering by means of a comparatively small number of interrelated laws of the great variety of distinct, *prima facie* unconnected, phenomena. So much for orthodox Hegelianism.

Like Hegel, Marx treats history as a phenomenology. In Hegel the Phenomenology of the human Spirit is an attempt to show, often with great insight and ingenuity, an objective order in the development of human consciousness and in the succession of civilizations that are its concrete embodiment. Influenced by a notion prominent in the Renaissance, but reaching back to an earlier mystical cosmogony, Hegel looked upon the development of mankind as being similar to that of an individual human being. Just as in the case of a man a particular capacity, or outlook, or way of dealing with reality cannot come into being until and unless other capacities have first become developed – that is, indeed, the essence of the notion of growth or education in the case of individuals – so races, nations, churches, cultures, succeed each other in a fixed order, determined by the growth of the collective faculties of mankind expressed in arts, sciences, civilization as a whole. Pascal had perhaps meant something of this kind when he spoke of humanity as a single, centuries old, being, growing from generation to generation. For Hegel all change is due to the movement of the dialectic, which works by a constant logical criticism, that is, struggle against, and final self-destruction of, ways of thought and constructions of reason and feeling which, in their day, had embodied the highest point reached by the ceaseless growth (which for Hegel is the logical self-realization) of the human spirit; but which, embodied in rules or institutions, and erroneously taken as final and absolute by a given society or outlook, thereby become obstacles to progress, dying survivals of a logically 'transcended' stage, which by their very one-sidedness breed logical antinomies and contradictions by which they are exposed and destroyed. Marx translated this vision of history as a battlefield of incarnate ideas into social terms, of the struggle between classes. For him alienation (for that is what Hegel, following Rousseau and Luther and an earlier Christian tradition, called the perpetual self-divorce of men from unity with nature, with each other, with God, which the struggle of thesis against antithesis entailed) is intrinsic to the social process, indeed it is the heart of history itself. Alienation occurs when the results of men's acts contradict their true purposes, when their official values, or the parts they play, misrepresent their real motives and needs and goals. This is the case, for example, when something that men have made to respond to human needs – say, a system of laws, or the rules of musical composition – acquires an independent status of its own, and is seen by men, not as something created by them to satisfy a common social want (which may have disappeared long ago), but as an objective law or institution, possessing eternal, impersonal authority in its own right, like the unalterable laws of Nature as conceived by scientists and ordinary men, like God and His Commandments for a believer. For Marx the capitalist system is precisely this kind of entity, a vast instrument brought into being by intelligible material demands – a progressive improvement and broadening of life in its own day, that generates its own intellectual, moral, religious beliefs, values and forms of life. Whether those who hold them know it or not, such beliefs and values merely uphold the power of the class whose interests the capitalist system embodies; nevertheless, they come to be viewed by all sections of society as being objectively and eternally valid for all mankind. Thus, for example, industry and the capitalist mode of exchange are not timelessly valid institutions, but were generated by the mounting resistance by peasants and artisans to dependence on the blind forces of nature. They have had their moment; and the values these institutions generated will change or vanish with them.

Production is a social activity. Any form of co-operative work or division of labour, whatever its origin, creates common purposes and common interests, not analysable as the mere sum of the individual aims or interests of the human beings involved. If, as in capitalist society, the product of the total social labour of a society is appropriated by one section of that society for its own exclusive benefit, as a result of an inexorable historical development, which Engels, more explicitly- (and much more mechanistically) than Marx, attempts to describe, this goes against 'natural' human needs – against what men, whose essence as human beings is to be social, require, in order to develop freely and fully. According to Marx, those who accumulate in their hands the means of production, and thereby also its fruits in the form of capital, forcibly deprive the majority of the producers – the workers – of what they create, and so split society into exploiter and exploited; the interests of these classes are opposed; the well-being of each class depends on its ability to get the better of its adversary in a continuous war, a war that determines all the institutions of that society. In the course of the struggle technological skills develop, the culture of the class-divided society becomes more complex, its products grow richer, and the needs which its material progress breeds, more varied and more artificial – that is, more 'unnatural'. Unnatural, because both the warring classes became 'alienated', by the conflict which has replaced co-operation for common ends, from the integrated common life and creation that, according to this theory, is demanded by the social nature of man. The monopoly of the means of production held by a particular group of men enables it to bind its will on the others and to force them to perform tasks alien to their own needs. Thereby the unity of society is destroyed, and the lives of both classes become distorted. The majority – that is the propertyless proletarians – now work for the benefit, and according to the ideas, of others: the fruit of their labour as well as its instruments are taken from them; their mode of existence, their ideas and ideals correspond not to their own real predicament – that of human beings artificially prevented from living as their natures demand (namely as members of a unified society, capable of understanding the reasons for doing what they do, and of enjoying the fruits of their own united, free and rational activity) – but to the aims of their oppressors. Hence their lives rest on a lie. Their masters, in their turn, whether consciously or not, cannot help seeking to justify their own parasitic existence as being both natural and desirable. In the course of this, they generate ideas, values, laws, habits of life, institutions (a complex which Marx sometimes calls 'ideology'), the whole purpose of which is to prop up, explain away, defend, their own privileged, unnatural, and therefore unjustified, status and power. Such ideologies – national, religious, economic and so on, are forms of collective self-deception; the victims of the ruling class – the proletarians and peasants – imbibe it as part of their normal education, of the general outlook of the unnatural society, and so come to look upon it, and accept it, as objective, just, necessary, a part of the natural order which pseudo-sciences are then created to explain. This, as Rousseau had taught, serves to deepen still further human error, conflict and frustration.

The symptom of alienation is the attribution of ultimate authority, either to some impersonal power – say the laws of supply and demand – from which the rationality of capitalism is represented as being logically deducible, or to imaginary persons or forces – divinities, churches, the mystical person of the king or priest, or disguised forms of other oppressive myths, whereby men, torn from a 'natural' mode of life (which alone makes it possible for entire societies to perceive the truth and live harmoniously), seek to explain their unnatural condition to themselves. If men are ever to liberate themselves, they must be taught to see through these myths. The most oppressive of all, in Marx's demonology, is bourgeois economic science, which represents the movement of commodities or of money – indeed the process of production, consumption and distribution – as an impersonal process, similar to those of nature, an unalterable pattern of objective forces before which men can only bow, and which it would be insane to attempt to resist. Deterministic as he was, Marx nevertheless resolved to show that the conception of any given economic or social structure as a part of an unchangeable world order was an illusion brought about by man's alienation from the form of life natural to him – a typical 'mystification', the effects of purely human activities masquerading as laws of nature; it would be removed ('unmasked') only by other, equally human activities – the application of 'demystifying' reason and science; but this is not sufficient; such delusions are bound to persist so long as the relations of production – that is, the social and economic structure by which they are generated – are as they are; these can be altered only by the weapon of revolution. These liberating activities may themselves be determined by objective laws, but what these laws determine is the activity of human thought and will (particularly of men taken in the mass), and not merely the movement of material bodies, obeying their own inexorable patterns that are independent of human decisions and actions. If, as Marx believed, human choices can affect the course of events, then, even if these choices are themselves ultimately determined and scientifically predictable, such a situation is one in which Hegelians and Marxists think it legitimate to call men free, since such choices are not, like the rest of nature, mechanically determined.

Because the historical function of capitalism, and its relation to the interests of a specific class, are not understood, it comes not to enrich but to crush and distort the lives of millions of workers, and indeed of their oppressors too, like everything that is not rationally grasped and therefore blindly worshipped as a fetish. Money for instance, which played a progressive role in the days of liberation from barter, has now become an absolute object of pursuit and worship for its own sake, brutalizing and destroying man whom it was invented to liberate. Men are divorced from the products of their own toil and from the instruments with which they produce: these acquire a life and status of their own, and in the name of their survival or improvement, living human beings are oppressed and treated like cattle or saleable commodities. This is true of all institutions, churches, economic systems, forms of government, moral codes, which, through being systematically (and, at certain stages of the class struggle, necessarily) misunderstood, become more powerful than their inventors, monsters worshipped by their makers – the blind, unhappy Frankensteins whose lives they frustrate and twist. At the same time, merely to see through or criticise this predicament, which the young Hegelians thought sufficient, will not destroy it. To be effective, the weapons with which one fights, among them ideas, must be those called for by the historical situation – neither those that served a previous period, nor those for which the historical process has not yet called. Men must ask themselves, first and foremost, what stage the class war – which is the dialectic at work – has reached, and then act accordingly. This is to be 'concrete' and not timeless, or idealistic or 'abstract'. Alienation – the substitution of imaginary relations between, or worship of, inanimate objects or ideas for real relations between, or respect for, persons – will come to an end only when the final class – the proletariat – defeats the bourgeoisie. Then the ideas which this victory will generate will automatically be those expressive of, and beneficial to, a classless society; that is, all mankind. Neither institutions nor ideas which rest on falsifying the character of any section of the human race, and so leading to (or expressive of) their opposition, will survive. Capitalism, under which the labour power of human beings is bought and sold, and the workers are treated merely as sources of labour, is plainly a system which distorts the truth about what men are and can be, and seeks to subordinate history to a class interest, and is therefore due to be superseded by the gathering power of its indignant victims which its own victories call into existence. All frustration, for Marx, is the product of alienation – the barriers and distortions that are created by the inevitable war of classes, and shut out this or that body of men from the harmonious co-operation with one another for which their nature craves.

For Marx, no less than for earlier rationalists, man is potentially wise, creative and free. If his character has deteriorated beyond recognition, that is due to the long and brutalizing war in which he and his ancestors have lived ever since society ceased to be that primitive communism out of which, according to the current anthropology, it has developed. Until this state is reached again, embodying, however, all the conquests, technological and spiritual, which mankind has won in the course of its long wandering in the desert, neither peace nor freedom can be obtained. The French Revolution was an attempt to bring this about by altering political forms only – which was no more than the bourgeoisie required, since it already possessed the economic reality: and, therefore, all it succeeded in doing (as indeed was its appointed historical task at the stage of development at which it occurred) was to establish the bourgeoisie in a dominant position by finally destroying the corrupt remnant of an obsolete feudal regime. This task could not but be continued by Napoleon, whom no one could suspect of wishing consciously to liberate humanity; whatever his personal motive for acting as he did, the demands of his historical environment inevitably made him an instrument of social change; by his agency, as Hegel had indeed perceived, Europe advanced yet another step towards the realisation of its destiny.

The gradual freeing of mankind has pursued a definite, irreversible direction: every new epoch is inaugurated by the liberation of a hitherto oppressed class; nor can a class, once it has been destroyed, ever return. History does not move backwards, or in cyclical movements: all its conquests are final and irrevocable. Most previous ideal constitutions were worthless because they ignored actual laws of historical development, and substituted in their place the subjective caprice or imagination of the thinker. A knowledge of these laws is essential to effective political action. The ancient world gave way to the medieval, slavery to feudalism, and feudalism to the industrial bourgeoisie. These transitions were not peaceful, but sprang from wars and revolutions, for no established order gives way to its successor without a struggle. And now only one stratum remains submerged below the level of the rest, one class alone remains enslaved, the landless, propertyless proletariat, created by the advance of technology, perpetually assisting classes above itself to shake off the yoke of the common oppressor, always, after the common cause has been won, condemned to be oppressed by its own former allies, the new victorious class, by masters who were themselves but lately slaves. The proletariat is on the lowest possible rung of the social scale: there is no class below it; by securing its own emancipation the proletariat will therefore emancipate mankind. It has, unlike other classes, no specific claim, no interests of its own which it does not share with all men as such: for it has been stripped of everything but its bare humanity; its very destitution causes it to represent human beings as such – what it is entitled to is the minimum to which all men are entitled. Its fight is thus not a fight for the natural rights of a particular section of society: for natural rights are but the ideal formulation of the bourgeois attitude to the sanctity of private property; the only real rights are those conferred by history, the right to act the part which is historically imposed upon one's class. The bourgeoisie, in this sense, has a full right to fight its final battle against the masses, but its task is hopeless: it will necessarily be defeated, as the feudal nobility was defeated in its day. As for the masses, they fight for freedom not because they choose, but because they must, or rather they choose because they must: to fight is the condition of their survival; the future belongs to them, and in fighting for it, they, like every rising class, fight against a foe doomed to decay, and thereby for the whole of mankind. But whereas all other victories placed in power a class itself doomed to ultimate disappearance, this conflict will be followed by no other, being destined to end the condition of all such struggles, by abolishing classes as such; by dissolving the state itself, hitherto the instrument of a single class, into a free, because classless, society. The proletariat must be made to understand that no real compromise with the enemy is possible: that, while it may conclude temporary alliances with him in order to defeat some common adversary, it must ultimately turn against him. In backward countries, where the bourgeoisie itself is still fighting for power, the proletariat must throw in its lot with it, asking itself not what the ideals of the bourgeoisie may be, but what it is *compelled* to do in the particular situation; and must adapt its tactics to this. And while history is determined – and the victory will, therefore, be won by the rising class whether any given individual wills it or not – how rapidly this will occur, how effectively or painlessly, how far in accordance with the conscious popular will, depends on human initiative, on the degree of understanding of their task by the masses and the courage and efficiency of their leaders.

To make this clear, and to educate the masses for their destiny is, therefore, according to Marx, the whole duty of a contemporary philosopher. But, it has often been asked, how can a precept, a command to do this or that, be deduced from the truth of a theory of history? Historical materialism may account for what does in fact occur, but cannot, precisely because it is concerned solely with what is, provide the answer to questions of value, that is, tell us what ought to be. Marx does not explicitly draw this distinction, which has been brought to the forefront of philosophical attention by Hume and Kant, but it seems clear that for him (he follows Hegel on this) judgements of fact cannot be sharply distinguished from those of value: all one's judgements are conditioned by practical activity in a given social milieu which, in its turn, are functions of the stage reached by one's class in its historical evolution: one's views as to what one believes to exist and what one wishes to do with it, modify each other. If ethical judgements claim objective validity, they must be definable in terms of empirical activities and be verifiable by reference to them. He does not recognize the existence of a non-empirical, purely contemplative or specifically moral intuition or moral reason. The only sense in which it is possible to show that something is good or bad, right or wrong, is by demonstrating that it accords or discords with the historical process – the collective progressive activity of men – that it assists it or thwarts it, will survive or will inevitably perish. All causes permanently lost or doomed to fail, in the complex but historically determined ascent of mankind, are, by that very fact, made bad and wrong, and indeed this is what constitutes the meaning of such terms. But this is a dangerous empirical criterion, since causes which may appear lost may, in fact, have suffered only a temporary setback, and will in the end prevail.

His view of truth in general derives directly from this position. He is sometimes accused of maintaining that, since a man is wholly determined to think as he does by his social environment, even if some of his statements are objectively true, he cannot know it, being conditioned to think them true by material causes, not by their truth. Marx's statements on this subject are vague to a degree; but in general it may be said that he would have accepted the normal interpretation of what is meant by saying that a theory or a proposition of natural science or of ordinary sense experience is true or false. But he was scarcely interested in this, the most common, type of truth discussed by modern philosophers. He was concerned with the reasons for which social, moral, historical verdicts are thought true or false, where arguments between opponents can not so easily be settled by direct appeal to empirical facts accessible to both. He might have agreed that the bare proposition that Napoleon died in exile would have been accepted as equally true by a bourgeois and a socialist historian. But he would have gone on to say that no true historian confines himself to a list of events and dates: that the plausibility of his account of the past, its claim to be more than a bare chronicle, depends, at the very least, upon his choice of fundamental concepts, his power of emphasis and arrangement, that the very process of selection of material betrays an inclination to stress this or that event or act as important or trivial, adverse or favourable to human progress, good or bad. And in this tendency the social origin and environment and class affiliation and interests of the historian tell only too clearly.

This attitude seems to underlie his Hegelian view of rationality as entailing knowledge of the laws of necessity. Marx scarcely ever embarks on any kind of philosophical analysis; the general line of his theories of knowledge, of morals, of politics has to be inferred from scattered observations and from what he takes for granted, accepts without question. His use of such notions as freedom or rationality, his ethical terminology, seem to rest on some such view as the following (for which chapter and verse cannot be quoted, but which his orthodox disciples, Plekhanov, Kautsky, Lenin, Trotsky, no less than more independent followers like Lukács and Gramsci, embody in their thought): if you know in what direction the world process is working, you can either identify yourself with it or not; if you do not, if you fight it, you thereby compass your own certain destruction, being necessarily defeated by the forward advance of history. To choose to do so deliberately is to behave irrationally. Only a wholly rational being is wholly free to choose between alternatives: where one of these irresistibly leads to his own destruction, he cannot choose it freely, because to say that an act is free, as Marx employs the term, is to deny that it is contrary to reason. The bourgeoisie as a class is indeed fated to disappear, but individual members of it may follow reason and save themselves (as Marx might have claimed to have done himself) by leaving it before it finally founders. True freedom is unattainable until society has been made rational, that is, has overcome the contradictions which breed illusions and distort the understanding of both masters and slaves. But men can work for the free world by discovering the true state of the balance of forces, and acting accordingly; the path to freedom thus entails knowledge of historical necessity. Marx's use of words like 'right', or 'free', or 'rational', whenever he does not slip insensibly into ordinary usage, owes its eccentric air to the fact that it derives from his metaphysical views; and therefore diverges widely from that of common speech, which is largely intended to record and communicate something scarcely of interest to him – the subjective experience of class-perverted individuals, their states of mind or of body as revealed by the senses or in self-consciousness.

Such in outline is the theory of history and society which constitutes the often 'implicit' metaphysical basis of communism. It is a wide and comprehensive doctrine which derives its structure and basic concepts from Hegel and the Young Hegelians, and its dynamic principles from Saint-Simon, its belief in the primacy of matter from Feuerbach, and its view of the proletariat from the French communist tradition. Nevertheless it is wholly original; the combination of elements does not in this case lead to syncretism, but forms a bold and coherent system, with the wide range and the massive architectonic quality that is at once the greatest pride and the fatal defect of all forms of Hegelian thought. But it is not guilty of Hegel's reckless and contemptuous attitude towards the results of the scientific research of his time; on the contrary, it attempts to follow the direction indicated by the empirical sciences, and to incorporate their general results. Marx's practice did not always conform to this theoretical ideal, and that of his followers sometimes did so even less: while not actually distorted, the facts are sometimes made to undergo peculiar transformations in the process of being fitted into the intricate dialectical pattern. It is by no means a wholly empirical theory, since it does not confine itself to the description of the phenomena and the formulation of hypotheses concerning their structure and behaviour; the Marxist doctrine of movement in dialectical collisions is not a hypothesis liable to be made less or more probable by the evidence of facts, but a pattern, uncovered by a non-empirical, historical method, the validity of which is not questioned. To deny this would be tantamount, according to Marx, to a return to 'vulgar' materialism, which, ignoring the crucial discoveries of Hegel and indeed Kant, recognizes only those connections as real for which there is the corrigible evidence of the physical senses.

In the sharpness and the clarity with which this theory formulates its questions, in the rigour of the method by which it proposes to search for the answers, in the combination of attention to detail and power of wide comprehensive generalization, it is without parallel. Even if all its specific conclusions were proved false, its importance in creating a wholly new attitude to social and historical questions, and so opening new avenues of human knowledge, would be unimpaired. The scientific study of historically evolving economic relations, and of their bearing on other aspects of the lives of communities and individuals, began with the application of Marxist canons of interpretation. Previous thinkers – for example, Vico, Hegel, Saint-Simon – drew up general schemata, but their direct results, as embodied, for instance, in the gigantic systems of Comte or Spencer, are at once too abstract and too vague, and are remembered in our day only by historians of ideas. The true father of modern economic history, and, indeed, of modern sociology, in so far as any one man may claim that title, is Karl Marx. If to have turned into truisms what had previously been paradoxes is a mark of genius, Marx was richly endowed with it. His achievements in this sphere are necessarily ignored in proportion as their effects have become part of the permanent background of civilized thought.

6 Concerning the Limitation of the Materialistic Theory of History

Benedetto Croce

Historical materialism, if it is to express something critically acceptable, can . . . be neither a new *a priori* notion of the philosophy of history, nor a new method of historical thought; it must be simply a *canon* of historical interpretation. This canon recommends that attention be directed to the so-called economic basis of society, in order that the forms and mutations of the latter may be better understood.

The concept canon ought not to raise difficulty, especially when it is remembered that *it implies no anticipation of results*, but only an aid in seeking for them; and is entirely of empirical origin. When the critic of the text of Dante's *Comedia* uses Witte's well-known canon, which runs: '*the difficult reading is to be preferred to the easy one*', he is quite aware that he possesses a mere instrument, which may be useful to him in many cases, useless in others, and whose correct and advantageous employment depends entirely on his caution. In like manner and with like meaning it must be said that historical materialism is a mere *canon*; although it be in truth a canon *most rich in suggestion*.

But was it in this way that Marx and Engels understood it? And is it in this way that Marx's followers usually understand it?

Let us begin with the first question. Truly a difficult one, and offering a multiplicity of difficulties. The first of these arises so to speak, from the *nature of the sources*. The doctrine of historical materialism is not embodied in a classical and definite book by those authors, with whom it is as it were identified; so that,

From Benedetto Croce, *Historical Materialism and the Economics of Karl Marx*, translated by C. M. Meredith, with an Introduction by A. D. Lindsay (London: Howard Latimer Ltd, 1913), pp. 77–93.

to discuss that book and to discuss the doctrine might seem all one thing. On the contrary it is scattered through a series of writings, composed in the course of half a century, at long intervals, where only the most casual mention is made of it, and where it is sometimes merely understood or implied. Anyone who desired to reconcile all the forms with which Marx and Engels have endowed it would stumble upon contradictory expressions, which would make it impossible for the careful and methodical interpreter to decide what, on the whole, historical materialism meant for them.

Another difficulty arises in regard to the weight to be attached to their expressions. I do not think that there has yet been a study of what might be called Marx's *forma mentis*; with which Engels had something in common, partly owing to congeniality, partly owing to imitation or influence. Marx, as has been already remarked, had a kind of abhorrence for researches of purely scholastic interest. Eager for knowledge of *things* (I say, of concrete and individual things) he attached little weight to discussions of *concepts* and the *forms of concepts*; this sometimes degenerated into an exaggeration in his own concepts. Thus we find in him a curious opposition between statements which, interpreted strictly, are erroneous; and yet appear to us, and indeed are, loaded and pregnant with truth. Marx was addicted, in short, to a kind of *concrete logic*.[1] Is it best then to interpret his expressions literally, running the risk of giving them a meaning different from what they actually bore in the writer's inmost thoughts? Or is it best to interpret them broadly, running the opposite risk of giving them a meaning, theoretically perhaps more acceptable, but historically less true?

The same difficulty certainly occurs in regard to the writings of numerous thinkers; but it is especially great in regard to those of Marx. And the interpreter must proceed with caution: he must do his work bit by bit, book by book, statement by statement, connecting indeed these various indications one with another, but taking account of differences of time, of actual circumstances, of fleeting impressions, of mental and literary habits; and he must submit to acknowledge ambiguities and incompleteness where either exists, resisting the temptation to confirm and complete by his own judgement. It may be allowed, for instance, as it appears to me for various reasons, that the way in which historical materialism is stated above is the same as that in which Marx and Engels understood it in their inmost thoughts; or at least that which they would have agreed to as correct if they had had more time available for such labours of scientific elaboration, and if criticism had reached them less tardily. And all this is of importance up to a certain point, for the interpreter and historian of ideas; since for the history of science, Marx and Engels are neither more nor less than

---

1 The over-abused Dühring was not mistaken when he remarked that in Marx's works expressions occur frequently 'which appear to be universal without being actually so' (Allgemein aussehen ohne es zu sein). *Kritische Geschichte der Nationalökonomie und des Socialismus* (Berlin, 1871), p. 527.

they appear in their books and works; real, and not hypothetical or possible persons.[2]

But even for science itself, apart from the history of it, the hypothetical or possible Marx and Engels have their value. What concerns us theoretically is to understand the various possible ways of interpreting the problems proposed and the solutions thought out by Marx and Engels, and to select from the latter by criticism those which appear theoretically true and welcome. What was Marx's intellectual standpoint with reference to the Hegelian philosophy of history? In what consisted the criticism which he gave of it? Is the purport of this criticism always the same for instance in the article published in the *Deutsch-französische Jahrbücher*, for 1844, in the *Heilige Familie* of 1845, in the *Misère de la philosophie* of 1847, in the appendix to *Das Kommunistische Manifest* of 1848, in the preface to the *Zur Kritik* of 1859, and in the preface to the 2nd edition of *Das Kapital* of 1873? Is it so again in Engels' works in the *Antidühring*, in the article on Feuerbach etc.? Did Marx ever really think of substituting, as some have believed, *Matter* or material fact for the Hegelian *Idea*? And what connection was there in his mind between the concepts *material* and *economic*? Again, can the explanation given by him, of his position with regard to Hegel – 'the ideas determined by facts and not the facts by the ideas' – be called an inversion of Hegel's view, or is it not rather the inversion of that of the ideologists and doctrinaires?[3] These are some of the questions pertaining to the

---

2   Gentile, *Una critica del materialismo storico* in the *Studi storici* of Crivellucci, vol. VI, 1897, pp. 379–423, throws doubt on the interpretation offered by me of the opinions of Marx and Engels, and on the method of interpretation itself. I gladly acknowledge that in my two earlier essays I do not clearly point out where precisely the textual interpretation ends and the really theoretical part begins; which theoretical exposition, only by conjecture and in the manner described above, can be said to agree with the inmost thoughts of Marx and Engels. In his recent book, *La Filosofia di Marx*, (Pisa, Spoerri, 1899) (in which the essay referred to is reprinted), Gentile remarks (p. 104), that, although it is a very convenient practice, and in some cases legitimate and necessary 'to interpret doctrines, by calling a part of their statement worthless or accidental in form and external and weak, and a part the real substance and essential and vital, it is yet necessary to justify it in some way'. He means certainly, 'justify it as historical interpretation', since its justification as correction of theory cannot be doubtful. It seems to me that even historically the interpretation can be justified without difficulty when it is remembered that Marx *did not insist* (as Gentile himself says) on his metaphysical notions; and did certainly insist on his historical opinions and on the political policy which he defended. Marx's personality as a sociological observer and the teacher of a social movement, certainly outweighs Marx as a metaphysician which he was almost solely as a young man. That it is worth the trouble to study Marx from all sides is not denied, and Gentile has now admirably expounded and criticized his youthful metaphysical ideas.

3   I confess that I have never been able to *understand* – however much I have considered the matter – the meaning of this passage (which ought, however, to be very evident, since it is quoted so often without any comment), in the preface to the second edition of *Das Kapital*: 'Meine dialektische Methode ist der Grundlage nach von der Hegel'schen nicht nur verschieden, sondern ihr direktes Gegentheil. Für Hegel is *der Denkprocess*, den er sogar unter dem Namen *Idee* in ein selbständiger subjeckt verwandelt, der Demjurg des Wirklichen, das nur seine aüssere Erscheinung bildet. Bei mir ist umgekehrt *das Ideelle* nichts Andres als das im Menschenkopf umgesetzte und

history of ideas, which will be answered some time or other: perhaps at present the time has not yet arrived to write the history of ideas which are still in the process of development.[4]

But, putting aside this historical curiosity, it concerns us now to work at these ideas in order to advance in theoretical knowledge. How can historical materialism justify itself scientifically? This is the question I have proposed to myself, and to which the answer is given by the critical researches referred to at the beginning of this paragraph. Without returning to them I will give other examples, taken from the same source, that of the Marxian literature. How ought we to understand scientifically Marx's *neodialectic*? The final opinion expressed by Engels on the subject seems to be this: the dialect is the rhythm of the development of things, *i.e.* the inner law of things in their development. This rhythm is not determined *a priori*, and by metaphysical deduction, but is rather observed and gathered *a posteriori*, and only through the repeated observations and verifications that are made of it in various fields of reality, can it be presupposed that all facts develop through negations, and negations of negations.[5] Thus the dialect would be the discovery of a great natural law, less empty and formal than the so-called *law of evolution* and it would have nothing in common with the old Hegelian dialect except the name, which would preserve for us a historical record of the way in which Marx arrived at it. But does this natural rhythm of development exist? This could only be stated from observation, to which indeed Engels appealed in order to assert its existence. And what kind of a law is one which is revealed to us by observation? Can it ever be a law that governs things absolutely, or is it not one of those which are now called tendencies, or rather is it not merely a simple and limited generalization? And this recognition of rhythm through negations of negations, it is not some rag of the old metaphysics, from which it may be well to free ourselves.[6] This is the investigation needed for the progress of science. In like manner should other statements of Marx and Engels be criticized. What, for example, shall

---

ubersetzte Materielle.' (*Das Kapital*, vol. I, p. xvii.) Now it seems to me that the *Ideelle* of the last phrase has *no relation* to the *Denkprocess* and to the Hegelian *Idea* of the preceding phrase . . . . some have thought that by the objections [I] stated, I intended to deny Marx's Hegelian inspiration. It is well to repeat that I merely deny its *logical relation* affirmed between the two philosophical theories. To deny Marx's Hegelian inspiration would be to contradict the evidence.

4 Answers to several of the questions suggested above are now supplied in the book already referred to, by Gentile: *La Filosofia di Marx*.

5 *Antidühring*, pt I, ch. xlii., especially pp. 138–45, which passage is translated into Italian in the appendix to the book by Labriola referred to above: *Discorrendo di socialismo e di filosophia*, cf. *Das Kapital*, vol. I, p. xvii, 'Gelingt dies und spiegelt sich nun das Leben des stoffs ideel wieder, *so mag es aussehen*, als habe man es mit einer Konstruction a priori zu thun.'

6 Lange, indeed, in reference to Marx's *Das Kapital*, remarked that the Hegelian dialectic, 'the development by antithesis and synthesis, might almost be called an *anthropological discovery*. Only in history, as in the life of the individual, development by antithesis *certainly does not accomplish itself so easily and radically, nor with so much precision and symmetry as in speculative thought*' (*Die Arbeiterfrage*, pp. 248–9).

we think of Engel's controversy with Dühring concerning the basis of history: whether this is *political force* or *economic fact*? Will it not seem to us that this controversy can perhaps retain any value in face of Dühring's assertion that political fact is that *which is essential historically*, but in itself has not that general importance which it is proposed to ascribe to it? We may reflect for a moment that Engel's thesis 'force protects (*schutzt*) but does not cause (*verursacht*) usurpation' might be directly inverted into another, that 'force *causes* usurpation, but economic interest *protects* it', and this by the well-known principle of the interdependence and competition of the social factors.

And the class war? In what sense is the general statement true that *history is a class war*? I should be inclined to say that history is a class war (1) when there are classes, (2) when they have antagonistic interests, (3) when they are aware of this antagonism, which would give us, in the main, the humorous equivalence that history is a class war only when it is a class war. In fact sometimes classes have not had antagonistic interests, and very often they are not conscious of them; of which the socialists are well aware when they endeavour, by efforts not always crowned with success (with the peasantry, for example, they have not yet succeeded), to arouse this consiousness in the modern proletariat. As to the possibility of the non-existence of classes, the socialists who prophesy this non-existence for the society of the future must at least admit that it is not a matter intrinsically necessary to historical development, since in the future, and without classes, history, it may well be hoped will continue. In short even the particular statement that 'history is a class war', has that limited value of a canon and of a point of view, which we have allowed in general to the materialist conception.[7]

The second of the two questions proposed at the beginning is: How do the Marxians understand historical materialism? To me it seems undeniable that in the Marxian literature, i.e. the writings of the followers and interpreters of Marx, there exists in truth a *metaphysical danger* of which it is necessary to beware. Even in the writings of Professor Labriola some statements are met with which have recently led a careful and accurate critic to conclude that Labriola understands historical materialism in the genuine and original sense of a metaphysic, and that of the worse kind, a metaphysic of the contingent.[8] But although I have myself, on another occasion, pointed out those statements and formulae which seem to me doubtful in Labriola's writings, I still think, as I thought then, that they are superficial outgrowths on a system of thought essentially sound; or to speak in a manner agreeing with the considerations developed above, that Labriola, having educated himself in Marxism, may have borrowed from it also some of its over-absolute style, and at times a certain

7 With regard to the *abstract* classes of Marxian economics and the *real* or *historical* classes, see some remarks by Sorel in the article referred to in the *Journal des Economistes*, p. 229. [Croce refers to Sorel's article 'Sur la théorie marxiste de la valeur,' *Journal des Economistes*, March 1897. Ed.]
8 Gentile, 'Critica del materialismo storico', in *Studi storici*, p. 421. cf. 400–1.

carelessness about the working out of concepts, which are somewhat surprising in an old Herbartian like himself,[9] but which he then corrects by observations and limitations always useful, even if slightly contradictory, because they bring us back to the ground of reality.

Labriola, moreover, has a special merit, which marks him off from the ordinary exponents and adapters of historical materialism. Although his theoretical formulae may here and there expose him to criticism, when he turns to history, i.e. to concrete facts, he changes his attitude, throws off as it were, the burden of theory and becomes cautious and circumspect: *he possesses, in a high degree, respect for history*. He shows unceasingly his dislike for formulae of every kind, when concerned to establish and scrutinize definite processes, nor does he forget to give the warning that there exists 'no theory, however good and excellent in itself, which will help us to a summary knowledge of every historical detail'.[10]

In his last book we may note especially a full inquiry into what could possibly be the nature of a *history of Christianity*. Labriola criticizes those who set up as an historical subject the *essence* of Christianity, of which it is unknown where or when it has existed; since the history of the last centuries of the Roman Empire shows us merely the origin and growth of what constituted the Christian society, or the church, a varying group of facts amidst varied historical conditions. This critical opinion held by Labriola seems to me perfectly correct; since it is not meant to deny (what I myself, do not deny) the justification of that method of historical exposition, which for lack of another phrase, I once called *histories by concepts*,[11] thus distinguishing it from the historical exposition of the life of a given social group in a given place and during a given period of time. He who writes the *history of Christianity*, claims in truth to accomplish a task somewhat similar to the tasks of the historians of *literature*, of *philosophy*, of *art*: i.e. to isolate a body of facts which enter into a fixed concept, and to arrange them in a chronological series, without however denying or ignoring the source which these facts have in the other facts of life, but keeping them apart for the convenience of more detailed consideration. The worst of it is that whereas literature, philosophy, art and so on are determined or determinable concepts, Christianity is almost solely a bond, which unites beliefs often intrinsically very diverse; and, in writing the history of Christianity, there is often a danger of writing in reality the history of a *name, void without substance*.[12]

But what would Labriola say if his cautious criticism were turned against that

---

9 Labriola has indeed an exaggerated dislike for what he calls the *scholastic*: but even this exaggeration will not appear wholly unsuitable as a reaction against the method of study which usually prevails among the mere men of letters, the niggardly scholars, the empty talkers and jugglers with abstract thought, and all those who lose their sense of close connection between science and life.

10 *Discorrendo di socialismo*, 1, ix.

11 *Intorno alla storia della cultura* (Kulturgeschichte in *Atti* dell Accad. Pont.; vol. xxv. 1895, p. 8.)

12 'If by Christianity is meant merely the sum of the beliefs and expectations concerning human

history of the origin of the family, of private property and of class distinctions, which is one of the most extensive historical applications made by the followers of Marx: desired by Marx, sketched out by Engels on the lines of Morgan's investigations, carried on by others. Alas, in this matter, the aim was not merely to write, as could, perhaps, have been done, a useful manual of the historical facts which enter into these three concepts, but actually an *additional history* was produced: A history, to use Labriola's own phrase, of the *essence* family, of the *essence* class and of the *essence* private property, with a predetermined cadence. A 'history of the family', to confine ourselves to one of the three groups of facts, can only be an enumeration and description of the particular forms taken by the *family* amongst different races and in the course of time: a series of particular histories, which unite themselves into a general concept. It is this which is offered by Morgan's theories, expounded by Engels, which theories modern criticism have cut away on all sides.[13] Have they not allowed themselves to presuppose, as an historical stage, through which all races are fated to pass, that chimerical matriarchate, in which the mere reckoning of descent through the mother is confused with the predominance of woman in the family and that of woman in society? Have we not seen the reproofs and even the jeers directed by some Marxians against those cautious historians who deny that it is possible to assert, in the present condition of the criticism of sources, the existence of a primitive communism, or a matriarchate, amongst the Hellenic races? Indeed, I do not think that throughout this investigation proof has been given of much critical foresight.

I should also like to call Labriola's attention to another confusion, very common in Marxian writings, between *economic forms of organization* and *economic epoch*. Under the influence of evolutionist positivism, those divisions which Marx expressed in general: the *Asiatic*, the *antique*, the *feudal* and the *bourgeois* economic organization, have become four historical *epochs: communism, slave organization, serf organization*, and *wage-earning organization*. But the modern historian, who is indeed not such a superficial person as the ordinary Marxians are accustomed to say, thus sparing themselves the trouble of taking a share in his laborious procedure, is well aware that there are four *forms* of economic organization, which succeed and intersect one another in actual history, often forming the oddest mixtures and sequences. He recognizes an Egyptian medievalism or feudalism, as he recognizes an Hellenic medievalism or feudalism; he knows too of a German *neo-medievalism* which followed the flourishing bourgeois organization of the German cities before the Reformation and the discovery of the New World; and he willingly compares the general

---

destiny, these beliefs', writes Labriola, 'vary as much, in truth, as in the difference, to mention only one instance, between the free will of the Catholics after the Council of Trent, and the absolute determination of Calvin!' (*Discorrendo di socialismo*, ix.)

13   Without referring to the somewhat unmethodical work of Westermarck, *History of Human Marriage*, see especially Ernst Grosse's book, *Die Formen der Familie und die Formen des Wirthschaft* (Freiburg in B., 1896).

economic conditions of the Greco-Roman world at its zenith with those of
Europe in the sixteenth and seventeenth centuries.

Connected with this arbitrary conception of historical epochs, is the other of
the inquiry into *the cause* (note carefully; into the cause) of the transition from
one form to another. Inquiry is made, for instance, into the *cause* of the abolition
of slavery, which must be the *same*, whether we are considering the decline of
the Greco-Roman world or modern America; and so for serfdom, and for
primitive communism and the capitalist system: amongst ourselves the famous
Loria has occupied himself with these absurd investigations, the perpetual
revelation of a single cause, of which he himself does not know exactly whether
it be the earth, or population or something else – yet it should not take much to
convince us (it would suffice for the purpose to read, with a little care, some
books of narrative history) that the transition from one form of economic, or
more generally, social, organization, to another, is not the result of a *single cause*,
nor even of a *group of causes which are always the same*; but is due to causes and
circumstances which need examination for each case since they usually vary for
each case. Death is death; but people die of many diseases.

But enough of this; and I may be allowed to conclude this paragraph by
reference to a question which Labriola also brings forward in his recent work,
and which he connects with the criticism of historical materialism.

Labriola distinguishes between historical materialism as an interpretation of
history, and as a general conception of life and of the universe (*Lebens-und-
Weltanschauung*), and he inquires what is the nature of the *philosophy immanent*
in historical materialism; and after some remarks, he concludes that this
philosophy is the *tendency to monism*, and is a *formal* tendency.

Here I take leave to point out that if into the terms *historical materialism two
different things* are intruded, i.e.: (1) a method of interpretation; (2) a definite
conception of life and of the universe; it is natural to find a philosophy in it, and
moreover with a tendency to monism, because it was included therein at the
outset. What close connection is there between these two orders of thought?
Perhaps a logical connection of *mental coherence*? For my part, I confess that I am
unable to see it. I believe, on the contrary, that Labriola, this time, is simply
stating *à propos* of historical materialism what he thinks to be the necessary
attitude of modern thought with regard to the problems of ontology; or what,
according to him, should be the standpoint of the socialist opinion in regard to
the conceptions of optimism and pessimism; and so on. I believe, in short, that
he is not making an *investigation* which will reveal the philosophical conceptions
underlying historical materialism; but merely a *digression*, even if a digression of
interest and importance. And how many other most noteworthy opinions and
impressions and sentiments are welcomed by socialist opinion! But why
christen this assemblage of new facts by the name of historical materialism,
which has hitherto expressed the well-defined meaning of a way of interpreting
history? Is it not the task of the scientist to distinguish and analyse what in
empirical reality and to ordinary knowledge appears mingled into one?

7   The Materialist Conception of History

Rudolf Hilferding

Marx called his conception of history the 'materialist' conception of history. That unfortunate designation has been responsible, in no small degree, for repeated misunderstandings and sterile polemics. But the use of this term is understandable. While transcending Hegel's philosophy Marx remained under the influence of this philosophy, and in 'negating' it he believed that he was still employing its dialectical method. He therefore opposed his 'materialist' conception to idealist speculation, whereas in reality, as Marx himself insists again and again, it is a matter of the opposition between scientific inquiry and philosophical speculation. The object of this inquiry makes Marx's conception of history a *sociological* conception of history. What that means requires closer analysis.

In his Preface to *A Contribution to the Critique of Political Economy*, Marx writes:

> I was led by my studies [of Hegel's system] to the conclusion that legal relations as well as forms of State could neither be understood by themselves, nor explained by the so-called general progress of the human mind, but that they are rooted in the material conditions of life. In the social production which men carry on they enter into definite relations that are indispensable and independent of their will; these relations of production correspond to a definite stage of development of their material powers of production. The totality of these relations of production constitutes the economic structure of society – the real foundation, on which legal and political superstructures arise and to which definite forms of social consciousness correspond. The mode of production of material life determines the general

From Rudolph Hilferding, *Das historische Problem*, translated by Tom Bottomore. Published by permission of Dr Peter Milford. The German text of this work, left unfinished at Hilferding's death in 1941, was first published, with an introduction by Benedikt Kautsky, in *Zeitschrift für Politik* (new series), vol. I, no. 4, December 1954, pp. 293– 324.

character of the social, political and spiritual processes of life. It is not the consciousness of men that determines their being, but, on the contrary, their social being determines their consciousness. At a certain stage of their development, the material forces of production in society come in conflict with the existing relations of production, or – what is but a legal expression for the same thing – with the property relations within which they had been at work before. From forms of development of the forces of production these relations turn into their fetters. Then occurs a period of social revolution. With the change of the economic foundation the entire immense superstructure is more or less rapidly transformed. In considering such transformations, the distinction should always be made between the material transformation of the economic conditions of production which can be determined with the precision of natural science, and the legal, political, religious, aesthetic or philosophical – in short, ideological – forms in which men become conscious of this conflict and fight it out. Just as our opinion of an individual is not based on what he thinks of himself, so can we not judge of such a period of transformation by its own consciousness; on the contrary, this consciousness must rather be explained from the contradictions of material life, from the existing conflict between the social forces of production and the relations of production.

In the first place, it should be emphasized again that this conception of history (erroneously called 'materialist') does not involve the ontological, metaphysical or epistemological problem of the relation between mind and matter, but only the question of a method which will enable us to attain a scientific knowledge of the historical process.

The relation of historical science to philosophy is exactly the same in principle as that of the physical sciences, biology or economics. It is the business of epistemology to draw conclusions from the current results of scientific inquiry, and to examine, let us say, what modifications the modern theory of relativity may entail for categories such as time, space and causality, or what philosophical world view – if metaphysical need cannot dispense with one – accords with the findings of social science. But if theology and philosophical speculation at one time laid down certain items of knowledge as being unalterable by scientific research and sought to impose their own methods of cognition as the only admissible ones, the relationship has now been *reversed*. Science forms, quite independently, its own methods of research, and its results constitute the data of epistemology. On the other side, the Marxian conception of history does not imply a commitment to a particlar epistemology or philosophical system any more than does, say, biology. What is irreconcilable with science of any kind is *dogma* established by speculation. But the question as to which elaboration of the findings of science in a theory of knowledge is the right one, conforming most closely with the results and the methods of research of science itself, is a separate question which has to be resolved by epistemology.

It is quite comprehensible, therefore, that a Marxist, like a natural scientist, when he adopts a particular position with regard to epistemological problems, cannot do so as a Marxist since he would then simply propound dogmatic epistemological conclusions of his own – but must do so as an epistemologist. This explains why Marxism as such cannot postulate a specific philosophical view, and why Marxists who concern themselves with these problems are in fact as little able to derive philosophical conclusions, in an *a priori* fashion, on the basis of their specific scientific perspective, as are other scientists. It is impossible to assign Marxism to any particular philosophical system.

The basic concept in Marx's conception of history is the *relation to production*. This is not a matter of a particular relation between an individual and a certain quantity of productive forces, or of the behaviour of an individual in the application of his tools and the use of the land, but the relation of people to each other, that is, the relationships of beings who are *socialized* because they produce, and by the manner in which they produce. The production relation is not, therefore, a mechanical, natural state of affairs, but a social condition 'entered' into by thinking, willing and acting human beings, or to put it more precisely perhaps, a condition in which they find themselves at any given time. Far from the 'forces of production' in their physical, natural state producing in some mystical way the corresponding forms of thought and volition, it is the social cooperation of human beings which turns wood, stones and land – in short, the products of nature – into *productive forces*, to the extent that this social cooperation allows at any given time.

It is the real human being, the thinking, willing and acting man, with his needs and interests, who constitutes the precondition for production relations. That is why the young Marx initially wanted to call his new conception, formulated in opposition to Hegel, 'naturalist' or 'humanist'. For the common element in philosophy after Hegel, which sought to develop his system in a more enlightened way while still working within its framework, was the attempt to substitute for the development of the world spirit the development of real human beings. What distinguishes Marx's thought from the humanism of Feuerbach and others, however, is that he replaces the abstract human being, with his ascribed qualities, by the real, historical human being, who has emerged in specific social conditions, and investigates the law-governed character of these social conditions. Concepts such as 'naturalist' and 'human-ist' would have been too narrow, whereas 'materialist', suitably redefined, might have expressed some kind of synthesis of these two concepts.

The production relation, therefore, is the relation of human beings to each other and to the existing forces of production. As such, it is always a property relationship as well, which is only 'a legal expression for the same thing', that is, a legal relationship. The law may be extremely primitive, still uncodified, existing only as a conventional or customary law, but without law there can be no social or production relations. 'Productive forces', then, do not create law or ideas of law in the sense in which, according to a certain kind of materialism based upon natural science (although this is more of a bogy than a theory), specific combinations or oscillations of matter manifest themselves as ideas. On the contrary, natural objects only become productive forces in a relation of production into which human beings enter, under existing, given natural conditions which they continually alter through their social behaviour. A production relation is always, therefore, at the same time a legal relation, and every economic structure has inherent in it a specific property, hence legal, relation.

A legal system, however, is always a power relation, i.e. a political relation, as well. Law presupposes the power to make it effective. Such power may be rudimentary and limited, traditional and based upon the natural tie of consanguinity, and exercised by one or several of the elders of the clan, but it goes hand in hand with the production relation and is one of its essential elements. It is the force which consciously regulates the production relation – the state power – and its scope and exercise are themselves rooted in the nature of the existing relations of production.[1]

The state is the conscious organization of society, endowed with executive power. By its very nature, therefore, it is a power organization. Its existence poses two problems.

Some social processes are directly subordinated to the commands of the state and are consciously regulated. Others remain outside the sphere of direct state regulation and function on the basis of their own laws, exempt from state control and in that sense autonomous; as for example, the economy, and also the whole of intellectual life in a liberal state (ideally conceived), even though this autonomy can only be exercised within the legal limits established and protected by the state. In every society the question arises concerning, first, the autonomous laws governing the spheres which are not controlled by the state, then the structure and interests of the state power itself, and finally the interdependence and interrelations of these two spheres. These are questions which arise, in principle, in every form of production relation, even the simplest. The struggle between the sphere free of state control and the state power may be of two kinds: it may be a struggle by the most powerful and preeminent group in the autonomous sector to influence or dominate the state, or a struggle against the state in order to maintain or extend the sphere which is free from state control by limiting the power of the state.

Second, the state develops into a separate power organization with its own

---

1   Friedrich Engels, on the basis of his studies of prehistory, restricted the concept of the state to organized political power in class societies. Important as the distinction between class and classless society is, it is not easy to see why the supreme organized political power necessarily present in every society should not be called a state, unless one wants to preserve the historically unjustified conception of a production relation unregulated by law and functioning without an executive organ of society. Nevertheless Engels' conception remained for a long time authoritative in the socialist vocabulary, particularly in Germany. It seemed beside the point to speak of a 'socialist state' or a 'people's state', since after the abolition of classes the 'state' would also disappear. It was customary to speak of a socialist society or community and to take a certain pride in being accused by opponents of hostility to the state.

organs. As a power organization it acquires a certain *independence vis-à-vis* society, or various sectors of society, and has its own interests: the maintenance and expansion of its power both at home and abroad, the furtherance of those developmental tendencies in the autonomous sphere which conform with its own interests, and the curbing of other tendencies. At the same time, however, the state is subject to the *influences* which emanate from the autonomous sphere of society. The state power is thus an independent factor with its own significance and capacity for action, but on the other hand also a product of society, the forces of which continually strive to determine its conduct. However, it is a mistake to overlook the distinctive importance of the state and to treat it simply as the executive organ of a social group. The interests of the state power should not simply be identified with the interests of a social group, at least not wholly or in every social situation. To a greater or lesser extent, and with varying degrees of effectiveness, the state power is an independent factor in historical development.

The struggles of social groups and classes are in part struggles among themselves, which take place in that sphere which is not controlled by the state and not consciously regulated by society (for example, struggles between workers' and employers' organizations over the division of the labour product, in conditions where freedom of association is legally established); in part, struggles by classes for a *share in the state power*. The power interests of the state are directly affected by the latter struggles, and it intervenes as an important independent factor whenever these interests so require. These interests of the state may indeed coincide with those of social groups, but this need not happen in every case, nor need its interests coincide completely. The result of such struggles, particularly when they have led to a strengthening of state power, can in turn change or modify the interests of those social groups themselves which appeared to dominate the state before the struggles erupted. Such a situation is most likely to occur when there is a certain equilibrium of class forces.

The 'production relation', therefore, is by no means a simple and natural affair. It is neither a mass of natural objects which can serve in production for the satisfaction of human needs, nor the relation of human beings to these objects. For this would remain a purely technical relation, which at the extreme might be conceived abstractly as the relationship of an isolated individual, but which could only develop in historical reality within society. The production relation is always the sum total of the interrelations among human beings, into which they enter, and in which they are placed, in order to be able to produce and so satisfy their needs, maintain and improve their lives. These are the interrelations of human beings socialized for and through production in a definite and specific way. The production relation, the economic structure, is not therefore something given by nature, but a social phenomenon, and as such it is always a legal and political relationship as well, the nature of which is determined by the needs of production. . . .

Marx never elaborated his conception of history in a systematic form. His emancipation from philosophy led at the same time to the rejection of any system such as that of Hegel's, in which not only was all previous knowledge summated, but the essence of future development could also be outlined. Marx's conception of history was intended as a *method of inquiry*, and as with every scientific method its value can only be judged, in the last resort, by applying it. The application of his method, as we have seen, has two aspects: an objective analysis of the production relation, and an account of how the state of affairs discovered by this means affects historically relevant action.

The objective analysis which Marx employed is to be found in *Capital*, and the social psychological consequences for capitalist society are then drawn out. The development of the forces of production, imposed by the capitalist laws of competition, concentration and accumulation, breaks through the capitalist laws of ownership, which cease to be a means of increasing the forces of production and become instead a fetter upon their growth. Social antagonisms become ever more acute. The classes which have emerged in the capitalist production relation enter into increasingly bitter conflict. The wage-earning class recognizes that its cultural and material emancipation requires that capitalism be overcome. As a result of the capitalist laws of motion themselves, its numbers and importance in the process of production grow, and along with this its class *consciousness*, the consciousness of its historical task. The working class develops its own political, legal and moral conceptions in opposition to the dominant ideas of bourgeois society. The conflict between these opposed ideas, which has grown out of the social situation and the divergence of interests, leads finally to a social revolution, in the course of a struggle for political power which is indispensable for the transformation of the social order.

Marx was unable to finish the chapter on classes which was to have completed *Capital* and provided a political and historical summing up. He refers to the three great classes of capitalist society: the landowners whose income derives from rent, the capitalists whose income comes from profit, and the wage workers whose income is derived from the wages of labour. But it is also evident from all Marx's formulations that he sees the basis of classes in the immediate process of production, distinguishes between them according to the principal forms of income, determined directly by the process of production, and attributes to them a specific class-consciousness determined by their position in the process of production.

This raises some crucial problems. In addition to the basic classes which are engaged in the production process and have their interests determined by it, the nature of the production relation gives rise to *other social groups*, whose function may be indispensable to the system of production and whose action can have a crucial importance. The most significant element is the state power, with all its different organs, which is indispensable to any production relation. Marx indicated again and again the great importance of 'force' in the origin and transformation of production relations, and his political goal – the conquest of political power by the working class – shows what immense significance he assigned to it. But he does not attribute any autonomy to this power. The state is conceived as the organization of the ruling classes, the nature of its policies being determined by their interests.

Now there are certainly some historical periods to which, in large measure, this conception applies. Such would be the case particularly when a class, with its particular interests, overshadows all other social groups; for instance during the first stage of assuming political power and establishing in a new form, or restructuring, the relations of production, and during the time when its rule is still little contested. During the classical period of English liberalism, for example, the interests of the bourgeoisie, and in particular those of industrial capital, in fact largely determined the policy of the English state. But that does not alter the fact that every state organization also has its *own interests*, the maintenance and promotion of its own power, which are not identical, and need not always coincide, with those of the ruling class. They are interests which may, under certain circumstances, be asserted very vigorously, since the state is a social organization armed with coercive power, and by virtue of its extensive apparatus – the army, the bureaucracy, the judiciary, teachers and professors, and perhaps, the church – is able to exert a great and direct social influence. The possibility of the state asserting its interests independently at any particular time depends upon specific political circumstances; it will be all the greater, the more it is the case, in a given stage of development, that classes or social groups neutralize each other in their endeavours, and in their exercise of the power which they can bring to bear upon the political leadership – in short, the more there prevails that 'equilibrium of class forces' of which Engels spoke.

The growing independence of the state power, its effort to realize its own specific interests in society, is most likely to be successfully achieved when it is a matter of maintaining or *strengthening its own existence*. The struggle against feudalism in order to establish the absolute monarchy, and therewith the modern state, was a struggle of the state power against the ruling class. This struggle was supported by the *bourgeoisie* – or more accurately, by a section of it – which was still a subordinate class. Naturally, a certain degree of economic development – which also meant bourgeois and urban development – had to be achieved, the productive forces of society and hence the growth of wealth outside the feudal sphere had to reach a certain level, before the goal of centralizing the state became possible and could thus be envisaged. Bourgeois wealth had to be in a position to supply the means for creating and maintaining standing armies and a modern bureaucracy, and for developing transport and communications. Only through the development of this economic base did the creation of the modern state become possible. But it was created by state power and its interests. It was supported by that section of the nascent bourgeoisie – by industrial, and to some extent by commercial, capital – which had a strong and conscious interest in the establishment of a centralized unitary state, the abolition of guild restrictions and internal tariff barriers etc., whereas the bourgeoisie of the guilds, and the peasantry which was still dominated by feudal lords, remained passive. But the initiator and sponsor of this political development, which was crucial for the transformation of the existing production relation and for the establishment of modern capitalism, was the independent power of the state, which made it possible for economic development to get under way.

The creation of the *modern state*, and along with it the political and legal preconditions indispensable to capitalist development, was thus made possible by the development of the production relation. But it was not the product either of the bourgeoisie or of its class struggle. It would be economic mysticism to maintain that it was the bourgeoisie alone which created the modern state, however much it subsequently made the state 'its own' in the course of its struggles. That this policy of the state served the interests of the bourgeoisie does not prove that it grew out of those interests – *post hoc* is not *propter hoc* – even though they paralleled and were linked with the really decisive interests: namely, those of the state. At this stage bourgeois ideologists – philosophers, teachers of law and cameralists – supported absolutism, and the mercantilist system in its early form is an expression of the bond between the most progressive section of the bourgeoisie and the interest of the state. The formulation of the new ideas was important and even indispensable for the systematic implementation of state policy and for the sublimation of the state's interests into the general interest. But the historical *causa movens* was the power interest of the state organization.

The growing independence of the state's own interest emerges particularly strongly in external political crises, when what is involved is either the defence of the state's existence or the extension of its power. The state power then appears directly as the general interest of all social groups, and the conflicts among them diminish in face of the common danger, giving way to mutual cooperation.

Finally, the manner in which the state power is exercised is also affected by the structural combination of its various organs, and by its social recruitment. The latter is itself influenced by the historical process in which the modern state emerged. Where, as in Prussia, this ends with a compromise between the monarchy and the aristocracy, the leading positions in the army and the administration remain the preserve of the aristocracy, which is thus able to retain some of its political power, though in a changed form. In Western Europe, on the other hand, the dominance of the bourgeoisie in the army and the administration was accomplished much more fully. Just as the pattern of recruitment varies greatly between different countries, so also does the position of the bureaucracy, and its degree of independence from political influences. In Prussia, the bureaucracy carried on a stubborn fight to defend its position, even against the government, and achieved complete success with the enactment of a statute which protected careers against any outside intervention, and in particular made dismissal dependent upon review by a commission constituted by the bureaucracy itself, so that it became practically impossible to get rid of an official. In Imperial Germany the government was dominated by the bureaucratic and military elites; the bureaucracy was not controlled by political power, but on the contrary largely determined the exercise of political power. In Western Europe, on the other hand, the bureaucracy had far less independence in relation to political bodies, and notably to the parliaments, which governed directly and effectively.

The increasing independence of the state power is by no means adequately expressed in present-day systems of government. It is much more easily embodied in an absolute monarchy than in a liberal or democratic regime. But whatever the regime, it depends upon the relation of classes to the state power and to each other. The significance of the struggle for parliamentary government was precisely to subject the state power to the influence of society – that is to say, to a political will which is the product of the existing class struggle – and so to restrict its independence as much as possible, or at the extreme to abolish such independence. As a result of the 'equilibrium of class forces', but also as a consequence of the growing autonomy of the state power during the war, the state eventually became more independent than ever before.

The manner in which the bourgeoisie confronted the state, and the extent to which it could make the state an instrument of its interests, varied substantially in different countries and led to considerable differences in the relationship between the state and classes. In Germany the state power was far more independent, and hence the assertion of pure power interests was much stronger than in Western Europe. This differentiation in the relationship with class also affects the position of the bureaucracy. In England a high degree of political neutrality is expected from members of the civil service; the civil servant cannot be a candidate in elections without first resigning from the service. The German bureaucracy expresses at almost every level a hierarchical, authoritarian ideology, and represents a closed status group, immune to any outside influence; if an official is elected he retains his office and his career prospects. In France the bureaucracy is extensively politicized, and this is even more the case in the United States, where until recently a career civil service scarcely existed. Modern developments, involving the assumption of new responsibilities, especially in the economic and social field, have enhanced the qualitative as well the quantitative importance of the state apparatus.

Since Marx did not provide an explicit analysis of the concept of class, nor an account of the development of classes, there is no basis for a polemic. But it seems clear at least that the structure of groups in a society may be far more complicated than is suggested by the division into classes, if this is limited to the basic classes. The differentiation of the principal classes according to type of income is correct from an economic point of view, but is inadequate in social terms. This is evident in the case of landowners, for both peasants and large landowners would be included in the class, despite the very great tension between these groups under certain circumstances. The same is true, though perhaps to a lesser extent, of the other two classes; the highly paid engineer and the factory worker are both wage labourers in economic terms, but they may differ greatly in social position. The economic, qualitative equality of a type of income may well lead to entirely different social positions according to the size of that income.

In addition to the three types of income arising directly from production there are derived incomes; incomes which are transferred to others by those who receive rent, profit or wages. According to Marx these include the income (profit) from commercial and interest-bearing capital, and also the wages of workers and employees in commerce and the banks. It is clear that the distinction between original and derived income is economically important, but it may not be crucial, by itself, in determining the orientation of social interests. There are, furthermore, those social groups which have been described rather superficially as 'pre-capitalist classes', namely peasants and artisans.

An analysis limited to the basic classes runs the risk, when it is carried over into the social field, of neglecting, in the first place, the conflicts of interest which arise within a class and may have great political and historical significance, such as those between commercial, bank and industrial capital, between peasants and large landowners, between workers in old handicraft establishments and those of modern factories, as happened in England at the time of the industrial revolution. Second, it may fail to consider as independent forces such social groups as the various agencies of the state, or the intellectuals, and simply subsume their interests under those of one or other of the basic classes. Third, it may ignore those social groups which are located between the basic classes, such as the peasants and the middle strata, which are themselves further differentiated. An analysis which differentiates along economic lines tends only too readily to subsume all the interests which are active in society under the interests of the basic economic classes; it thus fails to meet the requirements of historical analysis, and perhaps also of political analysis. For this reason it is more appropriate to speak of 'social groups'; and Marx himself, in such historical writings as *The Class Struggles in France* and *The Eighteenth Brumaire*, provided a model of this kind of analysis.

8 Marx and the 'Asiatic Mode of Production'

George Lichtheim

III

In January 1859, when writing the *Preface* to the *Critique of Political Economy*, Marx for the first (and last) time gave a summary of his method that indicates the exact relationship in which the economic process ('the mode of production of material life') stands to the historical process generally; and it is here, towards the close of the now classic formulation of the 'materialist conception of history', that he introduces his four historical stages: 'In broad outlines, Asiatic, ancient, feudal and modern bourgeois modes of production can be designated as progressive epochs in the economic formation of society'.[1] He was never again to display a similar degree of certainty in assigning their relative place to those forms of society which had embodied their characteristic features in definite stages of recorded history. Yet the general standpoint laid down in the *Preface* was not superseded or even substantially modified. (The qualifications introduced by Engels in the *Anti-Dühring* and the *Origins of the Family* are not, in my opinion, of basic importance.[2]) There are four, and only four, major

From George Lichtheim, 'Marx and the "Asiatic mode of production"', *St Antony's Papers*, no. 14: *Far Eastern Affairs*. © George Lichtheim, 1963.

1 *Selected Works*, vol. I, p. 363. The translation fails to convey the Hegelian ring of the original. Since an exact rendering of Hegel's observations on world history into English is a stylistic impossibility, one is left with the bare statement that Marx echoes Hegel not only in distinguishing four major epochs of world history but also in the confident Europeanocentrism with which he pronounces sentence upon the three preceding ones.

2 For a different view cf. Karl A. Wittfogel, *Oriental Despotism: A Comparative Study of Total Power* (New Haven, Conn., 1957), pp. 382ff.

historical epochs, the Asiatic being the first, and each corresponds to a definite social order which in turn lays the foundation for the succeeding one. These two aspects are internally related, but must none the less for analytical purposes be considered separately.[3]

To start, then, with the 'Asiatic mode' taken by itself, we have already seen what features can be said to distinguish it. [These features, mentioned earlier in the essay, are those outlined by Marx in a series of articles on India in the *New York Daily Tribune* during 1853: dispersion of population, provision of irrigation by central government, absence of private property in land. These articles, and others by Marx on non-European societies, have been reprinted in Shlomo Avineri (ed.), *Karl Marx on Colonialism and Modernization* (New York, 1968). Ed.] In his unsystematic fashion, Engels had suggested two: climatic conditions and the pervasive habits of an Oriental government. Marx expanded these hints into a system by tracing the peculiar character of Oriental society to the absence of private ownership in land.[4] He related this to the overriding role of the central government by suggesting that under the 'Asiatic system' the State was the 'real landlord'.[5] So far as private property in land is concerned we are left in no doubt what Marx thought of its role in dissolving the 'Asiatic mode', since in the second and concluding of his important *Tribune* articles on British rule in India he expressly describes it as 'the great *desideratum* of Asiatic society',[6] for the sake of which the infamies practised by the Indian *zamindar* and *ryotwar* systems, 'abominable as they are', should none the less be regarded as a step towards the emancipation of Indian society. Now what of the role played by the State? That in Asia it was the 'real landlord' Marx never doubted. For proof we have the passage in *Capital*, vol. III, where he refers to the situation of the producers being confronted not by a private landowner, 'but rather, as in Asia, under direct subordination to a state which stands over them as their landlord and simultaneously as sovereign'.[7] These characteristics of 'Asiatic society' – state control over the producer, and absence of private property in land – are presumably related to the strategic role of the central government in administering

3 It seems to me to be a decided weakness of Wittfogel's treatment of the subject that he fails to do this.

4 Engels's notion that the failure of Oriental society to develop private landed ownership was 'mainly due to the climate' is a trifle naïve, and looks back to Hegel, or even Montesquieu: one of the many instances of his tendency to relapse into ordinary cause-and-effect explanation, in the manner of the Enlightenment. The point cannot be pursued here; the reader of Hegel's *Vorlesungen*, vol. I, pp. 178ff., can easily discover where Engels obtained his basic notions about Oriental history. Marx, though equally inclined to take a Hegelian view of the historical process, relied for his factual information upon the classical economists, down to and including J. S. Mill, and upon British Blue Books and other official or semi-official sources.

5 NYDT [*New York Daily Tribune*, see editor's note above], 5 August 1853; cf. *Gesammelte Werke*, vol. 9, p. 218; this article has for some reason not been included in any English-language collection known to the writer.

6 NYDT, 8 August 1853; cf. *Selected Works*, vol. I, p. 353.

7 Quoted after the Moscow, 1960, English-language edition, p. 771.

the irrigation system, but how does this complex interrelationship come about *historically?* Engels never bothered about such difficult questions, but from Marx we are entitled to expect an answer. Let us see how far he provided one.

An indirect clue is afforded by his observation that where the small peasants 'form among themselves a more or less natural production community, as they do in India . . . the surplus labour for the nominal owner of the land can only be extorted from them by other than economic pressure, whatever the form assumed may be.'[8] This is followed by the remark about the state-sovereign doubling as landlord, so that taxes and ground-rents coincide. Marx then continues: 'Under such circumstances there need exist no harder political or economic dependence than that common to all subjection to that state. The state is here the supreme landlord. Sovereignty here consists in the ownership of land concentrated on a national scale. Conversely, no private ownership of land exists, although there is both private and common possession and use of land.'[9]

Does this point in the direction of a theory of conquest or some other form of political usurpation which blocks the emergence of true 'private ownership' of land, leaving the subject peasant population only with 'possession and use'? The puzzling thing is that the immediately following sentence states: 'The specific economic form in which unpaid surplus labour is pumped out of (the) direct producers determines the relationship of rulers and ruled, as it grows directly out of production itself and in turn reacts upon it as a determining element. Upon this, however, is founded the entire formation of the economic community which grows up out of the production relations themselves, (and) therewith simultaneously its specific political form.'[10] Other parts of the same lengthy passage refer to serfdom and similar forms of socio-economic bondage. It must be borne in mind that vol. III of *Capital* was pieced together by Engels from unfinished drafts. Even so it remains uncertain how Marx envisaged the historical genesis of a relationship which counterposed the State as supreme landlord to the peasant-producer. He makes it quite clear, however, that it is the dominance of the State which excludes genuine private ownership of land, i.e. the precondition of feudalism. If anything defines 'the Orient' according to Marx (and Engels) it is this supremacy of the State, which reduces the landowners to the role of merely 'nominal landlords' as Marx calls them.[11]

---

8 *Capital,* vol. III, p. 771. Marx here appends a footnote which adds: 'Following the conquest of a country, the immediate aim of the conqueror was also to convert its people to his own use. Cf. Linguet (*Théorie des lois civiles, etc.,* London, 1767). See also Möser.' It is not quite clear whether this refers to Indian conditions or whether it is meant to stand indifferently for all cases where peasant proprietors fall under some form of non-economic exploitation.

9 Ibid., pp. 771–2 (cited after the German text).

10 *Capital,* vol. III, p. 772; for the original text cf. *Das Kapital* (Berlin, 1949), vol. III, pp. 841–82. The authorized English translation published in Moscow is both wooden and inaccurate.

11 The above passage makes it clear that this refers to the original pre-conquest Indian landowners, and not only to the *zamindars,* as might be supposed from Marx's characterization of the latter as tax-gatherers imposed by the British government upon the wretched Bengali peasants (cf. NYDT, 5 August 1853).

There cannot then have been any genuine Oriental feudalism, at any rate not in India and China, the two Asian countries to which Marx had given some systematic attention. That he regarded their problems as broadly similar appears from a passage in *Capital*, vol. III, where he refers to the impact of European commerce upon Eastern societies:

> The obstacles presented by the internal solidity and organization of precapitalistic, national modes of production to the corrosive influence of commerce are strikingly illustrated in the intercourse of the English with India and China. The broad basis of the mode of production here is formed by the unity of small-scale agriculture and home industry, to which in India we should add the form of village communities built upon the common ownership of land, which incidentally was the original form in China as well. In India the English lost no time in exercising their direct political and economic power, as rulers and landlords, to disrupt these small economic communities. English commerce exerted a revolutionary influence on these communities and tore them apart only insofar as the low prices of its goods served to destroy the spinning and weaving industries which were an ancient integrating element of this unity of industrial and agricultural production. Even so this work of dissolution proceeds very gradually. And still more slowly in China, where it is not reinforced by direct political power. The substantial economy and saving in time afforded by the association of agriculture with manufacture put up a stubborn resistance to the products of the big industries whose prices include the *faux frais* of the circulation process which pervades them. Unlike the English, Russian commerce, on the other hand, leaves the economic ground-work of Asiatic production untouched.[12]

The interest of this passage is that it shows Marx, in the 1860s and while at work on *Capital*, reverting to the theme of his early newspaper articles. He does so also in a footnote in which the 'absurd (in practice infamous) economic experiments' conducted by the British in India are duly condemned, with special reference to the creation of 'a caricature of large-scale English estates' in Bengal.[13] Yet we have seen that in 1853 he had described private property in land as 'the great *desideratum* of Asiatic society', and expressly mentioned the *zamindars*. There is of course no contradiction if one bears in mind that for Marx the rupture of India's ancient stagnation involved the payment of a terrible price in exploitation and dislocation. But the new stress in *Capital* on

---

12 Cited after the Moscow edition, pp. 328–9; Engels's qualifying footnote (appended in 1894, i.e. almost thirty years after Marx had written these lines), about Russian commerce having in the meantime become genuinely capitalistic, does not affect the substance of the argument. Incidentally, the Soviet translation is not merely scandalously bad but in parts positively misleading; e.g. the key sentence really ought to run as follows: 'Insofar as their commerce here revolutionizes the mode of production, it does so only as through the low price of their merchandise they destroy the spinning and weaving which constitutes an ancient and integrating part of this union of industrial-agricultural production and thus disrupt the communities.'
13 *Capital*, p. 328n.

the futility and absurdity of these 'economic experiments', together with the reference to the solidity of the ancient social structure built upon the union of farming and handicrafts, does strike rather a different note. When he remarks that 'in the north-west they (sc. the English) did all they could to transform the Indian economic community with common ownership of the soil into a caricature of itself',[14] he seems to be saying, or at least hinting, that but for this outside interference the village community might have evolved in a sounder direction. Then there is the passing reference to the economic savings inherent in small-scale enterprise, as against the *faux frais* of modern large-scale industry – this last a familiar theme in socialist literature since Fourier, but one to which Marx normally did not give a great deal of attention. Altogether the tone of this passage seems to anticipate his well-known observations upon the prospects of the Russian village community in the 1880s: there is a hint of 'Narodism' about it.[15]

It is, I think, a fair inference from these passages that while in the 1850s Marx was inclined to emphasize the progressive role of Western capitalism in disrupting Oriental stagnation, by the time he came to draft his major economic work he was less certain that traditional society embodied no positive factors. At any rate, it may be said that by the 1860s his attitude had become ambivalent. We now find him remarking upon the stability of the ancient village communities, in a manner suggesting that he saw some genuine virtue in their peculiar mode of life. At the same time his hostility to capitalism had deepened. This is worth stressing as a qualification of the familiar statement that he had by the 1860s lost some of his early revolutionary ardour. If one has in mind his early attachment to a rather Jacobinical view of the coming European revolution, it is true to say that he grew more moderate in the measure that he became the theorist of a genuine labour movement with democratic aims. But at the same time he sharpened his critique of bourgeois society and the operation of capitalism as an economic system. The *Manifesto*, rather paradoxically, had celebrated the triumphant march of capitalism at the same time that it proclaimed the proletariat's coming victory. By the time Marx wrote *Capital* he was more concerned with factory legislation than with the proletarian revolution, but this did not make him more tolerant of 'the system'; rather less so. The note of indulgence has vanished, and the tone has become one of unqualified hostility and contempt. In 1847 the bourgeoisie still gained some plaudits for battering down the Chinese walls of barbarism; by 1867 even the 'Asiatic mode' comes in for favourable comment, at any rate so far as the village community is concerned: it is valued as a bulwark against social disintegration.

14 Ibid.
15 For Lenin's view on this issue, which of course was central to the gradual emergence of Russian Marxism from its Populist chrysalis, see his rather agitated defence of the 'real' Marx against the Narodniks (who naturally quoted *Capital*, vol. III, when it suited them) in *The Development of Capitalism in Russia* (1900; new edn, Moscow, 1956, pp. 340ff.); cf. Lichtheim, *Marxism: An Historical and Critical Study* (London, 1961), pp. 325ff.

IV

Here, then, is something like a hiatus in the argument. To some extent the difficulty arises from the fact that the more strictly historical part of Marx's theory of Oriental society is to be found in the posthumously published draft for *Das Kapital*, the so-called *Grundrisse*.[16] Before turning to this theme it may be as well to note where he departs from his predecessors. There was an 18th century and early 19th century view of Asian society with which Marx was thoroughly familiar. It is briefly but succinctly set out in the *Wealth of Nations*, and it is amusing to find that Smith, like Marx, refers to Bernier's travels as a source.[17] Chinese isolationism and indifference to foreign trade attracted the unfavourable attention of Smith who thought that 'upon their present plan they have little opportunity of improving themselves by the example of any other nation; except that of the Japanese':[18] a nice example of historical foresight. China is classed with 'ancient Egypt and Indostan', and Smith makes the pertinent point that in both these countries the government paid much attention to the canal system.[19] He also observes that 'the sovereigns of China, of ancient Egypt, and of the different kingdoms into which Indostan has at different times been divided, have always derived the whole, or by far the most considerable part, of their revenue from some sort of land-tax or rent. . . . It was natural, therefore, that the sovereigns of those countries should be particularly attentive to the interests of agriculture, upon the prosperity or declension of which immediately depended the yearly increase or diminution of their own reve-nue'.[20] Later he remarks that 'the sovereigns of China, those of Bengal while under the Mahometan government, and those of ancient Egypt, are said accordingly to have been extremely attentive to the making and maintaining of good roads and navigable canals, in order to increase, as much as possible, both the quantity and value of every part of the produce of the land.'[21] He then goes on to discuss 'the loss of the sovereign from the abuse and depredation of his tax-gatherers' and the interest of 'the Mandarins and other tax-gatherers' in maintaining a system of payment in kind that enabled them to fleece the

16 Cf. *Grundrisse der Kritik der politischen Ökonomie (Rohentwurf) 1857–1858* (Berlin, 1953); originally published in two volumes (Moscow, 1939–41). Part of this draft (over 1,000 pages in print) was revised and published by Marx in 1859 under the title *Zur Kritik der politischen Ökonomie*; the bulk was reworked from 1863 onwards into what is now *Das Kapital*.
17 Cf. *Wealth of Nations* (Modern Library edn, New York, 1937), p. 688, where the title of Bernier's *Voyages contenant la description des états du Grand Mogol*, etc. (Amsterdam, 1710), is given as *Voyages de François Bernier*.
18 Ibid., p. 64.
19 Ibid., p. 646.
20 Ibid., p. 647.
21 Ibid., p. 789.

peasants and defraud the central government.[22] There are the elements here of a theory of Oriental society, but it cannot be said that Smith makes much of them. He is content to register various features of Indian or Chinese administration, without inquiring to what extent they constitute a whole. In the following generation, we find James Mill, in his *History of British India* (1820), referring to an 'Asiatic model of government' (vol. I, pp. 175ff.), while John Stuart Mill (*Principles of Political Economy*, 1848) already employs the term 'Oriental society' as distinct from European.[23] Marx was familiar with these writers. Where does he diverge from them?

Principally, it seems to me, in expanding their hints into a theory that is both historical and sociological.[24] Unfortunately the theory was never formulated in systematic fashion, but has to be pieced together from his published and unpublished writings, notably the *Grundrisse* of 1857–8, where it is, however, chiefly employed to bring out the contrast between Oriental society and Graeco-Roman antiquity. By drawing upon all these scattered sources (including a very early work, the *German Ideology* of 1845–6, which throws out some interesting hints about slavery and feudalism), we arrive at something like the following:

The various stages in the development of the social division of labour correspond to different forms of property.[25] The 'first form' is communal and proper to 'the undeveloped stage of production where a people sustains itself by hunting and fishing, by cattle-raising or at most by farming'.[26] At this stage, the division of labour is rudimentary and consists for the most part in a further development of the primitive division of functions inherent in the family. 'The social order therefore limits itself to an extension of the family: patriarchal tribal chiefs, below them the members of the tribe, finally slaves. The slavery latent in the family develops gradually with the growth of population and needs, and with the extension of external intercourse, both of war and barter trade.'[27] This primitive tribal or communal organization is succeeded historically by a 'second form' which in the 1845–6 sketch is equated with 'the communal and state property of antiquity'. This is said to arise particularly

from the union of several tribes to a city through contact or conquest, and while retaining slavery. Side by side with communal property, mobile and subsequently

---

22 Ibid., p. 790.
23 Op. cit. (1909 edn), p. 20; Marx on the whole prefers the term 'Asiatic society', perhaps first used by Richard Jones in *An Essay on the Distribution of Wealth* (1831); cf. Wittfogel, p. 373.
24 I am obliged here to refer the reader to the chapter on Historical Materialism in *Marxism*, pp. 141ff., for a discussion of Marx's methodology. (The originality of his approach, and the basic difference between his theory and the unsystematic hints thrown out by his predecessors, seems to me to have been understressed by Wittfogel.)
25 Cf. *Die deutsche Ideologie, MEGA*, I/5, 11ff.
26 Ibid.
27 Ibid., p. 12.

immobile private property develops, but as an abnormal form subordinated to communal property. The citizens of the state possess power over their labouring slaves only collectively, and for this reason alone they are tied to the form of communal ownership. It is the joint private property (*das gemeinschaftliche Privateigentum*) of the active citizens who are compelled *vis-à-vis* the slaves to remain in this primitive (*naturwüchsige*) manner of association. Hence the entire organization of society based thereupon, and therewith the power of the people, decays in the same degree in which especially immobile private property develops. The division of labour is more highly developed. We already find the contrast of town and country. . . . The class relationship as between citizens and slaves is fully developed.[28]

Marx notes as a possible objection that 'the fact of conquest appears to contradict this whole conception of history', and goes on to demonstrate that 'for the conquering barbarian people, war itself is . . . a regular form of intercourse, which is exploited all the more energetically the more the growth of population together with the traditional . . . primitive mode of production arouses the demand for new means of production'.[29] This organization finds its ultimate development in Roman society, where 'slavery remains the basis of the entire production' and the plebeians 'stationed between free citizens and slaves never got beyond a *Lumpenproletariat*'. It is succeeded by the 'third form' of property, namely, 'feudal or estate ownership'.[30] In other words, by the European middle ages.

In 1845–6 Marx had not yet discovered Oriental society and the 'Asiatic mode'; consequently he mentions only three pre-modern stages: tribal society is succeeded by classical antiquity founded on slavery, and the latter by European feudalism. By 1859 the *Preface* to the *Critique of Political Economy* presents four stages corresponding to different forms of property: Asiatic society, antiquity, feudalism, and modern bourgeois society. Tribal society has disappeared, to be subsequently resurrected by Engels.[31] Now the 1859 work is based on the unpublished *Grundrisse* of 1857–8, and when we turn to this much-neglected source we obtain some light on how Marx had in the meantime come to regard the relationship of the Orient and the 'Asiatic mode' to primitive tribal society on the one hand, and to classical antiquity and European feudalism on the other. His economic studies had acquainted him with the researches of the British school, and what we now get is a picture in which the skeleton of the 'materialist conception of history' is fleshed out with economics.

28 Ibid., p. 12.
29 Ibid., pp. 12–13.
30 Ibid., p. 13.
31 Cf. the latter's *Origin of the Family* (1884). In passing it may be observed that Marx's sketch of 1845–6 supplies a very realistic hint at the emergence of slavery from within the tribal organization. Compare this with Engels's account of how and why 'the old classless gentile society' with its 'simple moral grandeur' succumbs to 'civilized' pressure from outside; cf. *Selected Works*, vol. II, p. 231.

True to his method, the approach remains historical. Marx begins by asking what are the 'forms which precede capitalist production',[32] and he replies that the historical presupposition of the latter is the 'separation of free labour from the objective preconditions of its realization. . . . Hence above all separation of the toiler from the soil as his natural laboratory: thus dissolution of small free landed property, as well as of the joint (*gemeinschaftlichen*) landed property resting upon the Oriental commune.'[33] 'In the first form of this landed property there appears a primitive (*naturwüchsige*) commonwealth as the precondition: (the) family and its extension to the tribe . . . or a combination of tribes. . . .' 'Tribal community (*die Stammgemeinschaft*), the natural community, appears not as the result but as the precondition of joint appropriation . . . and utilization of the soil.' 'The earth is the great laboratory, the arsenal, which provides the means as well as the materials of work, and likewise the location, the basis, of the community.'[34] The individual participates in ownership of the soil and the instruments of production only insofar as he is a member of this primitive commonwealth held together by the ties of consanguinity.

The real appropriation through the process of labour occurs under these presuppositions which are themselves not the product of labour, but appear as its natural or divine preconditions. This form, based on the same primitive relationship, can realize itself in many different ways. Thus it is not contradicted by the fact that in most of the Asiatic patterns (*Grundformen*) the encompassing unity, which stands above all these small communities, appears as the superior or as the sole proprietor, (and) the real communities only as hereditary possessors. Since the unity is the true owner and the real precondition of common ownership, it can appear as a particular something (*als ein Besonderes*) above the many real particular communities, where the individual is then in fact without property, or property . . . appears as though mediated for him through a grant by the total unity (*der Gesamteinheit*) – which is realized in the despot as the father of the many communities – to the individual through the intermediacy of the particular community. The surplus product . . . thus belongs inherently to this supreme unity. In the midst of Oriental despotism, and of the absence of ownership (*Eigentumslosigkeit*) which juridically seems to obtain therein, there thus exists in fact as the basis this tribal or communal ownership, generally produced by a combination of manufacture and agriculture within the small community, which thus becomes entirely self-sustaining and contains within itself all the conditions of reproduction and surplus production. Part of its surplus labour belongs to the higher unity which at last exists as a person, and this surplus labour makes its appearance both in tribute, etc., and in common labours for the glorification of the unity: in part the real despot, in part the imaginary tribal being, the god.[35]

32 *Grundrisse*, p. 375.
33 Ibid.
34 Ibid., pp. 375–6.
35 Ibid., pp. 376–7.

This kind of common ownership, held together at the top by the 'higher unity which at last exists as a person', appears under different historical variants: either the small communities maintain a separate existence and the individual works his plot independently, together with the members of his family; or again,

> the unity may extend to communalism at work itself, which may be a formalized system, as in Mexico, notably in Peru, among the ancient Celts, (and) some Indian tribes. Further, the communal form (*die Gemeinschaftlichkeit*) within the tribal organization may appear realized in a head of the tribal family, or rather as the mutual interrelationship of the heads of families. Thence either a more despotic or more democratic form of this commonwealth. The common preconditions of genuine appropriation through labour, *waterworks* (underlined by Marx), very important among the Asiatic people, means of communication, etc., thus appear as a work of the superior unity, the despotic government suspended above the small communities. Towns come into existence here only where there is a particularly favourable location for foreign trade; or where the head of state and his satraps exchange their revenue (surplus product) against labour, expend it as labour-funds.[36]

As against this centralized system – historically typified above all by the various Oriental despotisms – Graeco-Roman antiquity, with its development of private property in land, represents what Marx describes as 'the second form' wherein the original communal (tribal) organization raises itself to a higher socio-historical level. The lengthy process whereby the urban patriciate of independent landowners, which here monopolizes political power, builds up its peculiar institutions (ultimately resting upon slave labour, and constant war to acquire more slaves) and eventually brings about its own downfall, is described with many fascinating details, and – quite in accordance with Hegel, but also with Niebuhr and nineteenth-century historiography generally – the decline and fall of antiquity leads straight on to the Germanic middle ages:

'An (other) form of ownership by the labouring individuals, self-sustaining members of the community, of the natural conditions of their work, is the *German*. Unlike the specifically Oriental form, the member of the community is not as such a co-owner of the communal property . . . nor, unlike the Roman or Greek form . . . is the soil occupied by the community. . . .' (follows a brief analysis of the *ager publicus* as the specifically Roman institution, whereby the individual Roman citizen exercises his sovereign private ownership over a particular area of Roman soil).[37] As against these earlier forms, 'the German community' – which is treated by Marx as the original cell of the medieval body politic – represents something new: 'Ancient classical history is a history of cities, but of cities founded upon landed property and agriculture; Asiatic history is a kind of indifferent union of town and country (the great cities are to

36 Ibid., p. 377.
37 *Grundrisse* pp. 380–1.

be regarded merely as princely camps, as superfetations above the economic construction proper); the middle ages (German age) starts from the countryside as the seat of history, whose further development then proceeds through the antagonism of town and country; modern (history) is urbanization of the land, not as in antiquity ruralization of the town.'[38] Among the Germans, the coming-together of the clan chiefs does not subvert their original independence: 'The community appears as union, not as unity (*als Vereinigung, nicht als Verein*)', the (originally tribal, later feudal) landowners constituting themselves as 'independent subjects'.[39] 'The community does not therefore in fact exist as a *state* . . . as in antiquity, because it does not exist as a *city*. For the community to come into real existence, the free landed proprietors must come together in a meeting, whereas, e.g., in Rome it existed apart from these meetings, in the being of the city itself and the officials standing at its head.'[40] True, the medieval Germans also had their *ager publicus*, their commons, but it did not, as in Rome, appear 'as the peculiar economic existence of the state, side by side with the private owners'. It merely served as a 'supplement to individual ownership', and thus represents the sharpest possible contrast to the 'Asiatic form' where the individual has 'no ownership, only possession';[41] but it also contrasts sharply with the Graeco-Roman system, where the city has a life of its own, being the collective organization and quasi-ideal representation of the citizens in their public capacity, as distinct from their private existence. Thus, in the European middle ages, private property predominates from the start. 'The community exists only in the mutual relation of these individual landowners.'[42] Our modern liberties (Marx might have added, but did not) have their roots in the Germanic forests.

What he does add is an extremely interesting and subtle analysis of tribal and communal ownership in antiquity, interlarded with polemical excursions against Proudhon[43] which need not concern us here. When he returns to his original theme – tribal organization as the source of the subsequent threefold differentiation into Oriental, Graeco-Roman, and German-medieval forms of private and common ownership – it is to emphasize once more that the tribal system, 'wherein the community originally dissolves itself', recognizes no property save that held by members of the tribe, so that conquered tribes are automatically deprived of it. 'Slavery and serfdom are thus only further developments of the property rooted in the tribal system. They necessarily modify all its forms', though least of all in the 'Asiatic form', with its 'self-sustaining union of manufacture and agriculture on which this form

38 Ibid., p. 382.
39 Ibid., p. 383.
40 Ibid.
41 Ibid.
42 Ibid., p. 384.
43 Ibid., p. 384–92.

rests'.[44] What Marx describes as 'the general slavery of the Orient' (as distinct from the personal slavery of classical antiquity) appears as a special case of the institution of property. The latter – 'in its Asiatic, Slav, antique, German, form'[45] – originally signifies 'the relation of the labouring (producing) ... subject to the conditions of his production or reproduction'.[46] Historically this relationship takes different forms, depending upon the existence of the individual 'as a member of a tribe or community (whose property he is up to a certain point)': an interesting hint which hardly squares with the rather more idyllic picture subsequently painted by Engels. Man originally makes his appearance on earth as part of a primitive collective: 'a generic being, tribal being, herd animal – though by no means a *zoon politikon* in the political sense'.[47] He individualizes himself through the historical process, which is primarily a process of evolving various forms of communal and private property, i.e., various ways of organizing his social intercourse with nature and the – natural or artificial – preconditions of work. The different forms of this metabolism correspond to different stages of society, among which Oriental society is historically closer to man's primitive origins, having conserved some elements of primitive communism 'in the midst of Oriental despotism'. Hence the succession of stages – Asiatic, antique, feudal, modern – mirrors the gradual dissolution of the 'primitive unity', and the evolution of private ownership properly so called. The forcible disruption of the Indian or Chinese village community by European capital completes the process by rendering it truly global.

V

With this historical sketch in mind we can now return to our starting-point and try to establish whether Marx's and Engels's utterances on the subject of Oriental society are reducible to a consistent pattern.[48]

The picture in some ways is a puzzling one. Reference has already been made to the gradual change in Marx's attitude towards the Asian village community and its resistance to the battering-rams of Western capitalism. Now when one turns to the other structural element of the 'Asiatic mode of

44 Ibid., p. 392.
45 Ibid., p. 395.
46 Ibid.
47 Ibid., pp. 395–6.
48 I express a mere personal opinion when I say that the argument outlined in pp. 375–96 of the *Grundrisse* seems to me to be among the most brilliant and incisive of Marx's writings. Unfortunately it remained a mere sketch and, what is worse, it did not see the light until 1939–41. Had it been published around 1900, instead of remaining unknown until our days, one may suppose that Max Weber and his school would have found even better reason for relating themselves to Marx's researches. Marx in fact anticipates a good deal of what Weber had to say about Oriental society.

production', the centralized governmental despotism, it would seem as though Marx and Engels gradually deepened their hostility to this form of rule, to the point of discovering some positive virtues not only in private property but even in European feudalism and the Germanic middle ages. How else account for Marx's 1859 statement about 'Asiatic, ancient, feudal, and modern bourgeois modes of production' being 'progressive epochs in the economic formation of society'? It must be remembered that these words were written shortly after he had composed his unpublished draft of 1857–8, with its quasi-Hegelian stress on the element of personal freedom inherent in the rude institutions of the European middle ages. It must also be recalled that for Marx 'progressive' does not signify 'whatever happens to be going on', as it later did for his more thoughtless followers. 'Progress' in his sense stands for the unfolding of man's dormant powers. European feudalism is 'progressive' compared with Asiatic or Graeco-Roman society because thanks to its relatively healthy starting-point it embodies new potentialities of growth and human development; in Hegel's terminology, it represents 'a new principle'. These potentialities clearly have to do with a circumstance to which Marx alludes in passing in the *Grundrisse*: the fact that among the Germans political power did not at first exist separately from the individuals, but was simply the result of joint decisions taken in public. Engels was subsequently to go further by implying that the German barbarians rejuvenated Europe by infusing the remnants of their clan organization into the decaying fabric of the Roman Empire.[49] Sound Teutonic orthodoxy, one might say, as well as containing an indubitable amount of truth.[50] But exactly how does it relate to the more strictly theoretical concepts formulated by Marx and Engels?

There is no question that both men maintained and even accentuated their original aversion to Oriental rule considered as a political system. As we have seen, their first tentative utterances go back to the 1850s, when Marx still inclined on occasion to play off the moral superiority of the decaying Confucian empire against the crude materialist aims of the encroaching Europeans. These polemical sideswipes are, however, scarcely to be taken seriously. They relate back to the familiar eighteenth-century habit of contrasting the virtuous Chinese with the hypocritical Europeans: an amiable fantasy which Marx commonly ranked with other childish naïveties of the Rousseauist age. When he speaks as a theorist, the term 'semi-Asiatic' carries connotations which are both precise and unflattering. Moreover, it was gradually extended to Russia and became the standard reproach addressed to the Government of that country. In this respect Engels took the lead[51] but Marx followed suit in contrasting 'Russia' with 'Europe',[52] and thereafter consistently referred to the Tsarist government as a

---

49 *Origin of the Family*; cf. *Works*, vol. II, p. 277.
50 Cf. Marc Bloch, *Feudal Society* (London, 1961), pp. 145ff.
51 The article in the *New York Tribune* of 19 April 1853, in which Russia is first described as 'semi-Asiatic', was signed by Marx, but actually written by Engels; cf. *Gesammelte Werke*, vol. 9, p. 23.
52 NYDT, 5 August 1853; cf. *Gesammelte Werke*, vol. 9, p. 215.

despotism suspended above an unfree peasantry. The references are too numerous and familiar to need citing. Later in 1875 we find Engels classing Russia with the 'Asiatic mode' in an article where incidentally he comments on the village community.[53] The same point is briefly made in a better-known work, the *Anti-Dühring*: 'Where the ancient communes have continued to exist, they have for thousands of years formed the basis of the most barbarous form of state, Oriental despotism, from India to Russia.'[54] Lastly, there are Engels's writings of the 1890s, in which it is indeed suggested that Tsarist despotism is crumbling (and even that 'the young Russian bourgeoisie has the State entirely in its power'), but here too the surviving 'despotic autocracy of the Tsar' is related to 'the old communistic village community' – now in process of breaking up.[55]

In between, he and Marx had, however, given qualified support to the notion that the village community might become the starting-point of a socialist development. How was this to be accomplished? We have two statements by Marx, both regrettably brief. In his letter to Vera Zasulich of March 8, 1881, we find him ready to go some distance in accepting the Populist idea that the resistance of the village community to private capitalism might offer the emerging socialist movement a unique opportunity; though after stating that 'this community is the *point d'appui* of social regeneration in Russia', he is at pains to add that 'the pernicious influences which attack it from all sides' must be eliminated, so as 'to assure it of normal conditions for a spontaneous development'.[56] Then there is the preface to the Russian edition of the *Communist Manifesto*, dated January 21, 1882, with the quasi-Trotskyist suggestion that 'if the Russian Revolution becomes the signal for a proletarian revolution in the West, so that both complement each other, the present Russian common ownership of land may serve as the starting-point for a communist development'.[57] These hints point in the direction of a controversy which was destined to convulse the Russian socialist movement for decades, but they do not contribute much to the strictly theoretical concept of the 'Asiatic mode'. At most they imply that for Marx socialism offered a way out of the uncomfortable dilemma suggested by his researches into Oriental society: the

53 'Such a complete isolation of the individual (village) communities from each other . . . is the natural foundation of Oriental despotism, and from India to Russia this societal form, wherever it prevailed, has always produced despotism and has always found therein its supplement.' Cf. *Internationales aus dem Volksstaat (1871–75)*, (Berlin, 1894), p. 56.
54 *Anti-Dühring* (German edn) (Moscow, 1935), p. 165; cf. Foreign Languages Publishing House edn, (Moscow, 1954), p. 251.
55 Cf. *Volksstaat*, pp. 61–72.
56 Full text in *Marx–Engels Archiv*, vol. I, (Frankfurt, 1926), pp. 309–42; cf. Blackstock and Hoselitz, *The Russian Menace to Europe* (London, 1953), pp. 275ff.
57 *Selected Works*, vol. I, p. 24. In his 1894 gloss on this text, Engels pours a good deal of water into this heady wine; cf. 'Russia and the social revolution reconsidered', in Blackstock and Hoselitz, op. cit., pp. 229ff.

element of personal freedom, so plainly lacking in that society and equally so plainly at the roots of West European feudalism (and capitalism), might enter the system after the collapse of its 'political superstructure'. In different terms, the approaching fall of Tsarism presented an opportunity to develop the healthy core of the ancient communal organization, instead of disrupting it completely in the interest of capitalism.

It is noteworthy that Marx – and to some extent Engels – saw such an opportunity latent in Russia, but not in India or China: presumably because Russia was only 'semi-Asiatic'. It was not a genuinely European country, but it none the less possessed the germ of development, whereas 'the East' proper was stagnant. For the same reason, unfortunately, Russia was a permanent menace to Europe, and even its internal progress tended to make it more dangerous, because more aggressive and powerful.[58] The way out lay in a form of Europeanization which did away with the autocracy without – as the liberals would have it – simultaneously introducing Western capitalism. The commune – or what was left of it – was to be preserved as the future basis of a socialist society, or at any rate as an element of such a society. With this analysis the Populists were in agreement, and those among them who in the 1880s and 1890s gradually transformed themselves into Marxists could feel that they had not renounced the ideals and values which had originally brought them to socialism. Conversely, Marx for his part might think that by relating socialism back to pre-individualist, communal, forms of ownership, he had closed the circle of his argument: bourgeois society, so far from being 'natural' and permanent, was revealed to be simply one socio-economic formation among others.

The unsolved, or half-solved, problem lay in the genesis of the Oriental State. In his writings of the early 1850s Marx had stressed both its centralized character and its independence from the vast mass of scattered village communes. In the 1857–8 draft the roots of despotism in general are traced back to the tribal organization, with its tendency to 'realize' its internal unity in a personal ruler. Subsequently we find references to 'the state' as 'the supreme landlord', but no analysis of the means whereby the despotic sovereign builds up his power by surrounding himself with an administrative apparatus. From all this it is not difficult to conclude that Marx for some reason shirked the problem of the bureaucracy. Yet the latter's role is frequently alluded to in his other writings, notably in his diatribes against Bonapartism. His failure to make more of it in connection with the 'Asiatic mode' remains an oddity. Perhaps the

---

58 Cf. Marx, *Herr Vogt* (1859), in *Gesammelte Werke*, vol. 14, especially pp. 497–8: 'Incidentally, the emancipation of the serfs *in the sense of the Russian government* would multiply the aggressiveness of Russia a hundredfold. Its aim is simply the completion of the autocracy through the elimination of the barriers hitherto opposed to the great autocrat by the many little autocrats of the serf-based Russian gentry; as well as by the self-governing peasant communes whose material basis, the common ownership, is to be destroyed by the so-called emancipation.'

fact that he thought of it as a 'caste' as distinct from a 'class' of society lessened his interest in the subject; but though a possible explanation this is hardly an adequate defence.[59]

In his *Theories of Surplus Value* (1861–3) Marx quotes Richard Jones to the effect that 'the surplus revenue from the soil, the only revenues except those of the peasants of any considerable amount, were (in Asia, and more especially in India) distributed by the state and its officers'.[60] Taken together with his own previous observations on the importance of centrally controlled irrigation in Asia, and with Engels's subsequent remarks (mainly in the *Anti-Dühring*) about the emergence of a ruling class from within primitive society, the elements of a complete theory of Oriental despotism appear to be present. Why were they not fully exploited? Perhaps an indirect answer is afforded by a somewhat lengthy passage from Engels which demonstrates at once the enormous advance in understanding he and Marx had actually effected in relation to earlier writers, and the point where their investigations tailed off into an uncritical acceptance of the prevalent Victorian attitude in regard to state and society:

> It is not necessary for us to examine here how this independence of social functions in relation to society increased with time until it developed into domination over society; how he who was originally the servant, where conditions were favourable changed gradually into the lord; how this lord, depending on the conditions, emerged as an Oriental despot or satrap, the dynast of a Greek tribe, chieftain of a Celtic clan, and so on; to what extent he subsequently had recourse to force in the course of this transformation; and how finally the individual rulers united into a ruling class. Here we are only concerned with establishing the fact that the exercise of a social function was everywhere the basis of political supremacy; and further, that political supremacy has existed for any length of time only when it discharged its social functions. However great the number of despotisms which rose and fell in Persia and India, each was fully aware that above all it was the entrepreneur responsible for the collective maintenance of irrigation throughout the river valleys, without which no agriculture was possible there. It was reserved for the enlightened English to lose sight of this in India; they let the irrigation canals and sluices fall into decay, and are now at last discovering, through the regularly recurring famines, that they have neglected the one activity which might have made their rule in India at least as legitimate as that of their predecessors.[61]

Setting aside the polemical glance at the British government in India, what does this passage suggest, if not that Engels – and by implication Marx, since he

---

59 For a critique of Marx's and Engels's views on the subject of Oriental despotism see Wittfogel, *Oriental Despotism*, pp. 380ff.; it seems to me, though, that Wittfogel overdoes the theme of Marx's alleged theoretical backsliding in his later writings. The most one can say is that the earlier suggestions were not systematically developed.

60 R. Jones, *Literary Remains, Constituting of Lectures and Tracts on Political Economy* (London, 1859), pp. 448ff.; cf. Marx, *Theorien über den Mehrwert* (Stuttgart, 1921), vol. III, p. 501.

61 *Herr Eugen Dühring's Revolution in Science* (Moscow, 1954), p. 249.

had seen the text before publication – thought of the 'ruling class' in political terms, as the governing caste responsible for the exercise of those superior functions without which social life must come to a stop? The *Anti-Dühring* admittedly is a semi-popular tract primarily addressed to a working-class audience, but if Engels on this occasion expresses himself rather loosely, he does not contradict his or Marx's previous utterances. Political power arises from the exercise of a necessary social function: it then becomes independent of society (and of its own origins), but retains its roots in a collective need which it serves, *tant bien que mal*, until the social organism itself changes its character so as to require a different kind of 'superstructure'. The state, in short, is an epiphenomenon. Although it does have a life of its own, it is subservient to the real basic needs of society; consequently the long-run process can be analysed in terms of the latter.

In passing, it may be observed that Engels in the above passage identifies the 'ruling class' so completely with the governing caste as to provoke the rejoinder that on his assumptions Bismarck might have claimed to be a more legitimate representative of German society than the elected Reichstag. It is not at all clear how Engels would have met the argument that the political élite of a given society is, and must always remain, something different from, and superior to, the socially dominant class. It is true that in nineteenth-century Germany – and to some extent in Victorian England – the two coincided, inasmuch as the landed aristocracy had retained its political and social role, while steadily yielding economic power to the bourgeoisie. But this symbiosis was a peculiarity of European history, and its roots – as Marx observed in his 1857–8 sketch – lay in the relatively free and autonomous development of public life during the early middle ages. The Orient had never experienced anything of the kind, and since Engels had put his finger on the crucial role of the state – i.e. the bureacracy – in administering the central economic functions, it was really incumbent upon him to explain in what sense the governing caste was a 'ruling class'. Failure to clarify this matter was bound to obscure the entire problem of political power and the state in general.

At this point, however, we are on the threshold of the modern age, and for the same reason at the end of our brief investigation into the manner in which Marx and Engels, at the peak of the Victorian era, saw the problem of political power in an Eastern setting. It can hardly surprise a contemporary reader to find that they did not seriously examine the possibility of despotic rule in an industrial society: in other words, the problem of what we have learned to call totalitarianism. To have done so would have meant to overstep the presuppositions they shared with their contemporaries: chief among them the confident belief that in Europe, anyhow, the despotic reorganization of society from the top was excluded by the very nature of that society. If we have in recent years begun to doubt this certainty, we may nevertheless extract what comfort we can from Marx's belief that the inner principle of Western historical development has from the start been quite different from that of the East or of Graeco-

Roman antiquity. For my own part I am inclined to think that – in this as in most other matters – he was right, and that we are entitled to look upon European history as an evolution propelled by a dialectic of its own, to which there is no parallel in Oriental history. Needless to say, this Hegelian–Marxist view is incompatible with the notion that European, or Western, society is subject to a general law of growth and decay (or 'challenge and response' to employ the currently fashionable jargon) applicable to *all* major civilizations. On the contrary, it insists upon the West's uniqueness; and to that extent the present writer has no hesitation in calling himself a Hegelian.

Part II Science, Philosophy and Praxis

9   Marx's Concept of Man

Gajo Petrović

People often doubt the legitimacy of the question 'What is man?' in its general form. This question, they say, is sometimes posed by certain philosophies, but it is a false question, and it cannot be asked by Marxism. Different special sciences explore different aspects of man's activity; no aspect remains unexplored; and all 'special' sciences together give a complete picture of man. On the other hand, man in general, man as such, does not exist; there is only a concrete man of a concrete society; slave owner or slave, landlord or serf, bourgeois or worker.

Man is not, however, the sum of his parts or aspects, but an integral being; and no special science does or can answer the question of what he is as an integral being, that is, what makes him man and each of his activities or aspects human. Although man is not always and everywhere the same, although he historically changes, there is something that allows us to call a proletarian as well as a capitalist, a landlord as well as a slave-owner, a man.

What makes a man – man? What, if anything, makes somebody more and somebody less a man?

If Marx had bypassed these questions, they would still demand an answer. But nothing is more false than the assumption that Marx condemned discussions about man in general.

It is unnecessary to quote texts from the *Economic and Philosophical Manuscripts* because it is well known that Marx speaks there about man as man. But it is sometimes held that Marx later came to the conclusion that all general speculations about man are inadmissible. In support of this assumption some passages from *German Ideology* can be quoted. But is *German Ideology* Marx's last word in philosophy? Did not he also write *Capital?*

According to *Capital*, the labour process is

From *Marx in the Mid-Twentieth Century* by Gajo Petrović, pp. 72–4, 76–81. Copyright © 1967 by Gajo Petrović. Reprinted by permission of Doubleday and Company, Inc.

human action with a view to the production of use-values, appropriation of natural substances to human requirements; it is the necessary condition for effecting exchange of matter between man and Nature; it is the everlasting nature-imposed condition of human existence, and therefore is independent of every social phase of that existence, or rather, is common to every such phase. It was, therefore, not necessary to represent our labourer in connection with other labourers; man and his labour on one side, Nature and its materials on the other, sufficed. As the taste of porridge does not tell you who grew the oats, no more does this simple process tell you of itself what are the social conditions under which it is taking place, whether under the slave-owner's brutal lash, or the anxious eye of the capitalist, whether Cincinnatus carries it on in tilling his modest farm or a savage in killing wild animals with stones.[1]

Marx in *Capital*, then, stresses that we can speak not only about labourer, capitalist and slave-owner, but also about man, labour and nature in general.

In another place in *Capital* Marx writes against the Utilitarian Bentham:

> To know what is useful for a dog, one must study dog nature. This nature is not to be deduced from the principle of utility. Applying this to man, he who would criticize all human acts, movements, relations, etc., by the principle of utility, must first deal with human nature in general and then with human nature as modified in each historical epoch. Bentham makes short work of it. With the driest naïvete he takes the modern shopkeeper, especially the English shopkeeper, as the normal man. Whatever is useful to this queer normal man, and to his world, is absolutely useful. This yardstick, then, he applies to past, present and future.[2]

Marx thinks that a dog has its dog nature and man his human nature, but that man differs from dog by having a 'human nature in general' as well as one 'modified in each historical epoch'. He reproaches Bentham for regarding the modern shopkeeper as a normal man, ignoring in this way general human nature and its historical development.

Marx not only 'permits' discussion of human nature in general, in *Capital* he criticizes bourgeois society precisely because in it universal human nature cannot express itself, because in it 'a general or a banker plays a great part, but mere man [man as man], on the other hand, a very shabby part'.[3]

In accordance with this, Marx in the third volume of *Capital* opposes to capitalism a society in which the socialized man, the associated producers, will produce under conditions 'most adequate to their human nature and most worthy of it'.[4]

Marx thus without any hesitation speaks about human nature and about man

1 Marx, *Capital*, vol. I, pp. 204–5.
2 Ibid., p. 668.
3 Ibid., p. 51.
4 Ibid., vol. III, p. 954.

as man. [. . .] Just as the sense of Marx's question about man has been misunderstood, so has his answer to this question.

Expounding different conceptions of man, Max Scheler mentions as one of the five basic conceptions the positivistic, according to which man is an instinctive being, and as one of three sub-classes of positivistic conception the 'Marxist' or 'economic' conception, according to which man is determined by his impulse for food. He obviously does not know that, according to Marx, animals 'produce only under the compulsion of direct physical need, while man produces when he is free from physical need and only truly produces in freedom from such need'.[5]

A view similar to Scheler's is also found in some 'Marxists' who attribute to Marx Benjamin Franklin's definition of man as a tool-making animal. It is true that Marx quotes Franklin's definition with a certain sympathy in the first volume of *Capital*. But those who have noticed this often overlook the fact that in the same volume Marx characterizes this definition not as his, but as typically American. Of Aristotle's definition of man as a political animal he comments: 'Strictly, Aristotle's definition is that man is by nature a town-citizen. This is quite as characteristic of ancient classical society as Franklin's definition of man as a tool-making animal is characteristic of Yankeedom'.[6]

Marx believes that Aristotle's and Franklin's definitions of man are important – like Hegel, he thinks that no fundamental philosophical thought can be either simply false or worthless – but neither Aristotle's nor Franklin's definition is his.

When he rejects the traditional conception of man as a rational animal Marx does not do so simply because this gives reason the primary place, but first of all because he considers that neither reason nor political activity, neither production of tools nor any other special activity or property can be man's essence. Man is not a mechanical sum of his 'spheres' (economic, political, moral, artistic, etc.), and even in so far as it is possible to distinguish such 'spheres' they do not maintain for eternity the same relationships. Therefore, what makes a man man is not his 'main sphere', but his whole way of Being, the general structure of his relationship toward the world and toward himself. This way of Being, which is peculiar to man, Marx designates by the word 'praxis'. Man, for Marx, is the being of 'praxis'.

When we define man as praxis all questions are not answered; many only begin. First of all, what is praxis? Praxis is human activity. But a certain kind of activity is also peculiar to all animals. What is it that distinguishes praxis as human activity from animal activity? In answering this question people often lose what they gained in defining man as a being of praxis. Difficulties in answering the question are seen in Marx also.

About the activity of man and animal we read in Marx's *Economical and Philosophical Manuscripts* of 1844:

5 Fromm, *Marx's Concept of Man*, p. 102.
6 *Capital*, vol. I, p. 358.

The animal is one with its life activity. It does not distinguish the activity from itself.
It is *its activity*. But man makes his life activity itself an object of his will and
consciousness. He has a conscious life activity. It is not a determination with which
he is completely identified. Conscious life activity distinguishes man from the life
activity of animals.[7]

One can agree that man's life activity is conscious, whereas animals' is not. But
can one agree that it is first of all consciousness (or perhaps even only
consciousness) that distinguishes man's activity (praxis) from animal activity? If
man differs from animal by praxis, and if praxis differs from animal activity by
being conscious, then man differs from animal by his consciousness and we are
back to the traditional definition of man as a rational animal.

Is this unavoidable, or is it possible to give an interpretation of praxis that
would determine its general structure and also contain its determination as a
conscious and free activity?

I think that such is the interpretation of praxis as a universal-creative
self-creative activity by which man transforms and creates his world and
himself. Exactly such an interpretation prevails in Karl Marx.

In *Economic and Philosophical Manuscripts* he writes, for example:

> Animals construct only in accordance with the standards and needs of the species to
> which they belong, while man knows how to produce in accordance with the
> standards of every species and knows how to apply the appropriate standard to the
> object. Thus man constructs also in accordance with the laws of beauty.

It is precisely in his work upon the objective world that man proves himself as a
species-being. This production is his active species life. By means of it nature
appears as *his* work and *his* reality.

> The object of labour is, therefore the *objectification of man's species life*; he no longer
> reproduces himself merely intellectually, as in consciousness, but actively and in a
> real sense, and he sees his own reflection in a world that he has constructed.[8]

The interpretation of praxis as a universal-creative self-creative activity contains its determination as a free, conscious activity. From this conception, the
conception of man as a social history also follows. If man is a creative
self-creative being that constantly creates and changes himself and his world,
he is necessarily not always the same.

Animal species are also not always the same. But whereas an animal changes
by adapting to and transforming its environment without any plan or purpose,
man can by his creativity change purposefully his world and himself. 'In short,'
says Engels, 'the animal merely *uses* external nature and brings about changes in

7   Fromm, *Marx's Concept of Man*, p. 101.
8   Ibid., p. 102.

it simply by his presence; man by his changes makes it serve his ends, masters it.[9]

Therefore only man has a history. One can speak only figuratively of a 'history' of the animal kingdom. But man's history is not only the history of the transformation of nature; it is also and in the first place the history of man's self-creation: 'Since, however, for socialist man, *the whole of what is called world history* is nothing but the creation of man by human labour, and the emergence of nature for man, he therefore has the evident and irrefutable proof of his *self-creation*, of his own *origins*.'[10]

Just because man is praxis and history, he is also the future. If man's essence is universal-creative and self-creative activity by which he historically creates his world and himself, then, if he does not want to cease being man, he can never interrupt the process of his self-creation. This means that man can never be completely finished, that he is not man when he lives only in the present and in the contemplation of the past, but only in so far as he in the present realizes his future. Man is man if he realizes his historically created human possibilities.

At this point one can see clearly the difference between Marx and Hegel. For Hegel, man is also an active being, but he conceives man's activity primarily as an activity of self-consciousness, the final goal of which is the absolute knowledge of the absolute reality, a definitive completion of man and absolute. Absolute, which without man is only *an sich*, becomes through man *für sich*. Man's philosophical knowledge, which is at the same time the self-knowledge of the Absolute, means the end of human history. Man can be completed, and in Hegel's philosophy he is completed. For that reason he can also be fully described.

For Marx, man is an active being, but his activity is not the self-knowledge of the Absolute, but the transformation and creation of the world and of man himself. Therefore for Marx man can be never completed and never finally defined.

For that reason Marx's conception of man can never remain only a conception. Only to conceive man would mean only to conceive what man already was. But man is not only what he has been; he is in the first place what he can and ought to be. Marx's turn to praxis follows from this in the sense that his conception of man cannot remain a mere conception, but is also a criticism of alienated man who does not realize his human possibilities and a humanistic programme of struggle for humanness. Marx's conception of man can thus not be separated from his humanistic theory of alienation and de-alienation.

9   F. Engels, *Dialectics of Nature*, Foreign Publishing House (Moscow, 1954), p. 241.
10 Fromm, *Marx's Concept of Man*, p. 139.

10   Sociology and the Philosophy of Praxis

Antonio Gramsci

Historical materialism and sociology

One preliminary observation to be made is this: that the title does not correspond to the content of the book.[1] 'Theory of the philosophy of praxis' ought to mean a logical and coherent systematic treatment of the philosophical concepts generically known under the title of historical materialism (many of which are spurious and come from other sources and as such require to be criticized and eliminated). The first chapters should treat the following questions: What is philosophy? In what sense can a conception of the world be called a philosophy? How has philosophy been conceived hitherto? Does the philosophy of praxis renew this conception? What is meant by a 'speculative' philosophy? Would the philosophy of praxis ever be able to have a speculative form? What are the relationships between ideologies, conceptions of the world and philosophies? What is or should be the relationship between theory and practice? How do traditional philosophies conceive of this relationship? etc.

From Antonio Gramsci, *Selections from the Prison Notebooks*, edited and translated by Quintin Hoare and Geoffrey Nowell Smith (London: Lawrence and Wishart Ltd, 1971), pp. 425–36. Reprinted by permission of the publisher.

1   The title [of a book by Nikolai Bukharin] is *Theory of Historical Materialism*, and the sub-title *A Popular Manual of Marxist Sociology*. Gramsci goes on to argue below that only the sub-title is in any way an exact description of the content of Bukharin's work, and even then only 'on condition that one gives an extremely restricted meaning to the term "sociology"'. It should be noted that Gramsci himself vacillates slightly in his notion of what sociology is. His main targets would appear to be empiricism and positivism applied to the science of society, and the reflection of these doctrines, in the guise of 'materialism', in Bukharin's *Manual*. [Tr.] [Bukharin's book was published in English under the title *Historical Materialism: A System of Sociology*. Ed.]

The answer to these and other questions constitutes the 'theory' of the philosophy of praxis.[2]

In the *Popular Manual* there is not even a coherent justification offered of the premise implicit in the exposition and explicitly referred to elsewhere, quite casually, that the *true* philosophy is philosophical materialism and that the philosophy of praxis is purely a 'sociology'. What does this assertion really mean? If it were true, then the theory of the philosophy of praxis would be philosophical materialism. But in that case what does it mean to say that the philosophy of praxis is a sociology? What sort of thing would this sociology be? A science of politics and historiography? Or a systematic collection, classified in a particular ordered form, of purely empirical observations on the art of politics and of external canons of historical research? Answers to these questions are not to be found in the book. But only they could be a theory. Thus the connection between the general title *Theory of Historical Materialism* and the sub-title *Popular Manual of Marxist Sociology* is unjustified. The sub-title would be a more exact title, on condition that one gave an extremely restricted meaning to the term 'sociology'. In fact the question arises of what is 'sociology'. Is not sociology an attempt to produce a so-called exact (i.e. positivist) science of social facts, that is of politics and history – in other words a philosophy in embryo? Has not sociology tried to do something similar to the philosophy of praxis?[3] One must, however, be clear about this: the philosophy of praxis was born in the form of aphorisms and practical criteria for the purely accidental reason that its founder dedicated his intellectual forces to other problems, particularly economic (which he treated in systematic form); but in these practical criteria and these aphorisms is implicit an entire conception of the world, a philosophy.

Sociology has been an attempt to create a method of historical and political science in a form dependent on a pre-elaborated philosophical system, that of evolutionist positivism, against which sociology reacted, but only partially. It therefore became a tendency on its own; it became the philosophy of non-philosophers, an attempt to provide a schematic description and classification of historical and political facts, according to criteria built up on the model of natural science. It is therefore an attempt to derive 'experimentally' the laws of evolution of human society in such a way as to 'predict' that the oak tree will develop out of the acorn. Vulgar evolutionism is at the root of sociology, and sociology cannot know the dialectical principle with its passage from quantity to quality. But this passage disturbs any form of evolution and any law of

---

2 These questions are effectively those to which Gramsci himself attempts to give an answer in his own philosophical writings. [Tr.]

3 What Gramsci has in mind at this point is less the empiricism which is his most usual target than the attempts, notably by Max Weber but also by Pareto and Michels, to construct a general and comprehensive theory of man and society, under the general title (first coined by Auguste Comte) of 'sociology'. [Tr.]

uniformity understood in a vulgar evolutionist sense. In any case, any sociology presupposes a philosophy, a conception of the world, of which it is but a subordinate part. Nor should the particular internal 'logic' of the varying forms of sociology, which is what gives them a mechanical coherence, be confused with general theory, that is to say philosophy. Naturally this does not mean that the search for 'laws' of uniformity is not a useful and interesting pursuit or that a treatise of immediate observations on the art of politics does not have its purpose. But one should call a spade a spade, and present treatises of this kind for what they really are.

All these are 'theoretical' problems, while those that the author of the *Manual* considers as such are not. The questions which he poses are all of an immediate political and ideological order (understanding ideology as an intermediate phase between philosophy and day-to-day practice); they are reflections on disconnected and casual individual historical and political facts. One theoretical question arises for the author right at the beginning, when he refers to a tendency which denies that it is possible to construct a sociology of the philosophy of praxis and which maintains that this philosophy can be expressed only through concrete historical works. This objection, which is extremely important, is not resolved by the author except on the level of phrasemongering. Certainly the philosophy of praxis is realized through the concrete study of past history and through present activity to construct new history. But a theory of history and politics can be made, for even if the facts are always unique and changeable in the flux of movement of history, the concepts can be theorized. Otherwise one would not even be able to tell what movement is, or the dialectic, and one would fall back into a new form of nominalism.[4]

The reduction of the philosophy of praxis to a form of sociology has represented the crystallization of the degenerate tendency, already criticized by Engels (in the letters to two students published in the *Sozial. Akademiker*),[5] and which consists in reducing a conception of the world to a mechanical formula which gives the impression of holding the whole of history in the palm of its hand. This has provided the strongest incentive to the 'pocket-geniuses', with their facile journalistic improvizations. The experience on which the philosophy of praxis is based cannot be schematized; it is history in all its infinite variety

4 It is because he has not posed with any exactitude the question of what 'theory' is that the author has been prevented from posing the further question of what is religion and from offering a realistic historical judgement of past philosophies, all of which he presents as pure delirium and folly.

5 F. Engels. Letters to Josef Bloch and to Heinz Starkenburg, 21 September 1890 and 25 January 1894, published in *Der Sozialistischer Akademiker*, 1 and 15 October 1895. In the letter to Bloch, Engels writes: 'According to the materialist conception of history the determining moment in history is *ultimately* the production and reproduction of real life. More than this neither Marx nor I have ever asserted. If therefore somebody twists this into the statement that the economic moment is the only determining one, he transforms it into a meaningless, abstract and absurd phrase.' Both letters are in fact intended as correctives to the pseudo-Marxist reductionism which Gramsci is also concerned to attack. [Tr.]

and multiplicity, whose study can give rise to 'philology'[6] as a method of scholarship for ascertaining particular facts and to philosophy understood as a general methodology of history. This perhaps is what was meant by those writers who, as is mentioned in rather summary fashion in the first chapter of the *Manual*, deny that one can make a sociology of the philosophy of praxis and maintain rather that this philosophy lives only in particular historical essays (this assertion, in such a bald and crude form, is certainly erroneous and seems like a new and curious form of nominalism and philosophical scepticism).

To deny that one can construct a sociology, understood in the sense of a science of society, that is a science of history and politics, which is not coterminous with the philosophy of praxis itself, does not mean that one cannot build up an empirical compilation of practical observations which extend the sphere of philology as traditionally understood. If philology is the methodological expression of the importance of ascertaining and precising particular facts in their unique and unrepeatable individuality, one cannot, however, exclude the practical utility of isolating certain more general 'laws of tendency' corresponding in the political field to the laws of statistics or to the law of large numbers which have helped to advance various of the natural sciences. But the fact has not been properly emphasized that statistical laws can be employed in the science and art of politics only so long as the great masses of the population remain (or at least are reputed to remain) essentially passive, in relation to the questions which interest historians and politicians. Furthermore the extension of statistics to the science and art of politics can have very serious consequences to the extent that it is adopted for working out future perspectives and programmes of action. In the natural sciences the worst that statistics can do is produce blunders and irrelevances which can easily be corrected by further research and which in any case simply make the individual scientist who used the technique look a bit ridiculous. But in the science and art of politics it can have literally catastrophic results which do irreparable harm. Indeed in politics the assumption of the law of statistics as an essential law operating of necessity is not only a scientific error, but becomes a practical error in action. What is more it favours mental laziness and a superficiality in political programmes. It should be observed that political action tends precisely to rouse the masses from passivity, in other words to destroy the law of large numbers. So how can that law be considered a law of sociology? If one thinks about it even the demand for a planned, i.e. guided, economy is destined to break down the statistical law understood in a mechanical sense, that is statistics produced by the fortuitous putting together of an infinity of arbitrary individual acts. Planning of this kind must be based on statistics, but that is not the same thing. Human awareness

6 'Philology': Gramsci uses the word here partly in its conventional sense of the study of linguistic and historical documents (i.e. the primary sources of historiography and literary history) but partly in the sense resuscitated by Croce from the writings of Vico, which divides knowledge into philosophy as the science of the True and philology as the pursuit of the Certain. [Tr.]

replaces naturalistic 'spontaneity'. A further element which, in the art of politics, leads to the overthrow of the old naturalistic schema is the replacement by political organisms (parties) of single individuals and individual (or charismatic,[7] as Michels calls them) leaders. With the extension of mass parties and their organic coalescence with the intimate (economic-productive) life of the masses themselves, the process whereby popular feeling is standardized ceases to be mechanical and casual (that is produced by the conditioning of environmental factors and the like) and becomes conscious and critical. Knowledge and a judgement of the importance of this feeling on the part of the leaders is no longer the product of hunches backed up by the identification of statistical laws, which leaders then translate into ideas and words-as-force. (This is the rational and intellectual way and is all too often fallacious.) Rather it is acquired by the collective organism through 'active and conscious co-operation', through 'compassionality', through experience of immediate particulars, through a system which one could call 'living philology'. In this way a close link is formed between great mass, party and leading group; and the whole complex, thus articulated, can move together as 'collective man'.

Hendrik de Man's book,[8] if it has any value, has it precisely in this sense, in that he invites us to 'inform' ourselves in more detail about the real feelings of groups and individuals and not those that are assumed on the basis of sociological laws. But de Man has made no original discoveries, nor has he found any original principle which goes beyond the philosophy of praxis or scientifically proves it to be sterile or mistaken. He has elevated to the status of a scientific principle an empirical criterion of the art of politics which was already well known and had been applied, although it had perhaps been insufficiently defined and developed. But de Man has not even been able to establish the exact limits of his criterion, for he has finished up by just producing a new statistical law and, unconsciously and under another name, a new method of social mathematics and of external classification, a new abstract sociology.

Note. The so-called laws of sociology which are assumed as laws of causation (such-and-such a fact occurs because of such-and-such a law, etc.) have no causal value: they are almost always tautologies and paralogisms. Usually they are no more than a duplicate of the observed fact itself. A fact or a series of facts is described according to a mechanical process of abstract generalization, a relationship of similarity is derived from this and given the title of law and the law is then assumed to have causal value. But what novelty is there in that? The only novelty is the collective name given to a series of petty facts, but names are not an innovation. (In

7 The notion of 'charisma' as a quality which causes leaders to be followed in spite of their lack of legitimate or institutional authority derives in fact not from Michels but from Max Weber, who in turn took it from the jurist and church historian Rudolf Sohm. [Tr.]

8 *Au delà du Marxisme* (1929). [Tr.]

Michels' treatises[9] one can find a whole catalogue of similar tautological generalizations, the last and most famous being that about the 'charismatic leader'.) What is not realized is that in this way one falls into a baroque form of Platonic idealism, since these abstract laws have a strange resemblance to Plato's pure ideas which are the essence of real earthly facts.

The constituent parts of the philosophy of praxis

A systematic treatment of the philosophy of praxis cannot afford to neglect any of the constituent parts of the doctrines of its founder [Marx]. But how should this be understood? It should deal with all the general philosophical part, and then should develop in a coherent fashion all the general concepts of a methodology of history and politics and, in addition, of art, economics and ethics, finding place in the overall construction for a theory of the natural sciences. One widespread conception is that the philosophy of praxis is a pure philosophy, the science of dialectics, the other parts of it being economics and politics, and it is therefore maintained that the doctrine is formed of three constituent parts, which are at the same time the consummation and the transcending of the highest level reached around 1848 by science in the most advanced countries of Europe: classical German philosophy, English classical economics and French political activity and science. This conception, which reflects rather a generic search for historical sources than a classification drawn from the heart of the doctrine itself, cannot be set up in opposition, as a definitive scheme, to some other definition of the doctrine which is closer to reality. It will be asked whether the philosophy of praxis is not precisely and specifically a theory of history, and the answer must be that this is indeed true but that one cannot separate politics and economics from history, even the specialized aspects of political science and art and of economic science and policy. This means that, after having accomplished the principal task in the general philosophical part, which deals with the philosophy of praxis proper – the science of dialectics or the theory of knowledge, within which the general concepts of history, politics and economics are interwoven in an organic unity – it would be useful, in a popular manual, to give a general outline of each

9 See in particular 'Political Parties' (*Zur Soziologie des Parteiwesens*, 1911. English translation, from the Italian, 1915). Robert Michels (1876–1936) was a German sociologist of (originally) Social-Democratic leanings who emigrated first to Switzerland and then to Italy, where he became a naturalized citizen under the Mussolini regime. Michels is most famous for his 'iron law of oligarchy' and together with Mosca and Pareto is an originator of the theory of political elites. Despite Gramsci's evident contempt for Michels' method and distaste for his politics, it has been argued that there was a certain indirect influence of Michels and elite theory on his own theory of social and political structures in non-revolutionary periods. (See G. Galli, 'Gramsci e le teorie delle elites', in *Gramsci e la cultura contemporanea*, vol. II, pp. 201–17.) [Tr.]

moment or constituent part, even to the extent of treating them as independent and distinct sciences. On close examination it is clear that in the *Popular Manual* all these points are at least referred to, but casually and incoherently, in a quite chaotic and indistinct way, because there is no clear and precise concept of what the philosophy of praxis itself actually is.

Structure and historical movement

This fundamental point is not dealt with: how does the historical movement arise on the structural base? The problem is however referred to in Plekhanov's *Fundamentals*[10] and could be developed. This is furthermore the crux of all the questions that have arisen around the philosophy of praxis and without resolving this one cannot resolve the corresponding problem about the relationship between society and 'nature', to which the *Manual* devotes a special chapter. It would have been necessary to analyse the full import and conse- quences of the two propositions in the Preface to *A Contribution to the Critique of Political Economy* to the following effect:

1   Mankind only poses for itself such tasks as it can resolve;. . . the task itself only arises when the material conditions for its resolution already exist or at least are in the process of formation.
2   A social order does not perish until all the productive forces for which it still has room have been developed and new and higher relations of production have taken their place, and until the material conditions of the new relations have grown up within the womb of the old society. Only on this basis can all mechanism and every trace of the superstitiously 'miraculous' be eliminated, and it is on this basis that the problems of the formation of active political groups, and, in the last analysis, even the problem of the historical function of great personalities must be posed.

The intellectuals

It would be worth compiling a 'reasoned' catalogue of the men of learning whose opinions are widely quoted or contested in the book, each name to be accompanied by notes on their significance and scientific importance (this to be done also for the supporters of the philosophy of praxis who are certainly not quoted in the light of their originality and significance). In fact there are only the most passing references to the great intellectuals. The question is raised: would it not have been better to have referred only to the major intellectuals on the enemy side, leaving aside the men in the second rank, the regurgitators of second-hand phrases? One gets the impression that the author wants to combat

10 G. Plekhanov, *Fundamental Problems of Marxism*, 1908. [Tr.]

only the weakest of his adversaries and the weakest of their positions (or the ones which the weakest adversaries have maintained least adequately), in order to obtain facile verbal victories – for one can hardly speak of real victories. The illusion is created that there exists some kind of more than formal and metaphorical resemblance between an ideological and a politico-military front. In the political and military struggle it can be correct tactics to break through at the points of least resistance in order to be able to assault the strongest point with maximum forces that have been precisely made available by the elimination of the weaker auxiliaries. Political and military victories, within certain limits, have a permanent and universal value and the strategic end can be attained decisively with a general effect for everyone. On the ideological front, however, the defeat of the auxiliaries and the minor hangers-on is of all but negligible importance. Here it is necessary to engage battle with the most eminent of one's adversaries. Otherwise one confuses newspapers with books, and petty daily polemic with scientific work. The lesser figures must be abandoned to the infinite casebook of newspaper polemic.

A new science proves its efficacy and vitality when it demonstrates that it is capable of confronting the great champions of the tendencies opposed to it and when it either resolves by its own means the vital questions which they have posed or demonstrates, in peremptory fashion, that these questions are false problems.

It is true that an historical epoch and a given society are characterized rather by the average run of intellectuals, and therefore by the more mediocre. But widespread, mass ideology must be distinguished from the scientific works and the great philosophical syntheses which are its real cornerstones. It is the latter which must be overcome, either negatively, by demonstrating that they are without foundation, or positively, by opposing to them philosophical syntheses of greater importance and significance. Reading the *Manual* one has the impression of someone who cannot sleep for the moonlight and who struggles to massacre the fireflies in the belief that by so doing he will make the brightness lessen or disappear.

Science and system

Is it possible to write an elementary book, a handbook, a 'popular manual', on a doctrine that is still at the stage of discussion, polemic and elaboration? A popular manual cannot be conceived other than as a formally dogmatic, stylistically poised and scientifically balanced exposition of a particular subject. It can only be an introduction to scientific study, and not an exposition of original scientific researches, since it is written for young people or for a public which, from the point of view of scientific discipline, is in a condition like that of youth and therefore has an immediate need for 'certainties', for opinions which, at least on a formal level, appear as reliably true and indisputable. If the

doctrine in question has not yet reached this 'classical' phase of its development, any attempt to 'manualize' it is bound to fail, its logical ordering will be
purely apparent and illusory, and one will get, as with the *Popular Manual*, just a
mechanical juxtaposition of disparate elements which remain inexorably disconnected and disjointed in spite of the unitary varnish provided by the literary
presentation. Why not therefore pose the question in its correct theoretical and
historical terms and rest content with a book in which each of the essential
problems of the doctrine receives separate monographic treatment? This would
be more serious and more 'scientific'. But the vulgar contention is that science
must absolutely mean 'system', and consequently systems of all sorts are built
up which have only the mechanical exteriority of a system and not its necessary
inherent coherence.

The dialectic

The *Manual* contains no treatment of any kind of the dialectic. The dialectic is
presupposed, in a very superficial manner, but is not expounded, and this is
absurd in a manual which ought to contain the essential elements of the
doctrine under discussion and whose bibliographical references should be
aimed at stimulating study in order to widen and deepen understanding of the
subject and not at replacing the manual itself. The absence of any treatment of
the dialectic could have two origins. The first of these would be the fact that
philosophy of praxis is envisaged as split into two elements: on the one hand a
theory of history and politics conceived as sociology – i.e. one that can be
constructed according to the methods of natural science (experimental in the
crudest positivist sense); and on the other hand a philosophy proper, this being
philosophical alias metaphysical or mechanical (vulgar) materialism.

Even after the great debate which has taken place against mechanicism, the
author of the *Manual* does not appear to have changed very much his way of
posing the philosophical problem. It would appear from the contribution
presented at the London Congress on the History of Science that he continues
to maintain that the philosophy of praxis has always been split into two: a
doctrine of history and politics, and a philosophy, although he now calls the
latter dialectical materialism. But if the question is framed in this way, one can
no longer understand the importance and significance of the dialectic, which is
relegated, from its position as a doctrine of knowledge and the very marrow of
historiography and the science of politics, to the level of a sub-species of formal
logic and elementary scholastics. The true fundamental function and significance of the dialectic can only be grasped if the philosophy of praxis is
conceived as an integral and original philosophy which opens up a new phase of
history and a new phase in the development of world thought. It does this to the
extent that it goes beyond both traditional idealism and traditional materialism,
philosophies which are expressions of past societies, while retaining their vital

elements. If the philosophy of praxis is not considered except in subordination to another philosophy, then it is not possible to grasp the new dialectic, through which the transcending of old philosophies is effected and expressed.

The second origin would appear to be psychological. It is felt that the dialectic is something arduous and difficult, in so far as thinking dialectically goes against vulgar common sense, which is dogmatic and eager for peremptory certainties and has as its expression formal logic. To understand this better one can think of what would happen if in primary and secondary schools natural and physical sciences were taught on the basis of Einsteinian relativity and the traditional notion of a 'law of nature' was accompanied by that of a statistical law or of the law of large numbers. The children would not understand anything at all and the clash between school teaching and family and popular life would be such that the school would become an object of ridicule and caricature.

This motivation seems to me to act as a psychological brake on the author of the *Manual*; he really does capitulate before common sense and vulgar thought, since he has not put the problem in exact theoretical terms and is therefore in practice disarmed and impotent. The uneducated and crude environment has dominated the educator and vulgar common sense has imposed itself on science rather than the other way round. If the environment is the educator, it too must in turn be educated,[11] but the *Manual* does not understand this revolutionary dialectic. The source of all the errors of the *Manual*, and of its author (who does not seem to have changed his position, even after the great debate which apparently, or so it would appear from the text presented at the London Congress, resulted in his repudiating the book), consists precisely in this pretension to divide the philosophy of praxis into two parts: a 'sociology' and a systematic philosophy. Separated from the theory of history and politics philosophy cannot be other than metaphysics, whereas the great conquest in the history of modern thought, represented by the philosophy of praxis, is precisely the concrete historicization of philosophy and its identification with history.

11 Cf. the third of Marx's *Theses on Feuerbach*. [Tr.]

11 Philosophy and Sociology in Marx's Early Writings

Lucien Goldmann

Although it is obvious that Marx's thought is centred upon the idea of the unity of theory and practice there have not been wanting thinkers, ever since the time of Vorländer, Max Adler and Werner Sombart . . . who have insisted upon Marx's 'sociologism'; that is, upon the existence in his work of a positivist sociology, complemented by an ethical or political theory, which is no doubt based upon this sociology but nevertheless remains relatively autonomous.

Equally, there are to be found at the other extreme important thinkers such as the young Lukács, or Karl Korsch in his early writings, who affirm the strictly philosophical character of Marx's thought and his refusal to separate, even in a relative fashion, thought and practice.

Given this situation the most appropriate solution might appear to be an attempt to show that Marx actually adopted the third standpoint,[1] which does in fact seem to me to correspond both with his own thought and with the real situation of research in the social sciences. But this would also involve an undue simplification, for Marx's thought was not born in an instant like Minerva from the head of Jupiter, but was formed gradually, in a process which we can find

From Lucien Goldmann, *Marxisme et sciences humaines* (Paris: Éditions Gallimard, 1970), pp. 133–50. Translated by Tom Bottomore. Copyright © 1970 by Éditions Gallimard. Reprinted by permission of the publisher.

1 Goldmann begins his essay by outlining three possible conceptions of the relation between philosophy and sociology, the third of which is 'the standpoint according to which it is indeed impossible to separate factual judgements from value judgements, positive investigations from a world view, science from philosophy, theory from practice . . .', but which also recognizes that the two poles of investigation and action do not stand in a constant and immutable relation to each other, and that scientific inquiry may require, depending upon the context, either a more objective or a more committed approach. [Ed.]

expressed in his early writings. It would be valuable one day to undertake a thorough study of the way in which the problem that concerns us here was posed successively in Marx's writings between 1842 and 1845, or even 1847, before he had achieved a comprehensive formulation of his basic standpoint; a standpoint, moreover, which itself displays a number of variations in its application to specific research problems. In short, a genetic study of the problem of the relations between philosophy and sociology in Marx's early writings is an important task for future Marxological studies. Needless to say, I do not pretend to treat the subject exhaustively in the present essay, and at most I would like to propound some reflections . . . which may indicate a number of major issues and thus contribute to further research. . . .

Here, however, it is essential to make an additional comment. Even if the philosophical standpoint which explicitly asserts the impossibility of making a radical separation between factual judgements and value judgements is *not* philosophy in general but a specific philosophy which we call dialectical, it is still the case that if this dialectic conforms, as I believe, with reality, then all philosophical systems, including those which explicitly affirm the possibility, and even the necessity, of separating the theoretical from the normative, assertions in the indicative mood from hypothetical or categorical imperatives, contain within themselves a body of closely and intimately related factual assertions and valuations. That is to say that even if one finds in all Marx's early writings factual assertions and scientific analyses along with valuations and political or practical orientations, this does not mean in the least that these works had from the outset a dialectical character. The latter requires in effect an awareness of the inseparability of the two attitudes, a *consciousness* which is only to be found explicitly expressed in *The German Ideology* and above all in the *Theses on Feuerbach*. And it is striking that only when Marx has attained this awareness of the central core of dialectical thought do we find explicitly posed in his work the problem of the connection between theory and practice, and of the circular relation between social conditions and that which is conditioned by them. . . .

Terminology is undoubtedly very difficult to establish definitively in the social sciences, because of the dynamic character of the reality which they study and the impossibility of any non-genetic definitions. If however, taking this into account, we designate *sociology* as a science of society which aims to be objective and independent of the practical orientations of the investigator, and *historical materialism* as the dialectical conception which asserts the impossibility of separating these two kinds of human activity (one might equally well distinguish between 'historical sociology' and 'sociological history', but the double use of the term 'sociology' could lead to confusion), then it can be said that there is a highly important study to be made of the relations between sociology, morals or natural law, politics, and historical materialism in the various works in which the young Marx elaborated his ideas, up to *The German Ideology* and the *Theses on Feuerbach*.

In the present essay . . . I intend only to indicate four important aspects of this development, or more precisely to draw attention to Marx's fundamental standpoint on this problem in four texts: his articles in the _Rheinische Zeitung_, the _Critique of Hegel's Philosophy of the State_, the _Introduction to Hegel's Philosophy of Right_, and the _Theses on Feuerbach_.

Let me observe at once that it is in the articles in the _Rheinische Zeitung_ that Marx comes closest to the dualist position, which many interpreters have regarded as characterizing his work as a whole, a position which recognizes the existence of two more or less autonomous, though closely related, types of analysis: namely, on one side, a purely theoretical, sociological analysis, and on the other side, a normative analysis, dealing with political or moral questions. In fact, at the time when he was editing the _Rheinische Zeitung_ Marx, like many Young Hegelians, had moved away from Hegel's dialectical approach and drawn closer to a rationalist style of thought, related to the philosophy of the Enlightenment. Lukács, and later historians, have already analysed this movement of the Hegelian Left from dialectics to rationalism, or to use Lukács' expression, 'the return from Hegel to Fichte'. The most important historical factor which can explain this development is probably that all dialectical thought has to base itself upon reality, and the German reality of that period was not sufficiently revolutionary to justify a radical orientation. It was only the discovery of a real and effectively revolutionary force in the shape of the English and French proletariat which made it possible for Marx and Engels (and perhaps also Moses Hess to some extent, though this needs to be examined more fully) to return to a dialectical standpoint.

Be that as it may, the _political_ positions taken by the young Marx in his articles in the _Rheinische Zeitung_, it must be said bluntly, are not particularly original. They only express, though in a brilliant style, the ideas of democratic radicalism and individualistic rationalism. The state should represent society as a whole, and such representation is only possible if freedom of expression – which means freedom of the press – is assured. The collusion between the state and private interests with their established privileges is a real evil which must be unceasingly denounced as one of the most dangerous abuses of political power.

The real originality of these articles seems to me to lie, on the contrary, in their extremely subtle and penetrating sociological analyses, which are of course closely interwoven with Marx's political views, but still retain an independent value. Considering that the articles were written in 1842, and that many of them are still of great interest today, one must recognize that they are the work of a thinker who demonstrated already, at that time, his exceptional quality.

The first series of articles, concerned with the debates in the Rhenish Diet on the freedom of the press, and the publication of these debates, embodies an extremely subtle analysis, of great methodological interest, of the relation between the structure of the arguments presented by various speakers and the social groups which they represent. Marx is not content, in fact, merely to note that the speakers oppose the freedom of the press, or advocate a very limited freedom, and to criticize their views in the name of his democratic rationalism. He also notes – and it is in this respect that his articles retain their interest today – that the arguments invoked by each speaker to support his view are characteristic of the specific categories of thought of his group. Thus, in the case of the speaker representing the princely order, Marx observes that he justifies censorship in terms of the existing state of affairs, a specious argument perhaps, but one which is characteristic of the general outlook of this order; though it must be added that the validity of the 'existing state of affairs' is not, for this speaker or for the group which he represents, a universal principle, but is valid only when it is a matter of asserting the authority of governments and restricting the liberties of the people. That is why this same speaker, after having observed that censorship is good because it already exists, and is even developing in the German federation generally, feels obliged to add that the existence of freedom of the press in England, Holland and Switzerland, far from providing a sound argument for the validity of such freedom is, on the contrary, a doubtful argument to the extent that this freedom, where it exists, has 'arisen from particular circumstances', or has had 'pernicious' consequences.

The speaker representing the nobility begins by affirming that he is in favour of freedom to publish the debates in the Diet, on condition, however, that the decision on whether to publish them should be left to the Diet itself, so that there will be the maximum freedom of debate, without any 'external' pressures. Marx justly remarks that in this argument the notion of liberty, far from being the universal liberty of rationalism, becomes that of 'liberties', which is the term that the aristocracy of the sword or of the robe has always used to characterize its privileges. The speaker does not regard the Diet as an assembly of representatives of the provinces, and subject to their control, but rather – in the manner of the early French parliaments – as a privileged corporation similar to the body which he himself represents, which has to defend its 'liberties', that is to say, the free exercise of its privileges. Turning to the question of the freedom of the press, the same speaker expresses his opposition to it, giving as his specific, and specious, reason that since, according to him, human beings are by nature wicked, any kind of freedom of expression which allowed the 'bad' press as well as the 'good' press to appear freely would incur the risk of ensuring the triumph of the former, which would have a much stronger influence on public opinion; it being understood, of course, that for him the 'good' press is that which ensures the defence of individual privileges. In effect, he defines an 'ill-disposed outlook' as 'the arrogance which does not recognize authority in the church and in the state' and 'the envy which preaches the suppression of what the people call aristocracy'.

As Marx says,

> these gentlemen who do not regard liberty as a natural gift of the spread of universal reason, but only as a supernatural gift resulting from a particularly favourable

conjunction of the stars, because they want to recognize liberty only as the individual attribute of certain people or certain estates, are obliged in consequence to put universal reason and universal liberty in the category of those ill-disposed ideas and fantasies which characterize 'logically constructed systems'. In order to safeguard special liberties, i.e. privileges, they are led to proscribe the universal liberty of human nature.

Marx concludes his analysis with a quotation which expresses in a striking way the aristocratic perspective and its limitations. The speaker adds to his other arguments the view that 'to be able to speak and to write are purely mechanical talents'. It is well known indeed to what extent, for the aristocracy, writing and speaking were subsidiary activities.

The third speaker, finally, representing the bourgeoisie, declares himself in favour of the freedom of the press, but in a very peculiar fashion, since he explains that journalism is an occupation like any other and must be given the same freedom which is granted to all other professions. Thus he proposes to grant this freedom with the same restrictions as are imposed upon other occupations: namely, to accord the right of being a journalist only to a certain number of individuals whose competence will have been attested and who will have been granted a licence.

It is no exaggeration, I think, to say that, in the history of sociology, this study by Marx is one of the first examples of a sociological theory of knowledge, and that its methodological importance can scarcely be overestimated. It bears upon a central issue in any sociological study of human phenomena – namely, the general categories of thought which are specific to different social groups – which is, regrettably, either misunderstood or ignored in many sociological investigations, not only in the nineteenth century but even today.

Marx's articles on 'The leading article in no. 179 of the *Kölnische Zeitung*' formulate the basic principles of the sociology of thought in general, and of philosophical thought in particular. The following passage seems to me exceptionally striking:

> Philosophies do not spring up from the ground like mushrooms; they are the product of their age and of their people, whose most subtle, precious and hidden essence flows into philosophical ideas. The same spirit constructs philosophical systems in the heads of philosophers and railways with the hands of workers. Philosophy is not outside the world any more than the brain is outside man, even though it is not located in the stomach.

In his articles devoted to the thefts of wood Marx sketches, though certainly in an inadequate, undialectical fashion, the elements of the theory of reification, by showing how human relationships are transformed, in a society based upon private property, into qualities of objects; and in the particular case considered, how wood becomes more important than the men it oppresses and destroys. In these same articles there is a remarkable sociological analysis of the juridical sanctioning of recent social transformations, by means of an interpretation in terms of Roman law of the relationships inherited from the middle ages, when the notions of possession and property had an entirely different social content. I shall not discuss these last two studies further here, for the simple reason that the theory of reification, and also the justification of the expropriation of the customary rights of the peasants by the interpretation of the right of over-lordship as an absolute property right, are now well understood in the sociological literature.

The last series of articles, concerned with defending the correspondence from a wine grower of the Moselle region which the paper had published, and on which the authorities were demanding explanations, is again a noteworthy sociological analysis of the bureaucratic mentality, and of the structural reasons which necessarily incline it to misunderstand the nature of any protest against administrative measures and to support the administrative authority. Let me quote here Marx's comment that even when the administration desires to examine complaints objectively it is likely to confide the investigation to an official who is familiar with the problem, which means in most cases an official who has worked in the department concerned even if he is no longer employed there. Such an official is usually of fairly high rank; hence, the person who is to evaluate the complaint is not only a member of the department, and so tends to approve its actions, but also, very frequently has to assess measures which were taken either by himself or by one of his superiors.

The foregoing account shows the extent to which, in the period when Marx's thought was not very dialectical, but was close to the rationalism of the Enlightenment, there is to be found that dualism in his thought which some interpreters have claimed to discover in his later work; and equally, how far Marx, at that time, showed himself to be not only a militant supporter of radical democracy and a brilliant disciple of Enlightenment philosophy, but also a notable empirical sociologist. Let me add here that the value of all these sociological studies which I have mentioned consists, among other things, in the fact that they are studies in the sociology of knowledge, focused upon the mental categories specific to various social groups, and for that reason are capable of being incorporated later on, to a great extent, into a dialectical perspective. It is from this aspect, even at the time when Marx's thought is most remote from the dialectic, that it foreshadows, by its concentration upon the relation between structures of consciousness and social reality, its subsequent development.

The nature of the sociological studies in the *Rheinische Zeitung* can be characterized roughly in the following way. There exists for Marx a natural law and a natural morality upon which his political judgements are founded, and in the name of which he conducts his struggle. But this natural law and morality is confronted by a social reality which is full of abuses and errors, a reality which has to be explained sociologically; and Marx studies it in a *determined*, not a *genetic* way, focusing his analyses upon a *causal* explanation of the mental categories which form the consciousness of diverse social groups. Whether Marx is aware of it or not, this standpoint, like that of most of the Young Hegelians of the period, is at the opposite pole from dialectical thought.

It is in his next work, the *Critique of Hegel's Philosophy of the State*, that Marx is again confronted with the basic standpoint of dialectical thought. This is an extremely complex work, and there is no question of undertaking a detailed analysis of it here; what interests us for the present is the problem of the relations between theory and practice, sociology and politics, factual judgements and value judgements. But in approaching Hegel's thought, and regardless of the criticisms that he brings against it – which I shall consider later – Marx confronts a body of thought in which valuations are not formulated in terms of natural law or morality, but in terms of what is conceived as *reality*, even if this reality is not that which is directly and empirically given but the development of objective spirit and its advance toward the realization of freedom. It is important to note (and this is perhaps largely explicable by the historical context, in which *all the radicals wanted to be more or less Hegelian* even though opposing Hegel on political grounds) that Marx does not criticize Hegel from a political standpoint based upon natural law and morality, but asks what is the flaw in a system which bases its value judgements not upon the 'ought' but upon existing reality and arrives, in its philosophy of the state, at conclusions which are so strongly opposed to those of democratic radicalism, and are indeed a mere apologia for the existing social and political conditons in Germany. The central problem of the book, beyond all its particular analyses, is therefore that of an *immanent criticism* of the Hegelian system, and for that reason Marx is led to make an important step from Enlightenment rationalism toward dialectical thought.

In fact, from the very first pages of the book Marx points to the central issue which distinguishes Hegel's idealist dialectic from the future materialist dialectic of Marx and Engels, and makes the former an apologia for the existing state, the latter a revolutionary ideology. Marx's principal objection to Hegel is that he has inverted the real relation between subject and predicate by making spirit, which is above all a predicate, the subject of history, while reducing real human beings and the institutions created by their interrelations (the family, civil society, the state) to the status of predicates. This procedure, for reasons internal to it, is bound to reach a conservative conclusion, even if it is used in the most critical way and with the best intentions. There is, in fact, no way of gaining direct and immediate knowledge of objective spirit or of its short- or medium-term developmental tendencies (the thinker knows only the ultimate goal of its development). Thus the philosopher can only establish his political standpoint by means of a detour, by basing himself upon the so-called predicates, or in other words upon the existing institutions. That is why any honest use of an idealist dialectic, if it takes itself seriously and desires to avoid the dualism of 'being' and 'what ought to be', is bound to result in a conservative standpoint and an apologia for the existing social and political order. If value judgements have to be based upon the real subject of history, and if the latter can only be known through its empirical predicates which are conceived as *lacking any dynamism of their own*, then value judgements can only be a vindication of what is known positively about absolute spirit, that is to say, an apologia for what exists, which eliminates any valuation of possible change.

This fundamental criticism of the Hegelian system seems to me valid, and I do not see any objection which could be brought against it. At most, it might be added that a vindication of the existing reality may be progressive, and even revolutionary, when this reality is itself manifestly progressive or revolutionary, as was the case, for example, when it took the form of the Jacobin dictatorship or the Napoleonic empire; whereas it is necessarily reactionary during periods of conservative stabilization, as it was at the time when Hegel wrote his *Philosophy of Right* or when Marx wrote the work which we are engaged in studying.

Marx opposes to Hegel's error of inverting the real relation between subject and predicate the need for a scheme of thought which would be both positive and radical, and would see in real human beings and their social institutions (the family, civil society, the state) the genuine subject of historical action. But this requirement, pressed to its limit, was bound to lead Marx from the sociological/political dualism of his articles in the *Rheinische Zeitung* to historical materialism, for the idea of real human beings as the subjects of history, if it is conceived in a rigorous way, implies: (1) the need for a *genetic* study of social facts and social institutions, and; (2) the need to regard the theory itself as an element in human historical action, and to conceive the human beings and institutions which are studied as having a part, more or less directly, in the elaboration of the theory. In short, the need to reconstitute the relation between subject and predicate implied a kind of thought, both dialectical and positive, focused upon the close connection between theory and practice, and upon the total or partial identity of the subject and the object of thought and action.

Very frequently, however – indeed almost always – there is a considerable lag between the requirements immanent in the development of a theoretical standpoint and the effective realization of this development in the historical process and in the life of a thinker. The *Critique of Hegel's Philosophy of the State* already required the elaboration of a dialectical form of thought. But like most of the Young Hegelians Marx was too strongly attached to his radical, democratic and oppositional standpoint to be able to accept the requirements of dialectical thought, and particularly that of basing valuations exclusively upon the objective tendencies of the existing historical structures, so long as he had not discovered in these structures an objectively revolutionary force which would make it possible to reconcile the requirements of dialectical thought with the political attitudes of the Young Hegelians. In short, between the implicit requirement of a critique of Hegel's philosophy and the working out of dialectical materialism, there stood necessarily *the discovery of the English and French proletariat as revolutionary forces.*

　　　　　　　　　　　Lucien Goldmann

Even so, it must be remembered that the discovery of the proletariat as the subject and driving force of the socialist revolution did not result immediately in the elaboration of a monist and consistent form of dialectical thought. It is usual to locate the beginnings of historical and dialectical materialism in Marx's writings of 1843 and the first part of 1844, published in the *Deutsch-Französische Jahrbücher*, and especially in the *Critique of Hegel's Philosophy of Right. Introduction*. There is, however, an error in this interpretation which is not without interest for the development of Marxism after Marx. For although it is undeniable that this *Introduction* is the first of Marx's texts in which the idea of the proletariat as the class which is decisive for the achievement of a socialist revolution appears, it is far from being dialectical and takes a strictly dualist position.[2] Essentially, it is an attempt to synthesize the writings of 1842, which based the hopes for social and political reform upon the power of reason, supported by a natural morality and natural rights, with the dialectical requirements of the *Critique of Hegel's Philosophy of the State*, which sought to discover the active subject of history and progress in the real structures of society, not in the heaven of ideologies. Schematically expressed, the basic standpoint adopted in the *Introduction* asserts a duality between rational thought, which is the active force of history but remains powerless and ineffectual as long as it does not succeed in embodying itself in some material reality, and on the other side, this material reality, which is in itself, and in isolation, passive but may become, and does become, active when it is penetrated by rational thought. It will be enough to cite here a few passages: 'Revolutions need a *passive* element, a *material* basis. Theory is only realized in a people so far as it fulfils the needs of the people.' 'It is not enought that thought should seek to realize itself; reality must also strive towards thought.' 'It is clear that the arm of criticism cannot replace the criticism of arms. Material force can only be overthrown by material force; but theory itself becomes a material force when it has seized the masses.' 'The *emancipation of Germany* will be an *emancipation of man*. *Philosophy* is the *head* of this emancipation and the *proletariat* is its *heart*. Philosophy can only be realized by the abolition of the proletariat, and the proletariat can only be abolished by the realization of philosophy.'

It remains to ask why, not withstanding the passages just cited and the clearly dualist structure of the work as a whole, its transitional character, as a text which is dualist and not dialectical, has been so little emphasized in the later literature on Marx. It seems to me that the reason is to be found mainly in the fact that this literature itself had a dualist, non-dialectical character, and that what was called Marxism was essentially much closer to the standpoint of the *Introduction* than to that of the *Theses on Feuerbach*. In fact, it is enough to replace the word 'philosophy' in the *Introduction* by the word 'party' (and in both cases it

2 On this matter see the unpublished thesis of Michael Loewy, 'Revolution communiste et auto-émancipation du prolétariat dans l'oeuvre du jeune Marx.'

is really a matter of the group which elaborates an ideology) in order to arrive at a standpoint very close to that which Lenin formulated in *What is to be Done?*, but also close to the theoretical views, more or less clearly expounded, which corresponded with the actual practice of both German Social Democracy and the Bolsheviks; that is to say, of the two major sources of the development of Marxist theory.

The *Theses on Feuerbach* constitute, in the whole corpus of Marx's work, the first text which is rigorously monist and dialectical. In the history of European philosophy these two or three pages seem to me equal in importance to the most famous philosophical works, and I have no hesitation in comparing them with the *Discourse on Method*, the *Critique of Pure Reason*, and the *Phenomenology of Mind*. It is evident that an exhaustive analysis of this text would probably require a whole volume or more, and nothing of the kind can be attempted here. Let me simply note, in concluding this essay, that the *Theses on Feuerbach* pose in an uncompromising fashion the problem of the relations between theory and practice, factual judgements and valuations, knowledge of human phenomena and the transformation of the world; and that on this occasion Marx's response is strictly *monist* and *genetic*, asserting that the real subject of history is not the individual but the social group oriented toward indentification with the species.

The first thesis, subsequently confirmed by experimental studies, and notably by those of Jean Piaget, is one of the most radical affirmations of the unity of theory and practice, of knowledge and action, because it locates this unity not only at the level of consciousness and thought, but also at the more elementary level of sensation and perception: 'The chief defect of all previous materialism (including that of Feuerbach) is that things (*Gegenstand*), reality, the sensible world, are conceived only in the form of *objects* (*Objekt*) *of observation*, but not as human sense activity, not as *practical activity*, not *subjectively*.'

The third thesis asserts the impossibility of any determinist, or even simply objective, conception of social reality, given that such a standpoint always results in attempting to explain human thought and behaviour by social circumstances, whereas these circumstances themselves are created by human thought and behaviour. Every kind of thought and every theory is located within the historical process, and involves both cognitive endeavour and a practical intervention. As for the pretensions of an objective sociology, they correspond with the attempt 'to divide society into two parts, one of which is superior to society'.[3]

The sixth thesis reproaches Feuerbach, and by implication any objective sociology, with the lack of a genetic perspective. Finally, this same sixth thesis, and the ninth and tenth theses, underline the fact that the static and dualist standpoint results necessarily from the fundamental error of regarding the

3 It is easy to see the connection between sociologial objectivism and any fundamental division of society, or of the party, into two different groups: the passive masses and the active militants or theorists.

Lucien Goldmann

isolated individual as the subject of praxis, an error which leads to obscuring the historical character of praxis. The real subject is the collectivity, the human species. This is no doubt too general an assertion, but one which Marx will soon make precise by substituting for the abstract generic collectivity a more definite empirical reality, namely that of social classes.

12   Critique of Marx's Positivism

Albrecht Wellmer

My critique of the objectivism of Marx's philosophy of history was directed at a latently positivistic misconception, which, according to Habermas's thesis, arises from the part played in Marx's theory by the concept of labour. Of course it would be a basic misunderstanding of this thesis to suppose that Habermas's concept of 'instrumental behaviour' could conceal Marx's notion of production. It is well known that when Marx talks of 'production' in his economic analyses, he also means 'distribution', 'forms of intercourse' – which corresponds to 'communicative behaviour'.[1] Habermas also makes a distinction between the level of material analyses, on which Marx makes use of a concept of social practice incorporating labour *and* interaction,[2] and the level of historico-philosophical interpretation, on which Marx comprehends the self-production (that is, creation) of the human species solely on the basis of the logic of its activity in the production of objects:

> For his analysis of the development of socio-economic formations Marx uses a concept of the system of social labour containing more elements than are declared in the concept of the self-creating human species. Self-constitution through social work is conceived *on the categorical level* as a production process; and instrumental behaviour, work in the sense of productive activity, characterizes the dimension in which natural history runs its course. *On the level of his material investigations*, on the other hand, Marx always takes into account a social *praxis* incorporating work *and* interaction; the natural-historical processes are intermediated by the productive activity of the individual and the organization of its intercourse.[3]

From Albrecht Wellmer, *Critical Theory of Society* (New York: Herder and Herder, 1971), pp. 67–75, 94–9. Copyright © 1971 by The Continuum Publishing Corporation. Reprinted by permission of The Continuum Publishing Corporation.

1 Cf. Marx, *Grundrisse der Kritik der politischen Ökonomie* (Berlin, 1953), Introduction, pp. 16ff.
2 Cf. Jürgen Habermas, *Erkenntnis und Interesse*, (1968), p. 71.
3 Ibid., p. 71.

The epistemological implications of Marx's understanding of history lead to the misconception of ideology-critical social theory as a 'science' in the same sense as the natural sciences, which Marx in fact favoured.[4] The camouflaging of the difference between 'strict experimental science' and 'criticism',[5] between 'productive knowledge' and 'reflective knowledge', would necessarily have consequences in regard to the apprehension of the interplay of critical theory and revolutionary practice: Marx's self-conception provides the starting-points for an erroneously technocratic interpretation of his theory, which was then to become practical reality in the hands of the omniscient administrators of historical necessity.[6]

Of course the two levels of material analysis and categorical interpretation are not related as object- and meta-level. The categorical framework already includes an historico-philosophical articulation which allows the production of basic statements about the 'mechanism' of historical development. These pronouncements however have, as it were, no merely meta-theoretical status;[7] consequently, one might suppose that the contradiction between theory *qua* criticism and its objectivistic self-misconception has an inner-theoretical correlative in the form of a contradiction between the historical interpretation of historical materialism and the criticism of political economy. Of course this supposition, formulated in this global way, is *prima facie* implausible: historical

---

4 In his Preface to the second edition of *Capital* (vol. I), for example, Marx quotes (with approval) a Russian reviewer who compares Marx's method of economic analysis with a biology oriented to the history of evolution: 'Marx views the social movement as a process of natural history, governed by laws which are not only independent of the will, consciousness and intelligence of men, but on the contrary determine their volition, consciousness and intelligence' (*MA* [*Karl Marx–Ausgabe*, ed. H. J. Lieber, Darmstadt, 1962] vol. 4, p. xxix). Marx acknowledges the reviewer's description as a representation of his dialectical *method* (ibid., p. xxx); this is fatal in view of the following, far-reaching assertion by the reviewer: 'Consequently, Marx is concerned with only one thing: to show, by precise scientific investigation, the necessity of successive definite systems of social conditions, and to establish, as impartially as possible, the facts that serve him as starting-points and grounds. For this purpose it is wholly adequate if he proves, at one and the same time, the necessity of the present order and the necessity of another order into which the first must inevitably pass over, quite oblivious of whether men believe or do not believe it, are conscious or unconscious of it (ibid., p. xxix). These statements already show that a positivistic self-misconception cannot fail to affect even the material contents of the theory – here in particular the interpretation of the world-historical transition to the classless society. Subsequently, I try to demonstrate the inner context of theory that allowed Marx – not quite by accident – to let pass these statements by his St Petersburg reviewer.

5 Cf. Habermas, *Erkenntnis und Interesse*, p. 62.

6 Cf. Oskar Negt, Introduction to A. Deborin and N. Bukharin, *Kontroversen über dialektischen und mechanistischen Materialismus* (Frankfurt, 1969).

7 Otherwise one would only need to disengage Marx's statements about the scientific status of his theory and his 'meta-theory' of history from the body of the theory, and to allow them to speak for themselves as against their positivistic misinterpretations. It should soon become apparent that the matter is more complex than this.

materialism enters into the approach proper to the criticism of political economy, just as much as it is the result of that approach.[8]

In addition, the criticism of political economy becomes a *criticism of ideology*, inasmuch as it turns into what Lukács calls an 'historical criticism of economy'.[9] When Marx criticizes commodity-fetishism, he discovers behind the apparent natural qualities and the apparent social relations of things, the social relations of men, produced historically and both mediated and repressed from consciousness by coercive conditions; and behind the 'natural' characteristics of capital an historically produced class relationship.[10] Therefore there is a reciprocally consolidated relationship between historical materialism as a theory of socio-economic development mediated through class struggle, and the criticism of political economy. But if a 'modification' of Marx's interpretation of history actually becomes available and if this modified construct is not merely to have the status of a meta-theory of history (unauthoritative in regard to the material contents of the theory), then an inner-theoretical contradiction between the 'historical' and the 'ideology-critical' theoretical approaches nevertheless has to be established – unless criticism of the objectivistic traces in Marx's philosophy of history, especially his conception of the transition to the classless society, is to mean the total conception of theory. I believe it can be shown that, even to the extent of specific economic analyses, there is an unresolved contradiction between the 'modified' historical materialism (that is, that which traces the 'dialectics of morality' back to the dialectics of production) and the ideology-critical theoretical approach; and that, in particular, in contrast to this theoretical approach, 'modified' historical materialism results in an objectivistic concept of revolution that Marx has at some points explicitly acknowledged as his own.

I shall first of all indicate where this alleged contradiction is to be found. If, on this construction, the human *praxis* which constitutes and transforms society, and with it 'production' and the transformation of men's societal consciousness, appear ultimately as derivations and functions of their work in transforming nature, then the dialectical interplay between the world-historical process of formation of consciousness and social institutions on the one hand, and the historical development of productive forces on the other, must be misconceived as a functional relationship. Conditions of production, and ideologies that legitimize domination, then tacitly become second-order productive forces; their history can no longer be reconstructed in practical terms as that of a

---

8 For the first part of the assertion cf. K. Marx, *Grundrisse der Kritik der politischen Ökonomie* (Berlin, 1953), Introduction, esp. sections 2 and 3. The most effective evidence for the second part is the connection between the beginning and the end of *Capital*; cf. K. Kosik, *Dialektik des Konkreten* (Frankfurt, 1967), pp. 174ff.

9 Cf. Georg Lukács, 'Klassenbewusstsein', in *Geschichte und Klassenbewusstsein* (Amsterdam, 1967), p. 60.

10 Cf. *MA*, vol. 4, pp. 47ff.

progressive emancipation from the pressures of naturally effective social repression, instead their sole logic is that of another history: that of the technical conquest of external nature, that is, of the emancipation of men from the natural pressures that restrict them – but emancipation by means of the progressive reification of their 'essential powers' in material production. The dissolution of a false social consciousness of a kind that stabilizes domination (for Marx a constitutive aspect of the dissolution of relations of domination in the class struggle) cannot then be conceived as the result of a practical 'process of formation'; instead, it must itself reappear as the *product* of social work, that is, as the necessary by-product of socio-economic changes, which for their part were exacted solely by processes of technical innovation. But if the determining relationship between the development of productive forces, the transformation of forms of domination, and transformation of social consciousness, is constructed in this way, there are distinct consequences amounting to the establishment of an objectivistic theory of revolution. *First*, the immanent logic of a progressive technological self-objectification of men provides both the goal and the necessary result of human 'prehistory', namely, the complete rationalization of the process of social reproduction; *secondly*, the theoretical reconstruction of the prehistorical determining relationship between productive forces, conditions of production, and ideologies, becomes a task for strict experimental science; *thirdly*, there is the result that, in the capitalist process of production, the *subjective* conditions for a revolutionary transition to the classless society must be 'produced' at the very same time as the objective conditions; *fourthly*, and finally, the 'correct' proletarian consciousness can ultimately be none other than the consciousness of positive science: the freedom of proletarian men is attenuated and blunted to become insight into historical necessity, and their revolution can merely reduce and alleviate the 'birth pangs' of the new society.

Of course this theoretical relationship is not to be found in *this* form anywhere in Marx. But if the more or less evident 'distortions' of Marx's philosophy of history are seen in the perspective of decisions made in advance on the level of categorization, then they can be presented in terms of that theoretical relationship as their ideal limit value. This means, however, that the modification of Marx's construction of history potentially removes the basis of his critical social theory *qua* ideology-*criticism*. For this theory can only be a *critique* of ideology as a socially necessary illusion, if, as an historically explicative theory, it simultaneously reveals the contradiction between society as it is, and what it could and must be in terms of its technical possibilities and of the interpretations of the 'good life' acknowledged within it. This means that critical theory does not wish to replace an ideological consciousness with a scientific consciousness, but – of course by means of empirical and historical analyses – to assist the practical reason existing in the form of ideological consciousness to 'call to mind' its distorted form, and at the same time to get control of its practical-utopian contents. Ultimately, therefore, critical theory can prove itself only by initiating a reflective dissolution of false consciousness resulting in liberating *praxis*: the successful dissolution of false consciousness as an integrative aspect of emancipatory practice is the proper touchstone for its truth, because only in the process of this dissolution and resolution can it exist as the *acknowledged* truth of false consciousness. The truth of critical social theory is a *vérité à faire*; in the last resort it can demonstrate its truthfulness only by successful liberation: hence the hypothetico-practical status peculiar to the theory.

This hypothetico-practical status (and this is my thesis) is challenged by the basic assumptions of Marx's interpretation of history. In those basic assumptions, technical progress, the abrogation of 'dysfunctional' social repression and the dissolution of false consciousness are so indissolubly joined that the irresistible advance of technical progress, which starts with the capitalist mode of production, has to be interpreted as the irresistible advance towards the commonwealth of freedom. The building of the realm of freedom is therefore shifted back into the same continuum of historical necessity in which, for Marx, the prehistory of the human species had advanced. But on this assumption, the reasonableness of liberating practice can no longer be measured according to the degree to which it has already liberated from the existing coercive context those active individuals who have been enlightened as to their true interest, but only according to the extent to which they act on the basis of insight into the scientifically detectable regularities of the course of history. In this way, there is a potential elimination from the concept of liberating practice of that aspect of a reflective dissolution of false consciousness, which allows the practical realization of critical theory to be distinguished from the practical realization of a strictly experimental scientific theory: insight into the history and meaning of experienced social bondage and constraint, at which critical theory aims as the precondition of a process of collective emancipation, is indissolubly bound up with the transformation of attitudes, modes of behaviour and possibilities of experience; the dissolution of false consciousness mediated through practice *and* self-reflection is therefore at one and the same time transformation of consciousness and transformation of men.[11] Against this, a critical social theory which is misconceived as a strict experimental scientific theory can no longer anticipate the necessary transformation of men who want to transform society,

---

11 It is possible to interpret in this sense those statements of Marx's in which he anticipates the necessary transformation of the proletarians as the result of their liberating *praxis*. E.g., in the *Revelations about the Cologne Communist Trial*: 'Whereas we say to the workers: You have fifteen, twenty, or even fifty years of civil wars and national wars to endure, not only in order to change conditions, but in order to change yourselves and to fit yourselves for political rule, you say, on the contrary: "We must come to power immediately, or else lay ourselves down to rest" ' (*MA*, vol. 3, i, p. 454). Significantly, in this *political* document Marx stresses the emancipatory function of the class *struggle*. On the other hand, in so far as a modified historical materialism is brought to bear in his theory, precisely this liberating function of the class struggle is neglected in favour of the system-breaking function of objective class *antagonism*.

in the dimension of a self-enlightening *praxis*; instead it must rigorously distinguish between the transformation of consciousness and the transformation of attitudes and modes of behaviour: the first becomes knowledge of the economic law of movement of capitalist society, the second must be comprehended as the necessary result of the process of material production.

The basic thesis that I shall now try to establish in greater detail may be provisionally formulated thus: the union of historical materialism and the criticism of political economy in Marx's social theory is inherently contradictory. In particular, the basic assumptions of Marx's interpretation of history suggest, in contrast to the ideology-critical approach of the theory, an 'objectivistic' concept of revolution in a twofold sense: on the one hand, they determine the revolutionary *function* of critical theory as that of a post-ideological, 'positive' science, whereas on the other hand they lead to the camouflaging of the distinction between the *inevitable* and the practically necessary transformation of capitalist society, thus allowing the transition to the classless society to appear as the enforced result of the solution of problems proper to the capitalist system.

If this thesis is correct, then two misconceptions of Marx's theory which have certain practical consequences may depend on a theoretical relationship which is more or less latent in this theory itself; I shall call them the 'technocratic' and the 'evolutionist' misconceptions. According to the first misconception, under certain historic initial conditions socialism would have to be brought about by an exclusive, theoretically trained, revolutionary minority ruling by authoritarian measures; according to the second, it would have to be the enforced result of the development of capitalist society. In fact, as can easily be seen, there is only one misconception: namely, a 'mechanistic' misunderstanding of historical materialism, according to which the revolution becomes the mere question of more or less expenses on the bill of history – since the end-result of history is already settled. If, however, this error can find support in a theoretical realtionship latent in Marx's theory, then a meta-criticism of Marx's critique of political moralism is also requisite; at any rate to the extent that this critique, which struck at the Young Hegelians, early socialists and anarchists with equal severity, understood itself to be precisely the result of the development of socialism from utopia to *science*. . . .

'All collisions in history', says *The German Ideology*,[12] '. . . originate, in our view, in the contradiction between the productive forces and the form of intercourse.' 'This contradiction . . . had on every occasion to break out in a revolution, assuming at the same time various subsidiary forms: comprehensive collisions, collisions of different classes, contradiction of consciousness, battle of ideas, and so on, class warfare, and so on.' Marx distinguishes a basic form of

---

12 *MEW* [Karl Marx and Friedrich Engels, *Werke*, Berlin; Dietz Verlag, 1958 onwards], vol. 3, p. 73.

social contradiction from its 'subsidiary forms'; the mistake of written history in the past was that in any particular case it made one of these subsidiary forms the basis of social upheavals and historical development in general. 'From a restricted viewpoint one can isolate one of these subsidiary forms and see it as the basis of these revolutions – this is all the easier because the very individuals who started the revolutions had illusions about their own activity according to the extent of their education and the stage of historical development.'

In what sense can it be said now that a 'collision' between classes is the 'subsidiary form' of a contradiction between productive forces and forms of intercourse? Does it mean that this contradiction can be detected independently of the social conflicts in which it manifests itself, that is, as the dysfunctionality of a form of domination in regard, say, to the systematic goal of a development of the productive forces? Or does it mean only that the calling in question of a dominant order, manifest in class conflict, would only be possible and could only be resolved through the development of the productive forces? In one case, class conflict would be the necessary *consequence* of an 'objective' contradiction; in the other case, it would constitute it only *as* contradiction in the general sense. The incompatibility of these two possible interpretations, which are still left open here, is the incompatibility of two different versions of historical materialism made plain in the well-known formulations of the Preface to *A Contribution to the Critique of Political Economy*:

> In the social production of their life, men enter into certain necessary relations that are independent of their will, relations of production which correspond to a certain stage of development of their material productive forces. . . . At a certain stage of their development, the material productive forces of society come into conflict with the existing relations of production, or – what is only a legal expression for those same relations – with the property relations within which they have acted until now. These relations turn from forms of development of productive forces into their fetters. Then an epoch of social revolution commences. With the transformation of the economic basis, the whole immense superstructure is more slowly or more speedily transformed. When considering such transformations, one must always make a distinction between the material transformation of the economic conditions of production, which can be determined with natural scientific exactitude, and the legal, political, religious, artistic or philosophical, or, in short, the ideological forms in which men become conscious of this conflict and fight it out. Just as one does not judge an individual by what he thinks of himself, so such an epoch of trans-formation cannot be judged by its consciousness; instead, this consciousness must be explained on the basis of the contradictions of material life, of the existing conflict between the social productive forces and relations of production.[13]

Here Marx states clearly that social revolutions solve social systematic problems which are reflected in men's consciousness but which are defined – independently of

13 *MA*, vol. 6, pp. 838ff.

the interpretations of the individuals concerned – as conflicts 'of material life'; hence there are necessary solutions (independent of human volition) to such systematic problems in the shape of a transition to the next, higher mode of production, which in each particular case guarantees the further reproduction of society and the possibility of further development of the productive forces. Each stage of development of the productive forces allows, so to speak, only *one* definite institutionalization of the social reproduction process; hence the class struggle is necessary in order to carry out these institutionalizations, but it is at the same time merely the vehicle of an historical progress which advances to completion behind the backs of the warring classes, and whose unique logic is that of a progressive conquest of external nature by means of a species subject only apparently split into classes.

That is the first of the alternative possible interpretations proposed above; it appears irreconcilable with Marx's intentions. But the second possible interpretation, which takes into account the ideology-critical approach of the theory, is for its part equally incompatible with the text just cited. It would mean that a 'conflict' between the productive forces and forms of intercourse was always to be understood *also* as the protest of repressed individuals against forms of domination whose legitimations had become questionable, and against the burdens and deprivations demanded by such forms of dominations and experienced as capricious and unjust. It would be a conflict between the *possibility* of a 'good life' anticipated by these very individuals (admittedly on the basis of a definite stage of development of productive forces), and the social constraint that they experience in reality; between the demands of an inherited (that is, traditional) form of domination and the realizable demands of repressed classes. The social conflicts would be those of *material life*, because they would be grounded in the discrepancy between the possible fulfilment and the actual suppression of real needs; but they would be *conflicts* only because, through the interpretation and legitimation of their needs, social groups would put themselves in conflict with the traditional interpretations and legitimations of existing relations of domination. This would mean, however, that the forms in which men became conscious of their social conflicts, and in which they fought them out, would be not only an epiphenomenon of 'objective' conflicts between productive forces and conditions of production, but their constitutive aspect (*Moment*). The ideology-critical tracing back of these forms as forms of a distorted ethical context of relations could not be carried out solely by recourse to the 'transformation[s] of the economic conditions of production, which can be determined with natural scientific exactitude'; on the contrary, it would first of all require recourse to an immanently critical dissolution of their false consciousness.

Marx's formulations feature an ambiguity which is difficult to resolve, inasmuch as they can be interpreted according to differing theoretical approaches. Hence the programme of a transition from ideology to science, already indicated in the confrontation of an ideological consciousness requiring enlightenment with an explicative theory on the basis of facts 'which can be determined with natural scientific exactitude', as described by Marx in *The German Ideology*, also appears ambivalent. Nevertheless it is to be interpreted here in the perspective of our ideal-typical reinterpretation of a modified historical materialism.

The fact that Marx believes that the time has come for a transition from the 'ideological' to the 'scientific' method of observation of social reality is linked with his assumption that the capitalist process of production itself abolishes the traditional legitimations of domination, in so far as uprooted and pauperized men themselves are at last forced to 'contemplate their mutual relations with sober eyes'. For Marx, 'sober' means empirico-scientific, without any premises other than those which are 'open to confirmation in a purely empirical fashion'.[14] With the confrontation of ideology and science he returns to a certain extent from the shadowland of idealistic dialectics to the firm ground of the empiricist-materialistic tradition, whose enthusiasm for 'immediacy', especially that of Feuerbach's philosophy with its 'starting-point in the positive, the sensuously definite',[15] has left definite traces in this opposition. Nevertheless the influence of Feuerbach, whom Marx had already criticized in *The German Ideology* in regard to a return to insights of idealistic philosophy, has affected only the externals of Marx's thought; its essential content is already determined by the criticism of Feuerbach's materialism and of the whole materialistic tradition. The decisive indication of this is to be found in the second of the *Theses on Feuerbach*: 'The question whether human thinking can arrive at objective truth is not a theoretical but a *practical* question. Man has to prove the truth, that is, the reality and power, the "this-sidedness" of his thinking, in practice.'[16] However, for Marx the paradigm for a theoretical truth that proves itself in practice (that is, 'through the mediation of industry') was that of natural science.[17] This shows clearly the sole standpoint from which Marx was able to carry out a purely functional conjunction of ideologies and forms of domination: the standpoint of empirical science – the only one to have shown its practical truth in contrast to the destruction of ideological illusion. It is now evident how closely interwoven are Marx's interpretation of history, his modification of the concept of ideology and his pragmatic concept of theory, and how, from this reciprocal dependence of various aspects of his theory, the misconception that the end of ideology was identical with the transition from ideology to 'positive science' could arise. 'Where speculation ceases, there in real life, real, positive science begins – the representation of the practical activity, of the practical process of human development.'[18]

---

14 *The German Ideology*, p. 20.
15 Cf. *Economic and Philosophical Manuscripts, MA*, vol. 1, p. 639, pp. 603ff.
16 *MEW*, vol. 3, p. 5.
17 Cf. *Economic and Philosophical Manuscripts*, p. 603.
18 *MEW*, vol. 3, p. 27.

13   The Ethical Potential of Marx's Thought

Svetozar Stojanović

I

A Marxist ethics, at least one worthy of Marx's name, has yet to be constructed. Does this problem exist because of obstacles inherent in Marx's thought itself or perhaps simply because of certain external circumstances, such as the immaturity of Marx's followers? The following lines, written by Antonio Labriola, show that some Marxists have not even understood the ethical *problem* in Marxism:

> Ethics and idealism consist henceforth in this, to put the thought of science at the service of the proletariat. If this ethics does not appear moral enough for the sentimentalists, usually hysterical and silly, let them go and borrow altruism from its high priest Spencer who will give them a vague and insipid definition of it, such as will satisfy them.[1]

An examination of the reasons which might account for the non-existence of a Marxist ethics is a precondition for any more complete evaluation of Marx's philosophy. One of the criteria for evaluating a body of thought is its capacity of embracing all the key problems of man. It is not good for it to remain powerless before the moral dimension of social life.

How could it have happened that a revolutionary movement whose goal was the realization of the most radical humanistic ideals still lacks a developed ethics? To this very day Marxists have argued more about the causes of the

From Svetozar Stojanović, *Between Ideals and Reality: a Critique of Socialism and its Future*, translated by Gerson S. Sher (New York: Oxford University Press, 1973), pp. 137–55. Copyright © 1973 by Oxford University Press, Inc. Reprinted by permission of the publisher.

1 *Essays on the Materialistic Conception of History*, p. 75.

undeveloped state of their ethics than they have worked to develop one. Two reasons are commonly put forward for this – one socio-political, the other socio-psychological.

The state of the workers' movement, social democratic as well as communist, is usually cited as the first reason. Indeed, if 'the ultimate aim of socialism is nothing, but the movement is everything,'[2] it is difficult to find a place for ethics. On the other hand, Stalinism and contemporary Maoism have made a caricature of Marxist ethics: ethical theorists become the apologists of state policy.

The second, socio-psychological factor usually advanced to explain the lack of a Marxist ethics is the tendency of Marxists to postpone the formulation of a positive programme in times of revolutionary action. To this is usually added the observation that, although in 1844 he did intend to write a book on ethical problems, Marx himself did not have enough time to work on ethics. Marx, however, used his time for what he thought was more important. But if Marx did not have the time, this surely cannot be said of many of his followers. Nevertheless, to this very day we have not come upon a satisfactory Marxist ethics. A more complete explanation, apparently, will have to be sought in certain theoretical obstacles inherent to Marx's thought itself.

Throughout the history of Marxism and Marxology there have been two conflicting interpretations of Marx – ethical and a-ethical. This writer represents the view that Marx's thought contains ethical values which can serve as a point of departure for a Marxist ethics. But Marx also gave occasion for the contrary – a-ethical – interpretation. This ambivalence creates difficulties for any Marxist-oriented philosophy of morals. In addition, however, there is one more, significantly larger obstacle, i.e. Marx's understanding of historical determinism.

II

What evidence is there for those who claim that Marx's work has absolutely no ethical content?

Marx asserted that he had emerged from the province of speculation into the domain of 'real, positive science'.[3] He was attempting to establish a scientific socialism, as opposed to the moralizing-utopian socialism which had existed previously. Partisans of the a-ethical interpretation of Marx's thought usually refer to the following or similar passages:

Communists cannot preach any kind of *morality* at all, something that Stirner does

---

2 Eduard Bernstein, *Evolutionary Socialism*, p. 202.
3 *The German Ideology*, 1947, part I, p. 15.

altogether too much. They cannot pose any kind of moral demands at all to people: love one another, do not be egoists, etc. On the contrary, they know very well that egoism, just as well as self-sacrifice, *is* in specific conditions a necessary form of individual self-affirmation.[4]

Communism is for us not a stable state which is to be established, an *ideal* to which reality will have to adjust itself. We call communism the *real* movement which abolishes the present state of things.[5]

Law, morality, religion, are to it [the proletariat – S.S.] so many bourgeois prejudices, behind which lurk in ambush just as many bourgeois interests.[6]

Morality is 'impotence in action'. Every time one struggles with some vice it is defeated. But Rudolph cannot even raise himself to the standpoint of independent morality, which is based at least upon *human dignity*. To the contrary, his morality bases itself upon consciousness of human weakness. His *morality* is *theological*.[7]

In his letter to Engels of 4 November 1864,[8] Marx complained that the Mazzinists had forced him to throw two phrases into the Preamble of the Statutes of the International about 'duty and right' as well as about 'truth, morality, and justice', but added that in such a place they would do no damage.

In his letter to Sorge of 19 October 1877, Marx complained about those people who wanted to 'replace its [socialism's – Tr.] materialistic basis (which demands serious objective study from anyone who tries to use it) by modern mythology with its goddesses of Justice, Liberty, Equality and Fraternity'.[9]

The group which interprets Marx as an a-ethical thinker includes Werner Sombart, Benedetto Croce, Karl Kautsky, Max Adler, Rudolf Hildferding, the neo-Kantians, Lucien Goldmann, among others. Some of them hold that the absence of an ethical position is a shortcoming of Marx's thought and, therefore, seek to supplement Marx through Darwin (Kautsky), Darwin and Kant (Ludwig Woltmann), or Kant (the neo-Kantians).

III

Opposed to the group described above is an entire succession of theorists who think that Marx's thought has ethical content: Eduard Bernstein, Maximilien Rubel, Karl Popper, John Lewis, Eugene Kamenka and others. Once again I have cited non-Marxists as well as Marxists. This second group embraces both those who believe that Marx's doctrine is purely ethical and non-scientific, and those who claim that it is ethical only in one of its dimensions and scientific in the other.

4 'Die Deutsche Ideologie', part III, in *Werke*, 1959, vol. 3, p. 299.
5 *The German Ideology*, part I, p. 26.
6 *Communist Manifesto*, p. 44.
7 'Die Deutsche Ideologie', part III, p. 213.
8 Karl Marx and Frederick Engels, *Selected Correspondence* (Moscow, 1956), p. 182.
9 Ibid., pp. 375–6.

They also rely upon many passages from Marx, for example:

The criticism of religion ends with the doctrine that *man is the supreme being for man*.
It ends, therefore, with the *categorical imperative to overthrow all those conditions* in
which man is an abased, enslaved, abandoned, contemptible being. . . .[10]

The social principles of Christianity preach cowardice, self-contempt,
abasement, submission, humility, in short, all the qualities of the *canaille*, while the
proletariat, not wanting to be treated as *canaille*, needs its courage, pride, and sense
of independence much more than its daily bread.[11]

The standpoint of the old materialism is *civil* society; the standpoint of the new is
human society, or socialized humanity.[12]

Marx pleaded for a society 'in which the free development of each is the
condition for the free development of all'.[13] In the same document he often
used ethical expressions, such as 'naked self-interest and callous cash-
payment', 'oppression', 'degradation of personal dignity', 'shameless, direct and
brutal exploitation', 'inconsiderateness', 'the modern slavery of capital', 'subjugation', 'the masses of workers are slaves', and so on. Marx's *Capital* (especially
chapters IV, VII, and XXIII of the first volume) is also permeated with ethically
coloured formulations.

So is the following passage from *The Poverty of Philosophy* concerning
capitalism: 'This is the time when the very things which till then had been
communicated, but never exchanged; given, but never sold; acquired, but never
bought – virtue, love, conviction, knowledge, conscience, etc. – when everything, in short, passed into commerce. It is the time of general corruption, of
universal venality. . . .'[14]

In his *Critique of the Gotha Programme*, Marx compares bourgeois, socialist
and communist distribution of the social product, demonstrating the advantages
of the communist mode of distribution from the principle of social equality.

But there is no need to go on referring to passages from Marx's works. With
the books by Marek Fritzhand[15] and Eugene Kamenka,[16] in which Marx is
quoted and analysed in detail, I think that it has been definitively proved that
Marx's thought has an ethical dimension. From his earliest through to his latest
works, Marx wrote as an heir of the great European humanistic-ethical
tradition. Many non-Marxist thinkers as well have conceded this point.

How could it have been, and still be, that in the face of so many proofs to the
contrary, there have been interpreters of Marx's thought who have claimed that
it is a-ethical, and furthermore that it is not accidentally so but rather a-ethical

10 Marx, in Bottomore (ed.), *Karl Marx: Early Writings*, p. 52.
11 *Karl Marx, Friedrich Engels; Historisch-kritische Gesamtausgabe (MEGA)* (Berlin, 1932), I/6, 278.
12 'Thesis X on Feuerbach', in Marx and Engels, *Selected Works*, p. 30.
13 *Communist Manifesto*, p. 53.
14 Marx, *The Poverty of Philosophy* (New York, 1963), p. 34.
15 *Myśl Etyczna Młodego Marksa* (Warsaw, 1961).
16 *The Ethical Foundations of Marxism*.

in its very essence? In this connection, as we have seen, these interpreters refer to Marx's statement about the scientific character of his work and some of his thoughts on morality. As final proof they usually cite Marx's understanding of historical determinism – but we shall address ourselves to this topic in the next section.

From Marx's belief in the scientific character of his own teaching, of course, it does not at all follow that this teaching was not ethically coloured. The point is that Marx did not take 'science' to mean 'value-free' intellectual activity, which is what certain Marxologists have in mind when they speak of 'science'. Marx never drew the kind of distinction between cognitive and value statements which would place the latter outside the realm of science. We can never overlook the fact that Marx was a student of Hegel, and that Hegel had rejected Kant's dualism because he was convinced of the unity of the Is and the Ought, of *Sein* and *Sollen*.

No passage quoted by adherents of the a-ethical interpretation of Marx proves convincingly that moral values remained external to the content of his thought. On the contrary, there are many passages which prove the opposite. There is not a single passage of Marx's that *must* be interpreted in such a manner as to show that he was hostile to morality, but there are quite a few which unquestionably express a strong aversion to the *preaching* of moral values. At first glance it might seem as if the following lines, which we have already quoted above, are an exception in this respect: 'Law, morality, religion are to it [the proletariat – S.S.] so many bourgeois prejudices, behind which lurk in ambush just as many bourgeois interests.' But contextual analysis shows that this passage is hostile to the bourgeoisie and its invocation of morality rather than to morality as such.

Why was Marx against the preaching of morality? This cannot be explained in terms of his personal moral qualities, as Karl Popper tries to do when he writes: 'Marx, I believe, avoided an explicit moral theory, because he hated preaching. Deeply distrustful of the moralist who usually preaches water and drinks wine, Marx was reluctant to formulate his ethical convictions explicitly.'[17] Marx, for instance, had nothing against the personal moral standards of certain utopian socialists. But he criticized them none the less, as he wanted to transcend moralizing socialism with scientific socialism.

The moral preacher, according to Marx, operates on the assumption that 'a moral command to people to change their consciousness will really change their consciousness'.[18] The preacher is the personification of 'impotence in action'. This is the reason Marx decided in favour of a scientific investigation of existing society and reliance upon those forces which are interested in changing it at its very foundations. With complete devotion, he plunged into the task of establishing the regularities of capitalism and the forces which maintain it, the

17 *The Open Society and Its Enemies*, pp. 385–6.
18 'Die Deutsche Ideologie', part III, *Werke*, vol. 3, p. 232.

possibilities and tendencies pointing toward the transcendence of capitalism, as well as the task of discovering the identity of the agent of such revolution. Not believing in the efficacy of moral preaching, Marx insisted upon the need for radical changes in the social conditions which lead to immorality. His humanism is neither moralizing nor even primarily moral, although it does contain the moral dimensions as well; instead, it is practical and revolutionary. This humanism attempts to penetrate to the causes of an inhuman social order, and is not concerned primarily with consequences, unlike utopian socialism, which remains naïve and powerless. Marx's humanism, rather than relying upon its moral appeal and influence, relies upon something else much more basic – the *interests* of the working class. The task of Marx's theory is to contribute to the awakening of the working class's consciousness of its own interests.

Marx's intellectual position is not beyond moral values; but it is antimoralistic. Every moralist gives precedence to a moral judgement (rather than an examination of reality) and expects that this judgement in and of itself will move people to change reality. Moralism in practice corresponds to ethicism in theory.

Marx did make moral judgements about capitalism. Yet what was most important to him was scientific investigation into the nature of capitalism. In contrast to moralists, Marx held no illusions about the efficacy of moral judgements which do not coincide with real social interests, and although he evaluated capitalism from a humanistic standpoint, he did not feel the need to formulate and explicate the principles upon which he had based these judgements. Marx was a critic, and an ethical critic at that, but he was not a systematic ethical theorist. Should it not be possible, however, for those people who seek to construct a Marxist ethics to try to explicate, systematize, evaluate and employ his moral principles? This task is still no more than at its first stage, and no one has done more in this respect thant Marek Fritzhand, whom we have already mentioned.

Marxists are heirs to the clearly antimoralistic and anti-ethicist posture of Karl Marx. A Marxist ethics cannot consider its primary task to be to urge individuals to perfect themselves in a moral sense. A Marxist ethics must be the ethics of the revolutionary movement. Such an ethics finds its hope in moral revolution, but only as an aspect of social, and even more broadly, total humanist revolution. All this demands that a Marxist ethics be differentiated from classical normative ethics. Moreover, it should be recognized that Marxists have the best prospects of making new contributions in problems of social, rather than individual, ethics. Even so, they still cannot afford to lose sight of the ethical problems of the individual, such as for instance the meaning of life, happiness, love and hate, friendship and so on.

IV

That alongside of his understanding of historical determinism Marx also left a place for human praxis, freedom and self-realization is demonstrated by many of his texts, of which the following are illustrative:

> Men make their own history, but they do not make it just as they please; they do not make it under circumstances chosen by themselves, but under circumstances directly encountered, given and transmitted from the past.[19]

> History is nothing but the succession of the separate generations, each of which exploits the materials, the forms of capital, the productive forces handed down to it by all preceding ones, and thus on the one hand continues the traditional activity in completely changed circumstances and, on the other, modifies the old circumstances with a completely changed activity.[20]

> World history would indeed be very easy to make if the struggle were taken up only on condition of infallibly favourable chances. It would on the other hand be of a very mystical nature, if 'accidents' played no part. These accidents naturally form part of the general course of development and are compensated by other accidents. But acceleration and delay are very much dependent upon such 'accidents', including the 'accident' of the characters of the people who first head the movement.[21]

Still, Marx belonged to nineteenth-century science, in which the strict determinism of the natural science of the time was still the theoretical and methodological ideal for all the sciences. It should also be taken into consideration that in his philosophy of history, Marx's mentor, Hegel, treated people as instruments of the objective Spirit. All this had to have an impact upon Marx, who occasionally went to the extremes of absolute determinism:

> My standpoint, from which the evolution of the economic formation of society is viewed as a *process of natural history*, can less than any other make the individual responsible for relations whose creature he socially remains, however much he may subjectively raise himself above them.[22]

> But capitalist production begets, *with the inexorability of a law of Nature*, its own negation.[23]

Marx approvingly quoted one of *Capital*'s reviewers, who had written:

> Consequently, Marx only troubles himself about one thing: to show, by rigid scientific investigation, the necessity of successive determinate orders of social conditions, and to establish, as impartially as possible, the facts that serve him for fundamental starting-points. For this it is quite enough, if he proves, at the same time, both the necessity of the present order of things, and the necessity of another order into which the first must inevitably pass over; and this all the same, whether men believe or do not believe it, whether they are conscious or unconscious of it.

19 'The Eighteenth Brumaire of Louis Bonaparte', in Marx and Engels, *Selected Works*, p. 97.
20 *The German Ideology*, part I, p. 38.
21 Marx's Letter to L. Kugelmann of 17 April 1871; in Marx and Engels, *Selected Correspondence*, p. 320.
22 *Capital*, 'Preface to the First Geman Edition', vol. I, p. 10. My emphasis – S.S.
23 Ibid., p. 763. My emphasis – S.S.

Marx treats the social movement as a process of natural history, governed by laws not only independent of human will, but rather, on the contrary, determining that will, consciousness, and intelligence. . . .[24]

In the passage which follows, Marx advocates both strict determinism, according to which social laws function with 'iron necessity', but at the same time a milder form of determinism as well, which treats laws as 'tendencies': 'Intrinsically, it is not a question of the higher or lower degree of development of the social antagonisms that result from the natural laws of capitalist production. *It is a question of these laws themselves, of these tendencies working with iron necessity toward inevitable results.*'[25] And in the third volume of *Capital*,[26] Marx again puts forth the view that a law is only a tendency which can be annulled by contradictory tendencies.

And even when a society has got upon the right track for the discovery of the *natural laws of its movement – and it is the ultimate aim of this work, to lay bare the economic law of motion of modern society* – it can neither clear by bold leaps, nor remove by legal enactments, the obstacles offered by the successive phases of its normal development. But it can shorten and lessen the birth-pangs.[27]

There are, then, two interweaving and conflicting motifs in Marx's writings. While people are the subjects of the historical process, its course is independent of human consciousness and will. While man is a creative being, there is only one possible direction which history can take. While people can exert an influence upon historical events, they can exert such influence only upon the speed with which they take place, and not upon their general course. To be sure, this rule of blind historical forces over man was for Marx a sign that we are still in man's prehistory. In communism, associated humanity would determine the course of history.

Both as a philosopher and as a student of history, Marx had to give an account of the relationship between determinism and freedom. Experts on the history of human thought are aware that this is one of the so-called eternal philosophical problems, that the basic *types* of solutions had been outlined before the time of Marx, and that each of them has had its own powerful mode of argumentation and justification. Without being aware of it Marx continuously vacillated between two mutually exclusive positions.

Consequently, two different orientations branched off from Marx, orientations which have trailed through the history of Marxism to the present day. The majority of the Marxists of the Second International understood Marx as a theorist of strict determinism. At the same time, such a Marx had to be seen as an a-ethical thinker. Naturally, those Marxists who felt the absence of ethics to

24 Ibid., 'Afterword to the Second German Edition', p. 18. My emphasis – S.S.
25 Ibid., p. 8. My emphasis – S.S.
26 Ibid., vol. III, pp. 234–5.
27 Ibid., vol. I. 'Preface to the First German Edition', p. 10. My emphasis – S.S.

be a shortcoming had to seek a supplement to Marx's thought in other philosophies, above all in the philosophy of Kant.

Opposing himself to Western social democracy, Lenin gravitated toward the conception of Marx as a thinker of revolutionary-historical creativity. However, it must be pointed out that Lenin did not take note of the contradiction in Marx's understanding of historical determinism. Moreover, Lenin himself restated the idea that communism is historically inevitable while at the same time maintaining an activist posture. While in theory he often used severely deterministic language, in practice Lenin firmly insisted upon revolutionary consciousness and creativity. Perhaps no social movement more than the communist movement has insisted so vigorously upon the inevitability of its own goal and simultaneously upon the activism of organized fighters for that goal.

Faith in the inevitability of socialism had a diverse psychological effect upon the international workers' movement. Social democrats have rather passively expected capitalism to gradually arrive at its final crisis, while Leninists have actively pursued the destruction of capitalism with a great deal of self-confidence. Stalinists, in order to reassure their followers and render their opponents powerless, have made masterful use of the psychological effect of the concept of the inevitability of socialism. Faith in the inevitability of socialism, apparently, also fortifies the Maoists' conviction (in the spirit of indeterminism which they otherwise reject) that the determining nature of China's backwardness does not constitute an obstacle over which the organized masses cannot execute 'great leaps forward'.

V

Assuming that Marx's occasional extremely deterministic statements are true, that socialism is a historical inevitability, and that people can only speed up or slow down its advent: in that case, is a Marxist ethics possible?

The task of such ethics, among other things, would be morally to stimulate and obligate people to struggle for socialism. This effort of the ethical theorists, however, makes sense only if people can influence the course of history. Yet we have already quoted extensively from the Marx according to whom people have a weak impact upon the historical process and, therefore, bear little responsibility for the outcome of this process.

Precisely because he looked upon socialism as a historical inevitability, Marx did not feel the need to give an explicit ethical justification for it. Much less did he want to prescribe that people *ought* to try to bring about the triumph of socialism.

This has led a few interpreters – Karl Popper,[28] N. B. Mayo,[29] George L.

28 *The Open Society and Its Enemies.*
29 *Democracy and Marxism,* ch. 7.

Kline,[30] and others – to conclude that Marx took historical necessity as his ethical criterion. Since Popper's statement is the most fully elaborated, it seems most natural that his statement should be presented and evaluated here.

Popper characterizes Marx's position as 'moral positivism', or even more precisely, 'moral futurism', but immediately adds: 'Marx, I assert, would not seriously have defended moral positivism in the form of moral futurism if he had seen that it implies the recognition of future might as right.'[31] As evidence for his interpretation, Popper refers to the following passage from Engels: '. . . that morality which contains the maximum of durable elements is the one which, in the present, represents the overthrow of the present, represents the future: that is, the proletarian.'[32] But first of all, this passage does not prove that historical necessity was an ethical criterion for Engels. And secondly, even if it were to do so, this is Engels and not Marx. Popper did not quote Marx, and could not, because there are no passages in Marx's writings to justify such an interpretation. He read the ethical criterion implicit in Stalinism into Marx: that which triumphs in history is *ipso facto* moral.

Robert C. Tucker[33] rightly rejects Popper's interpretation, suggesting that Marx first arrived at the idea of a human society, and only later reached his convictions about its necessity. At this point we might also take note of another rather convincing counterproof offered by Tucker: it is hardly credible that anyone would be so disgusted by existing society, to the extent that Marx was, solely on the basis of the intellectual conviction that it would inevitably disappear and yield to communism. In my opinion, the idea of the humanistic foundation of communism led Marx *psychologically* to his conviction of its inevitability, and not conversely. As a great optimist he was convinced that the historical process would necessarily lead to a *human* society. However, these two matters – the historical necessity and the humanistic justification of communism – were *logically* independent of each other in his mind.

Because of its occasionally absolutely deterministic dimension, however, Marx's thought peculiarly does harm to the very cause it espouses. For a Marxist to be able to construct an ethics of revolutionary action, he must reject Marx's rigid determinism. Such determinism excludes human freedom, which is the *ratio essendi* of morality and ethics.

Many Marxists have accepted a milder variant of Marx's determinism. But it is by now high time to approach serious work on the formulation, development and justification of this position. In Marxism this point of view has merely been reiterated, with minor variations, yet other, non-Marxist philosophers have written many significant works on the problem of historical determinism and freedom. One could not say that they have solved this problem, of course, but it

30 *European Philosophy Today*, p. 132.
31 *The Open Society and Its Enemies*, p. 393.
32 *Anti-Dühring*, p. 104.
33 *Philosophy and Myth in Karl Marx*, p. 21.

is certain that they have made a considerable degree of progress in both the presentation of the problem and the argumentation of their positions.

The milder variant of determinism proceeds from the assumption that every historical situation bears within it more than one possibility. Yet possibilities are not unlimited, contrary to what Marxists who have fallen under the influence of existentialism may think, for the framework of possibilities is defined by the historical level achieved. Human freedom consists of the power to choose one of these possibilities and to commit oneself to its realization. Only when man possesses this power of choice is he morally responsible for the course of history. An ethics of revolutionary action is possible only on the basis of faith in the relative openness of the future.

However, even once one concludes that a Marxist ethics must renounce Marx's occasional absolute determinism, one need not in the least agree with Popper, who writes: '"Scientific" Marxism is dead. Its feeling of social responsibility and its love for freedom must survive.'[34] Today rigid determinism has been transcended in natural science as well as in social science. But even if science does not reveal inevitabilities in history, it is still capable of establishing historical possibilities and tendencies.

Socialism is one of these real possibilities and tendencies, but hardly an inevitability. Whether or not it will be realized depends upon human beings. Only a Marxism which sees socialism as a possibility can ethically obligate them to commit themselves to its realization.

After all the events of the past hundred years it is no longer possible to believe in the inevitability of socialism. At least two fundamental changes have occurred since Marx's time. First, a new form of class prehistory – statism – has been created, a form which Marx did not foresee; and second, man has accumulated such destructive forces in his hands that not even the existence of humanity can be taken for a certainty, much less the movement of history in any particular direction. Today it is not only possible for mankind to pass over from prehistory into true history; it may also pass over into de-history. What if it turns out that humanity has been trying to perform a task of Sisyphus? Or even worse – what if the stone destroys Sisyphus, and thus if the disappearance of the absurd is produced only at the price of the triumph of nothingness?

VI

Marx took possession of the pre-existing store of humanistic-ethical ideas, into which, among others, the ideals of the great democratic revolutions had found their way, and then radicalized, developed and made it concrete. The humanistic-ethical basis of his work is composed of the concepts of de-

34 *The Open Society and Its Enemies*, p. 397.

alienation, freedom, social equality and justice, the abolition of exploitation, the disappearance of social classes, the withering away of the state, the creation of self-managing associations of producers and so on. No satisfactory socio-political ethics today can steer clear of these values.

Marx's contribution to ethics must be sought in the radicalization and concretization of these values rather than in the formulation of a basic ethical criterion. To this day many Marxists have tried to find confirmation of such a criterion in Marx's writings, but to no avail.

At first the ethical criterion was sought in the abolition of exploitation and the interests of the proletariat. But one need not be very analytically minded to see that these principles cannot fulfil this role.

Marx's concept of exploitation embraces only a small portion of the moral phenomenon, and it is for this very reason that the abolition of exploitation could not be an ethical criterion. The attempt of certain Marxists to understand exploitation in a much broader sense, as *any situation* in which one person uses another *to his own advantage*, while avoiding the above-mentioned pitfall, introduces a second, no less dangerous one – excessive vagueness. Besides, ethics, particularly a Marxist ethics, cannot simply demand that people eliminate a situation in which each takes advantage of the other, but must rather demand instead something much more, something positive.

Lenin was in the habit of saying: 'We say that our morality is entirely subordinated to the interests of the proletariat's class struggle. Our morality stems from the interests of the class struggle of the proletariat.'[35] But when suggested as an ethical criterion, the interest of the proletariat has unavoidable weaknesses. Above all, the very notion of interest is extremely vague, and even Marx himself decisively rejected all utilitarian ethics. Some theorists have sought the solution in the difference between the immediate and historical interests of the proletariat. It is generally recognized that Marx clearly discriminated in favour of the latter. For him the proletariat's immediate interest was not even an unconditionally positive ethical value, much less a fundamental ethical criterion. The history of the proletariat and the proletarian movement indeed show how right Marx was to have a critical attitude toward its immediate interest.

However, to take the historical interest of the proletariat as the ethical criterion is to be caught unawares in a vicious circle. Analysis of Marx's writings demonstrates that the historical interest, as distinguished from the immediate interest of the proletariat, includes *by definition* the realization of the humanistic-ethical values enumerated above, thereby presenting us once more with the original question: which of these is the supreme ethical value that can serve as a basis for the supreme ethical criterion?

This vicious circle is not so conspicious as the one within which Lenin was

35 *Works*, in English (Moscow, 1950), vol. 31, p. 266.

188 *Svetozar Stojanović*

caught when he tried to define *communist* morality as that which 'serves to destroy the old exploiting society and to unite all the working people around the proletariat, which is building up a revolutionary, a *communist* society.'[36] For decades Soviet ethicists have retraced this circle. As illustration I refer to Shishkin: 'Marxism–Leninism sees the highest criterion of communist morality in the struggle for communism.'[37] But under the influence of Stalinism these ethicists went even 'farther' than Lenin by identifying the historical interest of the proletariat with the policies of their own Communist Party. They thus opened the door to the ethical degeneration of the party, as well as of the revolution.

More recently, certain Marxists have sought the supreme ethical criterion in de-alienation. This certainly represents theoretical progress, as the concept of de-alienation is more fundamental and complex than that of either the abolition of exploitation or realization of the interests of the proletariat. But this effort as well has failed to produce any satisfactory results.

In the second chapter of this book we analysed Marx's concept of de-alienation. On the formal level, de-alienation means the transcendence of the contradiction between human essence and human existence. On the level of content, the de-alienated person is creative, whole, free, sociable and multi-laterally developed. When we analyse such a complex concept as that of de-alienation, that is to say, we find multiple values contained within it, once again posing the question from which we had started: which of these values is most fundamental, so that it may serve as the basic ethical criterion?

'Creativity' and 'wholeness' even at first glance are unsatisfactory because what we need is precisely a measure by which we can judge when a person, even in his creativity and wholeness, is moral, and when he is not. Freedom, again, cannot be a moral *criterion* because it is a *presupposition* of morality. Moral judgement presupposes moral responsibility, and moral responsibility presupposes freedom. Besides, freedom itself is subordinate to an ethical evaluation (there are abuses as well as uses of freedom), and it therefore cannot be a measure for such an evaluation.

This means that only two of the above-mentioned notions remain – sociability and the multilateral development of human potentials. In his previously cited book, Fritzhand, after detailed analysis, extracts these two principles – the socialization and self-realization of man – as the axiological basis of Marx's work. But he did not succeed in finding one basic value in Marx which might serve as a rule of thumb when these two principles come into conflict. It is accurate to say that Marx was a sort of ethical perfectionist: he stood for the realization of every human potential which does not threaten man's social nature. But where is the border between egoistic self-realization

---

36 Ibid., vol. 31, p. 268. My emphasis – S.S.
37 *Osnovy kommunisticheskoi morali* (Foundations of Communist Morality) (Moscow, 1955), p. 95.

and socialization which does not smother individuality? Where does the free development of every individual as a 'condition for the free development of all' end and the development of an individual who threatens the freedom of others begin? How can we formulate a principle on the basis of which we can distinguish obligations of the free individual toward society from sociability which threatens human freedom?

Yet if Marx cannot help us to solve the problem of the fundamental ethical criterion, he still did articulate some important thoughts concerning individual ethical values. This fact should be put to good use in the construction of a Marxist ethics. A Marxist ethical theorist, of course, cannot afford to dwell too long on the establishment and systematization of Marx's contribution to ethics. Even if he extends his scope to other great socialist thinkers, which is undoubtedly necessary, he will still be no closer to a *living* ethics. Nothing can replace a critical analysis of the moral praxis of the revolutionary movement. Especially great prospects in this respect are offered by a humanistic-ethical critique of Stalinism.

14   Labour and Human Needs in a Society of Associated Producers

Agnes Heller

Now we can discuss the interaction between production and the structure of needs in the society of associated producers.

We have already noted that in his conception of the society of associated producers, Marx is working with an altogether new structure of needs. The primary role here is played by the need for labour (by which the whole theory stands or falls) and, as we have seen, by the need for surplus labour.

We know that the origin of the need for labour and its growth into a 'vital need' are not synonymous for Marx. In capitalism labour is a burden, (a) because it is performed under external compulsion, because it is alienated, and (b) because its specific nature offers no possibility of self-realization:

> He [Adam Smith] is right, of course, that, in its historic forms as slave labour, serf-labour and wage-labour, labour always appears as repulsive, always as external forced labour; and not-labour, by contrast, as 'freedom and happiness'. This holds doubly: for this contradictory labour; and, relatedly, for labour which has not yet created the subjective and objective conditions for itself . . . in which labour becomes attractive work, the individual's self-realization, which in no way means that it becomes mere fun, mere amusement, as Fourier, with Grisette-like naiveté, conceives it.[1]

From Agnes Heller, *The Theory of Need in Marx* (Giangiacomo Feltrinelli SpA), pp. 118–30. Reprinted by permission of the author.

1 *Grundrisse*, p. 611.

Marx uses the composition of music as an example of the kind of labour that is purely intellectual.

In the *Grundrisse* both conditions are satisfied: alienation is overcome and labour becomes *travail attractif*. Since with the production of material goods labour in the traditional sense ceases, all labour becomes essentially intellectual labour, the field for the self-realization of the human personality. It thus becomes the vital need, a determining (even if not the most determining) human need, and hence it also assumes a dominant role in the structure of needs. In this conception, there never can arise any question about 'why' human beings work.

In the framework of *Capital*, however, only one condition is satisfied: the alienation of labour ceases (in every aspect), but labour itself does not become *travail attractif*. In this interpretation labour in the society of associated producers is not free self-activity:

> In fact, the realm of freedom actually begins only where labour which is determined by necessity and mundane considerations cease; thus in the very nature of things it lies beyond the sphere of actual material production. . . . freedom in this field can only consist in socialized man, the associated producers, rationally regulating their interchange with nature, bringing it under their common control, instead of being ruled by it as by the blind forces of nature; and achieving this with the least expenditure of energy and under conditions most favourable to, and worthy of, their human nature. But it none the less still remains a realm of necessity. Beyond it begins that development of human energy which is an end in itself, the true realm of freedom, which, however, can blossom forth only with this realm of necessity as its basis. The shortening of the working day is its basic prerequisite.[2]

Three comments need to be made here. First, since according to the quotation from *Capital* only free time is the sphere of free self-activity, Marx is attributing an even greater importance here than in the *Grundrisse* to time-economy, to the reduction of the necessary working time and to the rationalization of production. Secondly, since labour is not itself *travail attractif*, it may be asked why people work. Thirdly, I would like to emphasize that from this point of view the project here appears just as utopian, despite the fact that its presentation is more realistic, as in the *Grundrisse*; I believe it inconceivable that there should be such a huge abyss between the activity of labour and the activity of free time. The *Grundrisse*'s noble picture of the individual active in his free time who re-enters production a changed man would lose its relevance: production does not 'need' to be performed by 'changed', 'richer' human beings.

This discussion could take us far away from our real argument, so let us

2 *Capital*, vol. III, pp. 799–800.

return to the second question: why do people work? Assuming the structure of needs to be what it is today, the answer can only be conceived in terms of the general obligation to labour. But 'the obligation to labour' for Marx is characteristic only of a period of transition (the brief phase of the dictatorship of the proletariat). In the society of associated producers only nature can force people to do anything: no one can force anyone else (feudal lordship and serfdom are, in Marx's view, reciprocal determinations; there is no feudal lordship without serfdom and vice versa). In the first phase of communism (in which people share products according to their labour) there is naturally a form of obligation inherited from capitalism: in order to live, people must work. But when they share their goods according to their needs, and the labour time of each individual is not divided into necessary labour and surplus labour, then this form of obligation also ceases to exist. So why do human beings work? In *Capital*, Marx posits a structure of needs that is basically new, that transforms human beings into changed people, for whom 'social duty' is *not only an external but an internal motivation*: in this respect, 'Must' [*Müssen*] and 'Ought' [*Sollen*] now coincide. (I can only imagine this model in a society composed of communities. We shall see below how this hypothesis occurred to Marx.)

Only in *Capital* do we find a consistent conception of the interaction between material needs and production:

> It is only where production is under the actual predetermining control of society that the latter establishes a relation between the volume of social labour time applied in producing definite articles, and the volume of the social want to be satisfied by these articles.[3]

And further on:

> Secondly, after the abolition of the capitalist mode of production, but still retaining social production, the determination of value continues to prevail in the sense that the regulation of labour-time and the distribution of social labour among the various production groups, ultimately the book-keeping encompassing all this, become more essential than ever.[4]

And again:

> Surplus labour in general as labour performed over and above the given requirements, must always remain. . . . a definite quantity of surplus labour is required as insurance against accidents, and by the necessary and progressive expansion of the process of reproduction in keeping with the development of the needs and the growth of population, which is called accumulation from the viewpoint of the capitalist.[5]

3 Ibid., p. 184.
4 Ibid., p. 830.
5 Ibid., p. 799.

What then, according to this point of view, is the relationship between material needs and production?

Society produces *for* needs; hence the 'accidental' character of the market is eliminated. It is therefore possible, according to Marx, to avoid the 'waste' of material goods and productive capacities which characterizes capitalism and stems from the fact that production and needs are brought together only on the market. How are needs and production matched? The 'associated producers', as I have already indicated, will measure (*a*) needs and (*b*) their disposable labour time, and will fix (*c*) the labour time socially necessary for each activity. They will then divide up (and reallocate) the productive forces between various branches of production. They will, of course, also take into account the production that does not directly serve the satisfaction of needs (the expansion of production, insurance funds and – they are not mentioned here, but they appear in other passages – public investments that will satisfy needs only over a period of time).

What are the needs which must be measured and for which production must be undertaken? They are the 'true social needs' which are identified with 'necessary needs'.

But how can 'true social needs' be measured? It is assumed that the needs of individuals that are directly oriented towards consumption are, both qualitatively and quantitatively, roughly equal. It is therefore extraordinarily easy to account for them: with the aid of random samples, both quality and quantity can be determined. So far so good: but human beings in communist society, in Marx's view, are characterized above all else by the fact that their needs, considered *individually*, and the needs of different individuals, will be qualitatively and quantitatively extremely varied. If this is also true of material needs, the kind of measurement given in *Capital* is simply absurd. Even if a procedure were invented – it would be indeed a complex one – to carry it out, one could assert with some certainty that such a 'production for needs' would lead to a 'waste' of material goods and productive forces much greater than that to which the production of commodities (regulation by the market) has led or can lead. We would thus be saying that Marx did not apply the individualization of needs to the field of need for material goods. Only non-quantifiable types of need would become individual (and qualitatively different); quantifiable types of need (true material needs) would not become individual. This would lead to an extremely homogeneous and almost uniform image of the individual – if, that is, one accepts that Marx regarded material needs as playing a decisive role in the structure of needs of individuals. But Marx actually thought exactly the opposite: that for individuals in the society of associated producers, material needs occupy a subordinate role in the structure of needs, so that the development of a system of individual needs becomes possible notwithstanding their qualitative and quantitative 'equality'.

This conception is based upon relatively static needs which develop very slowly (at least where material needs are concerned). It does not even take into consideration the fact that, as we have said, purely qualitative needs (which are *eo ipso* individual) also call for material production, and that this raises further difficulties in 'calculating' them.

In this conception of material needs, a kind of 'egalitarianism' predominates. It is important to underline this point because 'egalitarianism' has no bitterer enemy than Marx himself. He holds that the concept of equality belongs to commodity production: in fact commodity production is 'realized equality'. Equality and inequality are reciprocally determined: where there is equality there is inequality, and vice versa. 'Equality' as a slogan and as a demand always remains within the horizon of bourgeois society. It abstracts from the uniqueness of the individual, and quantifies what is qualitatively diverse. In the society that develops the wealth of individuality – in communist society – 'equality' is not realized: equality and inequality as reciprocal determinations become meaningless and irrelevant. In order to demonstrate that this idea is constantly present in Marx's thought I shall cite two passages, one from a work of his youth, the other from a late work. In *The Holy Family* Marx writes:

> Proudhon did not succeed in giving this thought the appropriate development. The idea of 'equal possession' is a political-economic one and therefore itself still an *alienated* expression for the principle that the object as being for man, as the objectified being of man, is at the same time the existence of man for other men, his human relation to other men, the social relation of man to man.[6]

The idea of 'equal possession' therefore articulates, in an alienated manner (i.e. within the horizon of bourgeois society and with its terminology), the real aim, which is to overcome the alienated relations. In the *Critique of the Gotha Programme* Marx does not attack the concept of equal possession but that of equal right (equal right, as we know, will continue to subsist in the first phase of communism, which therefore will still be a bourgeois society in this respect): 'This equal right . . . is therefore a right to inequality in its content, like every right.'[7] This equality is 'abstraction', because it takes account of man only as worker. At the same time it abstracts from the effective needs of individuals, by furnishing them with equal amounts of goods from the social wealth according equal amounts of labour, whatever their needs actually are. Distribution according to needs, in contrast to distribution according to labour, overcomes both this equality and this inequality.

According to the *Critique of the Gotha Programme*, as we know, *no value* exists in the second phase of communism, and labour is not reduced to simple labour; at the same time Marx posits an extraordinary wealth of goods. Precisely for this reason there is no place for what we have called the 'egalitarian' aspect of communism. This is not the case in *Capital*, where we come across a 'saturation

6 *The Holy Family*, p. 60.
7 *Critique of the Gotha Programme*, in *Selected Works*, vol. II, p. 564.

model' regarding material goods. In Marx's conception, this kind of 'egalitarianism' is in no way identical with the equality of commodity production (equality of possession and of rights): the matter at issue is rather the relative equality of actual needs as regards material goods. These, as we know, are only limited by other (higher) needs of individuals. We ourselves cannot imagine any social order in which the need for material goods can become saturated relatively easily and where the individuality of needs develops exclusively through non-material needs. Today, we would call the conception which appears in *Capital* 'egalitarian'. However, the fact is that it was not an egalitarian one in Marx's eyes, and that he associated this model not with 'equality' but with the complete restructuring of the system of needs.

The great importance that Marx attached to the restructuring of the system of needs also appears clearly in two observations in the *Grundrisse* (in his maturity Marx considered such a restructuring to be a *sine qua non*; on this point there is no difference between *Capital* and the *Grundrisse*). He writes about workers in capitalism as follows:

> Through excessive exhaustion of their powers, brought about by lengthy, drawn-out monotonous occupations, they are seduced into habits of intemperance, and made unfit for thinking or reflection. They can have no physical, intellectual or moral 'amusements' other than of the worst sort.[8]

The intemperance follows from the fact that no capacity for physical, intellectual and moral 'amusements' can develop in the worker. In the 'society of associated producers', in which this capacity (qualitative needs) is well developed, 'intemperance' ceases. In another passage Marx expounds the problem with reference to the social whole. If society has attained a certain level of [material] wealth, then 'society [is] able to wait; . . . a large part of the wealth already created can be withdrawn both from immediate consumption and from production for immediate consumption.'[9] Let me repeat once again: for material needs, Marx is using something quite close to a 'saturation model', at least when he analyses the period after the attainment of a certain level of material wealth.

At this point the following question arises: who makes the decisions about how productive capacity should be allocated? Who decides, for example, how long the production of goods directly serving consumption can 'wait'? Marx's reply, of course, is *everyone* (this is precisely why he speaks of 'associated individuals'). But how can every individual make such decisions? Marx did not answer this question, because for him it did not arise. For us, however, in our times, it has become perhaps the most decisive question of all. The focal point

---

8 *Grundrisse*, p. 714. Marx is actually quoting Robert Owen.
9 Ibid., p. 707.

of contemporary Marxism is to work out models for this (or at least it ought to be).

Naturally, it is no accident that Marx did not even once formulate the question about 'how every individual can take part in decision-making'. We have already noted that in his opinion the category of interest will be irrelevant in the society of the future, and that there will therefore be no group interests, nor conflict of interests. The clear common interest of every member of society, apart from the satisfaction of necessary needs (which, as we have seen, still play a subordinate role in the structure of needs), will be the reduction of labour time. This is possible only through the maximum of rationalization. Consequently, every individual strives for the same thing, namely this maximum of rationalism; and the manner in which decision-making is carried on is of no consequence whatever. Whether the decisions are made by means of a referendum or through rotating representatives, every individual expresses the needs of all other individuals and it cannot be otherwise. In 'socialized' man, the human species and the individual represent a realized unity. Every individual represents the species and the species is represented in every individual. The needs of 'socialized' human beings determine production – and this means that the human species itself makes the decisions.

To put it in Hegelian terms, in Marx's society of associated producers the sphere of 'the objective spirit' goes up in smoke. We find no system of right, no institutions or politics there. What remains of the sphere of the 'objective spirit' of class society is elevated to the sphere of the 'absolute spirit'. For it is not only the pre-existing activities and objectivations (in an alienated form) of class society, such as art or philosophy, which are 'in conformity with the species for itself'. Morals too, and every human relationship, become 'in conformity with the species for itself'. To continue with the Hegelian analogy: the 'world spirit' is not only recognized in art and philosophy, but in every human relationship; every individual is representative of a conformity to the species that has become real and actual, he recognizes this representativeness in every other person, and presents himself as such in relation to them. All this is very well expressed in *The Holy Family*, where Marx speaks of morality in the future:

> Plato admitted that the law must be one-sided and must make abstraction of the individual. On the other hand, under human conditions punishment will really be nothing but the sentence passed by the culprit on himself. There will be no attempt to persuade him that violence from without, exerted by others, is violence exerted on himself by himself. On the contrary, he will see in other people his natural saviours from the sentence which he has pronounced on himself; in other words the relation will be reversed.[10]

10 *The Holy Family*, pp. 238–9.

In one of Kant's hypotheses he imagined 'the ideal society' to be that in which people make a contract to proceed according to the categoric imperative. From the point of view of his own philosophy that is in effect a contradiction: if it is a case of making a contract, morality is changed into legality. In Marx's eyes, the same model – at least from the philosophical standpoint – appears to be posed without any contradiction. If every individual represents conformity with species for itself, then the *need* of every individual (in this case, moral need) is involved at the level of this conformity. If his own particularity transgresses this conformity, he may therefore punish himself. The conflict between morality and legality is thus surmounted, since the opposition or opposed Being between morality and legality (which for Marx is found only in class society, in alienation) disappears.

The disappearance of legality and of all institutions does not of course imply the simple disappearance of objectivation. Quite the opposite. Only in communism (in the positive abolition of private property) is individual possession properly founded. Remember: needs are always directed towards objects. These objectivations are all 'for themselves' – except the sphere of production, which is in and for itself. Since we can no longer speak of material needs, but only of needs which 'stand outside them', every objectivation belongs to the realm of the 'absolute spirit'. Non-material needs are therefore all directed to the 'absolute spirit', to their objectivations, to their objects and to the allocation of these objects.

It is precisely for this reason that in the society of associated producers the need for 'free time', for 'leisure time', has such a leading role in man's system of needs. ('Leisure time' is not necessarily synonymous with 'free time': the latter can in fact be interpreted as a negative concept, as freedom from labour. For Marx, however, free time is 'leisure time', an unambiguously positive category: time for genuinely human, high-level activities – free activities.) Furthermore, artistic activity has a leading role in free-time activities, as the work of Marx's most creative periods clearly demonstrates. Artistic activity, which even in the era of class society is already drawn towards objectivations 'for themselves' and creates them, is the simplest and most illuminating example of what preoccupies Marx: the need for objectivations which are objectivations *for themselves* and which conform to the species, is the true human need of the members of the 'society of associated producers'.

Needs for objectivations (and objects) for themselves are purely qualitative needs, which are not quantifiable; furthermore, they are always needs to an end. This is formulated in the third volume of *Capital* as follows: beyond production 'begins that *development of human energy* which is an *end in itself*, the true *realm of freedom*'.[11] In activities which are directed towards objectivations for

11 *Capital*, vol. III, p. 800.

themselves, the true wealth of human beings develops, a universality of needs and capacities that satisfies qualitatively different (non-quantifiable) needs: 'Wealth is disposable time and nothing more.'[12]

The object for itself of needs can, as we have already noted, be not an objectivation but also the other person. Recall the *Economic and Philosophical Manuscripts* of 1844: in his human relationships, socialized man at all times makes qualities possible only for other men, and this is an end in itself; 'rich man' is man rich in human relationships. The question here is: does need for human beings also mean 'need for community'?

The question is of significance not only for the system of needs, but also for the whole social model. We have seen that in Marx's notion of the society of associated producers there is no place for the 'objective spirit', for the system of institutions. But should this also imply that there is no place for human integration?

For Marx, community (even on the smallest scale) is justifiable and relevant only when it appears as the immediate form of conformity to the species for itself, when it is an objectivation that conforms with the species for itself. There is no interest, and no conflict of interests: community, like the individual, can only be an *immediate* expression of such conformity to the species.

In the young Marx, community and the need for community undoubtedly appear as a *leitmotiv*. Remember his thoughts on the meetings of communist workers: 'But at the same time, as a result of this association, they acquire a new need – the need for society – and what appears as a means becomes an end.'[13] In the same work he also says: 'Although communal activity and communal enjoyment – i.e. activity and enjoyment which are manifested and directly revealed in real association with other men – will occur wherever such a direct expression of sociability stems from the true character of the activity's content and is adequate to its nature.'[14] Or again: 'In the same way, the senses and enjoyment of other men have become my own appropriation. Besides these direct organs, therefore, social organs develop in the form of society; thus, for instance, activity in direct association with others, etc., has become an organ for expressing my own life, and a mode of appropriating human life.'[15] 'Universal consciousness', reflection, philosophy, theory and thought must be rooted in this communal Being, and not 'grip the masses' merely after the event. 'My general consciousness is only the theoretical shape of that which the living shape is the real community, the social fabric, although at the present time general consciousness is an abstraction from real life and as such confronts it with hostility.'[16] This is why I stated earlier that, in Marx's view, not all

---

12 *Theories of Surplus Value*, vol. III, p. 255.
13 *Economic and Philosophical Manuscripts of 1844*, p. 137.
14 Ibid., p. 137. Translation modified.
15 Ibid., pp. 139–40. Translation modified.
16 Ibid., p. 137.

philosophy will cease under communism, but only the philosophy which counterposes the particular to that which conforms with the species, and which counterposes appearance to essence – the philosophy built on self-realizing values. It is social science instead which, according to this conception, would seem to cease. In fact there will no longer be any fetishism; in society essence and appearance will overlap. And so social science, which owes its existence to the contradiction between essence and appearance, will in effect be superfluous under communism according to Marx's view.

The idea of community and of the need for society, which is properly central in the works of his youth, moves somewhat into the background in his later works. We can see various reasons for this. First, there is his critique of the 'community' of natural societies and its 'limitedness'. Wherever Marx speaks of community – even in his earlier works – he is thinking of something different from 'natural communities'. He conceives the communities of the future as freely chosen, as made up of individuals who freely unite, as 'purely social' relations – a consequence of the pushing back of natural limits. However, as Marx devotes himself with increasing intensity to his analysis of the evolution of capitalism as alienated *evolution*, he puts increasing emphasis on the positive trend which capitalism has produced – amongst other things, by dissolving the natural communities. But there is another factor to be taken into account: that the presence of communities in the future society seemed so obvious to Marx that he did not see any necessity for discussing it separately. Very often he speaks of the society of the future as the 'society of cooperatives'! The existence of the 'community' and the 'need for community' in effect pass into the background; and in the few passages where he speaks of them, they appear as a 'natural' perspective. This is how he deals with it in the third volume of *Capital*, for example. Analysing the embryos of the future which exist in the present, he speaks of Robert Owen's cooperative factories:

> The cooperative factories of the labourers themselves represent, *within the old form, the first shoots of the new* . . . the capitalist stock companies, as much as the cooperative factories, should be considered as *transitional forms* from the capitalist mode of production to the associated one, with the only distinction that *the antagonism is resolved negatively in the one and positively in the other*.[17]

In the draft of a letter to Vera Zasulic, written in 1881, Marx expresses himself in a still more broad and unambiguous manner. The Russian rural community 'finds capitalism in a crisis that will end only with its elimination, and *with the return of the modern societies* to the "archaic" type of communal property; or, as an American author has said, the new system to which modern society is tending will be a revival in a superior form of an archaic social type. There is no need to be frightened of the expression "archaic".' Furthermore, in discussing

17 *Capital*, vol. III, p. 431.

those aspects of the communities of the future which will be different from the archaic communities, he points before all else to the fact that the former will not be based upon blood ties. This conception is in no way different from the position taken by Engels in his article of 1845, 'Description of the communist colonies that have originated in recent times and are still existing', in which he refers enthusiastically to the religious communes of the United States and predicts that they will spread. Marx was alarmed by the dissolution of the existing communities, because he recognized and treasured them as embryos of the form of intercourse and integration which in communism would become general.

In Marx's view, therefore, the 'everyday life' of man in the future society is not built around productive labour. On the contrary, productive labour occupies a subordinate position in the activities of everyday life; the centre of organization of life is represented by those activities and human relationships which conform with the species for itself. The needs directed towards these (qualitative needs-as-ends) will become man's primary needs, they will constitute his unique individuality and will limit needs for material goods. It is in this way that the personality that is 'deep' and rich in needs will be constituted.

Marx believed this change in the structure of needs to be 'natural' and 'obvious'. He took so little account of the possibility of conflicts that one thing must be repeated: although the change in Being is the decisive issue for him, there are quite a few Enlightenment aspects to be found in his conception. One will search in vain for the actual conflicts and problems of the transition which are so relevant for us and which are now a century old, but even so this 'pure' model has not lost its decisive significance for us.

Engels spoke with pride of the development of socialism from utopia to science. Today, science contains more than a few utopian elements. But as Ernst Bloch has so strikingly said, there are fertile and infertile utopias. There are many respects in which Marx's ideas on the society of associated producers and on the system of needs of united individuals are utopian, when measured against our own today and our own possibilities for action; they are none the less *fertile*. He establishes a norm against which we can measure the reality and value of our ideas, and with which we can determine the limitedness of our actions: it expresses the most beautiful aspiration of mature humanity, an aspiration that belongs to our Being.

Part III   Property and Social Classes

15 Towards a Sociological Analysis of Property Relations

András Hegedüs

There is a continual movement of growth in productive forces, of destruction in social relations, of formation in ideas; the only immutable thing is the abstraction of movement – *mors immortalis*.

Marx, The Poverty of Philosophy

One of the most characteristic features of the Marxist theory of society has been to prove the outstanding importance of the dominant property[1] relations in the life of concrete social and economic formations, and to deduce from these essential relations the existence of historical forces such as classes and class struggles. Marx explained how differing socio-economic formations develop and succeed each other primarily through the changes in property relations which result from these social struggles, and from the development of the forces of production; and he defined the periods of social progress mainly on the basis of the changes that occur in this respect. Therefore, if we wish to analyse the socialist societies of our time on a Marxist basis, our point of departure must be the property relations which have developed in them. And first of all we have to ask whether the problem of property (in the Marxist sense) exists in these countries as a vital existential problem for a particular class or stratum, just as the abolition of feudal property relations was an existential problem for the bourgeois classes, or just as in nineteenth-century Europe it was the fundamental interest of the working class to transform bourgeois property relations.

From András Hegedüs, *Socialism and Bureaucracy* (London: Allison and Busby, 1976), pp. 93–105. Reprinted by permission of Artijus on behalf of the author.

1 Throughout this essay the words 'property' and 'ownership', 'proprietor' and 'owner' are synonymous, whereas 'possession' is one of the *functions* of 'ownership'.

It is especially difficult to examine questions of this kind in the social sciences, because every conclusion which the researcher reaches on the basis of his examination of the facts may collide with certain ideological tenets and even with political interests. But they are the problems which most demand a scientific analysis of social relations, in the interests of both practice and the progress of scientific thought; and they demand that we go beyond the unquestioning adoption of positions.

Property relations as the 'organizing principle' of social relations

According to Marx, property relations are always embedded in society as a whole; that is to say, they do not consist solely in the ownership of objects, but are a kind of central point in the complex system of relationships between different classes and strata. Marx demonstrated that ownership of the means of production is the essential social relationship upon which all the complex interrelations among people are built. As early as *Moralising Critique and Critical Morals*, he wrote that bourgeois private property was 'the sum total of the bourgeois relations of production'. In Oskar Lange's words, this meant that 'the ownership of the means of production . . . is the foundation, or we might say the "organizing principle" which determined both the relations of production and the relations of distribution.'[2] In Marx's approach, the notion of property relations as essential social relations is one of the points of departure for any deep-going social analysis; it must be understood that they are embedded in social relations (mainly productive ones) as a whole. Marx wrote in *The Poverty of Philosophy*: 'To define bourgeois property thus is simply to give an exposition of all the social relations of bourgeois production. To try to give a definition of property as an independent relation, a category apart, an abstract and eternal idea, can be nothing but an illusion of metaphysics or of jurisprudence.'

This quotation gives rise to two seemingly topical questions. How can one describe socialist property, in socialism, without taking into account all the essential social relations which are dominant in these societies? Why should the attempt to do so be anything but 'an illusion of metaphysics and jurisprudence'?

If we want to know what are the essential social relations of socialist property relations, and whether a basic property problem exists in the socialist countries, then we must first survey all those social consequences in which these property relations are manifested, and in which they assume a concrete form. What I am therefore seeking are the phenomena through which property relations as essential social relations 'materialize' into decisions and social action, in the

2 See Oskar Lange, *Political Economy*.

same way that the immanent, essential attribute of the commodity, its value, expresses itself in the price. I term the exercise of property relations in this sense 'ownership-exercise',[3] and I include the following legal and practical capacities within the scope of this concept; (*a*) the capacity to direct people's activities as the executors of productive labour, i.e. the exercise of *power* and the directing of people; (*b*) the capacity for disposition over the means of production and the structure of production, i.e. the directing of objects; (*c*) the capacity to use, appropriate or at least distribute the surplus product; (*d*) the capacity to alienate and transfer by hereditary means the objects of property, the means of production or financial capital. And if it is not the owner in the juridical sense who practises these capacities, then the question of control over the practice of these rights arises.

In the course of history these capacities to decide and to act, which can be included in the concept of 'ownership-exercise', have not always belonged to the *juridical* owner; either through some legal provision or simply through social custom, the owner may not in fact practise some of the capacities which come under the concept of ownership-exercise – he may have assigned them to others, or they may have been assigned to others compulsorily by society. In various ways, and to a greater or lesser extent, a type of restricted ownership-exercise has arisen, separate from the juridical owner, mainly in respect of capacities (*a*), (*b*) and (*c*), though not of (*d*). I shall call this restricted type of ownership-exercise 'possession' or 'possessing', in accordance with Marx's terminology.

The essential difference between property and possession is often obliterated, both in everyday parlance and in scientific thinking. Marx spoke about the serf under feudalism being a direct producer who was not a proprietor but only a possessor, and whose surplus labour belonged to the land owner. But Oskar Lange, for example, took property to be a type of possession which is socially recognized and protected, and in fact he put the emphasis on possession:

> The fundamental relationship among men is brought about on the basis of possession of the means of production. What we are dealing with here is not chance possession, but possession recognized by the members of society, which is guarded by the socially recognized rules of human coexistence and perhaps by the sanctions meted out against the contravention of these rules, i.e. by custom and by law. This kind of possession is called property.[4]

But in history, property on the one hand, and possession as restricted ownership-exercise on the other, have often been separated in the way that I

---

3 This term translates a neologism in the Hungarian, *tulajdonlás*. It must be read throughout this essay in the light of Hegedüs's definition here. [Tr.]

4 Lange, *Political Economy*.

have explained. I therefore consider it justified to consider possession to be the manifestation of property relations as an essential relation, in which various forms and degrees of separation from the juridical proprietor may develop.

Unless we are to remain content with the abstractions of jurisprudence or ideology, we must first of all survey those consequences of socialist property relations which manifest themselves in ownership-exercise or possession. The analysis of these consequences is the most important aspect of the sociological examination of property relations, although it must be remembered that just as the price of goods is not exactly identical with their value, ownership-exercise and possession are also mere expressions of property relations as the essential relations of the whole society.

Property and power

When the notions of property and power are placed alongside each other, they revive debates which are centuries old. Without trying to give any exact definition, I mean by 'power' the legal and practical capacity, supplied by the division of labour, of individual persons or groups to influence the behaviour of other persons with consequences for the latter's livelihood, and to determine their own behaviour themselves. Thus essentially, though with some amplification, I adopt Max Weber's definition, according to which power is 'the chance for one or several persons to assert their own will, within some social relation, against the resistance of other participants'. It will be noted that this indicates a narrower interpretation of power as far as the concept of ownership-exercise is concerned; I exclude the power of objects or reified relations over man, or to use Marx's words, that 'inhuman power which rules over the capitalist too'.

The source of power is property; the source of property is power. The two viewpoints are sharply opposed to each other, and they are the expression of ideologies that have become political and material forces. Marx was faced with the problem that one of the most important outward forms of property relations as essential relations was the development of power relations. The answer which he gave to the question of the relationship between property and power, in his polemic with Heinzen, is still of importance for the sociological analysis of property relations. According to Marx, property relations have primacy over power:

> How the 'acquisition of money' changes into the 'acquisition of power' or 'property' into 'political domination', how between two kinds of power, instead of there being a firm difference (which Mr Heinzen sanctions as a *dogma*), there are on the contrary connections which go as far as being a union, of this Mr Heinzen may quickly convince himself if he takes a look at how the serfs *bought* their freedom, how the communes *bought* their municipal rights, how the bourgeois on the one hand wheedled the money out of the pockets of the feudal lords through

trade and industry and changed their landed property into fleeting bills of exchange, and how on the other hand they helped the absolute monarchy to victory over the great feudal lords who had been thus undermined, and how they *bought* their titles from them.[5]

In Marx's analysis of *capitalist* society, the supreme problematic was indeed the process through which the 'acquisition of money' turned into the acquisition of power, since the structure of capitalist society arose chiefly as a result of this process. But this in no way implies that the 'acquisition of power' is then *free* from the 'acquisition of money' (in this respect, it is relevant to recall the historical process through which the hierarchic order of the European feudal societies came into being). The mistake of the 'official' Marxism of the European social democratic parties consisted precisely in giving primacy to the property relations over the power relations in all circumstances, irrespective of the historical situation, on the assumption that the latter could always be 'bought' by the proprietor. But this kind of mechanical view is far removed from Marx's attitude to history. Marx gave primacy to the property relations in the ontological sense, and above all in the historical emergence of capitalist property: 'the political rule of the bourgeois class is a consequence of those modern production relations which are proclaimed as inevitable and eternal laws by the bourgeois economists.'[6] It must not be forgotten, either, that in the polemic between Marx and Heinzen, power still appeared primarily as political or (in other words) administrative power, which in the form of the state was apparently entirely separate from the property relations. Marx obviously considered it his main task to demonstrate the dependence of the bourgeois 'state', this apparently supreme power, on the property relations. He did not consider it worth debating whether property and power were identical or not: he called them a tautology, 'which is already contained in the words themselves', but continually emphasized that even in its narrower sense, property was the direct or indirect source of power.

In the modern capitalist societies, the separation of property from power is not limited to politics but extends to almost every sphere of social and private life, and has become to a large extent a characteristic of economic administration too. In modern capitalism, the proprietor does not only acquire power through the state, which through various mechanisms is separate from him, but he also gives power to others in his own internal sphere, i.e. in the management of the enterprise. One of the phenomena which is most deserving of the attention of Marxist analysis is this (partial) separation of property from power in the economic sphere; this is a conspicuous feature in the recent development of Western societies, and it marks them off not only from feudalism but also

5 See Marx, 'Moralizing critique and critical morals'. [Articles published in the *Deutsche Brüsseler Zeitung*, October/November 1847, Ed.]
6 Ibid.

from classical capitalism. The intrusion of political power into the economic sphere (the state sector) means a certain separation between the essential owner, the capitalist state and the institutions practising power (which belong to the category of ownership-exercise). And even if this does not change the dominant nature of bourgeois private property, it has brought about a very important modification in the property relations as essential relations, understood in Marx's terms, i.e. not divorced from the social relations but interpreted as an 'organizing principle'.

Property and power over objects

Disposition over the objective relations of the production process forms an integral part of the exercise of property rights (or what I have termed 'ownership-exercise'), and indicates first of all the determination of the structure of production (what shall be produced), the object of labour (what it shall be produced from), and the means of labour (how it shall be produced).

In pre-capitalist times the owner, or whoever personified him, was often faced with difficulties in his right of ownership-exercise, and was forced to transfer to others not only his power over people but also his power over objects. Typical cases of this were the 'bureaucratic' empires of antiquity and China, where the ruler, personifying the ownership of the state, transferred these rights to a hierarchically ordered state administration. European feudalism provided a basically different solution to this problem: the *seigneur* and the landlord retained their power over their vassals and serfs, but transferred to them almost entirely the right of disposition over objects. It was precisely this kind of feudalism which made it possible for bourgeois private property to emerge, and thereby provided the opportunity for a dynamism of development that was unprecedented in history.

The principal moment in the development of bourgeois private property, besides this disposition over objects, was the achievement of power by the bourgeoisie over itself, which relatively quickly became power over others. It is no accident that the main protagonist in this process was precisely the serf who disposed of these objects. But with the development of bourgeois private property, the right to dispose of objects to others began to be transferred too; the first instance of this was the development of the joint stock company. Although every shareholder in the joint stock company actually disposes of his shares as his property, is entitled to appropriate the surplus-value and may sell his shares at any time, the greater part of the ownership capacities nevertheless belongs to enterprise management: the majority of shareholders are unable to participate in ownership-exercise, and often they do not even have real control over the enterprise management which acts in their name. However, the real managers of capitalist enterprises lead the masses of shareholders to believe that they are capable to exercising real control over the managers; this is a special domain in the management of capitalist enterprises, the domain of 'expert manipulation'. (American literature on management sociology provides innumerable examples of this: see, for example, Reinhard Bendix's *Work and Authority in Industry*, 1956). The separation between the person of the proprietor and actual disposition over the relations of production also extends to the larger forms of private family property, and in this way the management apparatuses which have developed in the capitalist societies are able to exercise power (in the organization of production) and possession (in the objective relations of production) at the same time. In modern capitalism, this has been added to by the increased importance of state property; this gives to certain state organs the kinds of jurisdiction which the administrations of capitalist enterprises have.

Property and disposition over the surplus product

There is a close historical link between property, on the one hand, and disposition over the surplus product (the legal and practical capacity to appropriate it) on the other; this is one of the keys to the understanding of the property relations which exist in the current socialist societies. Ever since the possibility of producing a surplus product has existed, social struggles have in the last resort never been fought only for power or for disposition over the objective factors of production, but for the distribution of the surplus product; and the concrete property relations, power structures and various modes of ownership-exercise and possession have developed in this unceasing struggle.

In the course of history, disposition over the surplus product has not always belonged in the final analysis to the proprietor himself, because he has been forced to share this power of disposition either with authorities greater than himself (*seigneur*, monarch etc.) or with those to whom he has transferred (in the sense mentioned above) his power of ownership over persons or over the objective factors of production. This means, of course, that not only is the actual right of disposition over the surplus product divided, but the surplus product itself is divided too. From this it also follows that the 'division' is a permanent source of conflict between the groups taking part in ownership-exercise.

In classical capitalism, the capitalist himself by and large exercised the right to dispose of the surplus product, just as he held the power of disposition over persons and over the objective factors of production. But this independence was considerably clipped by developments in the last century. On the one hand the capitalist state has taken an increasingly active part in distributing the surplus value (either by siphoning it off or by direct intervention); and on the other hand, the managements of the capitalist enterprises have also been demanding to have a hand in it. (As many Western sociological studies can testify, managements are chiefly interested in the increase of reserve funds and investments, while the capitalists, especially the shareholders, are mainly interested in maximizing dividends.)

The inheritance of property, its alienation and control over possession

One of the most important elements in ownership-exercise is the inheritance and alienation of property, in which the property relations as essential social relations often attain their most pregnant form of expression. That is why I did not include this element in the notion of restricted possession which I applied to the other three capacities of ownership-exercise. The proprietor may transfer his personal power, the right of disposition over the objective conditions of production and the surplus product, or at least part of the latter; but if he renounces the right to alienate his property, he ceases to be a proprietor. On many occasions in history, however, these *sui generis* rights of the proprietor *as* proprietor have been restricted, in most cases in the name of some 'collective' proprietor above him.

The proprietor's control over the possessor must be included among his *sui generis* rights. When we examine the exercise of any kind of power based on property relations and the various forms of ownership-exercise and possession, we must always ask whether there exists some kind of real control over those who dispose of power and exercise possession in the name of the proprietor. And if the answer is yes, we must examine how far this control extends, who or which groups exercise it, and what are the historical roots of their right and capacity to control.

The evolution of the forces of production and property relations

The multi-faceted theory of property relations which can be found in Marx's works has been deprived of its concrete nature by the schematism which has become dominant in Marxist theory. It has been turned into the system of interconnections of some mystical power, which appears to rule over society as the laws of nature do over the material world. What has been obscured? The supreme importance of social struggle, in which the property relations assume their concrete form, and through which considerably differing types of ownership-exercise and possession develop, even at one and the same level of productive forces. Instead of supplying concrete historical analysis, the simplified conception of Marxism has given rise to interpretations stating that the evolution of productive forces changes the property relations by the force of a law of nature, as it were. The necessary result of this view is overemphasis on the importance of the economic sphere, an overemphasis which a great number of Marxists have long fought against, and notably Engels, Lukács and Gramsci.

Berlinguer[7] draws attention to Togliatti's remarks about Gramsci, that 'he never considered the economic structure to be a mysterious, hidden force from which the various situations developed automatically.' Lenin himself was opposed to the 'official' view on almost every principal question of the strategy and structure of revolutionary social democracy. Although the October revolution was not only victorious over the bourgeoisie but also rendered palpably obsolete the ossification of Marxism into a dogma, many of the tenets of this dogmatic Marxism nevertheless lived on in the country where socialism had become victorious; it was now difficult not only to analyse the new phenomena in capitalism, but also to carry out any realistic self-analysis of the new socialist societies. We cannot yet give a satisfactory answer to the question of how and by what means, and under the influence of what social forces, schematism had become one of the main planks of official science in the USSR by the end of the 1920s, reaching the textbooks themselves during the 1930s. It is impossible to ignore its influence on the Stalinist theory of socialism, and especially on the tenets referring to property relations. The latter, especially where they touched on the new property relations, were considered irrevocable; their effect on ownership-exercise and possession made any realistic analysis extremely difficult, because the official viewpoint was protected by the severest clauses of the penal code against any attempt at confrontation, however justifiable this confrontation might be.

While this view of socialist property relations was ossified into a dogma for decades, the abolition of private property not only occurred in an increasing number of new countries but also took on increasingly varied forms. In such circumstances it has become a task of primary importance, not only for the social sciences but also for social practice, to examine the newly developed property relations without deliberately overlooking the power structures that have sprung up, the actual possibilities of possession, and the consequent power of disposition over the surplus product.

In this study, I am looking for an answer to these questions only in respect of the present conditions in the *European* socialist countries, and not of an analysis *in general* of every society that has abolished private property. I stress this because, in my view, all the historical conditions are now ripe for overcoming once and for all the idea that property relations, the forms of ownership-exercise and possession and of state organizations, must necessarily be *identical* in every respect in all societies which have abolished private ownership of the means of production, and that every deviation from this pattern is some sort of negative phenomenon. In our era we must also overcome the notion, which was dominant for a time and which in itself was already a way of correcting the 'cult of personality' conception, that some variations which are a result of national characteristics can be recognized, but only within the scope of social laws that are considered to be generally and inevitably valid. In spite of the progressive

7 Enrico Berlinguer, at the Tenth Congress of the Italian Communist Party, 1962.

role that this notion has played in the past, it allows no room for the possibility that different solutions may occur as the result of complex processes of social struggle, and thus that one alternative or another, all differing significantly from each other but all surpassing bourgeois private property to the same extent, may be equally victorious. At the moment, however, when this happens in practice, it is considered by the defenders of the first alternative to be a violation of socialist principles.

The new property relations as the negation of bourgeois private property

What we know of the property relations which have developed in the socialist societies of Europe consists first of all in a negation: there is no private property, or to put it more precisely, a new property relationship has been created by the abolition of bourgeois private ownership of the means of production, and by various methods such as nationalization, mass collectivization etc. What this negation actually means can only be decided through a concrete analysis of reality; this is the only way we can find out how far and in what respects the new has in fact surpassed the old. History has seen many kinds of forces which are negative in their *effects*; however important the negation of the prevailing 'establishment' may be at any given time, we certainly cannot identify it automatically with progress or with the quest for power. The question can only be answered if we first take account of the role which bourgeois private property has played in history.

The emergence of bourgeois private ownership of the means of production undoubtedly released powerful forces on to the historical scene, and it was mainly for this reason that mankind's progress began to accelerate at an unprecedented rate. Protestant 'ethics' simply gave the ideological 'green light' to the development of this form of ownership. I believe this needs stressing, because the dogmatic and simplified version of Marxism often emphasizes only the negative consequences of bourgeois private property: its anti-humanism, and its inability to function with optimum efficiency. This is dangerous not only because it gives a false view of the (past or present) world which maintains private property, but also because it impairs the realistic analysis of those property relations which prevail in socialism, and hampers any attempt to judge whether what has happened is more than a simple negation and whether it may be considered (and if so, in what sense) to actually surpass the previous conditions.

The importance of bourgeois private property in the development of the productive forces can best be measured by using the historical example which comes from comparing the Asiatic mode of production with post-Renaissance European development. In those countries where, as a result of various historical circumstances, the Asiatic mode of production became the prevailing form, the development of the more advanced forms of private property was blocked (the reasons for this have been analysed sufficiently in the existing literature); it was mainly for this reason that the development of the productive forces was interrupted for a period of centuries. The development of bourgeois private property in Europe, however, brought with it not only an economic dynamism which had been inconceivable in the preceding historical periods, but also social movements which expected the 'common weal' to emerge from the abolition of private property and were ready to fight for this at whatever cost. From the eighteenth century onwards, Europe has been the scene of repeated social endeavours to replace private property with social forms of property, whether by means of specific social struggles or of utopian reforms. But however valuable these experiments have been for the history of mankind, in some way or other and after some period of time they have proved to be unviable. The same fate befell both Fourier's communistic communities and the noble ideas of the Paris Commune.

The overcoming of bourgeois private property has become a reality in our century, but it is far from being a historical necessity which occurs automatically. The progress of the productive forces and likewise of social relations has reached a level where it has become possible to dispense with and replace all the positive aspects which bourgeois property brought with it (and chiefly those to do with the dynamics of development), and to set in motion the kind of driving forces which were unable to evolve in the framework of private property. The relatively advanced level of the forces of production and of social relations in the twentieth century has enabled the previously anarchic and utopian socialist attempts at abolishing and surpassing bourgeois private property to develop into a force spanning the globe, which has now led to the development of new forms of government in many countries.

It follows from this that several kinds of state system may be built in accordance with the property relations which develop after the abolition of private property. Property relations never do determine the form of government unequivocally; this is valid not only for those societies built on private ownership of the means of production but also for the societies which surpass them. This is not because there are no extremely close links between the specific mode of ownership-exercise (the property relations as the outward form of the essential relations) and the state system. Rather, it is because after the abolition of private property, in systems of social economic management which differ according to the objective conditions of the society's existence and according to social struggles (i.e. the people who themselves make history), extremely varied forms have developed and will develop, both of ownership-exercise and of the state system.

This reveals itself in capitalism, too, although bourgeois private property is undoubtedly the dominant form which determines everything else. On the one hand there is a great variety of power structures and systems of siphoning off surplus value. On the other hand, it is also a fact that forms of ownership have developed or survived which differ essentially from each other in their mode of ownership-exercise (cooperative, institutional, state property etc.); that is to say, here too we may distinguish to a considerable extent between different types of ownership-exercise and possession. When Marx, in his analysis of classical capitalism, foresaw the possibility of abolishing private property and emphasized the historical inevitability of this change, he also sensed that an evolution was taking place within capitalist property relations too; for example, he looked at the development of joint stock companies and at the emergence of various kinds of cooperative in this light. However, history has taken a course which differs considerably from Marx's prognosis. In the more advanced countries, capitalism has been able to adapt itself to the development of the productive forces better than Marx had assumed. Meanwhile the conditions for socialist revolution became ripe in the less advanced countries too, and because of the consistent struggle of the revolutionary forces and the historical circumstances, the overcoming of private property occurred here first.

16   The Marxian Synthesis

Stanislaw Ossowski

The concept of social class in Marxian doctrine

The concept of social class is something more than one of the fundamental concepts of Marxian doctrine. It has in a certain sense become the symbol of his whole doctrine and of the political programme that is derived from it. This concept is expressed in the terms 'class standpoint' and 'class point of view', which in Marxist circles used until recently to be synonymous with 'Marxist standpoint' or 'Marxist point of view'. In this sense 'class standpoint' simply meant the opposite of 'bourgeois standpoint'.

According to Engels,[1] Marx effected a revolutionary change in the whole conception of world history. For Marx, so Engels maintained, had proved that 'the whole of previous history is a history of class struggles, that in all the simple and complicated political struggles the only thing at issue has been the social and political rule of social classes'.

The concept of social class is also linked with what Engels in the same article calls the second great discovery of Marx, to which he attaches so much importance in the history of science – the clarification of the relationship that prevails between capital and labour. Finally, it may be said that the concept of social class is bound up with the entire Marxian conception of culture as the superstructure of class interests.

The role of the class concept in Marxian doctrine is so immense that it is

From Stanislaw Ossowski, *Class Structure in the Social Consciousness* (New York: The Free Press, 1963; London: Routledge and Kegan Paul Plc, 1963), pp. 71–84. Copyright © 1963 by Stanislaw Ossowski. Reprinted by permission of Macmillan Inc. and Associated Book Publishers (UK) Ltd.

1 ME, vol. II, p. 149; the quotation comes from Friedrich Engels, *Karl Marx*. [ME refers to Karl Marx and Frederick Engels, *Selected Works in Two Volumes* (Moscow, 1951). Ed.]

astonishing not to find a definition of this concept, which they use so constantly, anywhere in the works of either Marx or Engels. One might regard it as an undefined concept of which the meaning is explained contextually. But in fact one has only to compare the various passages in which the concept of social class is used by either writer to realize that the term 'class' has for them a variable denotation: that is, that it refers to groups differentiated in various ways within a more inclusive category, such as the category of social groups with common economic interests, or the category of groups whose members share economic conditions that are identical in a certain respect. The sharing of permanent economic interests is a particularly important characteristic of social classes in Marxian doctrine, and for this reason it has been easy to overlook the fact that although it is, in the Marxian view, a *necessary condition* it does not constitute a *sufficient condition* for a valid definition of social class.

Marx left the problem of producing a definition of the concept of social class until much later. The manuscript of the third volume of his *magnum opus, Das Kapital*, breaks off dramatically at the moment when Marx was about to answer the question: 'What constitutes a class?' We do not know what answer he would have given if death had not interrupted his work. Nor do we know whether he would have attempted to explain the discrepancies in his earlier statements.

After the death of Marx, Engels did not take up the question which the manuscript of *Das Kapital* left unanswered. Lenin's later definition, which has been popularized by Marxist textbooks and encyclopaedias, links two different formulations but fails to explain how we are to regard them. Does the author see them as two equivalent definitions and does he link them in order to give a fuller characteristic of the designate of the concept of class? Or is the conjunction of the two formulations essential because the characteristics given in one of them are not necessarily conjoint to the characteristic given in the second? Independently of this, such metaphorical expressions as the 'place in the historically determined system of social production' may be variously interpreted and Lenin's definition is sufficiently loose to be applicable to all the shades of meaning found in the term 'class' as used by Marx and Engels.[2] Bucharin's definition,[3] which is also intended to reflect the Marxian conception of social class, affords room for even wider possibilities of interpretation, and it

---

2 'Classes are large groups of people which differ from each other by the place they occupy in a historically determined system of social production, by their relation (in most cases fixed and formulated in law) to the means of production, by their role in the social organization of labour and, consequently, by the dimensions and method of acquiring the share of social wealth of which they dispose. Classes are groups of people one of which can appropriate the labour of another owing to the different places they occupy in a definite system of social economy' (V. I. Lenin, *A Great Beginning*, in *The Essentials of Lenin*, 2 vols, London, 1947, p. 492).

3 N. Bucharin, *Historical Materialism, A System of Sociology* (London, 1926), p. 267 (English translation).

is only Bucharin's classification of social classes that enables one to grasp the denotation assigned by the author to the concept of social class.[4]

In using the concept of class based on economic criteria, Marx sometimes restricts the scope of this concept by introducing psychological criteria. An aggregate of people which satisfies the economic criteria of a social class becomes a class in the full meaning of this term only when its members are linked by the tie of class consciousness, by the consciousness of common interests, and by the psychological bond that arises out of common class antagonisms.[5] Marx is aware of the ambiguity and makes a terminological distinction between *Klasse an sich* and *Klasse für sich*, but he does not in general make much further use of these more narrowly defined concepts.

Marx sometimes uses a different term to denote a class which is not a class in the fullest sense because it lacks psychological bonds. For instance, he sometimes uses the term 'stratum'; on other occasions he avoids using a more general term and confines himself to the name of a specified group such as the 'small peasantry'. At times he may even call certain classes which are conscious of their class interests 'fractions' of a more inclusive class. In the case of capitalists and landowners, for instance, Marx sometimes sees them as two separate classes, at others as two fractions of a single class, the bourgeoisie.

All these discrepant uses of the term 'class' were probably the less important for Marx because, according to his theory, further social development would render them obsolete. This was to result from the growth of the social consciousness and from the predicted disappearance of the difference between the *Klasse an sich* and the *Klasse für sich* as well as from the progressive process of class polarization in the social structure.

The matter can however be put in a different way. We may take it that Marx, instead of providing a definition of social class which would make it possible to fix the scope of this concept, is giving the model of a social class, the ideal type which is to be fully realized in the future, in the last stage of the development of the capitalist system. In the period in which Marx wrote, the industrial

---

4 Ibid. pp. 282–4.

5 Cf. the following passages: 'The separate individuals form a class in so far as they have to carry on a common battle against another class' (K. Marx and F. Engels, *The German Ideology* (The Marxist-Leninist Library, vol. XVII, London, 1940, pp. 48–9). 'The organization of the proletarians into a class, and consequently into a political party' ('Manifesto of the Communist Party', ME, vol. I, p. 41). 'In so far as millions of families live under economic conditions of existence that separate their mode of life, their interests and their culture from those of the other classes, and put them in hostile opposition to the latter, they form a class. In so far as there is merely a local interconnection among these small-holding peasants, and the identity of their interests begets no community, no national bond and no political organization among them, they do not form a class. They are consequently incapable of enforcing their class interest' (ME, vol. I, p. 303; quotation from K. Marx). 'Bonaparte represented the most numerous class of the French society at that time, the small-holding (*Parzellen*) peasants' (ME, vol. I, p. 302; quotation from *The Eighteenth Brumaire of Louis Bonaparte*).

proletariat of Western Europe was approximating to the ideal type of a social class. Other social groups separated on the basis of economic criteria could be called classes only to a greater or lesser extent, and could approximate to the ideal type only in some respects. Hence endeavours to apprehend them by means of conceptual categories with sharply drawn boundaries of application must lead to confusion.

However that may be, one should, when considering the Marxian conception of class structure, remember that the component elements of this structure are confined to those groups which Marx calls 'classes' when contrasting them with 'strata', in which 'the identity of their interests (those of the members of a "stratum") begets no unity, no national union and no political organization'.

As we shall see below, the Marxian concept of social class involves certain conceptual complications which are more than a matter of terminology.

The basic dichotomy

Marx and Engels are above all the inheritors of the dichotomic perceptions found in folklore and of the militant ideology of popular revolutions. Reading their works, one never loses sight of the age-old conflict between the oppressing classes and the oppressed classes. I have already mentioned the dichotomic perceptions of the drama of history that appear in the *Communist Manifesto* and in Engels' work written three years earlier. The reader will recall the twofold way of conceiving human relations within the social structure in terms of a dichotomic division: the manifold polar division of the various oppressor and oppressed classes in earlier societies gives way to a single all-inclusive dichotomy. According to the forecast of the *Communist Manifesto*, the capitalist society was to achieve this dichotomy in full in the penultimate act of the drama, in the period that precedes the catastrophe. In approximating to such a dichotomy, the social structure of the capitalist world would then be nearing its end.

According to the founders of Marxian doctrine, the society in which they lived was characterized by a tendency to develop in the direction indicated above. In this society Marx discerned 'the inevitable destruction of the middle bourgeois classes and of the so-called peasant estate'.[6] In Engels' version, the era marked the accomplishment of 'the division of society into a small, excessively rich class and a large, propertyless class of wage-workers'.[7] The workers' rising in Paris on 22 June 1848 was regarded by Marx as 'the first great battle ... between the two classes that split modern society ... the war of labour and capital'.[8]

---

6 ME, vol. I, p. 75; quotation from K. Marx, *Wage, Labour and Capital*.
7 Ibid., p. 73; quotation from F. Engels' Introduction to Marx's *Wage, Labour and Capital*.
8 Ibid., pp. 147, 148; quotations from K. Marx, *The Class Struggles in France, 1848–1850*.

Two conceptions of the intermediate classes

Marx the revolutionary and Marx the dramatist of history developed a dichotomic conception of a class society. Marx the sociologist was compelled in his analysis of contemporary societies to infringe the sharpness of the dichotomic division by introducing intermediate classes. He could not overlook the 'mass of the nation ... standing between the proletariat and the bourgeoisie.'[9] These intermediate classes were a very important element in the pictures of his own era given us by Marx in his historical studies. Sometimes he speaks of 'intermediate strata' when giving a narrower definition of a social class. Elsewhere the term 'middle estate' appears, although in this context it does not denote an institutionalized group such as the French *tiers état*.

There is such a variety of social statuses and economic positions in these intermediate classes that it is difficult to confine them within a uniform scheme. The term 'intermediate classes' suggests a scheme of gradation. And in fact one sometimes finds in Marx's writings the conception of the intermediate classes as groupings of individuals occupying an intermediate position in the economic gradation in respect of their relation to the means of production, or to the variety of their social roles and sources of income. For instance, in the *Address of the Central Committee to the Communist League*, written by Marx and Engels in 1850, the petit bourgeoisie includes the small capitalists, whose interests conflict with those of the industrialists. And again, in his *The Civil War in France*, Marx refers to the 'liberal German middle class, with its professors, its capitalists, its aldermen and its penmen'.[10] Here he conceives of the middle class in the sense in which the term is used in England or the United States. A capitalist – that is to say an owner of the means of production – may belong to one class or another depending on the amount of capital he owns. One should however bear in mind that Marx is not thinking here of 'high society' nor of rows and columns in statistical tables. For him the amount of capital owned by an individual is associated with separate class interests.

It was not, however, this conception of an intermediate class that was incorporated in the set of basic concepts in the Marxian analysis of the capitalist society. In constructing his theoretical system, Marx set up the foundation for another conception of the class which occupies the intermediate position between the class of capitalists and the proletariat. This conception was not in fact formulated in its final form by either Marx or his pupils. It is nevertheless related to the scheme of class structure of the capitalist society that is

9 Ibid., p. 137.
10 Ibid., p. 447; quotation from the *Second Address of the General Council of the International Working Men's Association on the Franco-Prussian War*.

characteristic for Marx and Marxism, a scheme in which three social classes correspond to three kinds of relations to the means of production.

In this scheme the intermediate class, which Marx usually calls the 'petit bourgeoisie' regardless of whether reference is being made to urban or rural dwellers, is determined by the simultaneous application of two criteria. Each of these criteria taken separately forms the basis for a dichotomic division of social classes, although in a different way. One criterion is the ownership of the means of production. This is a criterion which, in a dichotomic scheme, divides society into propertied and propertyless classes. The second criterion is work, which, however, in contradistinction to Saint-Simon's conception, does not include the higher managerial functions in the capitalist enterprises. We have come across this second criterion in the dichotomic scheme as well. It divides society into working classes and idle classes. In this conception, the intermediate class consists of those who belong to both the overlapping categories; those who possess their own means of production and themselves make use of them.

Marxism applies still another version of this trichotomous division, a version which is usually not differentiated from the former one. In the first criterion of division (the ownership of the means of production) remains the same. On the other hand, the second criterion is not work but the fact of not employing hired labour. In this version, the intermediate class is more narrowly defined than in the earlier one. It does not include all those working people who possess their own means of production but only those who work on their own account without employing hired labour. According to this version, a wealthy farmer who employs two or three regular hired labourers, or who has small-holders working for him in exchange for an advance in cash or kind, is included in the class of rural capitalists. In the first version the petit bourgeoisie includes two strata; those who work in their own workshops and employ hired labour, and those who do not employ such labour. Sociologically speaking, the first version is more suited to describe some conditions, the second more suited to others; thus it depends on various circumstances which need not be discussed here. The combination of the two versions gives two functionally differentiated intermediate classes, as the diagram shows.

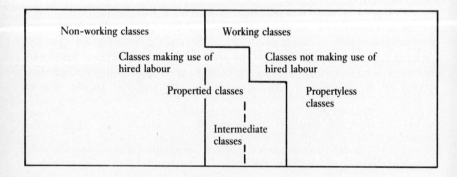

From the viewpoint of the Marxian assumptions concerned with the tendencies of development in capitalism, the position of the petit bourgeoisie, which is intermediate between the two basic classes, is sometimes interpreted in yet another way. The petit bourgeoisie is said to belong to the propertied class so far as present conditions are concerned, to the proletariat with regard to its future prospects. Thus not only the craftsman but also the small-holder are potential proletarians.[11]

There is also an economic gradation that corresponds to this trichotomous scheme. The capitalist class is that class which owns large-scale means of production or at least sufficient to make possible the employment of hired labour; the petit bourgeoisie consists of those who dispose of the means of production on a modest scale; while the proletariat is in principle the class that owns no means of production whatsoever. In this functional scheme, however, it is not the degree of wealth that determines the boundaries between classes but the social roles, namely their relation to the means of production, work and their relation to the hiring of labour. In the scheme of gradation referred to earlier, on the other hand, the middle class could also include *rentiers*, the owners of small industrial establishments and other capitalists with property not exceeding the limits of 'moderate wealth'.

A strict observance of functional economic criteria in distinguishing the three classes – capitalists, petit bourgeoisie and proletariat – leads, however, to conflicts with sociological criteria. For instance, an engineer would in his capacity as hired labour in a capitalistic establishment have to be included amongst the proletariat, as would a doctor employed in a private sanatorium. As we know, Marx associated the concept of the proletariat with the conception of a fundamental dichotomy. The proletarian is a man who is unprotected from the extremes of exploitation by any special qualifications which would prevent him from being replaced by another worker with equal physical strength. According to Marx's intentions, this criterion would exclude the engineer or doctor from the class of the proletariat.

Moreover, according to the Marxian assumption that a class is united by the common interests of its members in great social conflicts, yet another factor may help to correct a scheme based on 'relations to the means of production'. For instance, the salary of the engineer employed by the capitalist includes a portion of the 'surplus-value' produced by the workers and appropriated by the capitalist.

In summing up our discussion of this classical Marxian scheme of social roles in relation to the various ways of conceiving the social structure which were

11 Cf. Engels: *The Peasant Question in France and Germany*, ME, vol. I, pp. 384, 395. Bucharin, in developing Marx's theory of social classes, differentiates the category of classes intermediate between the two basic classes in a different way than is done in our scheme; he distinguishes intermediate classes, transition classes and classes of mixed types (*Historical Materialism*, pp. 283–4).

discussed earlier, we may consider it as an overlapping of a dichotomic view and a scheme of gradation. In this conception the intermediate class is determined by the boundaries of the two basic and antagonistic classes. It is separated from the others by virtue of the fact that these two basic classes are divided against each other, not by one single criterion, but by two or three criteria to which correspond class-groupings of varying extensions. The intermediate class is made up of people who are connected with each of the two basic classes but in differing respects. This connection exists both in the logical sense (characteristics which enter into the definition of two basic classes) and in the sociological sense. At the same time, as I have already pointed out, the petit bourgeoisie, as determined by its peculiar 'relations to the means of production', occupies a central position in the trichotomous economic gradation (the extent of ownership of the means of production).

A trichotomous functional scheme without an intermediate class

With Marx the revolutionary, the dichotomic conception of social structure is dominant. With Marx the theorist, we sometimes have to deal not only with the trichotomous scheme with a middle class between the two opposing classes but also with a scheme which is inherited from bourgeois economics. This is the trichotomous functional scheme of Adam Smith. This scheme appears rarely in the works of Marx and Engels,[12] but its importance is increased by the fact that it is the starting-point of the last chapter of the third volume of *Das Kapital*, the chapter which is devoted exclusively to an analysis of classes in modern society. This uncompleted chapter, entitled 'Classes', opens with the words:

> The owners merely of labour-power, owners of capital, and landowners, whose respective sources of income are wages, profit and ground-rent, in other words, wage-labourers, capitalists and landowners, constitute then three big classes of modern society based upon the capitalist mode of production.[13]

And a little further on, when he is dealing with the question 'What constitutes a class?' Marx again takes precisely this conception of the social structure as his starting-point.

In the dichotomic conception and in the trichotomous Marxian conception which I have discussed earlier the emphasis is placed on human relationships. In Smith's conception, on the other hand, the viewpoint of an economist rather than of a sociologist is dominant. The main stress falls on the relations of

---

12 Cf. *Ludwig Feuerbach and the End of Classical German Philosophy* (ME, vol. II, p. 356); Marx's letter to Engels of 30 April 1868 (K. Marx and F. Engels, *Selected Correspondence*, Moscow, n.d., pp. 245–50).
13 K. Marx, *Capital*, vol. III (Moscow, 1959), p. 862.

people to things. Clear economic categories, that is criteria concerned with relationships to things, leave no place in the social structure for the intermediate classes which a sociologist cannot overlook. In Adam Smith's scheme those who own their own means of production and yet work themselves do not form a separate class but belong to two or three classes simultaneously.

> It sometimes happens, indeed, that a single independent workman has stock sufficient both to purchase the materials of his work and to maintain himself till it be completed. He is both master and workman, and enjoys the whole produce of his own labour, or the whole value which it adds to the materials upon which it is bestowed. It includes what are usually two distinct revenues, belonging to two distinct persons, the profits of stock, and the wages of labour.[14]

Marx considers this point in the third volume of *Das Kapital*, and even accords it conditional approval.[15]

Thus we find two different trichotomous schemes of social structure in Marx, to both of which may be applied the definition of class as a group determined by the relation to the means of production. In the first case (capitalists, petit bourgeoisie, proletariat), the various classes have correspondingly *various relationships to the means of production*. In the second case (landowners, owners of capital and those who own nothing but their own labour), the classes are determined by the *relation to the various means of production*, the capacity to work being regarded here as a category of the means of production.

A multi-divisional structure

A functional scheme can contain more than three classes, as we saw with Madison [James Madison, *The Federalist*, no. 10 (1787)]. In Marx's writings a direct formulation which would conceive of social structure in terms of such a multi-divisional scheme is nowhere to be found. But if we bring together statements made in various works we find that even an image of this kind can be derived from his works. In his *German Ideology* we find the bourgeoisie and the

---

14 *Op. cit*, vol. I, Everyman's Library, p. 58.

15 'When an independent labourer – let us take a small farmer, since all three forms of revenue may here be applied – works for himself and sells his own product, he is first considered as his own employer (capitalist), who makes use of himself as a labourer, and second as his own landlord, who makes use of himself as his own tenant. To himself as wage-worker he pays wages, to himself as capitalist he gives the profit, and to himself as landlord he pays rent. Assuming the capitalist mode of production and the relations corresponding to it to be the general basis of society, this subsumption is correct, in so far as it is not thanks to his labour, but to his ownership of the means of production . . . that he is in a position to appropriate his own surplus labour' (*Capital*, vol. III, London, 1960, p. 853).

class of the large industrialists set against each other as classes of different and in a certain respect even opposite social functions; for the interests of the bourgeoisie are contained within national boundaries, while the large industrialists form a cosmopolitan class on an international scale.[16] In his *Class Struggles in France* Marx shows us how the class interests of the French financial aristocracy clash with those of the industrial bourgeoisie.[17] Marx attributes to the financial aristocracy the 'desire to enrich themselves not by production but by cleverly appropriating to themselves riches that already exist', and calls them ironically 'the *lumpenproletariat* on the heights of bourgeois society'.[18] Apart from these two rival classes, Marx mentions the petit bourgeoisie which is removed from political power. A year or so later, in his description of the same society in *The Eighteenth Brumaire*, Marx once again shifts the line dividing the bourgeoisie into two antagonistic factions. This antagonism, for which the ideological superstructure was the conflict between Orleanists and Legitimists, is seen as the outcome of the competition between capital and ownership of land.[19] These factions, based on the ownership of different types of wealth, are the two basic classes from Adam Smith's scheme.

If we now take the class differentiation of the rural population, as it is presented for instance by Engels in the introduction to his work *The Peasant Wars in Germany*,[20] and if we do not overlook the *lumpenproletariat* – which is not a 'class' according to the Marxian definition but a 'stratum' – 'a mass sharply differentiated from the industrial proletariat'[21] – a stratum which can play a specific role in social movements – we obtain an image in which the capitalist society is functionally differentiated into seven, eight or even nine classes or strata.

The overlapping of viewpoints

In his character of revolutionary economist and sociologist, Marx inherited all three basic types of conceiving the class structure which are encountered in the history of European thought. These are the dichotomic scheme, the scheme of gradation and the functional scheme. At the same time he introduced a characteristic way of conceiving this structure, by intersecting two or three dichotomic divisions. It is this latter way that has come to be regarded as the classic Marxian scheme, although Marx does not employ it when he is discussing the concept of class in the last pages of his greatest work.

16 K. Marx and F. Engels, *The German Ideology* (London, 1939), pp. 24–6.
17 'The mania to get rich not by production, but by pocketing the already available wealth of others.' *The Class Struggles in France 1848–1850*, ME, vol. I, pp. 128–9.
18 Ibid., p. 131.
19 K. Marx, *The Eighteenth Brumaire of Louis Bonaparte*, ME, vol. I, pp. 247–53.
20 F. Engels, Prefatory Note to *The Peasant War in Germany*, ME, vol. I, pp. 584–6.
21 *Class Struggles in France*, ME, vol. I, p. 142.

We have noted in Marx's writings two versions of this classic Marxian scheme, and also an explicit formulation of Adam Smith's trichotomous functional scheme; there is also an implied multi-class version of a functional scheme which recalls that of Madison. Thus it may be maintained that the works of Marx and Engels contain at least six different ways of conceiving the structure of contemporary capitalist societies. The definition of a social class which refers to the relations to the means of production is just as applicable to the classic Marxian scheme as it is to the schemes of Adam Smith and of Madison.

The schemes may differ, but this does not involve contradictory assumptions. The dichotomic aspect of the Marxian theory of classes indicates the direction in which capitalist societies will develop; seen in this perspective the multi-divisional schemes are intended to refer to transitory phenomena. But even without a reference to trends of development the Smithian scheme cited in the third volume of *Das Kapital* and elsewhere need not run counter to the basic dichotomy. It is sufficient to group landowners and owners of capital in a single more inclusive 'superior' category of 'propertied classes' and to set them against 'those who own nothing but their own labour' as the 'propertyless class'. The trichotomous scheme of gradation may be reconciled with the dichotomic conception by treating the middle class as a grouping resulting from over-lapping class extensions or as one determined by the boundaries of the two opposite classes.

We may still seek other explanations. In the Marxian image of capitalist society the dichotomy refers to the classes that participate in capitalist production, which, it should be noted, is not the only form of production in existing capitalist societies. The dichotomy is a basic scheme for the Marxian model of a capitalist society, with its two large classes which appear '*à l'intérieur de l'atelier capitaliste*', as Labriola puts it. But this dichotomous class division of capitalist society is not inconsistent with the existence of other social groups, so long as one accepts the view that other forms of relations of production and their corresponding classes have survived from the past within this society. The dichotomic scheme is intended to characterize capitalist society with regard to its dominant and peculiar form of relations of production, while the multi-divisional scheme reflects the actual social structure. . . .[22]

---

[22] 'Dire que le capitalisme est caracterisé par l'organisation autoritaire de la fabrique et la division en classes – capitalistes et salariés – qui en découle, ce n'est pas nier qu'avec le capitalisme survivent d'autres régimes économiques. . . . Si Marx s'occupait des deux grandes classes qui existent à l'intérieur de l'atelier capitaliste, il ne pouvait pour cela supprimer d'un trait de sa plume autoritaire petite bourgeoisie, groupes professionnels et autres métiers inclassables' (Arturo Labriola, *Karl Marx – L'économiste – Le socialiste*, Paris, 1909, pp. 185–6). Sorel points out that Marx frequently confuses logical constructions with his descriptions of actual phenomena, and conjectures that Marx did not always realize the abstract character of his theory of classes.

17   Class Consciousness

Georg Lukács

Marx's chief work breaks off just as he is about to embark on the definition of class. This omission was to have serious consequences both for the theory and the practice of the proletariat. For on this vital point the later movement was forced to base itself on interpretations, on the collation of occasional utterances by Marx and Engels and on the independent extrapolation and application of their method. In Marxism the division of society into classes is determined by position within the process of production. But what, then, is the meaning of class consciousness? The question at once branches out into a series of closely interrelated problems. First of all, how are we to understand class consciousness (in theory)? Second, what is the (practical) function of class consciousness, so understood, in the context of the class struggle? This leads to the further question: is the problem of class consciousness a 'general' sociological problem or does it mean one thing for the proletariat and another for every other class to have emerged hitherto? And lastly, is class consciousness homogeneous in nature and function or can we discern different gradations and levels in it? And if so, what are their practical implications for the class struggle of the proletariat?

I

In his celebrated account of historical materialism[1] Engels proceeds from the assumption that although the essence of history consists in the fact that 'nothing happens without a conscious purpose or an intended aim', to understand

1 *Feuerbach and the End of Classical German Philosophy*, SW [Marx/Engels, *Selected Works*, 2 vols, London: Lawrence and Wishart, 1950)] vol. II, pp. 354ff.

history it is necessary to go further than this. For on the one hand, 'the many individual wills active in history for the most part produce results quite other than those intended – often quite the opposite; *their motives, therefore, in relation to the total result are likewise of only secondary importance.* On the other hand, the further question arises: *what driving forces in turn stand behind these motives?* What are the historical causes which transform themselves into these motives in the brain of the actors?' He goes on to argue that these driving forces ought themselves to be determined, in particular those which 'set in motion great masses, whole peoples and again whole classes of the people; and which create *a lasting action resulting in a great transformation.*' The essence of scientific Marxism consists, then, in the realization that the real motor forces of history are independent of man's (psychological) consciousness of them.

At a more primitive stage of knowledge this independence takes the form of the belief that these forces belong, as it were, to nature and that in them and in their causal interactions it is possible to discern the 'eternal' laws of nature. As Marx says of bourgeois thought

> Man's reflections on the forms of social life and consequently also his scientific analysis of those forms, take a course directly opposite to that of their actual historical development. He begins post festum, with the results of the process of development ready to hand before him. The characters . . . have already acquired the stability of natural self-understood forms of social life, before man seeks to decipher not their historical character (for in his eyes they are immutable) but their meaning.[2]

This is a dogma whose most important spokesmen can be found in the political theory of classical German philosophy and in the economic theory of Adam Smith and Ricardo. Marx opposes to them a critical philosophy, a theory of theory and a consciousness of consciousness. This critical philosophy implies above all historical criticism. It dissolves the rigid, unhistorical, natural appearance of social institutions; it reveals their historical origins and shows therefore that they are subject to history in every respect including historical decline. Consequently history does not merely unfold *within* the terrain mapped out by these institutions. It does not resolve itself into the evolution of *contents*, of men and situations etc., while the *principles* of society remain eternally valid. Nor are these institutions the *goal* to which all history aspires, such that when they are realized history will have fulfilled her mission and will then be at an end. On the contrary, history is precisely *the history of these institutions*, of the changes they undergo *as* institutions which bring men together in societies. Such institutions start by controlling economic relations between men and go

2 *Capital*, vol. I, p. 75.

on to permeate all human relations (and hence also man's relations with himself and with nature etc.).

At this point bourgeois thought must come up against an insuperable obstacle, for its starting-point and its goal are always, if not always consciously, an apologia for the existing order of things or at least the proof of their immutability.[3] 'Thus there has been history, but there is no longer any',[4] Marx observes with reference to bourgeois economics, a dictum which applies with equal force to all attempts by bourgeois thinkers to understand the process of history. (It has often been pointed out that this is also one of the defects of Hegel's philosophy of history.) As a result, while bourgeois thought is indeed able to conceive of history as a problem, it remains an *intractable* problem. Either it is forced to abolish the process of history and regard the institutions of the present as eternal laws of nature which for 'mysterious' reasons and in a manner wholly at odds with the principles of a rational science were held to have failed to establish themselves firmly, or indeed at all, in the past. (This is characteristic of bourgeois sociology.) Or else, everything meaningful or purposive is banished from history. It then becomes impossible to advance beyond the mere 'individuality' of the various epochs and their social and human representatives. History must then insist with Ranke that every age is 'equally close to God', i.e. has attained an equal degree of perfection and that – for quite different reasons – there is no such thing as historical development.

In the first case it ceases to be possible to understand the *origin* of social institutions.[5] The objects of history appear as the objects of immutable, eternal laws of nature. History becomes fossilized in a *formalism* incapable of comprehending that the real nature of socio-historical institutions is that they consist of *relations between men*. On the contrary, men become estranged from this, the true source of historical understanding and cut off from it by an unbridgeable gulf. As Marx points out,[6] people fail to realize 'that these definite social relations are just as much the products of men as linen, flax, etc.'

In the second case, history is transformed into the irrational rule of blind forces which is embodied at best in the 'spirit of the people' or in 'great men'. It can therefore only be described pragmatically but it cannot be rationally understood. Its only possible organization would be aesthetic, as if it were a work of art. Or else, as in the philosophy of history of the Kantians, it must be seen as the instrument, senseless in itself, by means of which timeless, suprahistorical, ethical principles are realized.

---

3 And also of the 'pessimism' which *perpetuates* the present state of affairs and represents it as the uttermost limit of human development just as much as does 'optimism'. In this respect (and in this respect alone) Hegel and Schopenhauer are on a par with each other.
4 *The Poverty of Philosophy*, p. 135.
5 Ibid., p. 117.
6 Ibid., p. 122.

Marx resolves this dilemma by exposing it as an illusion. The dilemma means only that the contradictions of the capitalist system of production are reflected in these mutually incompatible accounts of the same object. For in this historiography with its search for 'sociological' laws or its formalistic rationale, we find the reflection of man's plight in bourgeois society and of his helpless enslavement by the forces of production. 'To them, *their own social action*', Marx remarks,[7] 'takes the form of the action of objects which rule the producers instead of being ruled by them.' This law was expressed most clearly and coherently in the purely natural and rational laws of classical economics. Marx retorted with the demand for a historical critique of economics which resolves the totality of the reified objectivities of social and economic life into *relations between men*. Capital and with it every form in which the national economy objectifies itself is, according to Marx, 'not a thing but a social relation between persons mediated through things'.[8]

However, by reducing the objectivity of the social institutions so hostile to man to relations between men, Marx also does away with the false implications of the irrationalist and individualist principle, i.e. the other side of the dilemma. For to eliminate the objectivity attributed both to social institutions inimical to men and to their historical evolution means the restoration of this objectivity to their underlying basis, to the relations between men; it does not involve the elimination of laws and objectivity independent of the will of man and in particular the wills and thoughts of individual men. It simply means that this objectivity is the self-objectification of human society at a particular stage in its development; its laws hold good only within the framework of the historical context which produced them and which is in turn determined by them.

It might look as though by dissolving the dilemma in this manner we were denying consciousness any decisive role in the process of history. It is true that the conscious reflexes of the different stages of economic growth remain historical facts of great importance; it is true that while dialectical materialism is itself the product of this process, it does not deny that men perform their historical deeds themselves and that they do so consciously. But as Engels emphasizes in a letter to Mehring,[9] this consciousness is false. However, the dialectical method does not permit us simply to proclaim the 'falseness' of this consciousness and to persist in an inflexible confrontation of true and false. On the contrary, it requires us to investigate this 'false consciousness' concretely as an aspect of the historical totality and as a stage in the historical process.

---

7 *Capital*, vol. I, p. 75 (my italics – G.L.). Cf. also Engels, *The Origin of the Family, Private Property and the State*, SW II, pp. 292–3.
8 *Capital*, vol. I, p. 766. Cf. also *Wage Labour and Capital*, SW II, p. 83; on machines see *The Poverty of Philosophy*, p. 149; on money, ibid., p. 89, etc.
9 *Dokumente des Sozialismus*, II, p. 76.

Of course bourgeois historians also attempt such concrete analyses; indeed they reproach historical materialists with violating the concrete uniqueness of historical events. Where they go wrong is in their belief that the concrete can be located in the empirical individual of history ('individual' here can refer to an individual man, class or people) and in his empirically given (and hence psychological or mass-psychological) consciousness. And just when they imagine that they have discovered the most concrete thing of all: *society as a concrete totality*, the system of production at a given point in history and the resulting division of society into classes – they mistake something wholly abstract for the concrete. 'These relations', Marx states, 'are not those between one individual and another, but between worker and capitalist, tenant and landlord, etc. Eliminate these relations and you abolish the whole of society; your Prometheus will then be nothing more than a spectre without arms or legs. . . .'[10]

Concrete analysis means then: the relation to society *as a whole*. For only when this relation is established does the consciousness of their existence that men have at any given time emerge in all its essential characteristics. It appears, on the one hand, as something which is *subjectively* justified in the social and historical situation, as something which can and should be understood, i.e. as 'right'. At the same time, *objectively*, it bypasses the essence of the evolution of society and fails to pinpoint it and express it adequately. That is to say, objectively, it appears as a 'false consciousness'. On the other hand, we may see the same consciousness as something which fails *subjectively* to reach its self-appointed goals, while furthering and realizing the *objective* aims of society of which it is ignorant and which it did not choose.

This twofold dialectical determination of 'false consciousness' constitutes an analysis far removed from the naïve description of what men in fact thought, felt and wanted at any moment in history and from any given point in the class structure. I do not wish to deny the great importance of this, but it remains after all merely the *material* of genuine historical analysis. The relation with concrete totality and the dialectical determinants arising from it transcend pure description and yield the category of objective possibility. By relating consciousness to the whole of society it becomes possible to infer the thoughts and feelings which men would have in a particular situation if they were *able* to assess both it and the interests arising from it in their impact on immediate action and on the whole structure of society. That is to say, it would be possible to infer the thoughts and feelings appropriate to their objective situation. The number of such situations is not unlimited in any society. However much detailed researches are able to refine social typologies there will always be a number of clearly distinguished basic types whose characteristics are determined by the types of position available in the process

10 *The Poverty of Philosophy*, p. 112.

of production. Now class consciousness consists in fact of the appropriate and rational reactions 'imputed' [*zugerechnet*] to a particular typical position in the process of production.[11] This consciousness is, therefore, neither the sum nor the average of what is thought or felt by the single individuals who make up the class. And yet the historically significant actions of the class as a whole are determined in the last resort by this consciousness and not by the thought of the individual – and these actions can be understood only by reference to this consciousness.

This analysis establishes right from the start the distance that separates class consciousness from the empirically given, and from the psychologically describable and explicable ideas which men form about their situation in life. But it is not enough just to state that this distance exists or even to define its implications in a formal and general way. We must discover, first, whether it is a phenomenon that differs according to the manner in which the various classes are related to society as a whole and whether the differences are so great as to produce *qualitative distinctions*. And we must discover, secondly, the *practical* significance of these different possible relations between the objective economic totality, the imputed class consciousness and the real, psychological thoughts of men about their lives. We must discover, in short, the *practical, historical function* of class consciousness.

Only after such preparatory formulations can we begin to exploit the category of objective possibility systematically. The first question we must ask is how far is it *in fact* possible to discern the whole economy of a society from inside it? It is essential to transcend the limitations of particular individuals caught up in their own narrow prejudices. But it is no less vital not to overstep the frontier fixed for them by the economic structure of society and establishing their position in it.[12] Regarded abstractly and formally, then, class consciousness implies a class-conditioned *unconsciousness* of one's own socio-historical and economic condition.[13] This condition is given as a definite structural relation, a definite formal nexus which appears to govern the whole of life. The 'falseness', the illusion implicit in this situation is in no sense arbitrary; it is simply the intellectual reflex of the objective economic structure. Thus, for example, 'the value or price of labour-power takes on the appearance of the price or value of labour itself. . .' and 'the illusion is created that the totality is paid labour. . . . In contrast to that, under slavery even that portion of labour which is paid for

---

11 In this context it is unfortunately not possible to discuss in greater detail some of the ramifications of these ideas in Marxism, e.g. the very important category of the 'economic persona'. Even less can we pause to glance at the relation of historical materialism to comparable trends in bourgeois thought (such as Max Weber's ideal types).

12 This is the point from which to gain an historical understanding of the great utopians such as Plato or Sir Thomas More. Cf. also Marx on Aristotle, *Capital*, vol. I, pp. 59–60.

13 'But although ignorant of this, yet he says it', Marx says of Franklin, *Capital*, vol. I, p. 51. And similarly: 'They know not what they do, but they do it', ibid., p. 74.

appears unpaid for.'[14] Now it requires the most painstaking historical analysis to use the category of objective possibility so as to isolate the conditions in which this illusion can be exposed and a real connection with the totality established. For if from the vantage point of a particular class the totality of existing society is not visible; if a class thinks the thoughts imputable to it and which bear upon its interests right through to their logical conclusion and yet fails to strike at the heart of that totality, then such a class is doomed to play only a subordinate role. It can never influence the course of history in either a conservative or progressive direction. Such classes are normally condemned to passivity, to an unstable oscillation between the ruling and the revolutionary classes, and if perchance they do erupt then such explosions are purely elemental and aimless. They may win a few battles but they are doomed to ultimate defeat.

For a class to be ripe for hegemony means that its interests and consciousness enable it to organize the whole of society in accordance with those interests. The crucial question in every class struggle is this: which class possesses this capacity and this consciousness at the decisive moment? This does not preclude the use of force. It does not mean that the class-interests destined to prevail and thus to uphold the interests of society as a whole can be guaranteed an automatic victory. On the contrary, such a transfer of power can often only be brought about by the most ruthless use of force (as e.g. the primitive accumulation of capital). But it often turns out that questions of class consciousness prove to be decisive in just those situations where force is unavoidable and where classes are locked in a life-and-death-struggle. Thus the noted Hungarian Marxist Erwin Szabó is mistaken in criticizing Engels for maintaining that the Great Peasant War (of 1525) was essentially a reactionary movement. Szabó argues that the peasants' revolt was suppressed *only* by the ruthless use of force and that its defeat was not grounded in socio-economic factors and in the class consciousness of the peasants. He overlooks the fact that the deepest reason for the weakness of the peasantry and the superior strength of the princes is to be sought in class consciousness. Even the most cursory student of the military aspects of the Peasants' War can easily convince himself of this.

It must not be thought, however, that all classes ripe for hegemony have a class consciousness with the same inner structure. Everything hinges on the extent to which they can become conscious of the actions they need to perform in order to obtain and organize power. The question then becomes: how far does the class concerned perform the actions history has imposed on it 'consciously' or 'unconsciously'? And is that consciousness 'true' or 'false'. These distinctions are by no means academic. Quite apart from problems of culture where such fissures and dissonances are crucial, in all practical matters

14 *Wages, Price and Profit*, SW I, pp. 388–9.

too the fate of a class depends on its ability to elucidate and solve the problems with which history confronts it. And here it becomes transparently obvious that class consciousness is concerned neither with the thoughts of individuals, however advanced, nor with the state of scientific knowledge. For example, it is quite clear that ancient society was broken economically by the limitations of a system built on slavery. But it is equally clear that neither the ruling classes nor the classes that rebelled against them in the name of revolution or reform could perceive this. In consequence the practical emergence of these problems meant that the society was necessarily and irremediably doomed.

The situation is even clearer in the case of the modern bourgeoisie, which, armed with its knowledge of the workings of economics, clashed with feudal and absolute society. For the bourgeoisie was quite unable to perfect its fundamental science, its own science of classes: the reef on which it foundered was its failure to discover even a theoretical solution to the problem of crises. The fact that a scientifically acceptable solution does exist is of no avail. For to accept that solution, even in theory, would be tantamount to observing society *from a class standpoint other than that of the bourgeoisie.* And no class can do that – unless it is willing to abdicate its power freely. Thus the barrier which converts the class consciousness of the bourgeoisie into 'false' consciousness is objective; it is the class situation itself. It is the objective result of the economic set-up, and is neither arbitrary, subjective nor psychological. The class consciousness of the bourgeoisie may well be able to reflect all the problems of organization entailed by its hegemony and by the capitalist transformation and penetration of total production. But it becomes obscured as soon as it is called upon to face problems that remain within its jurisdiction but which point beyond the limits of capitalism. The discovery of the 'natural laws' of economics is pure light in comparison with mediaeval feudalism or even the mercantilism of the transitional period, but by an internal dialectical twist they became 'natural laws based on the unconsciousness of those who are involved in them'.[15]

It would be beyond the scope of these pages to advance further and attempt to construct a historical and systematic typology of the possible degrees of class consciousness. That would require – in the first instance – an exact study of the point in the total process of production at which the interests of the various classes are most immediately and vitally involved. Secondly, we would have to show how far it would be in the interest of any given class to go beyond this immediacy, to annul and transcend its immediate interest by seeing it as a factor within a totality. And lastly, what is the nature of the totality that is then achieved? How far does it really embrace the true totality of production? It is quite evident that the quality and structure of class consciousness must be very different if, e.g. it remains stationary at the separation of consumption from

15 Engels, *Umriss zu einer Kritik der Nationalökonomie*, Nachlass [*Aus dem literarischen Nachlass von Karl Marx, Friedrich Engels und Ferdinand Lassalle*, 4 vols, edited by Franz Mehring (Stuttgart, 1902)] vol. I, p. 449.

production (as with the Roman *Lumpenproletariat*) or if it represents the formation of the interests of circulation (as with merchant capital). Although we cannot embark on a systematic typology of the various points of view it can be seen from the foregoing that these specimens of 'false' consciousness differ from each other both qualitatively, structurally and in a manner that is crucial for the activity of the classes in society.

18   The Proletariat

Shlomo Avineri

Only at this late stage does the proletariat appear in Marx's thinking and social criticism. Its appearance at this point has systematic significance, because it explains Marx's interest in the proletariat within the theoretical framework of this thought. As we shall see later in this chapter, the proletariat, for Marx, is not just a historical phenomenon: its suffering and dehumanization are, according to Marx, a paradigm for the human condition at large. It is not the proletarians' concrete conditions of life but their relation to an anthropological determination of man which primarily interest Marx. Consequently, though Marx is certainly not the first to discuss the proletariat and its position in industrial society, he is the first to relate it to general terms of reference which, for their part, draw very heavily on the Hegelian heritage and tradition.

Marx is fully cognizant of his debt to his predecessors, though there is a significant difference between his readily admitted indebtedness to French Restoration historians and his more ambivalent acknowledgement to Lorenz von Stein. Most of Marx's reading notes for the crucial summer of 1843, when his views on state and society took shape, deal with historical accounts of the role of social classes in the French Revolution, and most of his sources are naturally French; Marx even arranged an index to his various notebooks, according to the social background of the different constitutional instruments of the Revolution.[1] In 1852 Marx tells Weydemeyer that the 'bourgeois historians' discovered the role of the classes in determining developments in modern society.[2] Two years later, in a letter to Engels, he specifically refers to Thierry's

From Shlomo Avineri, *The Social and Political Thought of Karl Marx* (Cambridge: Cambridge University Press, 1968), pp. 52–63. Reprinted by permission of Cambridge University Press.

1 *MEGA*, I, 1/2, pp. 118–36; the index pp. 122–3.
2 Marx to Weydemeyer, 5 March 1852 (*Selected Correspondence*, p. 86).

contribution, but points out that like other Restoration historians Thierry overlooked the fact that social struggles did not end with the emergence and hegemony of the bourgeoisie. The real and final struggle, according to Marx, occurs at the moment of the bourgeoisie's victory, when it becomes a ruling class and ceases to be a *tiers état* alongside the clergy and the nobility.[3]

Marx's relation to Lorenz von Stein is more complex and remains controversial. Robert Tucker recently pointed out how much Marx's description of the proletariat draws on Stein's *Der Sozialismus und Kommunismus des heutigen Frankreichs*. In this Tucker follows several earlier writers who maintained that Marx had become acquainted with French socialist thinking through Stein's book, and that only later did he read the French authors themselves.[4] Others, however, maintain that, because of the writers' different levels of discussion and conceptualization, Stein's influence on Marx should be rather held at a minimum. It would indeed be difficult to suppose that Marx could be too impressed by Stein's somewhat simplistic arguments.[5]

It is difficult to take issue with these arguments if the problem is posed as if Stein were Marx's only conceivable source. Stein's book does not appear in Marx's reading lists of 1842 – but Marx's notes for that year include only books on art and mythology, and he certainly read books on history as well, so the notes as they survive cannot be considered comprehensive. Marx's remarks about Stein are none too clear. In *The Holy Family* Marx reproaches Bruno Bauer for concentrating in his discussion on French socialism and not paying any attention to the English working-class movement on the sole ground that Stein has nothing on it. Marx feels this is a serious weakness of Stein's book. In *The German Ideology*, however, Marx compares Stein's study quite favourably with Karl Grün's book on French and Belgian socialism, and points out that Grün's book is a muddled rehash of Stein's work.[6]

In contrast, Marx refers for the first time to 'a propertyless class' whose problems 'cry out to heaven in Manchester, Paris and Lyons' in an article in the *Rheinische Zeitung* in autumn 1842, a short time after the publication of Stein's book. Though this article ostensibly deals with one of Wilhelm Weitling's

3 Marx to Engels, 27 July 1854 (ibid., p. 105).

4 R. C. Tucker, *Philosophy and Myth in Karl Marx* (Cambridge, 1961), pp. 114–16; cf. G. Adler, 'Die Anfänge der Marxschen Sozialtheorie und ihre Beeinflussung durch Hegel, Feuerbach, Stein und Proudhon', *Festgabe für Adolf Wagner* (Leipzig, 1905), pp. 16ff.; P. Vogel, *Hegels Gesellschaftsbegriff und seine geschichtliche Fortbildung durch Lorenz Stein, Marx, Engels und Lassalle* (Berlin, 1925); B. Földes, *Das Problem Karl Marx – Lorenz Stein* (Jena, 1927).

5 F. Mehring, *Nachlass*, I, 186; S. Hook, *From Hegel to Marx*, new edition (Ann Arbor, 1962), p. 199. Hook, however, is mistaken in dating Stein's book at 1845, instead of 1842. For some recent valuable studies of Stein, see K. Mengelberg, 'Lorenz v. Stein and his Contribution to Historical Sociology', *Journal of the History of Ideas*, XXII, no. 2 (1961); J. Weiss, 'Dialectical Idealism and the Work of Lorenz v. Stein', *International Review of Social History*, VII, no. 1 (1963).

6 *The Holy Family*, p. 180; *The German Ideology*, pp. 534f. Engels refers to Stein's book in 1843 as 'dull drudgery' (*Werke*, I, 477).

books, Marx mentions here writings by Leroux, Considérant, Proudhon and Fourier. They are not mentioned by Weitling at all and Marx could not have read them in the original at that time. He probably got the information about them from Stein's book. But the problem, after all, is not biographical but methodological. Concentrating on the possible – and even quite probable – influence of Stein on Marx begs the question, assuming that Stein's book could have been Marx's only link with French socialist and communist ideas or with a sociological description of the proletariat in industrial society. This is clearly not the case, though some of the evidence has not always been considered. Stein's book caused a minor sensation in Germany, mainly because of the peculiar circumstances of its composition; but Stein was evidently not the first German author to raise the question of the proletariat. Volume XIII of Rotteck's and Welcker's *Lexikon der Staatswissenschaften*, published in 1842, includes the following statement in its entry on 'Revolution':

> But this is the content of history: no major historical antagonism disappears or dies out unless there emerges a new antagonism. Thus the general antagonism between the rich and the poor has been recently polarised into the tension between the capitalists and the hirers of labour on the one hand and the industrial workers of all kinds on the other; out of this tension there emerges an opposition whose dimensions become more and more menacing with the proportional growth of the industrial population.

Moreover, discussion of working-class conditions began in Germany many years before the problem existed in Germany itself and this discussion was started not by radicals or socialists, but by conservative romantics, who used it as an argument against *laissez-faire* liberalism. Two of the most reactionary German romantics, Adam Müller and Franz von Baader, took up the issue years before the radicals of Rotteck's or Welcker's stamp even considered it. In an essay published shortly after 1815, Adam Müller discussed the conditions of the working class in England in a language which seems to prefigure Marx's analysis in the *Economic-Philosophical Manuscripts* of 1844. Analysing Adam Smith, Müller arrives at the conclusion that political economy breaks the productive process, which should be unitary, into capital and labour.[7] In a work of 1816 Müller maintains that the division of labour emasculates the worker's personality:

> Man needs a many-sided, even an all-rounded, sphere for his activity, limited and restricted as this activity itself may be. . . . But if the division of labour, as it is now being practised in the big cities and the manufacturing and mining areas, cuts-up free man into wheels, cogs, cylinders and shuttles, imposes on him one sphere of activity in the course of his many-sided search for one object – how can one expect this segmented segment to be adequate to the full and fulfilled life or right

7 A. Müller, *Gesammelte Schriften* (München, 1839), I, p. 275.

and law? How can partial forms, which are cut out from the full circle of activity and are being divorced from one another, how can they fit into the full circle of political life and its laws? This is the miserable outcome of the division of labour in all the branches of private industry.[8]

Franz von Baader approaches the same issue in an essay written in 1835, which includes the term *proletair* in its title. Baader says that the moneyed classes impose the burden of taxation almost exclusively on the proletariat and make it simultaneously impossible for the proletarians to participate in political life and become full-fledged *citoyens*. According to Baader, the proletarians pay for the upkeep of the state but do not belong to it. He concludes that, according to the premises of political economy, capitalist competition is doomed to end in a monopoly that would leave the worker in a position far worse than that of the medieval serf:

> One can actually say that serfdom . . . is less terrible and more humane . . . than this reckless, defenceless and welfare-less freedom to which so many parts of the public are exposed in our so-called civilised and enlightened nations. Anyone who looks at this will have to admit that in what is called Christian and enlightened Europe, the civilisation of the few is generally made possible by the lack of civilisation and even barbarism of the many. We approach the state of ancient slavery and helotism far more than the Middle Ages.[9]

That both Müller and Baader sought to avoid this conclusion by a return to neo-feudal, corporative and romantic arrangements does not detract from the demonstration that Lorenz von Stein cannot be regarded as Marx's only source for his characterization of the industrial proletariat, much as Marx might have drawn from Stein's book some information about individual French writers. Marx draws on a mood and a general malaise prevalent at that time in intellectual circles in Germany among radicals and conservative romantics alike. It would be difficult – and utterly wrong – to choose one writer and make him responsible for moulding Marx's thought. Marx was responding to a *Zeitgeist*, and it was from a common stock far more than from any individual writer, that he drew his ideas and inspiration.

This common background also emphasizes Marx's specific contribution to this discussion of the working class, his suggestion that the condition of the proletariat should not be considered within the narrow historical circumstances of its emergence. Marx's intellectual *tour de force* must be approached by

8 A. Müller, 'Die heutige Wissenschaft der Nationalökonomie kurz und fasslich dargestellt', *Ausgewählte Abhandlungen*, ed. J. Baxa (Jena, 1921), p. 46.
9 F. v. Baader, 'Über das dermalige Misverhältnis der Vermögenlosen, oder Proletairs, zu den Vermögen besitzenden Klassen der Sozietät', *Schriften zur Gesellschaftsphilosophie*, ed. J. Sauter (Jena, 1925), p. 325.

confronting his description of the proletariat with the universal postulates of Hegel's political philosophy.

We have already seen that in the *Critique* Marx is aware that the class of 'immediate labour', though vital to the function of civil society, is not cared for by, nor integrated in, the general structure of society. Empirically Marx studied this phenomenon several months earlier when he discussed in some newspaper articles the situation of the village poor in the Rhineland. He comments that it seems inconsistent with Hegelian political philosophy for the village poor to be treated far better by the irrational countryside customs and traditions than by the rational arrangement of the institutional modern state: something must be wrong with the state if it fails to take account of this sector of the population.[10]

In the *Rheinische Zeitung* and in the *Critique* Marx is still obviously thinking in traditional terms of 'the poor'. This undifferentiated terminology shows that the issue has not yet been approached by philosophical speculation and insight. This happened only after Marx had finished his account of the Hegelian notion of the bureaucracy.

All of Marx's discussions about the bureaucracy conclude that the Hegelian postulate of a 'universal class' is an illusion of Hegel's inverted political world. The bureaucracy does not embody universality, but merely usurps it, using the pretexts of the commonwealth for its particular interests, which are no different from other class interests. But if Marx does not accept the Hegelian identification of bureaucracy with universality, he still retains the dialectical concept of a 'universal class', i.e. a partial social stratum which is, however, an ideal subject of the universal concept of the *Gemeinwesen*.

If Hegel's 'universal class' hypostatizes a given historical phenomenon into a self-fulfilling trans-historical norm, Marx uses it differently. For Marx the term will always be open to the dialectical dynamics of the historical process. He does not invest any one class with the attributes of universality: for him every generation, every historical situation, gives rise to a class which aspires to be the subject of society's general consciousness. Historical developments actually allow this class for a time to represent the *res publica*, society at large, but after a while, with changes in the distribution of social forces and in general conditions, this claim for universality no longer accords with the interests of society as a whole. The class which had hitherto represented society must vacate its place to a new class, which will henceforward claim that *it* represents society. 'Rising' classes are those whose claims for universality represent, at a given moment, the general will of society and realize the potential of its development. 'Declining' classes are those whose claim for universality is no longer valid and real. They cling to past glories and to present privileges derived from them. In these terms Marx sees the rise and decline of the feudal aristocracy, and applies the same analysis to the bourgeoisie. The Hegelian idea

---

10 *Rheinische Zeitung*, 27 October 1842 (*Werke*, I, 119).

of a 'universal class', stripped of its hypostasis, becomes, for Marx, a vehicle for historical explanation.

In the *Introduction to the Critique of Hegel's Philosophy of Right* Marx formulates this for the first time:

> No class in civil society can play this part unless it can arouse, in itself and in the masses, a moment of enthusiasm in which it associates and mingles with society at large, identifies itself with it, and is felt and recognised as the *general representative* of this society. Its aims and interests must genuinely be the aims and interests of society itself, of which it becomes in reality the social head and heart. It is only in the name of the general interest that a particular class can claim general supremacy . . . that genius which pushes material force to political power, that revolutionary daring which throws at its adversary the defiant phrase: *I am nothing and I should be everything.*[11]

And in *The German Ideology*:

> For each new class which puts itself in the place of one ruling before it, is compelled, merely in order to carry through its aims, to represent its interest as the common interest of all the members of society, that is, expressed in ideal form: it has to give its ideas the form of universality. . . . The class making a revolution appears from the very start . . . not as a class but as the representative of the whole of society.[12]

This tension between particularism and universality – between a class's appearance as a protagonist of the general will and its search for its own interests – comes to a head, according to Marx, with the emergence of the modern proletariat. It can be overcome only by the simultaneous abolition of the proletariat as a separate class and the disappearance of class differences in general. Marx does not postulate the abolition of class antagonisms because any economic mechanism points in that direction. No economic analysis precedes his dictum about the abolition of classes; they will be abolished (*aufgehoben*) because historical development has brought the tension between the general and the particular to a point of no return. The tension, according to Marx, is now radically general. It permeates every nook of society and cannot be transformed into just another change of the ruling class. Only a dialectical *Aufhebung* will give rise to a humanity with no dichotomy between the general and the particular.

Only because he sees in the proletariat the contemporary, and final, realization of universality, does Marx endow the proletariat with a historical significance and mission. He mentions the proletariat for the first time in the last section of the *Introduction to the Critique of Hegel's Philosophy of Right*,

11 *Early Writings*, pp. 55–6.
12 *The German Ideology*, pp. 61–2.

immediately after the passage cited above about the role of 'universal classes' in history. The reference to the proletariat is heavily loaded with allusions to its function as the ultimate 'universal class':

> A class must be formed which has *radical chains*, a class in civil society which is not a class of civil society, a class which is the dissolution of all classes, a sphere of society which has a universal character because its sufferings are universal, and which does not claim a *particular redress* because the wrong which is done to it is not a *particular wrong* but *wrong in general*. There must be formed a sphere of society which claims no *traditional* status but only a human status, a sphere which is not opposed to particular consequences but is totally opposed to the assumptions of the German political system; a sphere, finally, which cannot emancipate itself without emancipating itself from all the other spheres of society, without, therefore, emancipating all the other spheres, which is, in short, a *total loss* of humanity and which can only redeem itself by a *total redemption of humanity*. This dissolution of society, as a particular class, is the *proletariat*. . . .
>
> When the proletariat announces the *dissolution of the existing social order*, it only declares the *secret of its* own existence, for it *is* the *effective* dissolution of this order. When the proletariat demands the *negation of private property* it only lays down as a *principle for society* what society has already made a principle *for the proletariat*, and what the *latter* already involuntarily embodies as the negative result of society.[13]

The abolition (*Aufhebung*) of private property merely universalizes the situation the proletariat already experiences in society. Communism is not the starting-point of the discussion but its outcome as it emerges from philosophical principles. A political revolution, changing the balance of power within the social framework, will not do, because the proletariat remains in total alienation.[14] Hence the emancipation of the proletariat must be predicated on the emancipation of humanity, as the enslavement of the proletariat is paradigmatic to all forms of human unfreedom:

> From the relation of alienated labour to private property it also follows that the emancipation of society from private property, from servitude, takes the political form of the *emancipation of the workers*; not in the sense that only the latters' emancipation is involved, but because this emancipation includes the emancipation of humanity as a whole. For all human servitude is involved in the relation of the worker to production, and all the types of servitude are only modifications or consequences of this relation.[15]

The victory of the proletariat would mean its disappearance as a separate class. In this the proletariat, according to Marx, would differ from other classes,

---

13 *Early Writings*, pp. 58–9; cf. *The German Ideology*, pp. 86–7.
14 This is the crux of Marx's argument against the narrow view of a political revolution; see his article in *Vorwärts*, 8 August 1844 (*Werke*, I, 408).
15 *Early Writings*, pp. 132–3.

which, on attaining victory, still depended on the continuing existence of their opposite and complementary classes. The feudal baron needed a villein in order to be a baron; a bourgeois needs a proletarian in order to be a bourgeois – only the proletariat as a true, 'universal class' does not need its opposite to ensure its own existence. Hence the proletariat can abolish all classes by abolishing itself as a separate class and becoming co-eval with the generality of society. Even the programmatic and necessary connection between the proletariat and philosophy becomes possible, because both are universal, and because the proletariat carries out the universal postulates of philosophy: 'Just as philosophy finds its material weapons in the proletariat, so the proletariat finds its intellectual weapons in philosophy. . . . Philosophy is the head of this emancipation and the proletariat is its heart. Philosophy can only be realized by the abolition of the proletariat, and the proletariat can only be abolished by the realization of philosophy.'[16]

The universalistic nature of the proletariat does not disappear in Marx's later writings, when his discussion concentrates mainly on the historical causes of the emergence of the proletariat. What was at the outset a philosophical hypothesis is verified by historical experience and observation: the universalistic nature of the proletariat is a corollary of the conditions of production in a capitalist society, which must strive for universality on the geographical level as well.[17]

A careful reading of *The Communist Manifesto* brings the argument from universality to the surface. The proletariat as a 'universal', 'general', 'national' class can only be emancipated universally; its existence defies the norms of bourgeois society:

> In the conditions of the proletariat, those of old society at large are already virtually swamped. The proletarian is without property; his relation to his wife and children has no longer anything in common with the bourgeois family-relations; modern industrial labour, modern subjugation to capital, the same in England as in France, in America as in Germany, has stripped him of every trace of national character. . . .
>
> All previous historical movements were movements of minorities or in the interests of minorities. . . . The proletariat, the lowest stratum of our present society, cannot stir, cannot raise itself up, without the whole superincumbent strata of official society being sprung into the air. . . .
>
> The Communists are distinguished from other working-class parties by this only: 1. In the national struggles of the proletarians of the different countries, they put out and bring to the front the common interests of the entire proletariat, independently of all nationality. 2. In the various stages of development which the struggle of the working class against the bourgeoisie has to pass through, they always and everywhere represent the interests of the movement as a whole. . . .
>
> The working men have no country. We cannot take from them what they have

16 Ibid., p. 59.
17 *The German Ideology*, pp. 75–6.

not got. Since the proletariat must first of all acquire political supremacy, must rise to be the leading class of the nation, must constitute itself *the* nation, it is, so far, national, though not in the bourgeois sense of the word.

National differences and antagonisms between peoples are daily more and more vanishing, owing to the development of the bourgeoisie, to freedom of commerce, to the world market, to uniformity in the mode of production and in the conditions of life corresponding thereto.

The supremacy of the proletariat will cause them to vanish still faster. . . .[18]

This strong emphasis on the universal aspects of the proletariat recurs also in the Preamble to the General Rules of the International, drafted by Marx in 1864.[19] It is also behind Marx's opposition to Proudhonist mutualism, which he saw as an avoidance of this universalism. Appropriately enough, when Marx summarizes the deficiencies of the British labour class in 1870, he sees its inability to universalize its experience as its major weakness.[20]

This universalistic element in the proletariat can also explain the systematic nature of Marx's quarrel in the 1840s with Bruno Bauer and the 'True Socialists' about the role of the 'masses' in the struggle for emancipation. The disdain of Bauer and his disciples for the masses and their tendency to avoid complicity with the proletariat were motivated by a fear lest the general vision of liberty be replaced by advocacy of a particular class and espousal of its cause. For Marx, however, the proletariat was never a particular class, but the repository of the Hegelian 'universal class'. The debate about the place and significance of the proletariat was again conducted within the conceptual tradition of the Hegelian legacy.[21]

Nevertheless, because Marx's relation to the proletariat is not immediate but is reached through speculative considerations, he does not reveal much empathy or spiritual attachment to the members of the working class. Marx's sceptical view of the proletariat's ability to conceive its own goals and realize them without outside intellectual help has often been documented. It suits his remark that revolutions never start with the 'masses' but originate in elite groups.[22] Much as Marx always opposed those socialists who tried explicitly to dissociate themselves from the proletariat, a chief reason for the split in the League of Communists in 1850 was Marx's uncertainty about what would

18 *Selected Writings*, I, 44, 46, 51.
19 Ibid., p. 386.
20 *Werke*, XVI, 415.
21 Cf. D. Hertz-Eichenrode, 'Massenpsychologie bei den Junghegelianer', *International Review of Social History*, VII, no. 2 (1962), pp. 231–59. This excellent study does not, however, bring out the connection between Marx's view of the proletariat and his Hegelian background.
22 See Marx's article 'The Indian Revolt' (*New York Daily Tribune*, 16 September 1857): 'The first blow dealt to the French Monarchy proceeded from the nobility, not from the peasants. The Indian Revolt does not commence with the *ryots*, tortured, dishonoured and stripped naked by the British, but with the sepoys, clad, fed, petted and pampered by them.'

happen to the League if it were to be exclusively proletarian in membership. Marx's opponents within the League even went so far as to accuse him of trying to impose intellectual discipline on the proletarian movement; and Weitling was sometimes snubbed by Marx as the Tailor's King.[23]

This inquiry leads Marx to the conclusion that the conditions of the emergence of the proletariat guarantee their own overcoming. He couples this conclusion with the insight that the same forces produce poverty and wealth within society:

> Private property, as private property, as wealth, is compelled to maintain itself, and thereby its opposite, the proletariat, in existence. That is the positive side of the contradiction, self-satisfied private property. . . .
>
> The proletariat, on the other hand, is compelled as proletariat to abolish itself and thereby its opposite, the condition for its existence, what makes it the proletariat, i.e. private property. That is the negative side of the contradiction, its restlessness within its very self, dissolved and self-dissolving private property.[24]

23 Cf. *Werke*, VIII, 598–600. In a letter to Engels (20 July 1852) Marx has this to say about a group of German working-class men: 'Asses more stupid than these German workers do not exist' (*Werke*, XXVIII, 93).
24 *The Holy Family*, p. 51.

19 Social Classes and the State

Nicos Poulantzas

I

What are social classes in Marxist theory?

They are groupings of social agents, defined principally but not exclusively by their place in the production process, i.e. in the economic sphere. The economic place of the social agents has a principal role in determining social classes. But from that we cannot conclude that this economic place is sufficient to determine social classes. Marxism states that the economic does indeed have the determinant role in the mode of production or a social formation; but the political and the ideological (the superstructure) also have a very important role. In fact, whenever Marx, Engels, Lenin and Mao analyse social classes, far from limiting themselves to economic criteria alone, they make explicit reference to political and ideological criteria.

For Marxism, social classes involve in one and the same process both class contradictions and class struggle; social classes do not firstly exist as such, and only then enter into a class struggle. Social classes coincide with class practices, i.e. the class struggle, and are only defined in their mutual opposition.

The class determination, while it coincides with the practices (struggle) of classes and includes political and ideological relations, designates certain objective places occupied by the social agents in the social division of labour: places which are independent of the will of these agents.

It may thus be said that a social class is defined by its place in the ensemble of social practices, i.e. by its place in the social division of labour as a whole. This includes political and ideological relations. Social class, in this sense, is a concept which denotes the effects of the structure within the social division of

From Nicos Poulantzas, *Classes in Contemporary Capitalism* (Editions du Seuil; New Left Books, 1975), pp. 14–27. Reprinted by permission of Verso Books.

labour (social relations and social practices). This place thus corresponds to what I shall refer to as the structural determination of class, i.e. to the existence within class practices of determination by the structure – by the relations of production, and by the places of political and ideological domination/ subordination. Classes exist only in the class struggle.

This structural determination of classes, which thus exists only as the class struggle, must, however, be distinguished from class position in each specific conjuncture – the focal point of the always unique historic individuality of a social formation, in other words the concrete situation of the class struggle. In stressing the importance of political and ideological relations in determining social classes, and the fact that social classes only exist in the form of class struggle and practices, class determination must not be reduced, in a voluntarist fashion, to class position. The importance of this lies in those cases in which a distance arises between the structural determination of classes and the class positions in the conjuncture. . . .

(*a*) A social class, or a fraction or stratum of a class, may take up a class position that does not correspond to its interests, which are defined by the class determination that fixes the horizon of the class's struggle. The typical example of this is the labour aristocracy, which in certain conjunctures takes up class positions that are in fact bourgeois. This does not mean, however, that it becomes, in such cases, a part of the bourgeoisie; it remains, from the fact of its structural class determination, part of the working class, and constitutes, as Lenin put it, a 'stratum' of the latter. In other words, its class determination is not reducible to its class position.

If we now take the inverse case, certain classes or fractions and strata of classes other than the working class, and the petty bourgeoisie in particular, may in specific conjunctures take up proletarian class positions, or positions aligned with that of the working class. This does not then mean that they become part of the working class. To give a simple example: production technicians often have proletarian class positions, frequently taking the side of the working class in strikes, for instance. But this does not mean that they have then become part of the working class, since their structural class determination is not reducible to their class position. Moreover, it is precisely by virtue of its class determination that this grouping sometimes takes the side of the working class, and sometimes the side of the bourgeoisie (bourgeois class positions). Technicians no more form part of the bourgeoisie each time that they take up bourgeois class positions than they form part of the proletariat when they take up the positions of the latter. To reduce the structural determination of class to class position would be tantamount to abandoning the objective determination of the places of social classes for a 'relational' ideology of 'social movements'.

(*b*) It must be emphasized that ideological and political relations, i.e. the

places of political and ideological domination and subordination, are themselves part of the structural determination of class: there is no question of
objective place being the result only of economic place within the relations of
production, while political and ideological elements belong simply to class
positions. We are not faced, as an old error would have it, on the one hand
with an economic 'structure' that alone defines class places, and on the other
hand with a class struggle extending to the political and ideological domain.
This error today often takes the form of a distinction between '(economic)
class situation' on the one hand, and politico-ideological class position on the
other. From the start structural class determination involves economic,
political and ideological class struggle, and these struggles are all expressed
in the form of class positions in the conjuncture.

This also means that the analyses presented here have nothing in common
with the Hegelian schema with its class-in-itself (economic class situation,
uniquely objective determination of class by the process of production) and
class-for-itself (class endowed with its own 'class consciousness' and an
autonomous political organization = class struggle), which in the Marxist
tradition is associated with Lukács. This in turn implies:

(*a*)   That every objective class place in the productive process is necessarily
characterized by effects on the structural determination of this class in all
aspects, i.e. also by a specific place of this class in the political and ideological
relations of the social division of labour. For example, to say that there is a
working class in economic relations necessarily implies a specific place for
this class in ideological and political relations, even if in certain countries and
certain historical periods this class does not have its own 'class consciousness' or an autonomous political organization. This means that in such cases,
even if it is heavily contaminated by bourgeois ideology, its economic
existence is still expressed in certain specific material politico-ideological
practices which burst through its bourgeois 'discourse': this is what Lenin
designated, if very descriptively, as class instinct. To understand this, of
course, it is necessary to break with a whole conception of ideology as a
'system of ideas' or a coherent 'discourse', and to understand it as an
ensemble of material practices. This gives the lie to all those ideologies
arguing the 'integration' of the working class, and ultimately it means only
one thing: there is no need for there to be 'class consciousness' or
autonomous political organizations for the class struggle to take place, and to
take place in every domain of social reality.

(*b*)   'Class consciousness' and autonomous political organization, i.e. as far
as the working class is concerned, a revolutionary proletarian ideology and an
autonomous party of class struggle, refer to the terrain of class positions and
the conjuncture, and constitute the conditions for the intervention of classes
as social forces.

The principal aspect of an analysis of social classes is that of their places in the class struggle; it is not that of the agents that compose them. Social classes are not empirical groups of individuals, social groups, that are 'composed' by simple addition; the relations of these agents among themselves are thus not interpersonal relations. The class membership of the various agents depends on the class places that they occupy: it is moreover distinct from the class origin, the social origin, of the agents. The importance of these questions will become clear when we discuss the problem of the reproduction of social classes and their agents. Let us just signal here:

(*a*) in the relation between social classes and their agents, the pertinent question that needs to be posed is not that of the class to which this or that particular individual belongs (since what really matters are social groupings), nor that of the statistical and rigidly empirical boundaries of 'social groups' (since what really matters are the classes in the class struggle);

(*b*) the major factor in this respect is not that of 'social inequalities' between groups or individuals: these social inequalities are only the effect, on the agents, of the social classes, i.e. of the objective places they occupy, which can only disappear with the abolition of the division of society into classes. In a word, class society is not a matter of some inequality of 'opportunity' between 'individuals', a notion which implies that there is opportunity and that this depends wholly (or almost so) on the individuals, in the sense that the most capable and best individuals can always rise above their 'social milieu'.

In the determination of social classes, the principal role is played by place in the economic relations. What then does Marxist theory mean by 'economic'?

The economic sphere (or space) is determined by the *process* of production, and the place of the agents, their distribution into social classes, is determined by the *relations* of production.

Of course, the economic includes not only production, but also the whole cycle of production-consumption-distribution, the 'moments' of this appearing, in their unity, as those of the production process. In the capitalist mode of production, what is involved is the overall reproduction cycle of social capital: productive capital, commodity capital, money capital. In this unity, however, it is production which plays the determinant role. The distinction between the classes at this level is not, for example, a distinction based on relative sizes of income (a distinction between 'rich' and 'poor'), as was believed by a long pre-Marxist tradition and as is still believed today by a whole series of sociologists. The undoubted distinction between relative levels of income is itself only a consequence of the relations of production.

What then is the production process, and what are the relations of production which constitute it? In the production process, we find first of all the labour process: this refers to man's relation to nature in general. But the labour process always appears in a historically determined social form. It exists only in its unity with certain relations of production.

In a society divided into classes, the relations of production consist of a double relationship which encompasses men's relations to nature in material production. The two relationships are, first, the relationship between the agents of production and the object and means of labour (the productive forces); second, and through this, relations between men and other men, class relations.

These two relationships thus involve:

(*a*) The relationship between the non-worker (the owner) and the object and means of labour.
(*b*) The relationship between the immediate producer (the direct worker) and the object and means of labour.

The relationships have two aspects to them:

(*a*) Economic ownership: by this is meant real economic control of the means of production, i.e. the power to assign the means of production to given uses and so to dispose of the products obtained.
(*b*) Possession: by this is meant the capacity to put the means of production into operation.

In every society divided into classes, the first relationship (owners/means of production) always goes together with the first aspect: it is the owners who have real control of the means of production and thus exploit the direct producers by extorting surplus labour from them in various forms.

But this ownership is to be understood as real economic ownership, control of the means of production, to be distinguished from legal ownership, which is sanctioned by law and belongs to the superstructure. The law, of course, generally ratifies economic ownership, but it is possible for the forms of legal ownership not to coincide with real economic ownership. In this case, it is the latter which is determinant in defining the places of social classes, that is to say, the place of the dominant and exploiting class.

The second relationship – that between the direct producers (the workers) and the means and object of labour, defines the exploited class in the relations of production. It can take various forms, according to the various models of production in which it occurs.

In pre-capitalist modes of production, the direct producers (the workers) were not entirely 'separated' from the object and means of labour. In the case of the feudal mode of production, for instance, even though the lord had both legal and economic ownership of the land, the serf had possession of his parcel of land, which was protected by custom. He could not be purely and simply dispossessed by the lord; this was only achieved, as in England for example, by way of the whole bloody process of enclosures in the transition from feudalism to capitalism, what Marx referred to as the primitive accumulation of capital. In such modes of production, exploitation is predominantly by direct extraction of surplus labour, in the form of *corvée* payable in labour or in kind. In other words, economic ownership and possession are distinct in that they do not both depend on the same relationship between owners and means of production.

In the capitalist mode of production, by contrast, the direct producers (the working class) are completely dispossessed of their means of labour, of which the capitalists have the actual possession; Marx called this the phenomenon of the 'naked worker'. The worker possesses nothing but his labour-power, which he sells. It is this decisive modification of the place of the direct producers in the relations of production which makes labour itself into a commodity, and this determines the generalization of the commodity form, rather than the other way round: the fact that labour is a commodity is not the effect of a prior generalization of the celebrated 'commodity relations'. The extraction of surplus-value is thus achieved in this case not directly, but by way of the labour incorporated into commodities, in other words by the creation and monopolization of surplus-value. This entails the following:

The relations of production must be understood both as an articulation of the various relationships which constitute them, and in their union with the labour process: it is this which defines the dominant relation of exploitation characterizing a mode of production, and which determines the class that is exploited within this dominant relation. The property relationship should not be used alone, to denote negatively all those who do not dispose of economic ownership, i.e. all non-owners, as the class exploited within this dominant relation. The class exploited within this dominant relation (the basic exploited class: the working class in the capitalist mode of production) is that which performs the productive labour of that mode of production. Therefore in the capitalist mode of production, all non-owners are not thereby workers.

The production process, on the other hand, is defined not by technological factors, but by the relationships between agents and the means of labour, and hence between the agents themselves, in other words by the unity of the labour process, the productive forces and the relations of production. The labour process and the productive forces, including technology, do not exist in themselves, but always in their constitutive connection with the relations of production. Hence one cannot speak, in societies divided into classes, of 'productive labour' as such, in a neutral sense. In a society divided into classes, that labour is productive which corresponds to the relations of production of the mode in question, i.e. that which gives rise to the specific and dominant form of exploitation. Production, in these societies, means at the same time, and as one and the same process, class division, exploitation and class struggle.

It follows that it is not wages that define the working class economically: wages are a form of distribution of the social product, corresponding to market relations and the forms of 'contract' governing the purchase and sale of labour-power. Although every worker is a wage-earner, every wage-earner is certainly not a worker, for not every wage-earner is engaged in productive labour. If social classes are not defined at the economic level by a gradation of incomes (rich/poor), they are still less defined by the location of their agents in the hierarchy of wages and salaries. This location certainly has its value as an important index of class determination, but it is only the effect of the latter, just as are all those things that are generally referred to as social inequalities: the distribution of income, taxation etc. No more than other social inequalities is the wage differential a unilinear scale, a continuous and homogenous staircase, with or without landings, on which individuals or groups are located, certain groups at a 'higher' level, others at a 'lower' one: wage differentials are, rather, the *effect* of class barriers.

This being said, it is still necessary to emphasize that these class barriers and their extended reproduction have the effect of imposing specific and concentrated social inequalities on certain groupings of agents, according to the various classes in which they are distributed: in particular, on young people and on old people, not to enter here into the case of women, which is of a different order and, besides, more complex. This is because, in the case of women, what is involved is not simply certain overdetermined effects on them of the division of society into classes, but, more precisely, a specific articulation, within the social division of labour, of the class division and the sexual division.

The production process is thus composed of the unity of the labour process and the relations of production. But within this unity, it is not the labour process, including technology and the technical process, that plays the dominant role; the relations of production always dominate the labour process and the productive forces, stamping them with their own pattern and appearance. It is precisely this domination of the forces of production by the relations of production which gives their articulation the form of a *process* of production and reproduction.

This dominant role of the relations of production over the productive forces and the labour process is what gives rise to the constitutive role of political and ideological relations in the structural determination of social classes. The relations of production and the relationships which comprise them (economic ownership/possession) are expressed in the form of powers which derive from them, in other words class powers; these powers are constitutively tied to the political and ideological relations which sanction and legitimize them. These relations are not simply added on to relations of production that are 'already there', but are themselves present, in the form specific to each mode of production, in the constitution of the relations of production. The process of production and exploitation is at the same time a process of reproduction of the relations of political and ideological domination and subordination.

This implies, finally, that in the places of the social classes within the relations of production themselves, it is the social division of labour, in the form that this is given by the specific presence of political and ideological relations actually within the production process, which dominates the technical division of labour; we shall see the full consequences of this particularly in the question of the 'management and supervision' of the labour process, but also in that of the class determination of engineers and production technicians. Let us simply note here that it is by taking account of these basic Marxist propositions that we shall be able to grasp the decisive role of the division between manual labour and mental labour in the determination of social classes.

This is the right point to recall the basic distinction between mode of production and social formation: I shall restrict myself here to a few summary remarks, for this distinction has a theoretical importance which I shall have ample occasion to return to in the following essays.

In speaking of a mode of production, an abstract and formal object, one is still keeping to a general and abstract level, even though the concept mode of production itself already embraces relations of production, political relations and ideological relations: for example, the slave, feudal, capitalist modes of production etc. These modes of production, however, only exist and reproduce themselves within social formations that are historically determinate: France, Germany, Britain etc., at such and such a moment of the historic process. These social formations are always unique, because they are concrete and singular real objects.

Now a social formation comprises several modes – and also forms – of production, in a specific articulation. For example, European capitalist societies at the start of the twentieth century were composed of (i) elements of the feudal mode of production, (ii) the form of simple commodity production and manufacture (the form of the transition from feudalism to capitalism) and (iii) the capitalist mode of production in its competitive and monopoly forms. Yet these societies were certainly capitalist societies, in so far as the capitalist mode of production was dominant in them. In fact, in every social formation, we find the dominance of one mode of production, which produces complex effects of dissolution and conservation on the other modes of production and which gives these societies their overall character (feudal, capitalist etc.). The one exception is the case of societies in transition, which are, on the contrary, characterized by an equilibrium between the various modes and forms of production.

To return to social classes. If we confine ourselves to modes of production alone, we find that each of them involves two classes present in their full economic, political and ideological determination – the exploiting class, which is politically and ideologically dominant, and the exploited class, which is politically and ideologically dominated: masters and slaves in the slave mode of production, lords and serfs in the feudal mode of production. But a concrete society (a social formation) involves more than two classes, in so far as it is composed of various modes and forms of production. No social formation involves only two classes, but the two fundamental classes of any social formation are those of the dominant mode of production in that formation.

Social formations, however, are not the simple concretization or extension of modes and forms of production existing in their 'pure' form; they are not produced by the latter being simply 'stacked together' in space. The social formations in which the class struggle is enacted are the actual sites of the existence and reproduction of the modes and forms of production. A mode of production does not reproduce itself, or even exist, in the pure state, and still less can it be historically periodized as such. It is the class struggle in the social formations which is the motor of history; the process of history has these formations as its locus of existence.

This has considerable implications for the analysis of social classes. The classes of a social formation cannot be 'deduced', in their concrete struggle, from an abstract analysis of the modes and forms of production which are present in it, for this is not how they are found in the social formation. On the one hand, their very existence is affected by the concrete struggle that takes place within the social formation, and it is here in particular that we find the phenomenon of the polarization of other classes and class fractions around the two basic classes. In capitalist societies these are the bourgeoisie and the proletariat, which has decisive and very complex effects on these other classes, as well as on the two basic classes themselves. On the other hand, the classes of one social formation only exist in the context of the relations of this formation with other social formations, hence of the class relations of this formation with those of other formations. Here we have touched on the problem of imperialism and the imperialistic chain; imperialism, which precisely is the extended reproduction of capitalism, has its locus of existence in social formations, and not in the capitalist mode of production as such.

The Marxist theory of social classes further distinguishes *fractions* and *strata* of a class, according to the various classes, on the basis of differentiations in the economic sphere, and of the role, a quite particular one in these cases, of political and ideological relations. The theory also distinguishes social *categories*, defined principally by their place in the political and ideological relations: these include the state bureaucracy, defined by its relation to the state apparatuses, and the intellectuals, defined by their role in elaborating and deploying ideology. These differentiations, for which reference to political and ideological relations is always indispensable, are of great importance; these fractions, strata and categories may often, in suitable concrete conjunctures, assume the rule of relatively autonomous social forces.

It is none the less the case that we are not confronted here with 'social groups' external to, alongside, or above classes. The fractions are class fractions: the commercial bourgeoisie for example is a fraction of the bourgeoisie; similarly, the labour aristocracy is a fraction of the working class. Even social categories have a class membership, their agents generally belonging to several different social classes.

This is one of the particular and basic points of difference between the Marxist theory and the various ideologies of social stratification that dominate present-day sociology. According to these, social classes – whose existence all contemporary sociologists admit – would only be one form of classification, a partial and regional one (bearing in particular on the economic level alone) within a more general stratification. This stratification would give rise, in political and ideological relations, to social groups parallel and external to classes, on which they were superimposed. Max Weber already showed the way in this, and the various currents of political 'elite theory' need only be mentioned here.

The articulation of the structural determination of classes and of class positions within a social formation, the locus of existence of conjunctures, requires particular concepts. I shall call these *concepts of strategy*, embracing in particular such phenomena as class polarization and class alliance. Among these, on the side of the dominant classes, is the concept of the 'power bloc', designating a specific alliance of dominant classes and fractions; also, on the side of the dominated classes, the concept of the 'people', designating a specific alliance of these classes and fractions. These concepts are not of the same status as those with which we have dealt up till now: whether a class, fraction or stratum forms part of the power bloc, or part of the people, will depend on the social formation, its stages, phases and conjunctures. But this also indicates that the classes, fractions and strata that form part of these alliances do not for all that lose their class determination and dissolve into an undifferentiated type of merger or alliance. Just to take one example: when the national bourgeoisie forms part of the people, it still remains a bourgeoisie (leading to contradictions among the people); these classes and fractions do not dissolve into one another, as a certain idealist usage of the term 'popular masses', or even the term 'wage-earning class', might suggest.

II

We can now pose the question of the apparatuses, in particular the branches and apparatuses of the state, and the question of their relation to social classes. Here I shall confine myself to indicating certain of the roles played by the state apparatuses in the existence and reproduction of social classes.

The principal role of the state apparatuses is to maintain the unity and cohesion of a social formation by concentrating and sanctioning class domination, and in this way reproducing social relations, i.e. class relations. Political and ideological relations are materialized and embodied, as material practices, in the state apparatuses. These apparatuses include, on the one hand, the repressive state apparatus in the strict sense and its branches – army, police, prisons, judiciary, civil service; on the other hand, the ideological state apparatuses – the educational apparatus, the religious apparatus (the churches), the information apparatus (radio, television, press), the cultural apparatus (cinema, theatre, publishing), the trade union apparatus of class collaboration and the bourgeois and petty-bourgeois political parties etc., as well as in a certain respect, at least in the capitalist mode of production, the family. But as well as the state apparatuses, there is also the economic apparatus in the most strict sense of the term, the 'business' or the 'factory' which, as the centre of appropriation of nature, materializes and embodies the economic relations in their articulation with politico-ideological relations.

Given that the determination of classes involves political and ideological relations, and that the latter only exist in so far as they are materialized in the apparatuses, the analysis of social class (class struggle) can only be undertaken in terms of their relationship with the apparatuses, and with the state apparatuses in particular. Social classes and their reproduction only exist by way of the relationship linking them to the state and economic apparatuses; these apparatuses are not simply 'added on' to the class struggle as appendices, but play a constitutive role in it. In particular, whenever we go on to analyse politico-ideological relations, from the division between manual and mental labour to the bureaucratization of certain work processes and the despotism of the factory, we shall be concretely examining the apparatuses.

It remains none the less true that it is the class struggle that plays the primary and basic role in the complex relationship between class struggles and apparatuses, and this is a decisive point to note, given the errors of numerous present-day arguments on these questions. The apparatuses are never anything other than the materialization and condensation of class relations; in a sense, they 'presuppose' them, so long as it is understood that what is involved here is not a relation of chronological causality (the chicken or the egg). Now according to a constant of bourgeois ideology in the 'social sciences', which might be loosely referred to as the 'institutionalist-functionalist' current, it is apparatuses and institutions that determine social groups (classes), with class relations arising from the situation of agents in institutional relationships. This current exhibits in specific forms the couple idealism/empiricism, in the specific form of humanism/economism, both of which are characteristic of bourgeois ideology. This was already notably so with Max Weber; for him it was relations of 'power' which resulted in class relations, these 'power' relations having as their specific field and original locus of constitution relations within institutions or associations of the 'authoritarian' type (*Herrschaftsverbände*). This ideological lineage (and rooting a bit further back, one always comes across Hegel) has considerable repercussions, even in the most concrete questions, and permeates the whole of academic sociology in the currently dominant form of 'organization theory'. It is not restricted to the state apparatuses, but takes in the economic apparatus itself (the problem of the 'enterprise').

We can thus define both the relationship and the distinction between state power and state apparatuses. State apparatuses do not possess a 'power' of their own, but materialize and concentrate class relations, relations which are precisely what is embraced by the concept 'power'. The state is not an 'entity' with an intrinsic instrumental essence, but it is itself a relation, more precisely the condensation of a class relation. This implies that:

(*a*) the various functions (economic, political, ideological) that the state apparatuses fulfil in the reproduction of social relations are not 'neutral' functions *sui generis*, initially existing as such and later being simply 'diverted' or 'misappropriated' by the ruling classes; these functions depend on the state power inscribed in the very structure of its apparatuses, in other words on the classes and class fractions which occupy the terrain of political domination; (*b*) this political domination is itself bound up with the existence and functioning of the state apparatuses.

It follows that a radical transformation of social relations cannot be limited to a change in state power, but has to 'revolutionize' the state apparatuses themselves. In the process of socialist revolution, the working class cannot confine itself to taking the place of the bourgeoisie at the level of state power, but it has also radically to transform (to 'smash') the apparatuses of the bourgeois state and replace them by proletarian state apparatuses.

Here again, however, it is state power, directly articulated with the class struggle, that determines the role and the functioning of the state apparatuses.

(*a*) This is expressed, from the point of view of the revolutionization of the state apparatuses, by the fact that the working class and the popular masses cannot 'smash' the state apparatuses except by seizing state power.
(*b*) It is also expressed in the overall concrete functioning of the state apparatuses in every social formation. If the state apparatuses are not reducible to state power, it is none the less true that it is the particular configuration of the terrain of class domination, of state power (power bloc, hegemonic and governing classes or fractions etc., as well as class alliances and supporting classes) which determines, in the last instance, both the role of this or that apparatus or branch of the state in the reproduction of social relations, the articulation of economic, political and ideological functions within this apparatus or branch, and the concrete arrangement of the various apparatuses and branches. In other words, the role that this or that apparatus or branch of the state (eduction, army, parties etc.) plays in the cohesion of the social formation, the representation of class interests and the reproduction of social relations, is not a function of its intrisic nature, but depends on the state power.

More generally, any analysis of a social formation must take into direct consideration both the relations of class struggle, the power relations and the state apparatuses which materialize, concentrate and reflect these relations. Nevertheless, in the relationship between the class struggle and the apparatuses, it is the class struggle which is fundamental. It is not the 'institutional' forms and their modification which result in 'social movements', as for example current ideology about a 'blocked society' would have it, but rather the class struggle which determines the forms and modifications of the apparatuses.

These last points will stand out more clearly if one considers things from the point of view of the extended reproduction of social classes. In fact, social classes only exist in the context of the class struggle, with its historical and dynamic dimension. Classes, fractions, strata and categories can only be discerned, or even defined, by taking into consideration the historic perspective of the class struggle, and this directly raises the question of their reproduction.

A mode of production can only exist in social formations if it reproduces itself. In the last analysis, this reproduction is nothing other than the extended reproduction of its social relations: it is the class struggle that is the motor of history. Thus Marx says that, in the end, what capitalism produces is simply the bourgeoisie and the proletariat; capitalism simply produces its own reproduction.

Thus the site of the reproduction process is not, as a superficial reading of the second volume of *Capital* might suggest, the 'economic space' alone, and the process does not consist of a self-regulating automatism by which social capital is accumulated. Reproduction, being understood as the extended reproduction of social classes, immediately means reproduction of the political and ideological relations of class determination.

20 Karl Marx's 'Enquête Ouvrière'

Hilde Weiss

It appears from Marx's letter of 5 November 1880, addressed to Sorge, that the 'Enquête Ouvrière', published in the *Revue Socialiste* on 20 April 1880, was the work of Marx himself. He writes: 'I have prepared for him [Benoît Malon, the editor of the *Revue Socialiste*] the 'Questionneur' [sic] which was first published in the *Revue Socialiste* and afterwards distributed in a large number of copies throughout France.'[1] Only the detailed questionnaire, containing a hundred questions, and the accompanying text seem to have survived. A note in a later issue of the *Revue Socialiste*, the style of which suggests that it may have been written by Marx, indicates that some replies had been received, and that when a sufficient number had come in they would be published.[2] The journal *Egalité*, which was published during this period, and which Marx described in the same

From Hilde Weiss, 'Die "Enquête Ouvrière" von Karl Marx', *Zeitschrift für Sozialforschung*, V (Paris: Félix Alcan, 1936) pp. 76, 83–8, 91–7. Translated by Tom Bottomore. Reprinted by permission of Presses Universitaires de France.

1 'Twenty-five thousand copies of this appeal were printed and were sent to all labour organizations, socialist and democratic groups, French newspapers and individuals who requested copies.' (Note on the 'Enquête Ouvrière' in *Revue Socialiste*, April 20, 1880).

2 'Concerning the "Enquête Ouvrière". A number of our friends have already responded to our questionnaire, and we are grateful to them. We urge those of our friends and readers who have not yet replied to do so quickly. In order to make the survey as complete as possible we shall defer our own work until a large number of questionnaires has been returned. We ask our proletarian friends to reflect that the completion of these "cahiers du travail" is of the greatest importance, and that by participating in our difficult task they are working directly for their own liberation.' *Revue Socialiste*, 5 July 1880.

letter to Sorge as the first 'workers' paper' in France, repeatedly urged its readers to take part in the survey and included copies of the questionnaire.[3]

Marx's 'Enquête Ouvrière' differs in three respects from previous investigations of social conditions. First, as is clear from the statement of its purpose, and from the questions themselves, it aimed to provide an exact description of actual social conditions. Secondly, it proposed to collect information only from the workers themselves. Thirdly, it had a didactic aim; it was meant to develop the consciousness of the workers in the sense expounded in Marx's social theory.

Marx also intended that his 'Enquête Ouvrière' should diffuse among the general public a knowledge of the working and living conditions of the workers, and he had, therefore, some ulterior motives in undertaking his study. At the same time, however, his socialist views imposed upon him the obligation to depict as faithfully as possible the existing social misery. He assigns to social investigation the task of aiding the workers themselves to gain an understanding of their situation. For philanthropists the workers, as the most miserable stratum of society, were the object of welfare measures; but Marx saw in them an oppressed class which would become master of its own fate when once it had become aware of its situation. With the development of industrial capitalism, not only the misery of the proletariat, but also its will to emancipation increased. In his preface to the questionnaire Marx describes the 'Enquête Ouvrière' as a basis for 'preparing a reconstruction of society'.

However, it is not only in its aims that Marx's 'Enquête Ouvrière' differs from the private and official investigations that had preceded it, but also in the manner in which it was carried out. Earlier surveys, even if they had the intention, could not discover the real character of social evils, because they employed inadequate means to collect their information. They were addressed almost exclusively to factory owners and their representatives, to factory inspectors where there were such people, or to government officials (as in the case of Villeneuve-Bargement's inquiry).[4] Even where doctors or philanthropists who made such surveys went directly to working-class families, they were usually accompanied by factory owners or their representatives. Le Play, for example, recommends visits to working-class families 'with an introduction

---

3 'In its last issue the *Revue Socialiste* has taken the initiative in an excellent project. . . . The significance of an investigation of working-class conditions as they have been created by bourgeois rule is to place the possessing caste on trial, to assemble the materials for a passionate protest against modern society, to display before the eyes of all the oppressed, all wage-slaves, the injustices of which they are the constant victims, and thereby to arouse in them the will to end such conditions.' *L'Egalité*, April 28, 1880.

4 [Villeneuve-Bargement, *Economie politique chrétienne ou Recherches sur la nature et les causes du paupérisme en France et en Europe et sur les moyens de le soulager et de la prévenir*, 3 vols (Paris, 1834). Ed.]

from some carefully selected authority'; and he advises extremely diplomatic behaviour towards the family members, including the payment of small sums of money, or the distribution of presents, as a recompense. The investigator should 'praise with discrimination the cleverness of the men, the charm of the women, the good behaviour of the children, and discreetly hand out small presents to all of them'.[5] In the course of a thorough critical examination of survey methods that appears in Audiganne's account of the discussions in his circle of workers, it is said of Le Play: 'Never was a more misleading course embarked upon, in spite of the very best intentions. It is simply a question of the approach. A false viewpoint and a false method of observation give rise to a completely arbitrary series of suppositions, which bear no relation whatsoever to social reality, and in which there is apparent an invincible partiality for despotism and constraint.'[6] Audiganne indicates as one of the common mistakes in the conduct of surveys the pomp and ceremony which is adopted by investigators when they visit working-class families. 'If there is not a single tangible result produced by any survey carried out under the Second Empire, the blame must be assigned, in large measure, to the pompous manner in which they were conducted.'[7] Marx and Engels also described the methods by which workers were induced to give testimony through social research of this kind, even to the extent of presenting petitions against the reduction of their working hours.

Marx's questionnaire, which was addressed directly to the workers, was something unique. The article on social surveys in the *Dictionary of Political Economy* observes bluntly: 'Those who are to be questioned should not be allowed to participate in the inquiry.'[8] This justified Audiganne's criticism that 'people judge us without knowing us'.[9]

Marx asks the workers alone for information about their social conditions, on the grounds that only they and not any 'providential saviour' know the causes of their misery, and they alone can discover effective means to eliminate them. In the preface to the questionnaire he asks the socialists for their support, since they need, for their social reforms, exact knowledge of the conditions of life and work of the oppressed class, and this can only be brought to light by the workers themselves. He points out to them the historical role which the working class is called upon to play and for which no socialist utopia can provide a substitute.

This method of collecting information, by asking the workers themselves, represents a considerable progress over the earlier inquiries. It is, of course, understandable that Marx had to restrict himself to this method. Apart from the political and educational purposes which he wanted to combine with his

5 *Les Ouvriers Européens*, vol. I, p. 223.
6 Audiganne, *Mémoires d'un ouvrier de Paris, 1871–1872* (Paris, 1873), p. 61.
7 Ibid., p. 93.
8 *Dictionnaire de l'économie politique* (Paris, 1854), p. 706.
9 Audiganne, *Mémoires d'un ouvrier*, p. 1.

investigation, his method of obtaining information directly from the workers was intended to open the eyes of the public and of the state. From the point of view of modern social research in this field, the restriction of such an inquiry into working conditions to the responses of workers themselves would be considered inadequate. This method of inquiry is still vitally important in modern social surveys; but the monographs that were to have resulted from the 'Enquête Ouvrière' would need to be complemented, and their findings checked, by statistical materials, and by the data available from other surveys.
. . .

The didactic purpose of the 'Enquête Ouvrière' arises, as will be shown later, from the arrangement and formulation of the questions; but it is apparent also in the Preface, and especially in the title that Marx gives to the monographs which it is proposed to write on the basis of the replies to the questionnaire; he calls them 'cahiers du travail' ('labour-lists') in contrast to the 'cahiers de doléances' ('grievance-lists') of 1789. The specific character of his survey is shown by his coining of this new term, which is connected with a living tradition of the French workers, the petitions of the Third Estate. But while the 'cahiers de doléances' put forward trivial demands in a servile manner, the 'cahiers du travail' were meant to contain a true and exact description of the condition of the working class and of the path to its liberation. Moreover, the accomplishment of this programme is not to be left to the goodwill of a king; the workers are to struggle forthrightly and consciously for their human rights. It is not by chance that Marx also refers in this context to the 'socialist democracy', whose first task is to prepare the 'cahiers du travail'. The workers, who have to wage a class struggle and to accomplish a renewal of society, must first of all become capable of recognizing their own situation and of seeing the readiness of individuals to work together in a common cause.

The 'cahiers du travail', as I have noted, were not only to provide a better knowledge of working-class conditions, but were also to educate the workers in socialism. By merely reading the hundred questions, the worker would be led to see the obvious and commonplace facts that were mentioned there as elements in a general picture of his situation. By attempting seriously to answer the questions, he would become aware of the social determination of his conditions of life; he would gain an insight into the nature of the capitalist economy and the state, and would learn the means of abolishing wage labour and attaining his freedom. The questionnaire thus provides the outline of a socialist manual, which the worker can fill with a living content by absorbing its results.

Several of the questions are formulated in such a way – for instance, by the introduction of valuations – that the worker is led at once to the answer which the didactic purpose of the survey requires. Thus, Marx refers to the misuse of public power when it is a matter of defending the privileges of entrepreneurs; and a subsequent question asks whether the state protects the workers 'against the exactions and the illegal combinations of the employers'. The contrast is intended to make the worker aware of the class character of the state. Another example is provided by the case where workers share in the profits of the enterprise. The respondent is asked to consider whether business concerns with this apparently social orientation differ from other capitalist enterprises, and whether the legal position of the workers in them is superior. 'Can they go on strike? Or are they only permitted to be the humble servants of their masters?' (Question 99). It should be said, however, that only a relatively small proportion of the questions seek to influence opinion so directly.

It is far more significant, in relation to the two aspects of the survey, that Marx was successful in setting out the questions in a clear and practical manner. They are easily intelligible and deal with matters of direct concern to the worker. The simplicity and exactness of the questions in the 'Enquête Ouvrière' represent an advance over earlier surveys. Audiganne had observed quite rightly that these surveys asked questions that were far too comprehensive, abstract and complicated, and compromised the answers on important issues by introducing irrelevant questions.[10] For the same reasons, the various private investigations could provide no better picture of the real social conditions and attitudes of the workers.

The content of the questions posed in the earlier surveys, as well as their aims and techniques of inquiry, corresponded very closely with the interests of employers. For example, the question whether workers were paid wholly in cash, or whether a part of their wages were given in the form of goods or rent allowances, was asked both in the government survey of 1872 and in the 'Enquête Ouvrière'; but in the former case it was asked from the point of view of the employers, in the latter from the point of view of the workers. In the official survey, payments in the form of goods are treated as a 'supplement' to wages, but Marx regards every form of wage payment other than in cash as a method of reducing wages.

Since Marx's survey does represent an advance over earlier attempts, it is all the more surprising that very few replies to the questionnaire were apparently received.[11] Two reasons may explain this failure: first, the scope of the questionnaire, and second, the circumstances of the time. Even today, it is not easy for the average worker, in his spare time, to answer a questionnaire containing a hundred questions; and it was all the more difficult in a period when workers were being asked to do this for the first time. Their ability to write and to express themselves was still limited; they read very little, and their newspapers were published in small editions, as well as being hampered by the censorship. Second, the French labour movement was still in the period of

10 For one example among many, see Ducarre, *Rapport sur les conditions du travail en France* (Versailles, 1875), p. 195: 'What is the physical condition of the working population in your district, from the point of view of sanitary conditions, population increase, and expectation of life?' It is easy to imagine the prolixity of the replies.

11 It has proved impossible to find even the few replies that did arrive, in spite of an active search for them.

depression that followed the Paris Commune. Had there been at that time an independent labour movement, the survey could have been carried out much more effectively. It was, indeed, because of the backwardness of the labour movement and of the working class generally,[12] that Marx gave his survey the didactic purpose of awakening the workers to a realization of their condition. Thus Marx's survey had at the same time to create the circumstances in which an inquiry could be carried out.

The text of the questionnaire[13]

No government – whether monarchical or bourgeois-republican – has dared to undertake a serious investigation of the condition of the French working class, although there have been many studies of agricultural, financial, commercial and political crises.

The odious acts of capitalist exploitation which the official surveys by the English government have revealed, and the legislative consequences of these revelations (limitation of the legal working day to ten hours, legislation concerning the labour of women and children, etc.), have inspired in the French bourgeoisie a still greater terror of the dangers which might result from an impartial and systematic inquiry.

While awaiting the time when the republican government can be induced to follow the example of the English monarchical government and inaugurate a comprehensive survey of the deeds and misdeeds of capitalist exploitation, we shall attempt a preliminary investigation with the modest resources at our disposal. We hope that our undertaking will be supported by all those workers in town and country who realize that only they can describe with full knowledge the evils which they endure, and that only they – not any providential saviours – can remedy the social ills from which they suffer. We count also upon the socialists of all schools, who, desiring social reform, must also desire *exact* and *positive* knowledge of the conditions in which the working class, the class to which the future belongs, lives and works.

These 'labour-lists' ('cahiers du travail') represent the first task which socialist democracy must undertake in preparation for the regeneration of society.

The following hundred questions are the most important ones. The replies should follow the order of the questions. It is not necessary to answer all the questions, but respondents are asked to make their answers as comprehensive and detailed as possible. The name of the respondent will not be published unless specifically authorized, but it should be given together with the address, so that we can establish contact with him.

12 The reports compiled by workers on the occasion of the Vienna Exhibition (1873) show clearly how far the workers at that time were influenced by utopian ideas and by the views of employers.
13 Hilde Weiss notes that this was, to her knowledge, the first German translation of the 'Enquête Ouvrière'. An English translation of the questionnaire and of some passages from the prefatory statement was published in Bottomore and Rubel (eds), *Karl Marx: Selected Writings*. [Ed.]

The replies should be sent to the director of the *Revue Socialiste* (Monsieur Lécluse, 29 rue Royale, Saint-Cloud, near Paris).

The replies will be classified and will provide the material for monographs to be published in the *Revue Socialiste* and subsequently collected in a volume.

I

1 What is your occupation?
2 Does the workshop in which you are employed belong to a capitalist or to a joint-stock company? Give the names of the capitalist employers or of the directors of the company.
3 State the number of persons employed.
4 State their ages and sex.
5 What is the minimum age at which children (boys or girls) are employed?
6 State the number of supervisors and other employees who are not ordinary wage earners.
7 Are there any apprentices? How many?
8 Are there, in addition to the workers usually and regularly employed, others who are employed at certain periods?
9 Does your employer's industry work exclusively or primarily for the local market, for the national market, or for export?
10 Is the workshop in the country or in the town? Give the name of the place where it is situated.
11 If your workshop is in the country, does your industrial work enable you to live, or do you combine it with agricultural work?
12 Is your work done by hand or with the aid of machinery?
13 Give details of the division of labour in your industry.
14 Is steam used as motive power?
15 State the number of workshops in which the different branches of the industry are carried on. Describe the special branch in which you are employed, giving information not only about the technical aspects, but also about the muscular and nervous strain involved, and the general effects of the work on the health of the workers.
16 Describe the sanitary conditions in the workshop; size of the rooms, space assigned to each worker; ventilation, temperature, whitewashing of the walls, lavatories, general cleanliness; noise of machines, metallic dust, humidity, etc.
17 Is there any municipal or governmental supervision of the sanitary conditions in the workshops?
18 In your industry, are there any harmful fumes which cause specific illnesses among the workers?
19 Is the workshop overcrowded with machines?
20 Are the machines, the transmission system, and the engines supplying power, protected so as to avoid any accidents?
21 Enumerate the accidents which have occurred in your personal experience.
22 If you work in a mine enumerate the preventive measures taken by your employer to ensure adequate ventilation and to prevent explosions and other dangerous accidents.

23 If you are employed in a chemical works, in a factory, in the metal-working industry, or in any other industry which is particularly dangerous, enumerate the safety measures introduced by your employer.

24 How is your factory lighted (by gas, paraffin, etc.)?

25 In case of fire, are there enough emergency exits?

26 In case of accidents, is the employer obliged *by law* to pay compensation to the worker or his family?

27 If not, has he ever paid compensation to those who have met with an accident while working to enrich him?

28 Is there a medical service in your workshop?

29 If you work at home, describe the condition of your workroom. Do you use only tools, or do you use small machines? Are you helped by your children or by any other people (adults or children, male or female)? Do you work for individual clients or for a contractor? Do you deal directly with the latter, or do you deal with a middleman?

II

30 State your daily hours of work, and working days in the week.

31 State the holidays during the year.

32 What are the breaks in the working day?

33 Are meals taken at regular intervals or irregularly? Are they taken in the workshop or elsewhere?

34 Do you work during the meal breaks?

35 If steam power is used, when is the power turned on, and when is it turned off?

36 Is there any night work?

37 State the hours of work of children and young persons below the age of 16.

38 Are there shifts of children and young persons which replace each other during the hours of work?

39 Are the laws concerning the employment of children enforced by the government or the municipality? Are they respected by the employer?

40 Are there any schools for the children and young persons employed in your trade? If there are, what are the school hours? Who runs the schools? What is taught in them?

41 When work continues day and night how are the shifts organized?

42 What is the normal increase in hours of work during period of great industrial activity?

43 Are the machines cleaned by workers specially employed for this work, or are they cleaned gratuitously by the workers who are employed on them during the working day?

44 What are the regulations and the penalties for lateness? At what time does the working day begin, and at what time does it begin again after meals?

45 How much time do you spend in getting to work and in returning home?

III

46 What kind of work contract do you have with your employer? Are you engaged by the day, by the week, by the month, etc.?

47 What are the conditions laid down for giving or receiving notice?

48 In the event of the contract being broken, what penalty is imposed on the employer if it is his fault?

49 What penalty is imposed on the worker if it is his fault?

50 If there are apprentices, what are the terms of their contract?

51 Is your work regular or irregular?

52 In your trade, is the work seasonal, or is it, in normal times, spread more or less evenly over the year? If your work is seasonal, how do you live in the periods between working?

53 Are you paid time rates or piece rates?

54 If you are paid time rates, are you paid by the hour or by the day?

55 Is there additional pay for overtime work? What is it?

56 If you are paid piece rates, how are the rates fixed? If you are employed in an industry in which the work performed is measured by quantity or weight, as is the case in the mines, does your employer or his representatives resort to trickery in order to defraud you of a part of your earnings?

57 If you are paid piece rates, is the quality of the article made a pretext for fraudulent deductions from your wages?

58 Whether you are paid piece rates or time rates, when are you paid, or in other words how long is the credit which you extend to your master before receiving the price of the work carried out? Are you paid at the end of a week, a month, etc.?

59 Have you noticed that the delay in paying your wages makes it necessary for you to resort frequently to the pawnbroker, paying a high rate of interest, and depriving yourself of things which you need; or to fall into debt to shopkeepers, becoming their victim because you are their debtor? Do you know any instances in which workers have lost their wages through the bankruptcy of their employers?

60 Are wages paid directly by the employer, or by middlemen (sub-contractors, etc.)?

61 If wages are paid by sub-contractors, or other middlemen, what are the terms of your contract?

62 What is your daily and weekly wage rate in money?

63 What are the wages of women and children working with you in the same workshop?

64 What was the highest daily wage in your workshop during the past month?

65 What was the highest piece-rate wage ... ?

66 What was your wage during the same period, and if you have a family what were the wages of your wife and children?

67 Are wages paid entirely in money, or in some other way?

68 If you rent your dwelling from your employer, what are the conditions? Does he deduct the rent from your wages?

69 What are the prices of necessities such as:
   (*a*) rent of dwelling; conditions of letting; number of rooms, number of inhabitants, repairs and insurance: purchase and maintenance of furniture, heating, lighting, water;
   (*b*) food: bread, meat, vegetables, potatoes, etc., milk, eggs, fish, butter, oil, lard, sugar, salt, spices, coffee, chicory, beer, cider, wine, etc., tobacco;
   (*c*) clothing for parents and children, laundry, personal toilet, baths, soap, etc.;
   (*d*) various expenses: postage, loans and pawnbrokers' charges, children's school or apprenticeship fees, papers and books, contributions to friendly societies, or for strikes, cooperatives and defence societies;
   (*e*) expenses, if any, caused by your work;
   (*f*) taxes.
70 Try to draw up a budget of the weekly and annual income and expenditure of yourself and your family.
71 Have you noticed, in your personal experience, a greater rise in the price of the necessities of life, such as food and shelter, than in wages?
72 State the fluctuations in wage rates which are known to you.
73 State the wage reductions in periods of stagnation and industrial crisis.
74 State the wage increases in so-called periods of prosperity.
75 Note the interruptions of work resulting from changes of fashion and from particular and general crises. Give an account of your own experiences of involuntary unemployment.
76 Compare *the price of the article you produce*, or of the services you provide, with the price of your labour.
77 Quote any instance you know of workers being displaced by the introduction of machinery or by other improvements.
78 With the development of machinery and the productivity of labour, has the intensity and duration of work increased or diminished?
79 Do you know of any instance of an increase of wages in consequence of the progress of production?
80 Have you ever known any ordinary workers who were able to retire at the age of 50 and to live on the money acquired in their capacity as wage earners?
81 For how many years, in your trade, can a worker of average health continue to work?

IV

82 Are there any defence organizations in your trade, and how are they conducted? Send their statutes and rules.
83 How many strikes have occurred in your trade, in the course of your career?
84 How long did these strikes last?
85 Were they general or partial?
86 Was their aim an increase in wages, or were they organized to resist a wage reduction? Or were they concerned with the length of the working day, or caused by other factors?
87 What results did they achieve?

88 Say what you think of the actions of the *Prud'hommes* (arbitrators).[14]

89 Has your trade supported strikes by workers of other trades?

90 Give an account of the rules and penalties instituted by your employer for the government of his wage earners.

91 Have there been any combinations of employers for the purpose of imposing wage reductions, increasing working hours, or preventing strikes, or, in general, for getting their own way?

92 Do you know any instances in which the Government has misused the forces of the State, in order to place them at the disposal of employers against their employees?

93 Do you know any instances in which the Government has intervened to protect the workers against the exactions of the employers and their illegal combinations?

94 Does the Government apply against the employers the existing labour laws? Do its inspectors carry out their duties conscientiously?

95 Are there, in your workshop or trade, any friendly societies for cases of accident, illness, death, temporary incapacity for work, old age, etc.? Send their statutes and rules.

96 Is membership of these societies voluntary or obligatory? Are their funds controlled exclusively by the workers?

97 If the contributions are obligatory and under the control of the employers, are they deducted from wages? Is interest paid on these contributions? Are they returned to the worker when he leaves or is dismissed? Do you know any instances in which workers have benefited from so-called retirement funds controlled by the employers, but whose capital is derived from the workers' wages?

98 Are there any cooperative societies in your trade? How are they managed? Do they employ workers from outside in the same way as the capitalists do? Send their statutes and rules.

99 Are there any workshops in your trade, in which the workers are remunerated partly by wages and partly by a so-called participation in the profits? Compare the sums received by these workers with those received by workers where there is no so-called participation in profits. State the obligations of workers living under this system. Can they go on strike? Or are they only permitted to be the humble servants of their masters?

100 What is the general physical, intellectual, and moral condition of men and women workers employed in your trade?

101 General comments.

14 [The *conseil des prud'hommes* is a committee of arbitration in disputes between workers and employers. Ed.]

Part IV   Politics, Law and Ideology

21   Marx and the State

Ralph Miliband

I

As in the case of so many other aspects of Marx's work, what he thought about the state has more often than not come to be seen through the prism of later interpretations and adaptations. These have long congealed into *the* Marxist theory of the state, or into *the* Marxist–Leninist theory of the state, but they cannot be taken to constitute an adequate expression of Marx's own views. This is not because these theories bear *no* relation to Marx's views but rather that they emphasize some aspects of his thought to the detriment of others, and thus distort by over-simplification an extremely complex and by no means unambiguous body of ideas; and also that they altogether ignore certain strands in Marx's thought which are of considerable interest and importance. This does not, in itself, make later views better or worse than Marx's own: to decide this, what needs to be compared is not text with text, but text with historical or contemporary reality itself. This can hardly be done within the compass of an essay. But Marx is so inescapably bound up with contemporary politics, his thought is so deeply buried inside the shell of official Marxism and his name is so often invoked in ignorance by enemies and partisans alike, that it is worth asking again what he, rather than Engels, or Lenin or any other of his followers, disciples or critics, actually said and appeared to think about the state. This is the purpose of the present essay.

Marx himself never attempted to set out a comprehensive and systematic theory of the state. In the late 1850s he wrote that he intended, as part of a vast scheme of projected work, of which *Capital* was only to be the first part, to

From *The Socialist Register 1965*, edited by Ralph Miliband and John Saville (London: The Merlin Press Ltd, 1965), pp. 278–96. Reprinted by permission of The Merlin Press Ltd.

subject the state to systematic study.[1] But of this scheme, only one part of *Capital* was in fact completed. His ideas on the state must therefore be taken from such historical *pièces de circonstance* as *The Class Struggles in France*, the *Eighteenth Brumaire of Louis Bonaparte* and *The Civil War in France*, and from his incidental remarks on the subject in his other works. On the other hand, the crucial importance of the state in his scheme of analysis is well shown by his constantly recurring references to it in almost all of his writings; and the state was also a central preoccupation of the 'young Marx': his early work from the late 1830s to 1844 was largely concerned with the nature of the state and its relation to society. His most sustained piece of work until the 1844 *Economic and Philosophical Manuscripts*, apart from his doctoral dissertation, was his *Critique of the Hegelian Philosophy of Right*, of which only the *Introduction*, actually written after the *Critique* itself, has so far appeared in English.[2] It is in fact largely through his critique of Hegel's view of the state that Marx completed his emancipation from the Hegelian system. This early work of Marx on the state is of great interest; for, while he soon moved beyond the views and positions he had set out there, some of the questions he had encountered in his examination of Hegel's philosophy recur again and again in his later writings.

II

Marx's earliest views on the state bear a clear Hegelian imprint. In the articles which he wrote for the *Rheinische Zeitung* from May 1842 to March 1843, he repeatedly spoke of the state as the guardian of the general interest of society and of law as the embodiment of freedom. Modern philosophy, he writes in July 1842, 'considers the state as the great organism in which must be realized juridical, moral and political freedom and where the individual citizen, in obeying the laws of the state only obeys the natural laws of his own reason, of human reason.'[3]

On the other hand, he also shows himself well aware that this exalted view of the state is in contradiction with the real state's actual behaviour: 'a state which is not the realization of rational freedom is a bad state', he writes,[4] and in his article on the Rhineland Diet's repressive legislation against the pilfering of forest wood, he eloquently denounces the Diet's denial of the customary rights of the poor and condemns the assignation to the state of the role of servant of

1 K. Marx to F. Lassalle, 22 February 1858, and K. Marx to F. Engels, 2 April 1858 (*Selected Correspondence*, Moscow, n.d.), pp. 125, 126.
2 For the *Critique*, see *Marx/Engels Gesamtausgabe* (MEGA) (Moscow, 1927), I, 1/1, pp. 403–553; for the *Introduction*, first published in the *Franco-German Annals* of 1844, ibid., I, 1/1, pp. 607–21, and T. B. Bottomore (ed.), *Karl Marx: Early Writings* (London, 1963).
3 MEGA, I, 1/1, p. 249.
4 Ibid., p. 248.

the rich against the poor. This, he holds, is a perversion of the state's true purpose and mission; private property may wish to degrade the state to its own level of concern, but any modern state, in so far as it remains true to its own meaning, must, confronted by such pretensions, cry out 'your ways are not my ways, and your ideas are not my ideas'.[5]

More and more, however, Marx found himself driven to emphasize the external pressures upon the state's actions. Writing in January 1843 on the plight of the wine growers of the Moselle, he remarks that 'in the examination of the institutions of the state, one is too easily tempted to overlook the concrete nature of circumstances [*die sachliche Natur der Verhältnisse*] and to explain everything by the will of those empowered to act'.[6]

It is this same insistence on the need to consider the 'concrete nature of circumstances' which lies at the core of the *Critique of Hegel's Philosophy of Right*, which Marx wrote in the spring and summer of 1843, after the *Rheinische Zeitung* had been closed down. By then, his horizons had widened to the point where he spoke confidently of a 'break' in the existing society, to which 'the system of acquisition and commerce, of ownership and of exploitation of man is leading even more rapidly than the increase in population'.[7] Hegel's 'absurdity', he also writes in the *Critique*, is that he views the affairs and the activities of the state in an abstract fashion; he forgets that the activities of the state are human functions: 'the affairs of the state, etc., are nothing but the modes of existence and activity of the social qualities of men'.[8]

The burden of Marx's critique of Hegel's concept of the state is that Hegel, while rightly acknowledging the separation of civil society from the state, asserts their reconciliation in the state itself. In his system, the 'contradiction' between the state and society is resolved in the supposed representation in the state of society's true meaning and reality; the alienation of the individual from the state, the contradiction between man as a private member of society, concerned with his own private interests, and as a citizen of the state finds resolution in the state as the expression of society's ultimate reality.

But this, says Marx, is not a resolution but a mystification. The contradiction between the state and society is real enough. Indeed, the political alienation which it entails is the central fact of modern, bourgeois society, since man's political significance is detached from his real private condition, while it is in fact this condition which determines him as a social being, all other determinations

5 Ibid., p. 283.

6 Ibid., p. 360. Note also his contemptuous reference in an article of May 1842 on the freedom of the Press to 'the inconsistent, nebulous and timorous reasoning of German liberals, who claim to honour freedom by setting it up in an imaginary firmament, rather than on the solid ground of reality' (ibid., p. 220; A. Cornu, *Karl Marx et Friedrich Engels. Leur Vie et leur Oeuvre*, Paris, 1958, II, p. 17).

7 K. Marx to A. Ruge, May 1843, MEGA, I, 1/1, p. 565; see also K. Marx to A. Ruge, March 1843, *Selected Correspondence*, p. 25.

8 MEGA, I, 1/1, p. 424.

appearing to him as external and inessential: 'real man is the private man of the present constitution of the state'.[9]

But the mediating elements which are supposed, in Hegel's system, to ensure the resolution of this contradiction – the sovereign, the bureaucracy, the middle classes, the legislature – are not in the least capable, says Marx, of doing so. Ultimately, Hegel's state, far from being above private interests and from representing the general interest, is in fact subordinate to private property. What, asks Marx, is the power of the state over private property? The state has only the illusion of being determinant, whereas it is in fact determined; it does, in time, subdue private and social wills, but only to give substance to the will of private property and to acknowledge its reality as the highest reality of the political state, as the highest moral reality.[10]

In the *Critique*, Marx's own resolution of political alienation and of the contradiction between the state and society is still envisaged in mainly political terms, i.e. in the framework of 'true democracy'. 'Democracy is the solution to the riddle of all constitutions'; in it, 'the constitution appears in its true reality, as the free product of man'. 'All other political systems are specific, definite, particular political forms. In democracy, the formal principle is also the material principle'. It constitutes, therefore, the real unity of the universal and the particular.[11] Marx also writes: 'In all states which differ from democracy, the state, the law, the constitution are sovereign without being properly dominant, that is to say without materially affecting the other non-political spheres. In democracy, the constitution, the law, the state itself are only the people's self-determination, a specific aspect of it, in so far as that aspect has a political constitution.'[12]

Democracy is here intended to mean more than a specific political form, but Marx does not yet define what else it entails. The struggle between monarchy and republic, he notes, is still a struggle within the framework of what he calls the 'abstract state', i.e. the state alienated from society; the abstract political form of democracy is the republic. 'Property and all that makes up the content of law and the state is, with some modifications, the same in the United States as in Prussia; the republic in America is thus only a purely political form as is the monarchy in Prussia.'[13] In a real democracy, however, the constitution ceases to be purely political; indeed Marx quotes the opinion of 'some modern Frenchmen' to the effect that 'in a real democracy the political state disappears'.[14] But the concrete content of 'true democracy' remains here undefined.

9 Ibid., pp. 498–9. See also J. Hyppolite, *Etudes sur Marx et Hegel* (Paris, 1955), pp. 123ff., and M. Rubel, *Karl Marx. Essai de Biographie Intellectuelle* (Paris, 1957), pp. 58ff.
10 MEGA, I, 1/1, p. 519.
11 Ibid., pp. 434–5.
12 Ibid., p. 435.
13 Ibid., p. 436.
14 Ibid., p. 435.

The *Critique* already suggests the belief that political emancipation is not synonymous with human emancipation. The point, which is, of course, central to Marx's whole system, was made explicit in the two articles which he wrote for the *Franco-German Annals*, namely the *Jewish Question*, and the *Introduction* to a *Contribution to the Critique of Hegel's Philosophy of Right*.

In the first essay, Marx criticizes Bruno Bauer for confusing political and human emancipation, and notes that 'the limit of political emancipation is immediately apparent in the fact that the *state* may well free itself from some constraint, without man himself being *really* freed from it, and that the state may be a *free state*, without *man* being free'.[15] Even so, political emancipation is a great advance; it is not the last form of human emancipation, but it is the last form of human emancipation within the framework of the existing social order.[16] Human emancipation, on the other hand, can only be realized by transcending bourgeois society, 'which has torn up all genuine bonds between men and replaced them by selfishness, selfish need, and dissolved the world of men into a world of atomized individuals, hostile towards each other'.[17] The more specific meaning of that emancipation is defined in the *Jewish Question*, in Marx's strictures against 'Judaism', here deemed synonymous with trade, money and the commercial spirit which has come to affect all human relations. On this view, the political emancipation of the Jews, which Marx defends,[18] does not produce their social emancipation; this is only possible in a new society, in which practical need has been humanized and the commercial spirit abolished.[19]

In the *Introduction*, which he wrote in Paris at the end of 1843 and the beginning of 1844, Marx now spoke of 'the doctrine, that man is for man the supreme being' and of the 'categorical imperative' which required the overthrow of all conditions in which 'man is a degraded, enslaved, abandoned and contemptible being'.[20] But he also added another element to the system he was constructing, namely the proletariat as the agent of the dissolution of the existing social order;[21] as we shall see, this view of the proletariat is not only crucial for Marx's concept of revolution but also for his view of the state.

By this time, Marx had already made an assessment of the relative importance of the political realm from which he was never to depart and which also had some major consequence for his later thought. On the one hand, he does not wish to underestimate the importance of 'political emancipation', i.e.

15 Ibid., p. 582. Italics in original.
16 Ibid., p. 585.
17 Ibid., p. 605.
18 See S. Avineri, 'Marx and Jewish Emancipation', in *Journal of the History of Ideas*, vol. XXV (July–September 1964), pp. 445–50.
19 MEGA, I, 1/1, p. 606.
20 Ibid., p. 615.
21 Ibid., pp. 619ff.

of political reforms tending to make politics and the state more liberal and democratic. Thus, in *The Holy Family*, which he wrote in 1844 in collaboration with Engels, Marx describes the 'democratic representative state' as 'the perfect modern state',[22] meaning the perfect modern *bourgeois* state, its perfection arising from the fact that 'the public system is *not* faced with any privileged exclusivity',[23] i.e. economic and political life are free from feudal encumbrances and constraints.

But there is also, on the other hand, a clear view that political emancipation is not enough, and that society can only be made truly human by the abolition of private property. 'It is natural necessity, *essential human properties*, however alienated they may seem to be, and *interest* that holds the members of civil society together; *civil*, not *political* life is their *real* tie. It is therefore not the state that holds the *atoms* of civil society together . . . only *political superstition* today imagines that social life must be held together by the state, whereas in reality the state is held together by civil life.'[24] The modern democratic state 'is based on emancipated slavery, on bourgeois society . . . the society of industry, of universal competition, of private interest freely following its aims, of anarchy, of the self-alienated natural and spiritual individuality . . .';[25] the 'essence' of the modern state is that 'it is based on the unhampered development of bourgeois society, on the free movement of private interest'.[26]

A year later, in *The German Ideology*, Marx and Engels defined further the relation of the state to bourgeois society. 'By the mere fact that it is a *class* and no longer an *estate*,' they wrote, 'the bourgeoisie is forced to organize itself no longer locally but nationally, and to give a general form to its mean average interest'; this 'general form' is the state, defined as 'nothing more than the form of organization which the bourgeois necessarily adopt both for internal and external purposes, for the mutual guarantee of their property and interest.'[27] This same view is confirmed in the *Poverty of Philosophy* of 1847, where Marx again states that 'political conditions are only the official expression of civil society' and goes on: 'It is the sovereigns who in all ages have been subject to economic conditions, but it is never they who have dictated laws to them. Legislation, whether political or civil, never does more than proclaim, express in words, the will of economic relations.'[28]

This whole trend of thought on the subject of the state finds its most explicit expression in the famous formulation of the *Communist Manifesto*: 'The executive of the modern state is but a committee for managing the common

22 K. Marx and F. Engels, *The Holy Family* (Moscow, 1956), p. 154.
23 Ibid., p. 157. Italics in original.
24 Ibid., p. 163. Italics in original.
25 Ibid., p. 164.
26 Ibid., p. 166.
27 K. Marx and F. Engels, *The German Ideology* (New York, 1939), p. 59. Italics in original.
28 K. Marx, *The Poverty of Philosophy* (London, 1936), p. 70.

affairs of the whole bourgeoisie';[29] and political power is 'merely the organized power of one class for oppressing another'.[30] This is the classical Marxist view on the subject of the state, and it is the only one which is to be found in Marxism–Leninism. In regard to Marx himself, however, and this is also true to a certain extent of Engels as well, it only constitutes what might be called a primary view of the state. For, as has occasionally been noted in discussions of Marx and the state,[31] there is to be found another view of the state in his work, which it is inaccurate to hold up as of similar status with the first,[32] but which is none the less of great interest, not least because it serves to illuminate, and indeed provides an essential context for, certain major elements in Marx's system, notably the concept of the dictatorship of the proletariat. This secondary view is that of the state as independent from and superior to all social classes, as being the dominant force in society rather than the instrument of a dominant class.

III

It may be useful, for a start, to note some qualifications which Marx made even to his primary view of the state. For in relation to the two most advanced capitalist countries of the day, England and France, he often makes the point that, at one time or another, it is not the ruling class as a whole, but a fraction of it, which controls the state;[33] and that those who actually run the state may well belong to a class which is not the economically dominant class.[34] Marx does not suggest that this *fundamentally* affects the state's class character and its role of guardian and defender of the interests of property; but it obviously does introduce an element of flexibility in his view of the operation of the state's bias, not least because the competition between different factions of the ruling class may well make easier the passage of measures favourable to labour, such as the Ten Hours Bill.[35]

29 K. Marx and F. Engels, *Selected Works*, hereafter noted as SW (Moscow, 1950), I, p. 35.
30 Ibid., p. 51.
31 See, e.g., J. Plamenatz, *German Marxism and Russian Communism* (London, 1954), pp. 144ff.; J. Sanderson, 'Marx and Engels on the State', in the *Western Political Quarterly*, vol. XVI, no. 4 (December 1963), pp. 946–55.
32 As is suggested by the two authors cited above.
33 See, e.g., *The Class Struggles in France*, passim, *The Eighteenth Brumaire of Louis Bonaparte*, passim.
34 See, e.g., 'The Elections in Britain', in K. Marx and F. Engels, *On Britain* (Moscow, 1953), pp. 353ff. 'The Whigs are the *aristocratic representatives* of the bourgeoisie, of the industrial and commercial middle class. Under the condition that the bourgeoisie should abandon to them, to an oligarchy of aristocratic families, the monopoly of government and the exclusive possession of office, they make to the middle class, and assist it in conquering, all those concessions, which in the course of social and political developments have shown themselves to have become *unavoidable* and *undelayable*' (p. 353, italics in original).
35 Ibid., p. 368.

The extreme manifestation of the state's independent role is, however, to be found in authoritarian personal rule, Bonapartism. Marx's most extensive discussion of this phenomenon occurs in *The Eighteenth Brumaire of Louis Bonaparte*, which was written between December 1851 and March 1852. In this historical study, Marx sought very hard to pin down the precise nature of the rule which Louis Bonaparte's *coup d'état* had established.

The *coup d'état*, he wrote, was 'the victory of Bonaparte over parliament, of the executive power over the legislative power'; in parliament, 'the nation made its general will the law, that is, made the law of the ruling class its general will'; in contrast, 'before the executive power it renounces all will of its own and submits to the superior command of an alien will, to authority'; 'France, therefore, seems to have escaped the despotism of a class only to fall back beneath the despotism of an individual and, what is more, beneath the authority of an individual without authority. The struggle seems to be settled in such a way that all classes, equally impotent and equally mute, fall on their knees before the rifle butt.'[36]

Marx then goes on to speak of 'this executive power with its enormous bureaucratic and military organization, with its ingenious state machinery, embracing wide strata, with a host of officials numbering half a million, besides an army of another half million, this appalling parasitic body which enmeshes the body of French society like a net and chokes all its pores'.[37] This bureaucratic power, which sprang up in the days of the absolute monarchy, had, he wrote, first been 'the means of preparing the class rule of the bourgeoisie', while 'under the Restoration, under Louis Phillipe, under the parliamentary Republic, it was the instrument of the ruling class, however much it strove for power of its own'.[38] But the *coup d'état* had seemingly changed its role: 'only under the second Bonaparte does the state seem to have made itself completely independent'; 'as against civil society, the state machine has consolidated its position so thoroughly that the chief of the Society of December 10 [i.e. Louis Bonaparte] suffices for its head. . . .'[39]

This appears to commit Marx to the view of the Bonapartist state as independent of any specific class and as superior to society. But he then goes on to say, in an often quoted phrase: 'And yet the state power is not suspended in mid-air. Bonaparte represents a class, and the most numerous class of French society at that, *the small-holding peasants*'.[40] However, lack of cohesion makes these 'incapable of enforcing their class interests in their own name whether through a parliament or a convention';[41] they therefore require a representative

36 SW, I, p. 300.
37 Ibid., p. 301.
38 Ibid., p. 302.
39 Ibid., p. 302.
40 Ibid., p. 302. Italics in original.
41 Marx also notes that the identity of interest of the smallholding peasants 'begets no community,

who 'must at the same time appear as their master, as an authority over them, as an unlimited governmental power that protects them against the other classes and sends them rain and sunshine from above. The political influence of the small-holding peasants, therefore, finds its final expression in the executive power subordinating society to itself.'[42]

'Represent' is here a confusing word. In the context, the only meaning that may be attached to it is that the small-holding peasants *hoped* to have their interests represented by Louis Bonaparte. But this does not turn Louis Bonaparte or the state into the mere instrument of their will; at the most, it may limit the executive's freedom of action somewhat. Marx also writes that 'as the executive authority which has made itself an independent power, Bonaparte feels it his mission to safeguard "bourgeois order." But the strength of this bourgeois order lies in the middle class. He looks on himself, therefore, as the representative of the middle class and issues decrees in this sense. Nevertheless, he is somebody solely due to the fact that he has broken the political power of this middle class and daily breaks it anew'; and again, 'as against the bourgeoisie, Bonaparte looks on himself, at the same time, as the representative of the peasants and of the people in general, who wants to make the lower classes of the people happy within the frame of bourgeois society. . . . But, above all, Bonaparte looks on himself as the chief of the Society of 10 December, as the representative of the *lumpenproletariat* to which he himself, his *entourage*, his government and his army belong. . . .'[43]

On this basis, Louis Napoleon may 'represent' this or that class (and Marx stresses the 'contradictory task' of the man and the 'contradictions of his government, the confused groping about which seeks now to win, now to humiliate first one class and then another and arrays all of them uniformly against him. . . .'[44]); but his power of initiative remains very largely unimpaired by the specific wishes and demands of any one class or fraction of a class.

On the other hand, this does *not* mean that Bonapartism, for Marx, is in any sense neutral as between contending classes. It may *claim* to represent all classes and to be the embodiment of the whole of society. But it does in fact exist, and has been called into being, for the purpose of maintaining and strengthening the existing social order and the domination of capital over labour. Bonapartism and the Empire, Marx wrote much later in *The Civil War in France*, had succeeded the bourgeois Republic precisely because 'it was the only form of government possible at a time when the bourgeoisie had already lost, and the working class had not yet acquired, the faculty of ruling the

---

no national bond and no political organization among them', so that 'they do not form a class' (ibid., p. 302). For an interesting discussion of Marx's concept of class, see S. Ossowski, *Class Structure in the Social Consciousness* (London, 1963), ch. V. [Part is reprinted in this volume, pp. 215–25.]
42 SW, I, p. 303.
43 Ibid., pp. 308–9.
44 Ibid., p. 309.

nation'.[45] It was precisely under its sway that 'bourgeois society, freed from
political cares, attained a development unexpected even by itself'.[46] Finally,
Marx then characterizes what he calls 'imperialism', by which he means
Napoleon's imperial régime, as 'at the same time, the most prostitute and the
ultimate form of the State power which nascent middle-class society had
commenced to elaborate as a means of its own emancipation from feudalism,
and which full-grown bourgeois society had finally transformed into a means
for the enslavement of labour by capital'.[47]

In *The Origin of the Family, Private Property and the State*, written a year
after Marx's death, Engels also notes: 'By way of exception, however, periods
occur in which the warring classes balance each other so nearly that the state
power, as ostensible mediator, acquires, for the moment, a certain degree
of independence of both'.[48] But the independence of which he speaks would
seem to go much further than anything Marx had in mind; thus Engels refers
to the Second Empire, 'which played off the proletariat against the bourgeoisie and the bourgeoisie against the proletariat' and to Bismarck's German
Empire, where 'capitalists and workers are balanced against each other
and equally cheated for the benefit of the impoverished Prussian cabbage
junkers'.[49]

For Marx, the Bonapartist state, however independent it may have been
politically from any given class, remains, and cannot in a class society but
remain, the protector of an economically and socially dominant class.

IV

In the *Critique of Hegel's Philosophy of Right*, Marx had devoted a long and
involved passage to the bureaucratic element in the state, and to its attempt 'to
transform the purpose of the state into the purpose of the bureaucracy and the
purpose of the bureaucracy into the purpose of the state'.[50] But it was only in
the early 1850s that he began to look closely at a type of society where the state
appeared to be genuinely 'above society', namely societies based on the 'Asiatic
mode of production', whose place in Marx's thought has recently attracted
much attention.[51] What had, in the *Critique*, been a passing reference to the

45 K. Marx, *The Civil War in France*, SW, I, p. 470.
46 Ibid.
47 Ibid.
48 F. Engels, *The Origin of the Family, Private Property and the State*, SW, II, p. 290.
49 Ibid., pp. 290–1. For further comments on the subject from Engels, see also his letter to C.
Schmidt, 27 October 1890, in SW, II, pp. 446–7.
50 MEGA, I, 1/1, p. 456.
51 See, e.g., K. Wittfogel, *Oriental Despotism* (New Haven, Conn., 1957), ch. IX; G. Lichtheim,
'Marx and the "Asiatic Mode of Production"', in *St Antony's Papers*, no. 14, Far Eastern Affairs
(London, 1963). [Part is reprinted in this volume, pp. 121–38.] Also Karl Marx, *Pre-Capitalist*

'despotic states of Asia, where the political realm is nothing but the arbitrary will of a particular individual, where the political realm, like the material, is enslaved',[52] had, by 1859, become one of Marx's four main stages of history: 'In broad outlines', he wrote in the famous Preface to *A Contribution to the Critique of Political Economy*, 'Asiatic, ancient, feudal and modern bourgeois modes of production can be designated as progressive epochs in the economic formation of society.'[53]

The countries Marx was mainly concerned with in this connection were India and China, and also Russia as a 'semi-Asiatic' or 'semi-Eastern' state. The Asiatic mode of production, for Marx and Engels, has one outstanding characteristic, namely the absence of private property in land: 'this', Marx wrote to Engels in 1853, 'is the real key, even to the Oriental heaven. . . .'[54] 'In the Asiatic form (or at least predominantly so),' he noted, 'there is no property, but individual possession; the community is properly speaking the real proprietor';[55] in Asiatic production, he also remarked, it is the state which is the 'real landlord'.[56] In this system, he also wrote later, the direct producers are not 'confronted by a private landowner but rather, as in Asia, [are] under direct subordination to a state which stands over them as their landlord and simultaneously as sovereign'; 'the state', he went on, 'is then the supreme lord. Sovereignty here consists in the ownership of land concentrated on a national scale. But, on the other hand, no private ownership of land exists, although there is both private and common possession and use of land.'[57]

A prime necessity of the Asiatic mode of production, imposed by climate and territorial conditions, was artificial irrigation by canals and waterworks; indeed, Marx wrote, this was 'the basis of Oriental agriculture'. In countries like Flanders and Italy the need of an economical and common use of water drove private enterprise into voluntary association; but it required 'in the Orient, where civilization was too low and the territorial extent too vast to call into life voluntary associations, the interference of the centralized power of Government. Hence an economical function devolved upon all Asiatic governments, the functions of providing public works.'[58]

Economic Formations, with an introduction by E.J. Hobsbawm (London, 1964). This is a translation of a section of Marx's *Grundrisse der Kritik der Politischen Okonomie (Rohentwurf)* (Berlin, 1953).

52 MEGA, I, 1/1, p. 438.

53 SW, I, p. 329.

54 K. Marx to F. Engels, 2 June 1853, *Selected Correspondence*, p. 99.

55 K. Marx, *Pre-Capitalist Formations*, p. 79.

56 *New York Daily Tribune*, 5 August 1853, in Lichtheim, 'Asiatic Mode of Production', p. 94.

57 K. Marx, *Capital* (Moscow, 1962), vol. III, pp. 771–2.

58 K. Marx and F. Engels, *The First Indian War of Independence* (1857– 59) (Moscow, n.d.), p. 16. In *Capital* (Moscow, 1959), vol. I, p. 514, n. 2, Marx also notes that 'one of the material bases of the power of the State over the small disconnected producing organisms in India, was the regulation of the water supply'; also, 'the necessity for predicting the rise and fall of the Nile created Egyptian astronomy, and with it the dominion of the priests, as directors of agriculture' (p. 514, n. 1); for some further elaborations on the same theme, see also F. Engels, *Anti-Dühring* (Moscow, 1962), p. 248.

Finally, in the *Grundrisse*, Marx speaks of 'the despotic government which is poised above the lesser communities',[59] and describes that government as the 'all-embracing unity which stands above all these small common bodies . . . since the *unity* is the real owner, and the real pre-condition of common ownership, it is perfectly possible for it to appear as something separate and superior to the numerous real, particular communities . . . the despot here appears as the father of all the numerous lesser communities, thus realizing the common unity of all.'[60]

It is therefore evident that Marx does view the state, in the conditions of Asiatic despotism, as the dominant force in society, independent of and superior to all its members, and that those who control its administration are society's authentic rulers. Karl Wittfogel has noted that Marx did not pursue this theme after the 1850s and that 'in the writings of the later period he emphasized the technical side of large-scale waterworks, where previously he had emphasized their political setting'.[61] The reason for this, Professor Wittfogel suggests, is that 'obviously the concept of Oriental despotism contained elements that paralysed his search for truth';[62] hence his 'retrogressions' on the subject. But the explanation for Marx's lack of concern for the topic would seem much simpler and much less sinister; it is that he was, in the 1860s and the early 1870s, primarily concerned with Western capitalism. Furthermore, the notion of bureaucratic despotism can hardly have held any great terror for him since he had, in fact, worked through its nearest equivalent in capitalist society, namely Bonapartism, and had analysed it as an altogether different phenomenon from the despotism encountered in Asiatic society. Nor is it accurate to suggest, as does Mr Lichtheim, that 'Marx for some reason shirked the problem of the bureaucracy' in post-capitalist society.[63] On the contrary, this may be said to be a crucial element in Marx's thought in the late 1860s and in the early 1870s. His concern with the question, and with the state, finds expression in this period in his discussion of the nature of political power in post-capitalist societies, and particularly in his view of the dictatorship of the proletariat. This theme had last occupied Marx in 1851–2; after almost twenty years it was again brought to the fore by the Paris Commune, by his struggles with anarchism in the First International and by the programmatic pronouncement of German Social Democracy. It is to this, one of the most important and the most misunderstood aspects of Marx's work on the state, that we must now turn.

---

59 *Pre-Capitalist Economic Formations*, p. 71.
60 Ibid., p. 69. Italics in original.
61 K. Wittfogel, *Oriental Despotism*, p. 381.
62 Ibid., p. 387.
63 Lichtheim, 'Asiatic Mode of Production', p. 110.

V

It is first of all necessary to go back to the democratic and representative republic, which must be clearly distinguished from the dictatorship of the proletariat: for Marx, the two concepts have nothing in common. An element of confusion arises from the fact that Marx bitterly denounced the class character of the democratic republic, yet supported its coming into being. The contradiction is only apparent; Marx saw the democratic republic as the most advanced type of political regime in *bourgeois society*, and wished to see it prevail over more backward and 'feudal' political systems. But it remained for him a system of class rule, indeed the system in which the bourgeoisie rules most directly.

The limitations of the democratic republic, from Marx's point of view, are made particularly clear in the *Address of the Central Committee of the Communist League* which he and Engels wrote in March 1850. 'Far from desiring to revolutionize all society for the revolutionary proletarians,' they wrote, 'the democratic petty bourgeois strive for a change in social conditions by means of which existing society will be made as tolerable and comfortable as possible for them.' They would therefore demand such measures as 'the diminution of state expenditure by a curtailment of the bureaucracy and shifting the chief taxes on to the big landowners and bourgeois . . . the abolition of the pressure of big capital on small, through public credit institutions and laws against usury . . . the establishment of bourgeois property relations in the countryside by the complete abolition of feudalism.' But in order to achieve their purpose they would need 'a democratic state structure, either constitutional or republican, that will give them and their allies, the peasants, a majority; also a democratic communal structure that will give them direct control over communal property and over a series of functions now performed by the bureaucrats.'[64] However, they added, 'as far as the workers are concerned, it remains certain that they are to remain wage workers as before; the democratic petty-bourgeois only desire better wages and a more secure existence for the workers . . . they hope to bribe the workers by more or less concealed alms and to break their revolutionary potency by making their position tolerable for the moment.'[65]

But, Marx and Engels go on, 'these demands can in no wise suffice for the party of the proletariat'; while the petty-bourgeois democrats would seek to bring the revolution to a conclusion as quickly as possible, 'it is our interest and our task to make the revolution permanent, until all more or less possessing classes have been forced out of their position of dominance, until the proletariat

---

64 K. Marx and F. Engels, *Address of the Central Committee to the Communist League*, SW, I, p. 101.
65 Ibid., p. 101.

has conquered state power, and the association of proletarians, not only in one country but in all the dominant countries of the world, has advanced so far that competition among the proletarians of these countries has ceased and that at least the decisive productive forces are concentrated in the hands of the proletarians. For us the issue cannot be the alteration of private property but only its annihilation, not the smoothing over of class antagonisms but the abolition of classes, not the improvement of existing society but the foundation of a new one.'[66]

At the same time, while the demands and aims of the proletarian party went far beyond anything which even the most advanced and radical petty-bourgeois democrats would accept, the revolutionaries must give them qualified support and seek to push the democratic movement into even more radical directions.[67] It was, incidentally, precisely the same strategy which dictated Marx's later attitude to all movements of radical reform, and which led him, as in the *Inaugural Address* of the First International in 1864, to acclaim the Ten Hours Act or the advances of the cooperative movement as the victories of 'the political economy of labour over the political economy of property'.[68]

In 1850, Marx and Engels had also suggested that one essential task of the proletarian revolutionaries would be to oppose the decentralizing tendencies of the petty-bourgeois revolutionaries. On the contrary, 'the workers must not only strive for a single and indivisible German republic, but also within this republic for the most determined centralization of power in the hands of the state authority'.[69]

This is not only the most extreme 'statist' prescription in Marx's (and Engels's) work – it is the only one of its kind, leaving aside Marx's first 'Hegelian' pronouncements on the subject. More important is the fact that the prescription is intended *not* for the proletarian but for the bourgeois democratic revolution.[70] In 1850, Marx and Engels believed, and said in the *Address*, that the German workers would not be able 'to attain power and achieve their own class interest without completely going through a lengthy revolutionary development'.[71] The proletarian revolution would see the coming into being of an altogether different form of rule than the democratic republic, namely the dictatorship of the proletariat.

In a famous letter to J. Weydemeyer in March 1852, Marx had revealed the cardinal importance he attached to this concept by saying that, while no credit

---

66 Ibid., p. 102.
67 Ibid., p. 101.
68 Ibid., pp. 307–9.
69 Ibid., p. 106.
70 It is, in this connection, of some interest that Engels should have thought it necessary to add a Note to the 1885 edition of the Address, explaining that this passage was based on a 'misunderstanding' of French revolutionary experience and that 'local and provincial self-government' were not in contradiction with 'national centralization' (ibid., p. 107).
71 Ibid., p. 108.

was due to him for discovering the existence of classes in modern society or the struggles between them, 'what I did that was new was to prove (1) that the *existence of classes* is only bound up with *particular historical phases in the development of production*, (2) that the class struggle necessarily leads to the *dictatorship of the proletariat*, (3) that this dictatorship itself only constitutes the transition to *abolition of all classes* and to a *classless society*'.[72]

Unfortunately, Marx did not define in any specific way *what* the dictatorship of the proletariat actually entailed, and more particularly what was its relation to the state. It has been argued by Mr Hal Draper in an extremely well documented article that it is a *'social description*, a statement of the class character of the political power. It is not a statement about the forms of the government machinery'.[73] My own view, on the contrary, is that, for Marx, the dictatorship of the proletariat is *both* a statement of the class character of the political power *and* a description of the political power itself; and that it is in fact the nature of the political power which it described which guarantees its class character.

In the *Eighteenth Brumaire*, Marx had made a point which constitutes a main theme of his thought, namely that all previous revolutions had 'perfected this [state] machine instead of smashing it. The parties that contended in turn for domination regarded the possession of this huge state edifice as the principal spoils of the victors.'[74] Nearly twenty years later, in *The Civil War in France*, he again stressed how every previous revolution had consolidated 'the centralized State power, with its ubiquitous organs of standing army, police, bureaucracy, clergy and judicature'; and he also stressed how the political character of the state had changed 'simultaneously with the economic changes of society. At the same pace at which the progress of modern history developed, widened, intensified the class antagonism between capital and labour, the State power assumed more and more the character of the national power of capital over labour, of a public force organized for social enslavement, of an engine of class despotism. After every revolution marking a progressive phase in the class struggle, the purely repressive character of the State power stands out in bolder and bolder relief.'[75]

As Mr Draper notes, Marx had made no reference to the dictatorship of the proletariat in all the intervening years. Nor indeed did he so describe the Paris Commune. But what he acclaims above all in the Commune is that, in contrast to previous social convulsions, it sought not the further consolidation of the state power but its destruction. What it wanted, he said, was to have 'restored to the social body all the forces hitherto absorbed by the State parasite feeding

72 K. Marx to J. Weydemeyer, 5 March 1852, *Selected Correspondence*, p. 86. Italics in original.
73 H. Draper, 'Marx and the dictatorship of the proletariat', in *New Politics*, vol. I, no. 4, p. 102. Italics in original.
74 SW, I, p. 301.
75 Ibid., pp. 468–9.

upon, and clogging the free movement of, society'.[76] Marx also lays stress on the Commune's popular, democratic and egalitarian character, and on the manner in which 'not only municipal administration but the whole initiative hitherto exercised by the State was laid into the hands of the Commune'.[77] Moreover, while the communal form of government was to apply even to the 'smallest country hamlet', 'the unity of the nation was not to be broken, but, on the contrary, to be organized by the Communal Constitution, and to become a reality by the destruction of the State power which claimed to be the embodiment of that unity independent of, and superior to, the nation itself, from which it was but a parasitic excrescence'.[78]

In notes which he wrote for *The Civil War in France*, Marx makes even clearer than in the published text the significance which he attached to the Commune's dismantling of the state power. As contributing evidence of his approach to the whole question, the following passage from the Notes is extremely revealing:

> This [i.e. the Commune] was a Revolution not against this or that, legitimate, constitutional, republican or Imperialist form of State power. It was a Revolution against the *State* itself, of this supernaturalist abortion of society, a resumption by the people for the people of its own social life. It was not a revolution to transfer it from one fraction of the ruling class to the other but a Revolution to break down this horrid machinery of Classdomination [sic] itself . . . the Second Empire was the final form(?) [sic] of this State usurpation. The Commune was its definite negation, and, therefore, the initiation of the social Revolution of the nineteenth century.[79]

It is in the light of such views that Marx's verdict on the Commune takes on its full meaning: this 'essentially working-class government', he wrote, was 'the political form at last discovered under which to work out the economic emancipation of labour'.[80]

It is of course true that, while Engels, long after Marx's death, did describe

76 Ibid., p. 473.
77 Ibid., p. 471.
78 Ibid., p. 472.
79 *Marx–Engels Archives* (Moscow, 1934), vol. III (VIII), p. 324. Italics in original. I am grateful to Mr M. Johnstone for drawing my attention to these Notes. Note also, e.g., the following: 'Only the Proletarians, fired by a new social task to accomplish by them for all society, to do away with all classes and class rule, were the men to break the instrument of that class rule – the State, the centralized and organized governmental power usurping to be the master instead of the servant of society. . . . It had sprung into life against them. By them it was broken, not as a peculiar form of governmental (centralized) power, but as its most powerful, elaborated into seeming independence from society expression and, therefore, also its most prostitute reality, covered by infamy from top to bottom, having centred in absolute corruption at home and absolute powerlessness abroad' (ibid., p. 326). The peculiar English syntax of such passages is obviously due to the fact that they are only notes, not intended for publication.
80 SW, I, p. 473.

the Paris Commune as the dictatorship of the proletariat,[81] Marx himself did not do so. The reason for this would seem fairly obvious, namely that, for Marx, the dictatorship of the proletariat would be the outcome of a socialist revolution on a national scale; the Commune, as he wrote in 1881, was 'merely the rising of a city under exceptional conditions', while 'the majority of the Commune was in no wise socialist, nor could it be'.[82] Even so, it may justifiably be thought that the Commune, in its de-institutionalization of political power, did embody, for Marx, the essential elements of his concept of the dictatorship of the proletariat.

Precisely the opposite view has very generally come to be taken for granted; the following statement in Mr Lichtheim's *Marxism* is a typical example of a wide consensus: 'His [Marx's] hostility to the state was held in check by a decidedly authoritarian doctrine of political rule during the transition period: prior to being consigned to the dustbin of history, the state was to assume dictatorial powers. In different terms, authority would inaugurate freedom – a typically Hegelian paradox which did not worry Marx though it alarmed Proudhon and Bakunin.'[83]

The trouble with the view that Marx had a 'decidedly authoritarian doctrine' is that it is unsupported by any convincing evidence from Marx himself; and that there is so much evidence which directly runs counter to it.

Marx was undoubtedly the chief opponent of the anarchists in the International. But it is worth remembering that his central quarrel with them concerned above all the manner in which the struggle for a socialist revolution ought to be prosecuted, with Marx insisting on the need for political involvement within the existing political framework, against the anarchists' all or nothing rejection of mere politics; and the quarrel also concerned the question of the type of organization required by the international workers' movement, with Marx insisting on a *degree* of control by the General Council of the International over its affiliated organizations.

As for the role of the state in the period of transition, there is the well-known passage in the 'private circular' against the anarchists issued by the General Council in 1872, *Les Prétendues Scissions dans l'Internationale*, and most probably written by Marx:

> What all socialists understand by anarchism is this: as soon as the goal of the proletarian movement, the abolition of class, shall have been reached, the power

---

81 'Of late,' Engels wrote in an Introduction to the 1891 edition of *The Civil War in France*, 'the Social-Democratic philistine has once more been filled with wholesome terror at the words: Dictatorship of the Proletariat. Well and good, gentlemen, do you want to know what this dictatorship looks like? Look at the Paris Commune. That was the Dictatorship of the Proletariat' (SW, I, p. 440).
82 K. Marx to F. Domela-Nieuwenhuis, 22 February 1881, in *Selected Correspondence*, p. 410.
83 G. Lichtheim, *Marxism* (London, 1961), p. 374.

of the state, whose function it is to keep the great majority of the producers beneath the yoke of a small minority of exploiters, will disappear, and governmental functions will be transformed into simple administrative functions. The Alliance [i.e. Bakunin's Alliance of Socialist Democracy] turns the thing upside down. It declares anarchism in the ranks of the workers to be an infallible means for disrupting the powerful concentration of social and political forms in the hands of the exploiters. Under this pretext, it asks the International, when the old world is endeavouring to crush our organization, to replace organization by anarchism. The international police could ask for nothing better.[84]

This can hardly be construed as an authoritarian text; nor certainly is Marx's plaintive remark in January 1873 quoted by Lenin in *State and Revolution* that 'if the political struggle of the working class assumes violent forms, if the workers set up this revolutionary dictatorship in place of the dictatorship of the bourgeoisie, they commit the terrible crime of violating principles, for in order to satisfy their wretched, vulgar, everyday needs, in order to crush the resistance of the bourgeosie, instead of laying down their arms and abolishing the state, they give the state a revolutionary and transitory form.'[85]

Nor is there much evidence of Marx's 'decidedly authoritarian doctrine' in his marginal notes of 1875 on the Gotha Programme of the German Social-Democratic Party. In these notes, Marx bitterly attacked the programme's references to 'the free state' ('free state – what is this?') and this is well in line with his belief that the 'free state' is a contradiction in terms; and he then asked: 'What transformation will the state undergo in communist society? In other words, what social functions will remain in existence there, that are analogous to present functions of the state?' Marx, however, did not answer the question but merely said that it could only be answered 'scientifically' and that 'one does not get a flea-hop nearer to the problem by a thousandfold combination of the word people with the word state'.[86] He then goes on: 'Between capitalist and communist society lies the period of the revolutionary transformation of the one into the other. There corresponds to this also a political transition period in which the state can be nothing but *the revolutionary dictatorship of the proletariat.*'[87]

This does not advance matters much, but neither does it suggest the slightest 'authoritarian' impulse. In the *Critique of the Gotha Programme*, Marx as always before, made a sharp distinction between the democratic republic and the dictatorship of the proletariat, and Engels was clearly mistaken when he wrote in 1891 that the democratic republic was 'even the specific form of the

---

84 G. M. Stekloff, *History of the First International* (London, 1928), pp. 179–80, and J. Freymond, (ed.), *La Première Internationale* (Geneva, 1962), II, p. 295.
85 V. I. Lenin, *State and Revolution* (London, 1933), p. 54.
86 K. Marx, *Critique of the Gotha Programme*, SW, II, p. 30.
87 Ibid., p. 30. Italics in original.

dictatorship of the proletariat'.[88] On the contrary, Marx's critical attitude towards the democratic republic in the *Critique of the Gotha Programme* shows that he continued to think of the dictatorship of the proletariat as an altogether different and immeasurably freer form of political power. 'Freedom', he wrote in the *Critique of the Gotha Programme,* 'consists in converting the state from an organ superimposed upon society into one completely subordinated to it.'[89] This would seem a good description of Marx's view of the state in the period of the dictatorship of the proletariat. No doubt, he would have endorsed Engels's view, expressed a few weeks after Marx's death, that 'the proletarian class will first have to possess itself of the organized political force of the state and with this aid stamp out the resistance of the capitalist class and reorganize society'.[90] But it is of some significance that, with the possible exception of his remark of January 1873, referred to earlier, Marx himself always chose to emphasize the liberating rather than the repressive aspects of post-capitalist political power; and it is also of some interest that, in the notes he made for *The Civil War in France,* and which were not of course intended for publication, he should have warned the working class that the 'work of regeneration' would be 'again and again relented [sic] and impeded by the resistance of vested interests and class egotisms', but that he should have failed to make any reference to the State as an agent of repression. What he did say was that 'great strides may be [made] at once through the communal form of political organization' and that 'the time has come to begin that movement for themselves and mankind'.[91]

The fact is that, far from bearing any authoritarian imprint, the whole of Marx's work on the state is pervaded by a powerful anti-authoritarian and anti-bureaucratic bias, not only in relation to a distant communist society but also to the period of transition which is to precede it. True, the state is necessary in this period. But the only thing which, for Marx, makes it tolerable is popular participation and popular rule. If Marx is to be faulted, it is not for any authoritarian bias, but for greatly understating the difficulties of the libertarian position. However, in the light of the experience of socialist movements since Marx wrote, this may perhaps be judged a rather less serious fault than its bureaucratic obverse.

88 Quoted in Lenin, *The State and Revolution*, p. 54. Lenin's own comment is also misleading: 'Engels', he writes, 'repeats here in a particularly striking manner the fundamental idea which runs like a red thread through all of Marx's works, namely, that the democratic republic is the nearest approach to the dictatorship of the proletariat' (ibid., p. 54). Engels's phrase does not bear this interpretation; and whatever may be said for the view that the democratic republic is the nearest approach to the dictatorship of the proletariat, it is not so in Marx.
89 SW, II, p. 29.
90 F. Engels to P. Van Patten, 18 April 1883, *Selected Correspondence*, p. 437.
91 *Marx–Engels Archives*, p. 334.

22 The Economic and Social Functions of the Legal Institutions

Karl Renner

Our inquiry . . . is not concerned with positive legal analysis, the systematic exposition of legal institutions, a field which has been amply covered by others. Nor are we investigating the problems of the creation of law. We shall refrain from analysing the questions as to how the norms originate which make up the legal institutions, how a legal norm grows from its economic background, and what are the economic causes of the creation of legal norms. This field, it is true, has not been cultivated, but we shall keep away from it. We propose to examine only the economic and social effect of the valid norm as it exists, so long as the norm does not change.

Those acquainted with socialist literature will at once perceive that we have taken as our subject the mutual relations between law and economics. The traditional Marxist school conceives the economic relations as the substructure and the legal institutions as the superstructure. 'Substructure' and 'superstructure' are metaphors, borrowed from architecture; it is obvious that they serve only to illustrate the connection, not to define it in exact terms. This superstructure, according to Marx's well-known formula,[1] comprises not only

From Karl Renner, *The Institutions of Private Law and Their Social Functions* (London: Routledge and Kegan Paul Plc, 1949), pp. 55–60. Reprinted by permission of Associated Book Publishers (UK) Ltd.

1 Preface to Marx's *Critique of Political Economics*, trans. N. I. Stone, N.Y. London, 1904. 'The sum total of these relations of production constitutes the economic structure of society – the real foundations on which rise legal and political superstructures.'

law but also ethics and culture, in fact every ideology. This terminology must therefore apply to many facts other than those relevant to the law, whose structures are completely different and must be separately defined. The relation between the philosophy of an age and the economic substructure of that age is obviously determined by key concepts quite different from those of legal norm, exercise of a right and the like. We must desist, therefore, from attempting to give a general exposition of the Marxist concept of superstructure. We must recognize that each of these social phenomena, which in their general aspects are quite aptly illustrated by Marx's metaphor, requires a specific investigation. We attempt this investigation in regard to law.

Our previous explanations have made it clear that the relation is not merely one of cause and effect. It would be no solution of our problem to say that the economic structure generates the norm. Such an assumption could apply only to one of the fields of learning, that concerned with the creation of laws. Yet the mechanism by which economy as the causal factor brings about the effect of law is obscure and unexplored. It probably would not become intelligible by any ultimate abstraction, such as the application of the primitive categories of cause and effect, nor does Stammler's formula [Rudolf Stammler, *Wirtschaft und Recht nach der materialistischen Geschichtsauffassung* (Leipzig, 1896)] of the regulating form and the regulated substance make it any clearer. In the second province, that of positive legal analysis, the concepts of cause and effect generally mean little; the main concern here is obviously that of motive, means and ends, and the appropriate method of explanation is teleological, not causal. If we were to describe the superstructure of the law in the third field (that of the economic and social efficacy of the norms) as exclusively the effect of the social and economic substructure, our conclusions would be proved to be absurd by the very facts to which they refer.

It is mere platitude to say that laws can influence economy sufficiently to change it and can therefore be considered as causes of economic results. Marx, of course, was the last person to deny this. 'The influence of laws upon the conservation of the relations of distribution and consequently their influence upon production must be specifically determined'.[2] Laws are made with the intention of producing economic results, and as a rule they achieve this effect. Social life is not so simple that we can grasp it, open it and reveal its kernel like

---

Friedrich Engels, Preface to Marx's *Der achtzehnte Brumaire*, 3rd edn, Hamburg, 1885: 'The law according to which all struggle, whether in the political, religious, philosophical or any other ideological field, is in fact only the more or less clear expression of struggles among social classes whose existence and hence collisions are again conditioned by the degree of development of their economic position, their methods of production and their manner of exchange dependent thereon.' And many other passages. . . .

2 *Neue Zeit*, p. 744. This quotation and those that follow come from Marx's Introduction to the *Grundrisse*. The Introduction was first published by Karl Kautsky in the journal *Neue Zeit*, 21 (1903), from which Renner quotes. [Ed.]

a nut, by placing it between the two arms of a nutcracker called cause and effect. Although he was much occupied with legal problems, Marx never found time to 'determine the influence of the laws' (as above); yet he saw the problem clearly as is proved in particular by the following methodological hint: 'The really difficult point to be discussed here, however, is how the relations of production as relations of the law enter into a disparate development. An instance is Roman civil law in its relations to modern production'.[3] We make use of this hint in the formulation of our problem.

1   Law which continues unchanged in relation to changing economic conditions.
2   Changed economic conditions in relation to the new norms and the new law.

Our study, however, will be concerned with the first part of the problem only.

We start with a definite legal system based upon a definite economic foundation as it appears at a given moment of history. All economic institutions are at the same time institutions of the law. All economic activities are either, like sale and purchase, acts-in-the-law, or, like farming one's own land, the mere exercise of a right; or if neither, like the work of a mill-hand at his loom, even though they are extra-legal activities, they are nevertheless performed within definite legal conditions. We see that the act-in-the-law and the economic action are not identical.

The process of eating has a physiological, an economic and a volitional aspect but it is not an act of will with the qualities of an act-in-the-law. Yet the conditions under which it takes place are determined to some extent by the law.

The circulation of goods in a capitalist society is mediated by sale and purchase and by ancillary contracts: these are transactions for which the law of obligations provides various forms. Production, however, is not in itself an act-in-the-law. It can be the mere exercise of the right of ownership, as in the case of the peasant. In the capitalist factory, however, the legal aspect of production is more complicated. For the capitalist, production is the exercise of his right of ownership, since factory and machines are his property. For the worker it is the fulfilment of a legal obligation which has been established by the contract of employment. In so far as it is the latter, it is an act-in-the-law; in so far as it is the former, it is the mere exercise of a right. Thus a simple economic category is equivalent to a combination of various legal categories, there is no point-to-point correspondence. A number of distinct legal institutions serves a single economic process. They play a part which I will call their economic function.

Yet every economic process which in theory is an isolated unit is only part of the whole process of social production and reproduction. If the economic

3 Ibid., p. 779

function is related to this whole, it becomes the social function of the legal institution.

A comprehensive exposition of the functions fulfilled by the legal institutions at every stage of the economic process has been given in *Das Kapital*, Marx's principal work. No other investigator, either before or after him, was more aware of their importance for even the most minute details of this process. We shall see that no other economic theory gives so much insight into the connections between law and economics. Marx's predecessors and successors either refused to recognize the problem or could not do it full justice.

If we regard a social order as static and confine our attention to a certain moment of history, then the legal norms and the economic process merely appear as mutually conditioned and subservient to one another. Within the economic structure economic process and legal norm appear as the same thing: the former seen as an external, technico-natural event, the latter as an inherent relation of wills, seen from the point of view of individual will-formation. We call the external, technico-natural process the substratum of the norm. This sounds very plausible. But we can no more study the laws of gravity from a stone in a state of rest than we can learn the art of cooking from the cook who was pricked by the Sleeping Beauty's spindle. All that we can observe is that in a state of rest legal and economic institutions, though not identical, are but two aspects of the same thing, inextricably interwoven. We must define and describe this coexistence.

This observation, however, only stresses the fact that they are mutually determined. We must study the process in its historical sequence, the gradual transition of a social order from a given stage to the next. The inherent laws of development can only be revealed if the events are seen in motion, in the historic sequence of economic and legal systems. If we examine two consecutive periods, chosen at random, we may obtain results which, though they apply to these particular periods of transition, cannot claim to be generally valid. To decide the function of the law in general, we have to study inductively all social orders as they appear in the course of history, from the most primitive to the most highly developed. By this method we obtain the general categories of the social order and at the same time the general functions of the law.

This procedure is legitimate in spite of the fact that every individual stage of development has its specific nature and is subject to its peculiar laws. Marx frequently refers to general principles of this kind, declaring them to be justified. 'All periods of production have certain characteristics in common . . . production in general is an abstract concept, but a reasonable one in that it really establishes and emphasizes what is common, and thus saves us repetition.' '. . . a unity brought about by the fact that the subject, mankind, and the object, nature, are always the same'. Yet Marx disparages these general abstractions in economics often enough to fortify our objections against them.

4 Ibid., p. 712.

One of his reasons was the tendency of economists, which still exists, to regard the categories of the capitalist order as eternal and sacrosanct. Another reason lies in the limitations of his own task, viz., to explore and describe one individual period only. 'Yet it is the very difference from what is general and common which is the essential element of a particular development.' If Marx had concentrated upon the definition of peculiar characteristics of one epoch as he found them, he might have given a description in the manner of a research student, but the laws of social development would have remained hidden from him. Marx, however, seeks to explain the specific historical phenomenon alongside with previous individual forms as being merely an individual manifestation of the general principle. In this way he discovers inherent connections within the development.

The following may serve as an example: 'Surplus labour is a general social phenomenon as soon as the productivity of human labour power exceeds the immediate needs of life, but its appearance in the feudal epoch differs from that in the capitalist epoch – in the former it is villeinage, in the latter surplus-value.'

We cannot dispense in our inquiry with a general survey of the functions performed by the legal institutions. Every individual function which is historically determined is correlated to the whole and can only be clearly understood within its context. A diagrammatic exposition of the functions at least clears the field. A concrete detail cannot be demonstrated otherwise than by relating it to the general whole. 'A phenomenon is concrete because it integrates various determining factors, because it is a unity of multiplicity. If it is thought out, it appears as the product and result of an integrating process.'

23   Ideology and Theory

Leszek Kolakowski

Let me attempt to establish in very general terms what I understand by the concept 'ideology', and how ideology is distinguished in particular from science.

By ideology I understand the sum of conceptions which enables a social group (a social class, for example, but not only a class) to systematize the *values* in which the mystified consciousness and the activity of this group are expressed. This is not an exact definition but simply a preliminary characterization that helps us to describe the ways in which ideology is differentiated from scientific work. In other words: the social function of ideology is to consolidate belief in the values which are essential to the fruitful activity of the group. Thus, ideology is not, and cannot be, 'pure' theory, for the knowledge of reality as such cannot incite anyone to activity. Ideology incorporates value judgements or descriptive judgements, which are either the mystified expression of belief in certain values, or else are subordinated to the affirmation of beliefs and values. Patriotism, for example, or nationalism (conceived not as a sentiment but as a conviction of the value of the 'people' or the 'nation'), is an ideology. The slogans of liberty and equality are ideological, as are those of fatherland, honour and eternal bliss. Socialism, democracy and liberalism are ideologies that incorporate political values.

The distinction between ideology and science is not a distinction between falsehood and truth. They are distinguished by their social function and not by their degree of veracity. I am using the concept of ideology, therefore, roughly in the sense in which Marx used it, but not in the sense in which it is employed in current Marxist literature. For Marx, the concept of ideology comprises a

From Leszek Kolakowski, *Der Mensch ohne Alternative: Von der Möglichkeit und Unmöglichkeit, Marxist zu sein* (Munich: R. Piper and Co. Verlag, 1960), pp. 24–9. Translated by Tom Bottomore. Reprinted by permission of Geisenheyner and Crone, Stuttgart, on behalf of the author.

negative judgement; it always signifies a distorted consciousness. That does not mean, however, that an ideology must be simply an assemblage of false beliefs; it is determined by its function, which is the organization of values. Thus the acceptance of an ideology is not a pure intellectual act, but is a practical affirmation, an embryonic activity. Since all political action needs an ideology, it is impossible to get rid of ideology as a social phenomenon.

A special instance of ideology is myth, which is characterized by the following qualities: a myth is the sum of stories concerning particular occurrences such as the history of the gods or of individual men. The mythic character of such a story is, however, independent of its accuracy, and is determined by the function which it fulfils. The mythic character of the Gospels is quite independent of the answer to the question whether Christ was a historical figure or not. There was also a myth about Napoleon, and about Stalin, even though they were evidently historical figures. Every people, and every political movement, creates its own myths, which are the *concrete systematization of values*; that is, an assemblage of values which are embodied not in abstractions, but in particular individuals and situations, and which serve to unify the social group which generated them. Myth is also the collective awareness of a common origin; legendary tales serve to elaborate a quasi-familial bond between those who believe in the myth, a bond between the members of a community who trace their physical or spiritual origins to the same figures that embody the appropriate values.

Another special instance of ideology is utopia (in the comprehensive sense of the word) – that is, a body of acknowledged values concerning social relations that are considered unrealizable but are formulated as a programme. (The legend of paradise or of the Golden Age is a myth, but the vision of the millennium is a utopia.) The utopian character of values, like the mythic character of particular legends, is independent of the knowledge as to whether they are realizable or not. In this sense, the idea of socialism is also a utopia – which does not mean that socialism is impossible. Whereas myth in its social-psychological function organizes the group around its existing values, utopia organizes the hope that values will be realized in social institutions. As yet, no social mass movement has appeared without a utopia, and none has been able to renounce myths.

With this introduction we can now turn to those particular features associated with the rise of Marxism and its development into an ideology. The specific and historically unique antinomy presented in the evolution of Marxism consists in the fact that this doctrine, which revealed how social consciousness is mystified through the pressure of political circumstances, and which proclaimed the complete liberation of consciousness from myth, has itself become a victim of such mystification.

The uniqueness of this situation is that we have here a case in which a genuinely scientific theory, which grew out of the rationalist tradition and was deeply rooted in the intellectual, not the religious, life of European culture, has become the ideal superstructure of an organized political mass movement. In this way, however, the Marxist idea that social consciousness reflects an inverted image of reality, as in a camera obscura, was subsequently reduced to the axiom that this mystification has its source only in class consciousness; that it is either the product of intellectual immaturity (as in the case of those oppressed classes which existed before the proletariat) or else simply a conscious deceit (in the case of the possessing class).

In both cases, the interpretation of the social consciousness was preeminently idealistic, since it attributed the distorted picture of the world which was formed in men's heads to a quality of these heads – to ignorance or the wish to deceive. In both cases, therefore, the essence of Marx's thought – the theory of alienation – was lost. Instead, there emerged the very optimistic conviction that the working class, which, as a 'class for itself', is incarnated exclusively in the Party and automatically liberated from all mystifications, no longer has any reason to hanker after a distorted view of the world once it has created a political organization. This conception is understandable, since it then follows that the Party, which is the materialized spirit of the class, has already achieved a total emancipation, or quite simply, that it is never wrong. In practice, therefore, Marx's theory of alienation is replaced, as the result of a perfectly comprehensible tendency, by a dogma of infallibility.

In this situation the problem of the distorting influence that political organization itself exercises upon the theoretical consciousness could not emerge within Marxist thought. In earlier mass movements it did not emerge because they had only an ideology in Marx's sense, and this was not created from scientific ideas. At their inception they adopted a flexible ideology which was not regulated by any scientific laws. Now, however, it became necessary to make a scheme of thought that was originally scientific responsive to the pressure of the organization – that is, to remove all rational control.

The religious ideologies could never pass from a scientific to a religious stage, because they were never scientific; from the outset, therefore, they were easily capable of adaptation to every requirement of the social situation. But the development of Marxism has transformed a science into a mythology, into a soft and malleable material from which the backbone of reason has been eliminated. The development occurred in a typically ideological way, but because of the tradition in which it originated it was concealed behind a scientific facade. The outcome was a striving for a 'total' culture which was thoroughly permeated by an ideology employing scientific slogans, although it had long since ceased to be founded upon scientific laws. (Nevertheless, there were still very valuable scientific by-products created in opposition to institutional Marxism. The methodological advances made by Marx were not wholly forgotten, and they provided, indeed, an inspiration for great scientific achievements. An example is to be found in the works of G. Lukács.)

The rise of institutional Marxism confirmed Marx's theory of alienation. It illustrated, in particular, the destructive effects of the political organization upon scientific thought when thought came into conflict with ideology. The association of thought and ideology, which should have formed a symbiosis, ended as the parasitic existence of ideology, the cells of which spread through scientific thought and endangered its life. This should not provoke either indignation or condemnation, since it is the natural tendency of a political organization. Once it has been created as a social fact, the organization has at least one interest of its own: to maintain an inner 'belongingness' by opposing bitterly every attempt at disintegration. The organizational bond is in opposition to the class bond, for the existence of the class is given by the objective situation (Marx's 'class in itself'). A disintegration of consciousness is fatal to the organization, and so its ideology has to be protected from rational control.

Science, on the other hand, promotes in the course of its development just this principle of social control, of the independence of its content from political pressure – the principle of objectivity, revisionism, permanent criticism, and continual confrontation of all possible viewpoints. Thus ideology and science are in perpetual conflict with each other, and this conflict cannot be eliminated by expressions of goodwill, for goodwill does not abolish social regularities. The transformation of Marxism into an institution was not a 'lapse' which can be put aside by a 'sincere repentance' like a sin in the confessional.

24 Ideology

Jürgen Habermas

By the middle of the nineteenth century the capitalist mode of production had developed so fully in England and France that Marx was able to identify the locus of the institutional framework of society in the relations of production and at the same time criticize the legitimating basis constituted by the exchange of equivalents. He carried out the critique of bourgeois ideology in the form of *political economy*. His labour theory of value destroyed the semblance of freedom, by means of which the legal institution of the free labour contract had made unrecognizable the relationship of social force that underlay the wage–labour relationship. Marcuse's criticism of Weber is that the latter, disregarding this Marxian insight, upholds an abstract concept of rationalization, which not merely fails to express the specific class content of the adaptation of the institutional framework to the developing systems of purposive-rational action, but conceals it. Marcuse knows that the Marxian analysis can no longer be applied as it stands to advanced capitalist society, with which Weber was already confronted. But he wants to show through the example of Weber that the evolution of modern society in the framework of state-regulated capitalism cannot be conceptualized if liberal capitalism has not been analysed adequately.

Since the last quarter of the nineteenth century two developmental tendencies have become noticeable in the most advanced capitalist countries: an increase in state intervention in order to secure the system's stability, and a growing interdependence of research and technology, which has turned the sciences into the leading productive force. Both tendencies have destroyed the particular constellation of institutional framework and sub-systems of purposive-rational action which characterized liberal capitalism, thereby eliminating the conditions relevant for the application of political economy in

From Jürgen Habermas, *Toward a Rational Society* (Boston: Beacon Press, 1970), pp. 100–14.

the version correctly formulated by Marx for liberal capitalism. I believe that Marcuse's basic thesis, according to which technology and science today also take on the function of legitimating political power, is the key to analysing the changed constellation.

The permanent regulation of the economic process by means of state intervention arose as a defence mechanism against the dysfunctional tendencies which threaten the system, that capitalism generates when left to itself. Capitalism's actual development manifestly contradicted the capitalist idea of a bourgeois society, emancipated from domination, in which power is neutralized. The root ideology of just exchange, which Marx unmasked in theory, collapsed in practice. The form of capital utilization through private ownership could only be maintained by the governmental corrective of a social and economic policy that stabilized the business cycle. The institutional framework of society was repoliticized. It no longer coincides immediately with the relations of production, i.e. with an order of private law that secures capitalist economic activity and the corresponding general guarantees of order provided by the bourgeois state. But this means a change in the relation of the economy to the political system: politics is no longer *only* a phenomenon of the superstructure. If society no longer 'autonomously' perpetuates itself through self-regulation as a sphere preceding and lying at the basis of the state – and its ability to do so was the really novel feature of the capitalist mode of production – then society and the state are no longer in the relationship that Marxian theory had defined as that of base and superstructure. Then, however, a critical theory of society can no longer be constructed in the exclusive form of a critique of political economy. A point of view that methodically isolates the economic laws of motion of society can claim to grasp the overall structure of social life in its essential categories only as long as politics depends on the economic base. It becomes inapplicable when the 'base' has to be comprehended as in itself a function of governmental activity and political conflicts. According to Marx, the critique of political economy was the theory of bourgeois society only as *critique of ideology*. If, however, the ideology of just exchange disintegrates, then the power structure can no longer be criticized *immediately* at the level of the relations of production.

With the collapse of this ideology, political power requires a new legitimation. Now since the power indirectly exercised over the exchange process is itself operating under political control and state regulation, legitimation can no longer be derived from the unpolitical order constituted by the relations of production. To this extent the requirement for direct legitimation, which exists in precapitalist societies, reappears. On the other hand, the resuscitation of immediate political domination (in the traditional form of legitimation on the basis of cosmological world views) has become impossible. For traditions have already been disempowered. Moreover, in industrially developed societies the results of bourgeois emancipation from immediate political domination (civil and political rights and the mechanism of general elections) can be fully ignored only in periods of reaction. Formally democratic government in systems of state-regulated capitalism is subject to a need for legitimation which cannot be met by a return to a pre-bourgeois form. Hence the ideology of free exchange is replaced by a substitute programme. The latter is oriented not to the social results of the institution of the market but to those of government action designed to compensate for the dysfunctions of free exchange. This policy combines the element of the bourgeois ideology of achievement (which, however, displaces assignment of status according to the standard of individual achievement from the market to the school system) with a guaranteed minimum level of welfare, which offers secure employment and a stable income. This substitute programme obliges the political system to maintain stabilizing conditions for an economy that guards against risks to growth and guarantees social security and the chance for individual upward mobility. What is needed to this end is latitude for manipulation by state interventions that, at the cost of limiting the institutions of private law, secure the private form of capital utilization *and bind the masses' loyalty to this form.*

In so far as government action is directed toward the economic system's stability and growth, politics now takes on a peculiarly negative character. For it is oriented toward the elimination of dysfunctions and the avoidance of risks that threaten the system: not, in other words, toward the *realization of practical goals* but toward the *solution of technical problems.* Claus Offe pointed this out in his paper at the 1968 Frankfurt Sociological Conference:

> In this structure of the relation of economy and the state, 'politics' degenerates into action that follows numerous and continually emerging 'avoidance imperatives': the mass of differentiated social-scientific information that flows into the political system allows both the early identification of risk zones and the treatment of actual dangers. What is new about this structure is . . . that the risks to stability built into the mechanism of private capital utilization in highly organized markets, risks that can be manipulated, prescribe preventive actions and measures that *must* be accepted as long as they are to accord with the existing legitimation resources (i.e., substitute programme).[1]

Offe perceives that through these preventive action-orientations, government activity is restricted to administratively soluble technical problems, so that practical questions evaporate, so to speak. *Practical substance is eliminated.*

Old-style politics was forced, merely through its traditional form of legitimation, to define itself in relation to practical goals: the 'good life' was interpreted in a context defined by interaction relations. The same still held for the ideology of bourgeois society. The substitute programme prevailing today,

---

1 Claus Offe, 'Politische Herrschaft und Klassenstrukturen', in Gisela Kress and Dieter Senghaas (eds), *Politikwissenschaft.* The quotation in the text is from the original manuscript, which differs in formulation from the published text.

in contrast, is aimed exclusively at the functioning of a manipulated system. It eliminates practical questions and therewith precludes discussion about the adoption of standards; the latter could emerge only from a democratic decision-making process. The solution of technical problems is not dependent on public discussion. Rather, public discussions could render problematic the framework within which the tasks of government action present themselves as technical ones. Therefore the new politics of state interventionism requires a depoliticization of the mass of the population. To the extent that practical questions are eliminated, the public realm also loses its political function. At the same time, the institutional framework of society is still distinct from the systems of purposive-rational action themselves. Its organization continues to be a problem of *practice* linked to communication, not one of *technology*, no matter how scientifically guided. Hence, the bracketing out of practice associated with the new kind of politics is not automatic. The substitute programme, which legitimates power today, leaves unfilled a vital need for legitimation: how will the depoliticization of the masses be made plausible to them? Marcuse would be able to answer: by having technology and science *also* take on the role of an ideology.

Since the end of the nineteenth century the other developmental tendency characteristic of advanced capitalism has become increasingly momentous: the scientization of technology. The institutional pressure to augment the productivity of labour through the introduction of new technology has always existed under capitalism. But innovations depended on sporadic inventions, which, while economically motivated, were still fortuitous in character. This changed as technical development entered into a feedback relation with the progress of the modern sciences. With the advent of large-scale industrial research, science, technology and industrial utilization were fused into a system. Since then, industrial research has been linked up with research under government contract, which primarily promotes scientific and technical progress in the military sector. From there information flows back into the sectors of civilian production. Thus technology and science become a leading productive force, rendering inoperative the conditions for Marx's labour theory of value. It is no longer meaningful to calculate the amount of capital investment in research and development on the basis of the value of unskilled (simple) labour power, when scientific-technical progress has become an independent source of surplus-value, in relation to which the only source of surplus-value considered by Marx, namely the labour power of the immediate producers, plays an ever smaller role.[2]

As long as the productive forces were visibly linked to the rational decisions and instrumental action of men engaged in social production, they could be

2 The most recent explication of this is Eugen Löbl, *Geistige Arbeit – die wahre Quelle des Reichtums*, translated from the Czech by Leopold Grünwald.

understood as the potential for a growing power of technical control and not be confused with the institutional framework in which they are embedded. However, with the institutionalization of scientific-technical progress, the potential of the productive forces has assumed a form owing to which men lose consciousness of the dualism of work and interaction.

It is true that social interests still determine the direction, functions and pace of technical progress. But these interests define the social system so much as a whole that they coincide with the interest in maintaining the system. *As such* the private form of capital utilization and a distribution mechanism for social rewards that guarantees the loyalty of the masses are removed from discussion. The quasi-autonomous progress of science and technology then appears as an independent variable on which the most important single system variable, namely economic growth, depends. Thus arises a perspective in which the development of the social system *seems* to be determined by the logic of scientific-technical progress. The immanent law of this progress seems to produce objective exigencies, which must be obeyed by any politics oriented toward functional needs. But when this semblance has taken root effectively, then propaganda can refer to the role of technology and science in order to explain and legitimate why in modern societies the process of democratic decision-making about practical problems loses its function and 'must' be replaced by plebiscitary decisions about alternative sets of leaders of administrative personnel. This technocracy thesis has been worked out in several versions on the intellectual level.[3] What seems to me more important is that it can also become a background ideology that penetrates into the consciousness of the depoliticized mass of the population, where it can take on legitimating power.[4] It is a singular achievement of this ideology to detach society's self-understanding from the frame of reference of communicative action and from the concepts of symbolic interaction and replace it with a scientific model. Accordingly the culturally defined self-understanding of a social life-world is replaced by the self-reification of men under categories of purposive-rational action and adaptive behaviour.

The model according to which the planned reconstruction of society is to proceed is taken from systems analysis. It is possible in principle to comprehend and analyse individual enterprises and organizations, even political or economic sub-systems and social systems as a whole, according to the pattern of self-regulated systems. It makes a difference, of course, whether we use a

3 See Helmut Schelsky, *Der Mensch in der wissenschaftilichen Zivilisation*; Jacques Ellul, *The Technological Society*; and Arnold Gehlen, 'Über kulturelle Kristallisationen', in *Studien zur Anthropologie und Soziologie*; and 'Über kulturelle Evolution', in *Die Philosophie und die Frage nach dem Fortschritt*, M. Hahn and F. Wiedmann (eds).

4 To my knowledge there are no empirical studies concerned specifically with the propagation of this background ideology. We are dependent on extrapolations from the findings of other investigations.

cybernetic frame of reference for analytic purposes or *organize* a given social system in accordance with this pattern as a man-machine system. But the transferral of the analytic model to the level of social organization is implied by the very approach taken by systems analysis. Carrying out this intention of an instinct-like self-stabilization of social systems yields the peculiar perspective that the structure of one of the two types of action, namely the behavioural system of purposive-rational action, not only predominates over the institutional framework but gradually absorbs communicative action as such. If, with Arnold Gehlen, one were to see the inner logic of technical development as the step-by-step disconnection of the behavioural system of purposive-rational action from the human organism and its transferral to machines, then the technocratic intention could be understood as the last stage of this development. For the first time man can not only, as *homo faber*, completely objectify himself and confront the achievements that have taken on independent life in his products; he can in addition, as *homo fabricatus*, be integrated into his technical apparatus if the structure of purposive-rational action can be successfully reproduced on the level of social systems. According to this idea the institutional framework of society – which previously was rooted in a different type of action – would now, in a fundamental reversal, be *absorbed* by the sub-systems of purposive-rational action, which were embedded in it.

Of course this technocratic intention has not been realized anywhere even in its beginnings. But it serves as an ideology for the new politics, which is adapted to technical problems and brackets out practical questions. Furthermore it does correspond to certain developmental tendencies that could lead to a creeping erosion of what we have called the institutional framework. The manifest domination of the authoritarian state gives way to the manipulative compulsions of technical-operational administration. The moral realization of a normative order is a function of communicative action oriented to shared cultural meaning and presupposing the internalization of values. It is increasingly supplanted by conditioned behaviour, while large organizations as such are increasingly patterned after the structure of purposive-rational action. The industrially most advanced societies seem to approximate the model of behavioural control steered by external stimuli rather than guided by norms. Indirect control through fabricated stimuli has increased, especially in areas of putative subjective freedom (such as electoral, consumer, and leisure behaviour). Socio-psychologically, the era is typified less by the authoritarian personality than by the destructuring of the superego. The increase in *adaptive behaviour* is, however, only the obverse of the dissolution of the sphere of linguistically mediated interaction by the structure of purposive-rational action. This is paralleled subjectively by the disappearance of the difference between purposive-rational action and interaction from the consciousness not only of the sciences of man, but of men themselves. The concealment of this difference proves the ideological power of the technocratic consciousness.

In consequence of the two tendencies that have been discussed, capitalist society has changed to the point where two key categories of Marxian theory, namely class struggle and ideology, can no longer be employed as they stand.

It was on the basis of the capitalist mode of production that the struggle of social classes as such was constituted, thereby creating an objective situation from which the class structure of traditional society, with its immediately political constitution, could be *recognized* in retrospect. State-regulated capitalism, which emerged from a reaction against the dangers to the system produced by open class antagonism, suspends class conflict. The system of advanced capitalism is so defined by a policy of securing the loyalty of the wage-earning masses through rewards, that is, by avoiding conflict, that the conflict still built into the structure of society in virtue of the private mode of capital utilization is the very area of conflict which has the greatest probability of remaining latent. It recedes behind others, which, while conditioned by the mode of production, can no longer assume the form of class conflicts. In the paper cited, Claus Offe has analysed this paradoxical state of affairs, showing that open conflicts about social interests break out with greater probability the less their frustration has dangerous consequences for the system. The needs with the greatest conflict potential are those on the periphery of the area of state intervention. They are far from the central conflict being kept in a state of latency, and therefore they are not seen as having priority among dangers to be warded off. Conflicts are set off by these needs to the extent that disproportionately scattered state interventions produce backward areas of development and corresponding disparity tensions:

> The disparity between areas of life grows above all in view of the differential state of development obtaining between the actually institutionalized and the possible level of technical and social progress. The disproportion between the most modern apparatuses for industrial and military purposes and the stagnating organization of the transport, health and educational systems is just as well known an example of this disparity between areas of life as is the contradiction between rational planning and regulation in taxation and finance policy and the unplanned, haphazard development of cities and regions. Such contradictions can no longer be designated accurately as antagonisms between classes, yet they can still be interpreted as results of the still dominant process of the private utilization of capital and of a specifically capitalist power structure. In this process the prevailing interests are those which, without being clearly localizable, are in a position, on the basis of the established mechanism of the capitalist economy, to react to disturbances of the conditions of their stability by producing risks relevant to the system as a whole.[5]

The interests bearing on the maintenance of the mode of production can no longer be 'clearly localized' in the social system as class interests. For the power

5 Offe, 'Politische Herrschaft und Klassenstrukturen'.

structure, aimed as it is at avoiding dangers to the system, precisely excludes 'domination' (as immediate political or economically mediated social force) exercised in such a manner that one class subject *confronts* another as an identifiable group.

This means not that class antagonisms have been abolished but that they have become *latent*. Class distinctions persist in the form of sub-cultural traditions and corresponding differences not only in the standard of living and life-style but also in political attitude. The social structure also makes it probable that the class of wage earners will be hit harder than other groups by social disparities. And finally, the generalized interest in perpetuating the system is still anchored today, on the level of immediate life chances, in a structure of privilege. The concept of an interest that has become *completely* independent of living subjects would cancel itself out. But with the deflection of dangers to the system in state-regulated capitalism, the political system has incorporated an interest – which transcends latent class boundaries – in preserving the compensatory distribution façade.

Furthermore, the displacement of the conflict zone from the class boundary to the underprivileged regions of life does not mean at all that serious conflict potential has been disposed of. As the extreme example of racial conflict in the United States shows, so many consequences of disparity can accumulate in certain areas and groups that explosions resembling civil war can occur. But unless they are connected with protest potential from other sectors of society no conflicts arising from such underprivilege can really overturn the system – they can only provoke it to sharp reactions incompatible with formal democracy. For underprivileged groups are not social classes, nor do they ever even potentially represent the mass of the population. Their *disfranchisement* and pauperization no longer coincide with *exploitation*, because the system does not live off their labour. They can represent at most a past phase of exploitation. But they cannot through the withdrawal of cooperation attain the demands that they legitimately put forward. That is why these demands retain an appellative character. In the case of long-term non-consideration of their legitimate demands underprivileged groups can in extreme situations react with desperate destruction and self-destruction. But as long as no coalitions are made with privileged groups, such a civil war lacks the chance of revolutionary success that class struggle possesses.

With a series of restrictions this model seems applicable even to the relations between the industrially advanced nations and the formerly colonial areas of the Third World. Here, too, growing disparity leads to a form of underprivilege that in the future surely will be increasingly less comprehensible through categories of exploitation. Economic interests are replaced on this level, however, with immediately military ones.

Be that as it may, in advanced capitalist society deprived and privileged groups no longer confront each other *as* socio-economic classes – and to some extent the boundaries of underprivilege are no longer even specific to groups and instead run across population categories. Thus the fundamental relation that existed in all traditional societies and that came to the fore under liberal capitalism is mediatized, namely the class antagonism between partners who stand in an institutionalized relationship of force, economic exploitation and political oppression to one another, and in which communication is so distorted and restricted that the legitimations serving as an ideological veil cannot be called into question. Hegel's concept of the ethical totality of a living relationship which is sundered because one subject does not reciprocally satisfy the needs of the other is no longer an appropriate model for the mediatized class structure of organized, advanced capitalism. The suspended dialectic of the ethical generates the peculiar semblance of *post-histoire*. The reason is that relative growth of the productive forces no longer represents *eo ipso* a potential that points beyond the existing framework with emancipatory consequences, in view of which legitimations of an existing power structure become enfeebled. For the leading productive force – controlled scientific-technical progress itself – has now become the basis of legitimation. Yet this new form of legitimation has cast off the old shape of *ideology*.

Technocratic consciousness is, on the one hand, 'less ideological' than all previous ideologies. For it does not have the opaque force of a delusion that only transfigures the implementation of interests. On the other hand today's dominant, rather glassy background ideology, which makes a fetish of science, is more irresistible and farther-reaching than ideologies of the old type. For with the veiling of practical problems it not only justifies a *particular class's* interest in domination and represses *another class's* partial need for emancipation, but affects the human race's emancipatory interest as such.

Technocratic consciousness is not a rationalized, wish-fulfilling fantasy, not an 'illusion' in Freud's sense, in which a system of interaction is either represented or interpreted and grounded. Even bourgeois ideologies could be traced back to a basic pattern of just interactions, free of domination and mutually satisfactory. It was these ideologies which met the criteria of wish-fulfilment and substitute gratification; the communication on which they were based was so limited by repressions that the relation of force once institutionalized as the capital–labour relation could not even be called by name. But the technocratic consciousness is not based in the same way on the causality of dissociated symbols and unconscious motives, which generates both false consciousness and the power of reflection to which the critique of ideology is indebted. It is less vulnerable to reflection, because it is no longer *only* ideology. For it does not, in the manner of ideology, express a projection of the 'good life' (which even if not identifiable with a bad reality, can at least be brought into virtually satisfactory accord with it). Of course the new ideology, like the old, serves to impede making the foundations of society the object of thought and reflection. Previously, social force lay at the basis of the relation between capitalist and wage labourers. Today the basis is provided by structural conditions which predefine the tasks of system maintenance: the private form of capital utilization and a political form of distributing social rewards that guarantees mass loyalty. However, the old and new ideology differ in two ways.

First, the capital–labour relation today, because of its linkage to a loyalty-ensuring political distribution mechanism, no longer engenders uncorrected exploitation and oppression. The process through which the persisting class antagonism has been made virtual presupposes that the repression on which the latter is based first came to consciousness in history and *only then* was stabilized in a modified form as a property of the system. Technocratic consciousness, therefore, cannot rest in the same way on collective repression as did earlier ideologies. Second, mass loyalty today is created only with the aid of rewards for *privatized needs*. The achievements in virtue of which the system justifies itself may not in principle be interpreted politically. The acceptable interpretation is immediately in terms of allocations of money and leisure time (neutral with regard to their use), and mediately in terms of the technocratic justification of the occlusion of practical questions. Hence the new ideology is distinguished from its predecessor in that it severs the criteria for justifying the organization of social life from any normative regulation of interaction, thus depoliticizing them. It anchors them instead in functions of a putative system of purposive-rational action.

Technocratic consciousness reflects not the sundering of an ethical situation but the repression of 'ethics' as such as a category of life. The common, positivist way of thinking renders inert the frame of reference of interaction in ordinary language, in which domination and ideology both arise under conditions of distorted communication and can be reflectively detected and broken down. The depoliticization of the mass of the population, which is legitimated through technocratic consciousness, is at the same time men's self-objectification in categories equally of both purposive-rational action and adaptive behaviour. The reified models of the sciences migrate into the socio-cultural life-world and gain objective power over the latter's self-understanding. The ideological nucleus of this consciousness is *the elimination of the distinction between the practical and the technical*. It reflects, but does not objectively account for, the new constellation of a disempowered institutional framework and systems of purposive-rational action that have taken on a life of their own.

The new ideology consequently violates an interest grounded in one of the two fundamental conditions of our cultural existence: in language, or more precisely, in the form of socialization and individuation determined by communication in ordinary language. This interest extends to the maintenance of intersubjectivity of mutual understanding as well as to the creation of communication without domination. Technocratic consciousness makes this practical interest disappear behind the interest in the expansion of our power of technical control. Thus the reflection that the new ideology calls for must penetrate beyond the level of particular historical class interests to disclose the fundamental interests of mankind as such, engaged in the process of self-constitution.[6]

6 See my essay 'Erkenntnis und Interesse' in *Technik und Wissenschaft als 'Ideologie'*. It will appear in English as an appendix to *Knowledge and Human Interests*. [See Bibliographical References. Ed.]

If the relativization of the field of application of the concept of ideology and the theory of class be confirmed, then the category framework developed by Marx in the basic assumptions of historical materialism requires a new formulation. The model of forces of production and relations of production would have to be replaced by the more abstract one of work and interaction. The relations of production designate a level on which the institutional framework was anchored only during the phase of the development of liberal capitalism, and not either before or after. To be sure, the productive forces, in which the learning processes organized in the sub-systems of purposive-rational action accumulate, have been from the very beginning the motive force of social evolution. But, they do not appear, as Marx supposed, *under all circumstances* to be a potential for liberation and to set off emancipatory movements – at least not once the continual growth of the productive forces has become dependent on scientific-technical progress that has *also* taken on functions of *legitimating political power*. I suspect that the frame of reference developed in terms of the analogous, but more general relation of institutional framework (interaction) and sub-systems of purposive-rational action ('work' in the broad sense of instrumental and strategic action) is more suited to reconstructing the socio-cultural phases of the history of mankind.

Bibliographical References

[*Note:* The Bibliography does not include works for which full references are given in footnotes. Nor does it include the works of Marx and Engels, for which the contributors cite various editions.]

Adams, H. P., *Karl Marx in his Earlier Writings*. London: Allen and Unwin, 1940.

Adler, Max, *Kausalität und Teleologie im Streite um die Wissenschaft*. Vienna: Wiener Volksbuchhandlung, 1904.

—— *Lehrbuch der materialistischen Geschichtsauffassung* (1930–2). Republished with the addition of a third volume under the title *Soziologie des Marxismus*. Vienna: Europa Verlag, 1964.

Althusser, Louis, *Lenin and Philosophy and Other Essays*. London: New Left Books, 1971.

Althusser, Louis, and Balibar, Étienne, *Reading Capital*. London: New Left Books, 1970.

Anderson, Perry, *Passages from Antiquity to Feudalism*. London: New Left Books, 1974.

—— *Lineages of the Absolutist State*. London: New Left Books, 1974.

Avineri, Shlomo, *The Social and Political Thought of Karl Marx*. Cambridge: Cambridge University Press, 1968.

Baran, Paul, and Sweezy, Paul, *Monopoly Capital*. New York: Monthly Review Press, 1966.

Barrett, M., *Women's Oppression Today: Problems in Marxist Feminist Analysis*. London: New Left Books, 1980.

Bastide, Roger (ed.), *Sens et usage du terme structure*. Brussels: Mouton, 1962.

Bauer, Otto, 'Marxismus und Ethik', *Die Neue Zeit*, 24 (2) (1905–6). English trans. in Bottomore and Goode (eds), *Austro-Marxism*.

—— *Die Nationalitätenfrage und die Sozialdemokratie*. Vienna: Wiener Volksbuchhandlung, 1907; 2nd enlarged edn, 1924.

Benton, Ted, *Philosophical Foundations of the Three Sociologies*. London: Routledge and Kegan Paul, 1977.

Bernstein, Eduard, *Evolutionary Socialism*. New York: Schocken Books, 1961.

Bhaskar, Roy, *A Realist Theory of Science*. Brighton: Harvester Press, 2nd edn, 1978.

—— *The Possibility of Naturalism: A Philosophical Critique of the Contemporary Human Sciences*. Brighton: Harvester Press, 1979.

Birnbaum, Norman, *Toward a Critical Sociology*. New York: Oxford University Press, 1971.

Blumenberg, Werner, *Karl Marx*. London: New Left Books, 1972.

Bottomore, Tom (ed.), *Karl Marx: Early Writings*. New York: McGraw-Hill, 1964.

—— *Marxist Sociology*. London: Macmillan, 1975.

—— (ed.), *A Dictionary of Marxist Thought*. Oxford: Basil Blackwell, 1983.

—— *The Frankfurt School*. Chichester and London: Ellis Horwood/Tavistock, 1984.

—— *Theories of Modern Capitalism*. London: Allen and Unwin, 1985.

Bottomore, Tom and Rubel, Maximilien (eds) (1956), *Karl Marx: Selected Writings in Sociology and Social Philosophy*. Harmondsworth: Penguin Books, 1963.

Bottomore, Tom and Goode, Patrick (eds), *Austro-Marxism*. Oxford: Clarendon Press, 1978.

Brym, Robert J., *Intellectuals and Politics*. London: Allen and Unwin, 1980.

Bukharin, Nikolai, *Historical Materialism: A System of Sociology*. New York: International Publishers, 1925.

Cieszkowski, August von, *Prolegomena zur Historiosophie*. Berlin, 1838.

Cornu, Auguste, *Karl Marx et Friedrich Engels*. Paris: Presses Universitaires de France, 1955–70.

Croce, Benedetto, *Historical Materialism and the Economics of Karl Marx*. London: Howard Latimer, 1913.

Djilas, M., *The New Class*. London: Thames and Hudson, 1957.

Dühring, Eugen, *Kritische Geschichte der Nationalökonomie und des Sozialismus*. Berlin: T. Grieben, 1871.

Easton, L. and Guddat, K. (eds), *Writings of the Young Marx on Philosophy and Society*. New York: Anchor Books, 1967.

Ellman, M., 'Did the agricultural surplus provide the resources for the increase in investment in the USSR during the First Five Year Plan?', *Economic Journal* (December 1975).

Ellul, Jacques, *The Technological Society*. New York: Vintage Books, 1967.

Forde, Daryll, and Radcliffe-Brown, A. R. (eds), *African Systems of Kinship and Marriage*. London: Oxford University Press, 1950.

Fromm, Erich (ed.), *Socialist Humanism*. Garden City, NY: Doubleday and Co., 1965.

—— *Marx's Concept of Man*. New York: Frederick Ungar, 1961.

Gans, E., *Rückblicke auf Personen und Zustände*. Berlin, 1836.

Gehlen, Arnold, *Studien zur Anthropologie und Soziologie*. Berlin, 1963.

Godelier, Maurice, *Rationality and Irrationality in Economics*. London: New Left Books, 1974.

—— *Perspectives in Marxist Anthropology*. Cambridge: Cambridge University Press, 1977.

Goldmann, Lucien, *The Hidden God*. London: Routledge and Kegan Paul, 1964.

—— *Marxisme et sciences humaines*. Paris: Gallimard, 1970.

Gough, Ian, 'State expenditure in advanced capitalism', *New Left Review* (July/August 1975).

Gramsci, Antonio, *Selections from the Prison Notebooks*, edited and translated by Quintin Hoare and Geoffrey Nowell Smith. London: Lawrence and Wishart, 1971.

Habermas, Jürgen, *Knowledge and Human Interests*. London: Heinemann, 1972.

—— *Legitimation Crisis*. London: Heinemann, 1976.

Hahn, M., and Wiedmann, F. (eds), *Die Philosophie und die Frage nach dem Fortschritt*. Munich, 1964.

Hilferding, Rudolf (1910), *Finance Capital*. London: Routledge and Kegan Paul, 1981.

Jay, Martin, *The Dialectical Imagination*. Boston: Little, Brown and Co., 1973.

Kamenka, Eugene, *The Ethical Foundations of Marxism*. London: Routledge and Kegan Paul, 1962.

Kline, George L., *European Philosophy Today*. Chicago: University of Chicago Press, 1965.

Kolakowski, Leszek, *Marxism and Beyond*. London: Pall Mall Press, 1969.
—— *Main Currents of Marxism*. 3 vols. Oxford: Clarendon Press, 1978.
Konrád, G. and Szelényi, I., *The Intellectuals on the Road to Class Power*. Brighton: Harvester Press, 1979.
Korsch, Karl (1923), *Marxism and Philosophy*. London: New Left Books, 1970.
—— *Karl Marx*. London: Chapman and Hall, 1938. (Revised German edition, Frankfurt: Europäische Verlagsanstalt, 1967).
Kosik, Karel, *Dialectics of the Concrete*. Dordrecht and Boston: D. Reidel, 1976.
Kress, Gisela, and Senghaas, Dieter (eds), *Politikwissenschaft*. Frankfurt-am-Main: Suhrkamp, 1969.
Kühne, Karl, *Economics and Marxism*. 2 vols. London: Macmillan, 1979.
Kuhn, A., and Wolpe, A. M. (eds), *Feminism and Materialism*. London: Routledge and Kegan Paul, 1978.
Labriola, Antonio, *Essays on the Materialistic Conception of History*. Chicago: Charles H. Kerr, 1908.
Lange, Oskar, *Political Economy*, vol. I. London: Pergamon Press, 1963.
Larrain, Jorge, *The Concept of Ideology*. London: Hutchinson, 1979.
Leach, Edmund, *Political Systems of Highland Burma*. London: Bell and Sons, 1964.
Lévi-Strauss, Claude, *The Savage Mind*. London: Weidenfeld and Nicolson, 1966.
—— *The Elementary Structures of Kinship*. London: Eyre and Spottiswoode, 1968.
—— *Conversations with G. Charbonnier*. London: Jonathan Cape, 1969.
—— *Totemism*. Harmondsworth: Penguin Books, 1969.
—— *From Honey to Ashes*. London: Jonathan Cape, 1973.
Lichtheim, George, *From Marx to Hegel and Other Essays*. London: Orbach and Chambers, 1971.
Löbl, Eugen, *Geistige Arbeit – die wahre Quelle des Reichstums*. Vienna, 1968.
Lukács, Georg (1923), *History and Class Consciousness*. London: Merlin Press, 1971.
McLellan, David, *The Young Hegelians and Karl Marx*. London: Macmillan, 1969.
—— (ed.), *Karl Marx: The Early Texts*. Oxford: Basil Blackwell, 1971.
—— (ed.), *Marx's Grundrisse*. London: Macmillan, 1971.
Mandel, Ernest, *Late Capitalism*. London: New Left Books, 1975.
Mannheim, Karl, *Ideology and Utopia*. London: Routledge and Kegan Paul, 1936.
Marcuse, Herbert, *Reason and Revolution: Hegel and the Rise of Social Theory*. New York: Oxford University Press, 1941.
—— *One-Dimensional Man*. London: Routledge and Kegan Paul, 1964.
Marković, Mihailo, and Cohen, Robert S., *Yugoslavia: The Rise and Fall of Socialist Humanism*. Nottingham: Spokesman Books, 1975.
Marković, Mihailo and Petrović, Gajo (eds), *Praxis: Yugoslav Essays in the Philosophy and Methodology of the Social Sciences*. Dordrecht: D. Reidel, 1979.
Mayo, N. B., *Democracy and Marxism*. New York: Oxford University Press, 1955.
Mészáros, Istvan (ed.), *Aspects of History and Class Consciousness*. London: Routledge and Kegan Paul, 1971.
Michels, Robert, *Political Parties*. New York: Free Press, 1966.
Miliband, Ralph, *The State in Capitalist Society*. London: Weidenfeld and Nicolson, 1969.
—— *Marxism and Politics*. Oxford: Oxford University Press, 1977.

Mills, C. Wright, *The Marxists*. New York: Dell Publishing Co., 1962.

Musil, Robert, *The Man Without Qualities*, vol. I. London: Secker and Warburg, 1953.

Nadel, F., *The Theory of Social Structure*. London: Cohen and West, 1957.

Nomad, Max, *Rebels and Renegades*. New York: Macmillan, 1932.

O'Connor, James, *The Fiscal Crisis of the State*. New York: St Martin's Press, 1973.

Offe, Claus, *Strukturprobleme des kapitalistischen Staates*. Frankfurt-am-Main: Suhrkamp, 1972.

—— 'The theory of the capitalist state and the problem of policy formation', in L. Lindberg et al. (eds), *Stress and Contradiction in Modern Capitalism*, London: D.C. Heath, 1975.

O'Malley, Joseph (ed.), *Karl Marx: Critique of Hegel's 'Philosophy of Right'*. Cambridge: Cambridge University Press, 1971.

Outhwaite, William and Mulkay, Michael (eds), *Social Theory and Social Criticism*. Oxford: Basil Blackwell, 1987.

Palloix, C., 'The self-expansion of capital on a world scale', *Review of Radical Political Economy*, 9 (2) (1977).

Plekhanov, G. V., *Fundamental Problems of Marxism*. London: Martin Lawrence, 1929.

Popper, Karl, *The Open Society and Its Enemies*. London: Routledge and Kegan Paul, 1945.

Poulantzas, Nicos, *Classes in Contemporary Capitalism*. London: New Left Books, 1975.

Prawer, S. S., *Karl Marx and World Literature*. Oxford: Oxford University Press, 1976.

Richta, Radovan et al., *Civilization at the Crossroads*. White Plains, NY: International Arts and Sciences Press, 1969.

Rose, Gillian, *The Melancholy Science: An Introduction to the Thought of Theodor W. Adorno*. London: Macmillan, 1978.

Schelsky, Helmut, *Der Mensch in der wissenschaftlichen Zivilisation*. Cologne–Opladen: Westdeutscher Verlag, 1961.

Schmidt, Alfred, *The Concept of Nature in Marx*. London: New Left Books, 1971.

Schumpeter, J. A., *Capitalism, Socialism and Democracy*, 5th edn. London: Allen and Unwin, 1976.

Sekine, T., 'Uno-Riron: A Japanese contribution to Marxian political economy', *Journal of Economic Literature*, 13 (September 1975).

Simmel, Georg (1900), *Philosophy of Money*. London: Routledge and Kegan Paul, 1978.

Sombart, Werner, *Der moderne Kapitalismus*, 3 vols. Leipzig: Duncker and Humblot, 1902; 2nd edn, 1924–7.

Stein, Lorenz von (1842), *The History of the Social Movement in France, 1789–1850*. Totowa, NJ: Bedminster Press, 1964.

Taylor, John G., *From Modernization to Modes of Production: A Critique of the Sociologies of Development and Underdevelopment*. London: Macmillan, 1979.

Tönnies, Ferdinand (1887), *Community and Association*. London: Routledge and Kegan Paul, 1955.

—— (1921), *Karl Marx: His Life and Teachings*. Michigan: Michigan State University Press, 1974.

Touraine, Alain, *The Post-Industrial Society*. New York: Random House, 1971.
Tucker, Robert C., *Philosophy and Myth in Karl Marx*. Cambridge: Cambridge University Press, 1961.
Wallerstein, Immanuel, *The Modern World System*. New York: Academic Press, 1974.
Weber, Max (1904–5), *The Protestant Ethic and the Spirit of Capitalism*. London: Allen and Unwin, 1976.
—— *The Methodology of the Social Sciences*, edited by Edward A. Shils and Henry A. Finch. New York: The Free Press, 1949.
Wellmer, Albrecht, *Critical Theory of Society*. New York: Herder and Herder, 1971.

Contributors

LOUIS ALTHUSSER taught at the École Normale Supérieure in Paris. His best known writings are *For Marx*, *Reading Capital* and *Lenin and Philosophy*.

SHLOMO AVINERI has taught for many years at the Hebrew University of Jerusalem where he is now Professor of Political Theory. His works include *The Social and Political Thought of Karl Marx* and *Hegel's Theory of the Modern State*.

ISAIAH BERLIN was Chichele Professor of Social and Political Theory, University of Oxford, and subsequently President of Wolfson College, Oxford. He has been Visiting Professor in the University of Chicago, Harvard University and Princeton University. His writings include *Karl Marx*, *Historical Inevitability* and *Four Essays on Liberty*.

TOM BOTTOMORE taught for a number of years at the London School of Economics and Political Science, was Head of the Department of Political Science, Sociology, and Anthropology at Simon Fraser University in British Columbia, 1965–7, and Professor of Sociology in the University of Sussex, 1968–85. His writings include *Sociology: A Guide to Problems and Literature*, *Elites and Society*, *Classes in Modern Society*, *Political Sociology*, *Theories of Modern Capitalism*, and he has edited *A Dictionary of Marxist Thought*.

BENEDETTO CROCE (1866–1952) was the most influential Italian philosopher of his time, an interpreter of Vico and Hegel who devoted his attention especially to the philosophy of history and to aesthetics. His major writings include the four volumes of *Philosophy of Spirit*, *History as the Story of Liberty*, and his early essays on Marxism, collected in the volume *Historical Materialism and the Economics of Karl Marx*.

MEGHNAD DESAI is Professor of Economics at the London School of Economics and has written on various aspects of Marx's economic theory.

MAURICE GODELIER is Directeur d'études at the École des Hautes Études en Sciences Sociales, Paris. His writings include *Rationality and Irrationality in Economics* and *Perspectives in Marxist Anthropology*.

316   *Contributors*

LUCIEN GOLDMANN (1913–70) wrote extensively on Marxist method and on the sociology of literature. His writings include *The Hidden God, Recherches dialectiques*, and *Marxisme et sciences humaines*.

ANTONIO GRAMSCI (1891–1937) was one of the founders of the Italian Communist Party and its most original thinker. Arrested by the Fascist Government in 1926 he was sentenced first to internment and then to prison, where he remained for the next eight years and produced some of his most important works, subsequently published as *Quaderni del carcere*, 6 vols, Turin: Einaudi, 1948–51.

JÜRGEN HABERMAS is the most eminent thinker of the later Frankfurt School. He was Professor of Philosophy and Sociology at the University of Frankfurt and Director of the Max Planck Institute in Starnberg, before returning to the University of Frankfurt. Most of his major works have been translated into English, including *Knowledge and Human Interests* and *Legitimation Crisis*.

ANDRÁS HEGEDÜS was Prime Minister of Hungary in 1955–6, and from 1963 director of the Sociological Research Group in the Hungarian Academy of Sciences. After protesting against the Soviet invasion of Czechoslovakia in 1968 he was dismissed from this post and subsequently expelled from the Communist Party. He has written several works on socio-economic questions, including *Socialism and Bureaucracy*.

AGNES HELLER, a colleague, pupil and friend of Georg Lukács, was dismissed from her post at Budapest University in 1973 along with Ferenc Fehér and György Márkus. She left the country to take up a post at La Trobe University in Australia, and in 1985 was appointed Professor of Philosophy at the New School of Social Research, New York.

RUDOLF HILFERDING (1877–1941) was one of the principal Austro-Marxist thinkers. He became a leading figure in the German Social Democratic Party, and was Finance Minister in two governments of the Weimar Republic. In 1933 he was obliged to go into exile, and in February 1941, after being handed over to the German authorities by the Vichy government, he died in Paris in the hands of the Gestapo. His major works are *Böhm-Bawerk's Marx-Critique* and *Finance Capital*.

LESZEK KOLAKOWSKI taught philosophy in the University of Warsaw. He played a prominent part in the Polish revolt against Stalinism in October 1956, and became widely known as an original and critical Marx thinker. In 1966 he was expelled from the Polish Communist Party and was subsequently dismissed from his teaching post in Warsaw. He is now at All Souls College, Oxford. His writings include *Philosophy and Everyday Life, Religious Consciousness and the Church Affiliation*, and *Main Currents of Marxism* (3 vols).

GEORGE LICHTHEIM (1912–73) was well known as a writer on Marxism and on current politics. His works include *Marxism: An Historical and Critical Study, Marxism in Modern France, The Origins of Socialism* and *Imperialism*.

GEORG LUKÁCS (1885–1971) was one of the outstanding Marxist philosophers of this century. Minister for Education in the short-lived Hungarian Soviet of 1919, then in exile in Vienna and Moscow, he returned to Hungary in 1945 and became Professor of Aesthetics and Philosophy of Culture at Budapest University, but had to go into exile again for a brief period after taking part in the Hungarian revolt of 1956. His principal writings are *The Theory of the Novel, History and Class Consciousness, The Young Hegel* and *The Historical Novel*.

RALPH MILIBAND taught for many years at the London School of Economics and Political Science, was Professor of Politics in the University of Leeds and now teaches in the fall semester at York University, Toronto. He is coeditor of the annual *Socialist Register*, and his books include *Parliamentary Socialism* and *The State in Capitalist Society*.

STANISLAW OSSOWSKI (1897–1963) was Professor of the Theory of Culture at the University of Lodz, and afterwards at the University of Warsaw. During the German occupation of Poland and the following Stalinist period, he continued to teach sociology clandestinely. His best-known work (the only one available in English) is *Class Structure in the Social Consciousness*.

GAJO PETROVIĆ is Professor of Philosophy at the University of Zagreb and a leading member of the *Praxis* group. His writings include *English Empiricist Philosophy* and *Marx in the Mid-Twentieth Century*.

NICOS POULANTZAS (1936–79) was one of the leading younger members of the Marxist structuralist school in Paris. His best known works are *Political Power and Social Classes* and *Classes in Contemporary Capitalism*.

KARL RENNER (1870–1950) was a leader of the Austrian Social Democratic Party and a prominent member of the group of Marxist thinkers who became known as the 'Austro-Marxists'. He became Chancellor of the first Austrian Republic in 1918, and again in 1945 was appointed Chancellor (later President) of the second Republic. His principal writings are *The Institutions of Private Law and their Social Functions, Marxism, War and the International* and *Man and Society*.

JOSEPH A. SCHUMPETER (1883–1950) was one of the leading economists of his generation. Professor at the Universities of Graz and Bonn, he was subsequently Professor of Economics at Harvard University. His major works are *The Theory of Economic Development, Imperialism and Social Classes, Business Cycles, Capitalism, Socialism and Democracy* and *History of Economic Analysis.*

SVETOZAR STOJANOVIĆ was Chairman of the Department of Philosophy and Sociology at the University of Belgrade and a prominent member of the *Praxis* group. His best-known work in English is *Between Ideals and Reality.*

HILDE WEISS attended the universities of Berlin, Jena, Frankfurt and Paris, and published in 1936 *Les Enquêtes Ouvrières en France entre 1830 et 1848.* She later taught sociology at Brooklyn College, New York.

ALBRECHT WELLMER was one of the leading members of the postwar Frankfurt School, and is now Professor of Philosophy at the University of Konstanz. He is best known to English readers for his book *Critical Theory of Society.*

Index

of, 259; *cahiers du travail*, 261; didactic purpose of, 285–7; and earlier surveys, 260–1, 263; preface to, 18; response to, 262, 262n

epistemology, 112–13; *see also* knowledge

equality, 194–5

ethics, 64: and determinism, 181–6; dialectic of, 306–7; and freedom, 188; future of, and law, 196–7; Marxist, 177–89; preaching and, 180–1; Protestant, 212; and science, 177–80; and socialism, 184–5; and technocratic consciousness, 308

evolution, 76, 147–8: of capitalism, 199; misconception of, 172

exchange value, 11–12, 77, 300, 302

exploitation, 71, 250–1, 252: abolition of, 187; pre-capitalist, 249–50; and under-privileged, 306

false consciousness, 229–32: and ideology, 295–6

fetishism, 62n, 69, 79, 169, 199

feudal mode of production, 67, 249–50

feudal society, 13, 16, 109–10: in Kingdom of Franks, 52

feudalism, 68, 82, 127, 128, 131, 133, 205, 207, 208; absence in Orient of, 124; bourgeois struggle against, 117; and capitalism, 56; and class, 51–2, 239–40, 242; and reciprocity, 192; versus the state, 117

Feuerbach, Ludwig, 5, 45, 61, 101, 113: concept of 'practice' in, 62

Feuerbach, Theses on (Marx), 42, 61, 93, 157, 158, 161, 164–6, 175

Fichte, J. G., 5

Fourier, F. M. C., 125, 190, 213, 237

France, 101, 236, 237, 242, 277: Bonapartism in, 278–80; bureaucracy in, 119; Enlightenment in, 158, 161, 162, 200; labour movement in, 262–3; peasantry in, 17; social surveys in, 258, 259, 260, 263; *see also* French Revolution

Frankfurt School, 31–3, 37

Franklin, Benjamin, 143

free time, 14–15, 191, 197

freedom, 43, 98–101, 275: in bourgeois ideology, 66–7; and determinism, 183, 185; of expression, 158–60; and labour, 191; of labour, 299; and morality, 188; in the Middle Ages, 133; in the state, 275, 288–9

French Revolution, 4, 5, 61–2, 82, 98, 235

Fritzhand, Marck, 34, 179, 181, 188

Fromm, Erich: *Marx's Concept of Man*, 144, 145

functionalism, 72–3, 76, 80

futurism, moral, 185

Galli, G., 151n

Gans, Eduard, 4, 6n

Gehlen, Arnold, 304

German Ideology (Marx), 8, 93, 127, 141, 157–8, 172, 175, 180, 182, 217n, 223–4, 240, 242, 276

Germany, 82, 119, 227: under Bismarck, 83, 137, 280; class power in, 137; feudal lords in, 56; Marx on, 244n, 273n, 284; middle class in, 219; social democracy in, 24, 25, 282, 288; state power in, 119; working class conditions in, 237–8, 242

Gobineau, A. de, 53

Godelier, M., 39

Goldmann, Lucien, 178

Gotha Program, Critique of the (Marx), 179, 194–5, 288–9

Gough, Ian, 90–1

Gramsci, Antonio, 26n, 30–1, 37, 210–11: *Selections from the Prison Notebooks*, 146n

Great Peasant War (1525), 232

Greece, ancient, 76, 109–10, 130, 131

Grundrisse der Kritik der politischen Oekonomie (Marx), 2–3, 9–12, 13–15, 19–21, 126–9, 190–1, 282

Habermas, Jürgen, 34–6, 167

Hegel, G. W. F., 36, 111, 113, 116, 143, 158, 180, 182, 255, 306: concept of man of, 145; dialectic in, 31–2, 94; and Engels, 122n; history and, 93–4, 97–102, 121n, 130, 228; Idea in, 93, 106n; Marx's criticism of, 4–5, 6,